CONFEDERATE CITIES

 HISTORICAL STUDIES OF URBAN AMERICA

Edited by Lilia Fernández, Timothy J. Gilfoyle, Becky M. Nicolaides, and Amanda Seligman
James R. Grossman, editor emeritus

Also in the series:

CONFEDERATE CITIES

The Urban South during the Civil War Era

EDITED BY ANDREW L. SLAP
AND FRANK TOWERS

With a Foreword by David Goldfield

THE UNIVERSITY OF CHICAGO PRESS
CHICAGO AND LONDON

ANDREW L. SLAP is professor of history at East Tennessee State University.

FRANK TOWERS is associate professor of history at the University of Calgary.

The University of Chicago Press, Chicago 60637
The University of Chicago Press, Ltd., London
© 2015 by The University of Chicago
All rights reserved. Published 2015.
Printed in the United States of America

24 23 22 21 20 19 18 17 16 15   1 2 3 4 5

ISBN-13: 978-0-226-30017-7 (cloth)
ISBN-13: 978-0-226-30020-7 (paper)
ISBN-13: 978-0-226-30034-4 (e-book)
DOI: 10.7208/chicago/9780226300344.001.0001

Library of Congress Cataloging-in-Publication Data
    Confederate cities : the urban South during the Civil War era / edited by
Andrew L. Slap and Frank Towers ; with a foreword by David Goldfield.
        pages ; cm. — (Historical studies of urban America)
    Includes index.
    ISBN 978-0-226-30017-7 (cloth : alk. paper)—
ISBN 978-0-226-30020-7 (pbk. : alk. paper)—ISBN 978-0-226-30034-4 (ebook)
1. Urbanization—Confederate States of America—History—19th century.
2. Cities and towns—Confederate States of America—History—19th century.
3. United States—History—Civil War, 1861–1865. 4. Secession—Southern
States.   I. Slap, Andrew L., editor. II. Towers, Frank, editor. III. Goldfield,
David R., 1944–writer of foreword. IV. Series: Historical studies of urban
America.
    E487.C66   2015
    973.7'13—dc23

                                                          2015014450

♾ This paper meets the requirements of ANSI/NISO Z39.48-1992 (Permanence of
Paper).

FOR JEWEL AND NICOLE,
WHO TOLD US NOT TO DO THIS

CONTENTS

ACKNOWLEDGMENTS

Any book, especially a collaborative project such as this one, results from more than the work of its authors alone.

Andy Slap deserves credit for starting this project in 2009 at the encouragement of Pete Carmichael. David Moltke-Hansen, John Inscoe, and Bill Link have all been very helpful throughout the process. In 2010 Frank Towers joined the project and worked with Andy to organize a conference on "Southern Cities during the Civil War" held at the University of Calgary and in Banff, Alberta, in late May 2012.

Most of the essays in this volume began as papers presented at that meeting, which produced a lively discussion of the place of cities in southern Civil War history, and allowed contributors to share ideas about each other's work.

The conference was generously funded by the Canadian Social Sciences and Humanities Research Council, East Tennessee State University's Department of History, and at the University of Calgary the Faculty of Arts, the Calgary Institute for the Humanities (CIH), The Centre for Military and Strategic Studies, and the Department of History.

At the CIH, Wayne McCready, its former director, and Denise Hamel were especially helpful in organizing the meeting. Beau Cleland worked on local arrangements and Shannon Murray coordinated the editing and circulation of the conference proceedings. They also produced very helpful historiographic presentations for the meeting as did Courtenay Adams, James Phelan, Jarret Ruminski, and John Woitkowicz. Presenters-turned-authors benefited greatly from formal conference comments prepared by Marc Egnal, Elizabeth Jameson, Lynn Kennedy, Richard Reid, and Jewel Spangler. We also learned a lot from other presenters and attendees including Sharon Romeo, Mary DeCredico, Larry MacDonnell, and Kathleen Hilliard.

Thanks to Adam Arenson and Steven Nash who could not attend but did send in papers. Tyler Anbinder, Jacqueline Campbell, and Gregg Kimball assisted the project in its latter stages. Frank Towers is especially grateful to Scott Marler and Paul Quigley for their feedback on his essay. Andy Slap appreciates Tom Lee tutoring him on southern and urban history.

The late Michael Fellman joined in preliminary discussions of the book, including a meeting at the 2011 Southern Historical Association, and he was scheduled to participate in the conference. Tragically, health problems prevented his attendance. His death in the summer of 2012 was a great loss to the historical profession and to the study of US history in Canada in particular.

From 2012 to 2014 the manuscript went through several revisions. The University of Chicago Press was invaluable in that process. Robert Devens gave us an advanced contract, which helped tremendously in securing conference funding and adding contributors. Since then his successor, Tim Mennel, has been extremely patient and encouraging in bringing the book to publication. The same goes for series editor Tim Gilfoyle and the UCP editorial board. We also want to thank all the other people at the press who helped, including editorial assistants Russell Damian and Nora Devlin, promotions manager Ashley Pierce, and copyeditor Therese Boyd. The anonymous readers of the manuscript gave extremely helpful, insightful feedback on every essay and helped us to shape the book to better meet questions about the current state of Civil War–era urban history.

Finally the editors want to thank their wives. Nicole gives Andy the time and support he needs to take on a seeming ever-increasing number of projects. It has become a running joke that next semester will be easier. More important, though, when this project started Andy and Nicole had one three-year-old child and by the time it was published they had nine-year-old Abby and five-year-old Josh. Jewel Spangler provides Frank Towers with invaluable support. She not only joined in the 2012 conference but also puts up with Frank at home and at work, no mean feat, and tolerates his bad habit of overcommitting to multiple academic assignments. Every one of them is worthwhile but all together they make for chaos. Thankfully, this one is finished.

FOREWORD

DAVID GOLDFIELD

Walt Whitman could no longer abide the carnage. He had spent the better part of eighteen months shuttling from his office to hospitals in Washington, D.C. He had seen hundreds of young men die and limbs lopped off routinely by surgeons drenched in blood, and had heard the heartbreaking moans of soldiers for whom death could not come too soon. In November 1863, Whitman took a train to Brooklyn for a self-imposed furlough.

He quickly left the war behind. Passing through Baltimore and Philadelphia, Whitman marveled at the scenes out his train window. "It looks anything else but war, everybody well dressed, plenty of money, markets boundless & the best, factories all busy." He was witnessing the birth of America's future: the bustling, commercial, industrial behemoths that would propel the nation to the top rank of economic powers by the turn of the twentieth century. The Civil War in the urban North was not a battleground; it was an opportunity.

Southern cities, of course, fared differently. And in their tale is the story of the South after the war as well. Atlanta, Columbia, and Richmond, and many smaller urban places suffered significantly during the war. Not only the physical trauma of war's terrible swift sword, but also the human drama of urban residents, many of whom were women and children. What was it like to live under a state of siege? We know about the cave dwellers of Vicksburg and how they were reduced to eating rats. But the fare and accommodations were scarcely better in other cities torn asunder by war. We know that women occasionally revolted in the urban South. What impact did these conditions have on their children? We need to know more about the trials of these non-combatants and how it affected them after the war and how these experiences may have shaped southern policy into the twentieth century. We write too much of triumph and not enough about trauma.

Southern cities demonstrated, as cities are wont to do, remarkable resilience coming back to a semblance of normal life within a few years of the war's end. Scarlett O'Hara was not alone in abandoning farming for the enterprise of Atlanta. But Scarlett was hardly the only southerner who figured out the future was in red brick, not red dirt.

It was not surprising that the former slaves became the most urbanized group of southerners after the Civil War. There was an old saying dating back as far as medieval Europe that "city air makes you free." Frederick Douglass wrote about his relative freedom in Baltimore before the war compared to his residence on the farm. Former slaves lit out for the city, sometimes to look for relatives, sometimes to look for work, and often just to escape from the surveillance of whites.

It was also not surprising that southern whites, many of whom had just returned from a bloody and lost war, would take umbrage at these new residents jostling for space and work and lord knows what else. New Orleans, Memphis, Natchez, and other southern cities were flashpoints of racial tension and violence as southern whites sought to restore white supremacy, albeit without the institution of slavery, but with something as close to it as possible. And African Americans resisted. So the story of Reconstruction-era southern cities is the story of the war's continuation in another context until the Redemption secured the Rebel victory that they could not gain on the battlefield. In this, the cities were little different from the rural parishes of Louisiana or the small towns of Mississippi and South Carolina.

It is well to talk of black agency and of the heroism of their few white allies in these southern cities. But the contest was woefully unequal from the start, even during the relatively brief era of Congressional Reconstruction. Frederick Douglass may have engaged in a bit of hyperbole when he characterized the Emancipation Proclamation as a "stupendous fraud," when he spoke on its twenty-fifth anniversary, but conditions for most of the former slaves, and now their offspring, were only marginally better than under bondage. And when Douglass spoke those words in 1888, the worst was yet to come: the carnival of lynching, disfranchisement, the codification of racial segregation, and the triumph of white supremacy generally. For these results, not only the South, but also the nation must take full responsibility.

Which takes us back to the Civil War itself, because ultimately this is more than a book about southern cities; it is a book about the South and the nation. Several years after Appomattox Walt Whitman sensed that the war's ultimate bloody lesson would evaporate in forgetfulness. "Future years will never know the seething hell and the black infernal background . . . of the Secession War." He feared "the real war will never get into the books."

For more than a generation we have been immersed in the "battle-cry-of-freedom" school of the Civil War that depicts the conflict as a holy struggle between good and evil resulting in the liberation of four million human beings and the salvation of the Union. The self-congratulatory message has subsumed Whitman's real war. The story of the urban South in war and Reconstruction is the story of hope and heartbreak, of promise and betrayal, and ultimately, of tragedy. It is the story of America.

Historians and the Urban South's Civil War

ANDREW L. SLAP AND FRANK TOWERS

This volume explores the relationship between the Civil War and cities in the eleven slave states that formed the Confederacy. In separate essays, our contributors use the lens of the city to re-examine main themes of the Civil War era, such as the broad scope of the war, secession, gender, emancipation, and the new urban South created in the wake of the war's destruction. All of these topics have been the subject of a more general renaissance in Civil War studies that has bridged earlier thematic divides between military, political, and social history. Along with a more integrative approach to Civil War history, recent work by historians of the nineteenth-century South has dramatically revised our understanding of slavery's relationship to capitalist economics and cultural modernity.[1] As late as the 1980s conventional scholarly wisdom regarded slavery as a retrograde institution that hindered economic development while encouraging a paternalistic, antimodern politics and culture that among other things inhibited the growth of cities. As this earlier perspective has come under a wide-ranging critique cities have increasingly seemed like important places to study the Civil War–era South, rather than anomalous exceptions to a supposed agrarian norm. This volume adds to that current intellectual movement by showcasing the findings of recent studies that integrate southern cities into the history of the Civil War and debating the merits of this new understanding of slavery, the South, and its cities.

To understand the place of this volume in the broader arc of Civil War and southern historiography, it will help to consider some of the ways that southern cities mattered in the history of secession, the Confederacy, and Reconstruction. For example, despite the tendency of secession's advocates to idealize the social order of the rural plantation, many of them were urban intellectuals, like New Orleans's J. D. B. De Bow and Charleston's Robert Barnwell Rhett. These and other propagandists for disunion had good reason to live in cities. It was there that they found printing presses and skilled typesetters as well as other writers, politicians, and financiers willing to back their cause. Compared to plantations and villages, cities were also a much better place to coordinate high-volume communication with political agitators across the South.[2]

Cities not only hosted the plotters of secession, but also the legislative debates over disunion that followed Abraham Lincoln's election in November 1860. Those debates occurred in southern state capitals, every one of them a city or sizable town. Four months after the presidential election the Confederate government was created in Montgomery, Alabama, which became the new nation's first capital. On April 12, 1861, Confederates fired the first shots of the war in Charleston harbor. Attention then shifted to Richmond, Virginia, where a special session of the legislature had been debating secession since February. Lincoln's call for volunteers to suppress the rebellion gave Virginia secessionists the momentum they needed to convince the legislature to separate from the Union. Shortly thereafter the city of Richmond became the Confederate capital, the center of the new country's military and political organization.

As a consequence of its new status, Richmond's capture was one of the Union's main military objectives and its defense a measure of Confederate survival. In fact, many of the largest confrontations of the war occurred in Union efforts to capture Richmond, New Orleans, Vicksburg, Atlanta, and other Confederate cities. For its part, in 1864 the Confederacy launched futile campaigns to take Nashville and Washington, DC.

Along with their role in politics and fighting, cities hosted the Confederacy's impressive wartime industrialization. Tredegar Iron Works in Richmond more than tripled its workforce by 1863 and produced more than a thousand cannon for the Confederacy. In 1864 Confederate cotton mills in Georgia alone churned out more than a million yards of cloth per month, and that state's cities increased their populations from between 50 and 100 percent in a few years.[3] What foreign trade the Confederacy could transact came through those ports that held out against the Union blockade, most prominently Wilmington, North Carolina, which remained in Confederate hands until 1865. Cities were also a prime destination for refugees, whose numbers contributed to the surge in wartime urban population.

Given how important Confederate cities were to the Civil War, any account of their history needs to confront their neglect in popular memory and in the dominant academic interpretations of the Civil War. What follows is an explanation of how the public and prior generations of historians have described the relationship between southern cities and the Civil War.

Public amnesia on the urban dimensions of the Civil War stems in large part from Confederate partisans' efforts, begun immediately after the war, to portray their cause as a struggle to preserve a traditional rural way of life from the forces of modernity and the centralizing government that allegedly went with it. For these and other reasons, postwar southern writers and intellectuals purposefully propagated the vision of an agrarian South devoid of cities. One of the earliest and most influential was Edward A. Pollard, who published *The Lost Cause: A New Southern History of the War of the Confederates* in 1866. According to Pollard the Confederacy had lost only because it had been overwhelmed by northern men and materiel, an outcome linked to different urban trajectories for the two regions. While in the North "towns had become great cities, Southern cities had decayed or become stationary." In the decades before the conflict, Pollard asserted, "The South continued to decline; she had no manufacturers, no great cities, no shipping interests; and although the agricultural productions of the South were the basis of the foreign commerce of the United States, yet Southern cities did not carry it on."[4] These were Pollard's opinions, not objective fact, but they nonetheless helped shape perceptions of the South for generations to come.

Authors of southern fiction also burnished this anti-urban myth of southern history. The agrarian nature of the Old South became a key component in romanticizing it as morally superior to both the North and the postwar world. Thomas Nelson Page and a host of other writers idealized the plantation South in hundreds of short stories and novels that led to the creation of the Moonlight and Magnolias myth of the South in which cities played no part. In a work of nonfiction, Page explained that in the South of 1860, with "the people being almost universally agricultural, and there being no cities and no great difference of interests, the structure of society was naturally simple." Ironically, urbanization in the late nineteenth century created a huge audience for works depicting a golden agrarian age and helped to spread such myths far and wide. Even academics like the Southern Agrarians in the 1920s, who, ironically, lived in Nashville, a city of over 100,000 residents, looked back to the supposed benefits of a rural, farming society in the antebellum South and proclaimed its "absence of urban settlements."[5] Along with telling popular stories that sold books, these writers also shared a political interest in fighting off challenges to Jim Crow segregation. By claiming to defend a mythologized rural, tradition-bound southern way of life, segregationists repackaged their support for Jim Crow's injustices into a more palatable stand in favor of old-time country values in opposition to a vague fear of change associated with urbanization itself, an ideal that even genteel suburbanites fleeing congestion in northern cities could endorse.

After 1945, people continued to promote an image of an overwhelmingly rural Civil War South for a wide variety of purposes. During the civil rights struggle of the 1950s and '60s the idea of the South as rural and backward-looking turned up in the rhetoric of segregationists claiming to defend tradition as well as integrationists attacking Jim Crow as a vestige of an antiquated rustic culture. At the same time filmmakers and authors adopted the trope of the South as rural and slow to modernize as a reaction to the rapid urbanization and industrialization of the South after 1945.[6] More recently, the rhetorical narrative of the Confederacy as a rural society has been reinforced in well-known controversies over displaying the Stars and Bars, celebrating Confederate History Month, or using Confederate mascots for college sports teams. For example, a 2013 promotion for Confederate heritage in Georgia claimed that "the South was the most peaceful, rural, and Christian part of America before war and Reconstruction destroyed the pastoral way of life here." Here the speaker not only employs the narrative of the rural, premodern Old South but also weaves into that story a common belief that evangelical Christianity stands for a simpler set of rural cultural values in opposition to urban cosmopolitanism.[7]

Another way to gauge public interest in the rural Civil War is attendance at federally designated Civil War historic sites. In 2012, just over one-third of the more than 12 million visitors to Civil War sites managed by the US National Park Service (NPS) visited an urban Civil War site, despite the natural advantage the urban sites have being in the middle of large population centers. In addition, those included places like Grant's Tomb in New York City and Kennesaw Mountain, just outside Atlanta, where visitors learn little about the urban dimensions of the conflict.[8] Meanwhile, the NPS administered Richmond National Battlefield Complex, which includes the Chimbarazo Medical Museum and Tredegar Iron Works, both prime examples of what cities contributed to the Confederacy, received slightly less than 157,000 visitors, placing it last among the top twenty-five NPS Civil War sites. Suffice to say that despite their very real existence prior to 1865, southern cities have been neglected in popular historical narratives about the Civil War–era South.

For much of the twentieth century this neglect of Confederate cities in popular memory resonated with comprehensive histories of the South's Civil War written by scholars. In his massive 568-page study of the Confederacy published in 1950, E. Merton Coulter devoted only five pages to the urban experience, much of it about tavern life, and began that section declaring that "the Confederacy was overwhelmingly rural." Later that decade, Clement Eaton wrote that the Confederate Constitution expressed "the agrarian interests of the vast majority of the people." Historians who emphasized the South's social diversity concentrated on different types of farmers. To the extent that urban issues appear in standard accounts of the Confederacy, they are mainly limited to the question of crowd violence in response to economic scarcity as manifested in the Richmond bread riots of 1863.[9]

Recent textbooks on the Civil War recognize more diversity in the antebellum South, and typically discuss cities as one of the various subsets of southern society that challenged the plantation belts for dominance. However, in narrating the war, southern cities remain on the margins, despite efforts to better integrate comparatively new fields of research such as gender, nationalism, and Native Americans. For instance, the latest edition of a popular textbook history of the South states "towns and cities helped unify the diverse elements of the antebellum South," but then in its chapter on the Confederacy omits any discussion of cities.[10] Significantly, one of the few textbooks to devote a separate section to "Cities and the Civil War" is *The Evolution of American Urban Society*, a book now in its seventh edition that was coauthored by Howard P. Chudacoff, a pioneer of the new urban history of the 1960s.[11]

As aggregates of their field, textbooks tend to lag behind the latest scholarship, reflecting long-term trends rather than the latest changes. Ironically, the bulk of recent studies of the Civil War urban South have been written by historians trained in Civil War and southern history, not by scholars specializing in urban history, yet the history of slave-state cities continues to be treated in mainstream works as something more pertinent to urban specialists rather than to Civil War–era historians. This discrepancy reflects long-term patterns in the study of southern urban history, particularly during its heyday in the 1960s and '70s.

Despite their comparative absence in popular commemoration and synthetic histories of the Civil War, wartime southern cities have been the subject of professional scholarship dating to the late 1800s when participants in the war still wrote its history.[12] In the first half of the twentieth century, a time when history came into its own as a professional discipline, histories of Confederate cities either concentrated on battles or followed the urban biography model that treated the city as an organic unit that "lived through" the Civil War and, in most cases, Union occupation.[13] The

Confederate years also showed up as a chapter in longer urban biographies that traced a city's growth from infancy to the present day. As Carl Abbott has argued, urban biography owed less to the booster tradition of city promotion than to the Chicago School of sociology associated with Robert Park and his emphasis on "urban ecology," or the interplay of forces that in their totality shape a city. Although not as deeply invested in the political stands taken by the Lost Cause writers and the later Southern Agrarians, some of the South's urban biographers tended to treat the Confederate cause as a noble one defeated by the forces of northern industry and modernization, ideas that also resonated with their time.[14]

This biographical approach to urban history started to decline in the 1960s in favor of the self-styled "new urban history" that dominated the field into the 1980s. Attracted to quantitative and comparative methods, new urban historians focused on thematic subjects such as occupational mobility or migration on scales that ranged from discrete neighborhoods to datasets of multiple cities.[15] Although never as narrowly focused on social mobility and immigrant communities, historians writing about the urban South adopted the new urban history's interest in statistical methods and going beyond unitary histories of particular cities.[16]

As applied to the South, the new urban history reinforced Eugene D. Genovese's influential interpretation of the master-slave relationship as antithetical to bourgeois capitalism. Also writing in the 1960s, Genovese famously argued that the "premodern quality of the Southern world was imparted to it by its dominant slaveholding class," adding, "the planters, in truth, grew into the closest thing to feudal lords imaginable in a nineteenth-century bourgeois republic."[17] Although not as doctrinaire about the master-slave relationship, the new urban history nonetheless operated within the reigning paradigm of northern modernity and southern premodern distinctiveness. As such, new urban historians found that the South made a useful comparison point for studying the larger history of American urbanization. Perhaps the best example of this scholarship on the urban South was the first of the genre, Richard Wade's *Slavery in the Cities*, published in 1964. Wade brought together data from ten of the largest southern cities to explore urban slavery. His overarching thesis was that "as the cities grew, they produced conditions which first strained, then undermined, the regime of bondage in the South's metropolises."[18] According to Wade, cities did so because they were quintessentially modern settings characterized by complexity, mobility, and a greater degree of personal liberty than could be found in the countryside. In an even larger study of the urban South, Goldfield argued that slavery made for a distinctively southern city, one that was less typically urban than its northern counterparts because of large numbers of rural-born southerners, minimal industrialization, and economic subordination to commercial networks centered in New York and London.[19]

Among their many contributions, Wade, Goldfield, and other new urban historians tended to reinforce the case for the region as predominantly rural and for cities as tangential to the history of the Confederacy. Much of this scholarship argued that the urbanization in the South was either significantly slower than elsewhere in the modern world or antithetical to the dominant trends of slave society. Such findings informed the perspective of synthetic histories of the Confederacy and the slave South published in that era. Citing the work of the new urban historians, Elizabeth Fox-Genovese argued that "Southern society, as a whole, did not generate a city-system. Villages and small towns abounded but rarely crossed the threshold to urban status." Echoing the standard works on the Confederacy, she concluded, "the South as a whole did not include enough heavy concentrations of population to counterbalance its overwhelmingly rural character." Fox-Genovese and Eugene D. Genovese wrote in a later study that "while cities and towns were setting the tone and driving the development of northern society, the countryside continued to set the tone for southern towns and cities and control their development." Similarly, after summarizing Richard Wade's findings, Peter Kolchin concluded that "if cities were peripheral to antebellum Southern life, they were even more so to antebellum Southern slavery."[20] The new urban history thus reinforced an outlook among scholars that cities were outliers to the dominant trends in southern society. This point of view quite logically minimized the role of cities when historians influenced by this scholarship came to write about the South during the Civil War era.

Although many of its findings about the comparative differences between northern and southern cities remain relevant, as several essays in this volume demonstrate, by the mid-1980s the momentum behind the new urban history had faded in step with a general move away from quantification and social theories that informed other "new" fields of histories that had started in the 1960s. In the 1990s some urban historians shifted their attention to questions about politics and culture—for example, studies by Mary Ryan and Phillip Ethington explored the creation of a public sphere in Civil War–era American cities, whereas others continued to work with long runs of data on questions about ethnicity and social class.[21] At the end of the decade Timothy Gilfoyle concluded that "interpretive confusion" had characterized "urban history since 1980. The inclusion of topics ranging from cultural representations of cities found in fiction to empirical studies of the built environment fractured an already splintered and internally divided field."[22]

Gilfoyle could have added that scholars specializing in urban studies had lost interest in Civil War cities, particularly southern ones. For urban historians, the event-driven questions of the rise of suburbia and the decline of central cities after 1945 grew in significance, especially because they offered clues to explaining our present-day political and cultural order in ways that the nineteenth-century city could not. Indicative of this trend, work on the Civil War–era South has lately been missing from the *Journal of Urban History*, a six-issue-per-year periodical that is the leading publication for urban historians. Between 2004 and 2014 it published only two essays on the South before 1865, and has produced little on the nineteenth century in general. Similarly, since the year 2000, urban history book series by leading academic presses have published very little on the nineteenth century and nothing on the South in that era.[23]

Thus, it may come as a surprise to learn that since 2000 academic presses, almost all of them known for southern and Civil War history, have published over forty books on the Civil War–era urban South, more than double the number produced during the preceding fourteen-year period 1985–1999.[24] This trend corresponds to the aforementioned revision in historians' interpretation of slavery's relationship to nineteenth-century capitalism and the modernizing changes that went with it. Where earlier scholarship emphasized the absence of wages and the fixed costs associated with slave ownership as barriers to the spread of capitalism, more recent studies have shown the adaptability of slave labor to factories, railroads, and flexible work schedules; the importance of the slave-produced cotton trade for the development of the market economy; and the crucial role played by property rights in slaves in financing southern economic development.[25] This scholarship on slavery and capitalism has been accompanied by new studies on the southern middle class as well as the planters, all of which shows these white southerners immersed in Victorian cultural trends that crossed the Atlantic.[26]

These challenges to the portrayal of southern society as overwhelmingly agrarian have encouraged historians to view cities as necessary players in the slave economy and as one of several types of southern social formations rather than as exceptions to the norm. Commenting on men and women writing about the South in the twenty-first century, James Cobb observes "no longer encumbered by the obligation to explain why things did not work out as they did in the North, they have been able to confront southern history on its own terms, as it happened to southerners both across and within not just racial, but class and gender groupings as well."[27] Cobb's point also applies to the geographic binary of urban and rural. Consequently southern and Civil War historians, even those who are not primarily concerned with the debate over slavery's modernity, have become more receptive to looking at cities as places that can shed light on larger themes of the period.

This new openness to studying the nineteenth-century urban South has been abetted by social theorists' growing doubts about the validity of the very core concepts that had shaped urban studies as an interdisciplinary field for much of the twentieth century. Dating to nineteenth-century sociologists like Emile Durkheim, Max Weber, Georg Simmel, and Ferdinand Tönnies, mid-twentieth-century social theorists, including the Chicago School, defined cities by not only dense settlement but also by a specific mix of markets, government, and public space characteristic of the modern metropolitan giants of their day. Similarly, American sociologist Louis Wirth interpreted urbanism as a distinctive way of life characterized by impersonal, contractual, and competitive human relations, and German geographer Walter Christaller defined urban networks as a hierarchical relationship between cities that conceived of central places or primate cities, such as New York or London, dominating an extended chain of smaller cities.[28] As critics have pointed out, these definitions treated the largest cities of North America and Western Europe as ideal types against which the rest of world urban history could be judged. When examined from the perspective of postcolonial societies or twenty-first-century mega-cities, conventional definitions have given way to more open-ended understandings of what constitutes a city, how people live in urban settings, and the network connections between urban places.[29]

For US urban historians such debates never mattered as much as specific problems in American cities such as migration, racial and ethnic conflict, and municipal politics. Nonetheless, the loss of confidence in theories that made the big cities of the Western world the archetypal standard has cast doubt on the long-held assumption that smaller southern cities were therefore relatively unimportant to the South's history.

The waning power of the theories that undergirded past scholarship has not only stimulated new research into southern cities, but also changed the very nature of the research agenda. Armed with a compelling model of urbanism as an intrinsically cosmopolitan and individualist cultural ethos, "new urban historians" such as Wade could organize scholarly research around the central question of whether the illiberal institution of slavery was compatible with urbanism and, if not, what consequences that conflict had for the development of cities across the slave South. Shorn of such theoretical sureties about what it means to live in a city, much less what truly defines a city in the first place, today's wave of research into southern cities stands out for its lack of such a field-organizing debate. Rather than rebut the findings of that older scholarship, much of the most recent scholarship has simply discarded older, more dogmatic assertions about the place of cities in southern history in favor of a much more diverse approach to what kinds of things cities can reveal about the history of the South during the Civil War.

This volume highlights the important contributions of the last decade's writing on Confederate cities by showing how cities were at the forefront of change in the Confederacy with long-term consequences for the entire South. The timeworn analytical division of urban and rural helps to sort social experience but it also distorts the overlap between town and country produced by the circulation of people, information, and commodities between them. Although present before 1861, this back-and-forth intensified during the war, and thereby increased the reach of urban places into southern society.

The following chapters illustrate a range of ways that urban questions became central to broad challenges facing the Confederacy. For example, conflicts over gender could find expression in town in ways not possible in the countryside because urban places had the stores, brothels, taverns, and congested public spaces necessary for playing out individual expectations of manly and feminine conduct. For black southerners, who were even more likely to live in rural places than whites in 1860, cities and towns nonetheless played an outsized role in the struggle for freedom. Cities did so because they provided critical infrastructure, be it schools, jobs, or public gathering places for contesting the meaning of freedom. In one of the greater ironies of southern history, the ideological movement to save what its advocates claimed was a traditional rural society from the onslaught of urban modernity was carried out by city dwellers. And, of course, the beginnings of an urban industrial "New South" began in southern cities, however fitfully.

This new wave of scholarship also brings out the peculiar character of the urban South and in doing so sheds light on the distinctiveness of southern society as a whole. No matter how much more dynamic than previously thought, the slave states had fewer cities and factories than did the North, and that material difference caught the notice of almost every observer of the Civil War. Southern cities were different than northern ones both in size and because of slavery. But they were also notably different from the rural South. Slave-state cities were whiter, had more foreign-born immigrants, more non-enslaved African Americans, more industry, wage labor, print-ing presses, markets, and cosmopolitan culture than the rural South. These features made southern cities glaring outliers to the social ideal of the plan-tation and provided some secessionists with fodder for crafting a pastoral ideal of southern society.

The Civil War brought destruction to this late antebellum incarnation of the urban South. For cities, as well as the nation at large, emancipation was the most important change wrought by Confederate defeat. With free-dom, black southerners began moving to cities during the war and never stopped. Once there, African Americans built schools, claimed public space, and developed networks for their own advancement that outshone the ear-lier efforts of much smaller antebellum free black urban communities.

The war and its aftermath also spurred the growth of an urban network in the upland interior. A railroad boom funded by Reconstruction govern-ments spurred town building along an east-west traffic corridor in the in-terior with Atlanta at its center and new South towns such as Charlotte, Dallas, and Birmingham feeding into it. Meanwhile European immigration ground to a halt and failed to pick up after 1865, cutting the urban South off from most of the late nineteenth century's influx of southern and eastern Europeans who came to work in the factories of the North, which escaped the wartime destruction wreaked on southern industry. Although a few ports handled commerce through the blockade, Confederate cities turned inward to supply the needs of their fledgling nation and, in turn, to feed off the sustenance of Confederate farms. It would take capital from the North and Europe to spur a new wave of southern urban growth.

Thus instead of foreign-born immigrants, the postwar urban South drew on its nearby rural population for growth. This influx of near rural new-comers meant that the South's cities had a higher share of southern-born residents after 1865 than before. Their presence mattered not only for put-ting cities at the forefront of the battle over freedpeople's rights but also for connecting city dwellers to Confederate memory. Those connections made bound these cities to regional norms not shared elsewhere in the United States. By the early 1900s the difference between the urban South and other American cities was obvious to any traveler. Historian John Cell has noted the leading role played by cities in developing segregation. In his words, "Jim Crow, it seems, was not born and bred among 'rednecks' in the coun-try. First and foremost he was a city slicker."[30] Segregation imposed a strict, overt racial apartheid on the urban South that, although echoed in the daily life of the rest of the country, did not have the stigma of official sanction. With segregation came a conservative culture that made it more likely that

America's bohemia would thrive in northern cities rather than southern ones.[31]

More than a decade of new research in the Civil War–era urban South shows that the way the southern cities looked in 1900 can be traced back to the impact of the Civil War, and that the war cannot be fully understood without appreciating the role played by cities as crucibles of change. This new approach to the urban South has the advantage of bringing cities back into the history of the Civil War. Perhaps no single scholar better exemplifies the shift in attention than David Goldfield, pioneer of southern urban history and editor of the *Journal of Urban History*. Although still engaged in urban history, Goldfield has most recently written on the Civil War. In his foreword, Goldfield reminds us that "this is more than a book about southern cities; it is a book about the South and the nation." With this mission in mind, *Confederate Cities* showcases the renaissance in southern urban history even as it seeks to re-engage the big questions about cities and region that mattered to an earlier generation.

The book begins with two thematic essays by J. Matthew Gallman and David Moltke-Hansen that debate the big historiographic question about the urban South's modernity. These authors agree on the basic facts that cities in the late antebellum South were growing rapidly but that their size paled in comparison to the cities of the North. They differ in choosing what to emphasize from these trends—the external comparison with the North, or the internal dynamics of the urban South—and from this emphasis present two very different pictures of the Civil War–era urban South. Gallman starts by tracing urban development in the antebellum South and comparing it to what was happening in the North. He finds the institution of slavery pivotal, arguing that the economic importance of slavery and plantation agriculture caused southern towns to grow into small urban centers without becoming true cities like those in the North. Gallman contends that the South's limited urban network hurt the Confederacy's ability to wage war and meant that the southern cities did not constitute major strategic targets for the Union war effort. Moltke-Hansen, in contrast, looks at southern urbanization on its own terms and finds a more robust pattern of urban development flourishing underneath the shadows cast by the North. He contends that in the 1850s improved transportation and communication consolidated a networked South that reached its apotheosis in the new Confederate nation. One facet of this dynamism was the publishing network run through these cities by Confederate nationalists. For Moltke-Hansen, urban decline and decline as a trope of southern intellectual life had to wait for the postwar era.

The two essays on secession explore the complicated and often contradictory roles southern cities played in Confederate nation building. Frank Towers analyzes the intertwined and competing agendas of southern secessionists and urban boosters. While often critical of cities in their promotion of a new nation, southern secessionists appealed to the boosters of the urban South with promises that their particular city could become the "New York of the South." Urban boosters, meanwhile, sought to use the secession movement to advance their own transnational and cosmopolitan dreams for their city, even though it was often at odds with a Confederate nationalist vision of a self-sufficient, slave-based society that looked after the interests of its rural farmers and planters. Towers suggests that the tensions between cosmopolitan and rural, transnational and national, city and nation, undermined the effectiveness of Confederate nationalism as a means for unifying white southerners during the Civil War.

Lloyd Benson thinks southerners were better at negotiating the differences between urbanism and nation building. Taking a global comparative approach that puts gendered language at the forefront of his analysis, Benson examines the understudied question of Confederate unification; the post–Fort Sumter merger of Virginia and three other Upper South states with the seven existing states of the Confederacy. By placing southern cities in the context of the Atlantic world—comparing Richmond, Virginia, and Charleston, South Carolina, to cities in British North America and Europe also struggling at the same time with unification and emerging nation states—Benson shows how urban nationalists in all three would-be nations used metaphors of family and gender to promote the unification of the city and the countryside and thereby combine the cosmopolitan and the national. In the cities of the South, however, he finds that slavery and race served as a "trump card," making gendered rhetoric particularly effective in the nationalist deployment of gender and family rhetoric. Towers and Benson show how cities as symbols and as sites for political mobilization in their own right shaped the South's internal debate over secession and Union.

Among the major historiographic breakthroughs of the past two decades has been the explosion of studies on gender and the Civil War.[32] In this volume gender is the subject of not only Benson's essay, which uses gender primarily as a discursive category, but also essays by Michael Pierson and Keith Bohannon who explore gender as urban social experience. Pierson looks at how the bars and brothels of New Orleans constituted a recognizable urban, gendered landscape for northern soldiers like Spaulding—whom Pierson identifies as an adherent of a rough masculinity in opposition to evangelical manhood—and helped them to negotiate the South as a whole. Whereas Gallman insists that southern cities were not "northernized," Pierson argues that Spalding and his comrades easily recognized the gender and cultural milieu of New Orleans, providing both a sense of familiarity and the ability to continue their prewar gender roles while occupying the South. Bohannon, meanwhile, takes up perhaps the most celebrated example of women's activism in Confederacy, the 1863 bread riots, and revises some key claims about those events. He challenges recent interpretations of the riots as solely either an example of premarket values or, as Stephanie McCurry has recently argued, the politicization of women upset about government indifference.[33] Instead, Bohannon argues that all levels of government in the South were working to alleviate shortages of necessities and that it was the unique urban environment created during the first two years of the war that produced these riots on the Georgia homefront in 1863. Further challenging an understanding of bread riots as a manifestation of straightforward dissent against Jefferson Davis's government, Bohannon also brings out the rioters' anger at speculating merchants, many of them Jews, a group perceived as parasitical outsiders in southern towns at that time.

The effects of emancipation for African Americans and the urban South after the Civil War drive the three essays in the emancipation section. Hilary Green examines the Freedmen's Bureau schools in Mobile, Alabama, from 1865 to 1867. Building upon Mobile's urban infrastructure and tradition of antebellum Creole education, African Americans created an educational system in the city that they saw as a model for the entire state. Green argues that African Americans' struggle for education illustrates the transformative nature of the Civil War and the ways that African Americans defined the meanings of freedom and citizenship in the postwar urban South. Offering a different approach to the meanings of freedom and citizenship, Justin Behrend focuses on the political mobilization of African Americans in Natchez, Mississippi, and its relationship with the urban environment. Too often, he insists, historians both ignore agrarian cities like Natchez and see cities merely as a setting in which events take place and ideas are contested, not as places in which people interact with the urban environment. He contends that it was not emancipation that fundamentally altered urban life, but the political mobilization of ex-slaves, for once black men became involved in government the existing public spaces took on new meanings and the policies of the emancipated electorate reshaped the character of the city.

Andrew Slap analyzes how and why Memphis, Tennessee, became a majority African American city in the decades after the Civil War. While Green focuses on education and Behrend concentrates on political mobilization, Slap examines how African American military service helped reshape the postwar urban South. After the Civil War African American veterans lived in Memphis and other southern cities at a much higher rate than whites or other African Americans, disproportionately changing the demography of these cities. Slap suggests that social networks among African American veterans were both a cause and a consequence of these high rates of urbanization. The different effects of emancipation in various southern cities examined in the three essays helps to dehomogenize the African American experience and demonstrate the importance of place and local circumstances in determining the effects of emancipation in the urban South.

The two essays in the last section focus explicitly on how the Civil War created a new urban South. William Link examines the wartime experiences of arguably the most important and transformed city in Georgia during the war, Atlanta. The crucible of war transformed Atlanta from a growing mid-sized antebellum city into one of the principal industrial and transportation centers of the entire South. Much like Richmond, Virginia, Atlanta became a major objective of the Union Army, and Link contends that the invasion of North Georgia in 1864 fundamentally remade the city, both during the war and in the decades afterward. While the surge of immigrants, new wealth, and Union occupation all changed the city's social landscape, Link argues that the most profound transformation was the end of slavery and the expanded presence of African Americans in Atlanta. Compared to Atlanta, it took longer for the Civil War to unleash economic development in Hampton Roads, Virginia, as John Majewski shows in the last essay. He argues that a combination of slavery and environmental factors limited the region's economic development in the antebellum period, for the acidic soils discouraged the growth of densely populated hinterlands that could support industry and commerce while the inequality of slavery inhibited industrialization. The creation of truly national capital markets and networks after the war, Majewski contends, led to an infusion of northern capital that allowed the cities of Hampton Roads finally to build the railroads and other infrastructure needed to escape the confines of their sparsely settled hinterland and grow into dynamic commercial and industrial centers. In this respect, Majewski discounts recent arguments that the urban South had an internal dynamism capable of advancing without external capital and outside capitalists.

Taken together, the essays in this volume highlight new ways of connecting southern cities to the Civil War. This volume is marked by its thematic diversity—it looks at nationalism, gender, environment, education, and public space, among other topics—and its intellectual engagement with the origins and outcomes of the Civil War, with essays covering the entire gamut of the nineteenth century.

To be sure, the majority of our essays, like the majority of southern historians writing today, oppose the narrowest view of southern distinctiveness advocated by historians writing during the Cold War era. In that time, scholars with perspectives as wildly different as Louis Hartz and Eugene Genovese could agree that the South was opposed to the mainstream of American development. As noted above, that perspective regarded cities as outside of the main currents of southern history and much of the late twentieth-century scholarship on the urban South started from the premise that southern cities were underdeveloped. Since the 1990s, historians have rejected the strictest versions of this earlier interpretive framework and thereby opened the door for scholars to consider southern cities as part of the South rather than outliers to its history. This volume, which highlights the current renaissance in southern urban history, testifies to the renewed appreciation for *cities as southern*. Where an earlier generation shied away from cities as places to explore the Confederate experience, our authors show no such caution and display the many ways that urban history was also Confederate history.

As befitting a developing field, no defining interpretation characterizes this volume. Instead it showcases the diversity of new scholarship on the Civil War–era urban South and highlights the key points of debate in the broader revision of nineteenth-century southern history. In so doing, the contributors hope to bring greater attention to what has thus been a piecemeal accumulation of new scholarship on Confederate cities conducted largely outside the mainstream study of urban history. Perhaps now is the time to restore a once-fruitful connection between the study of the nineteenth-century South and the field of urban history.

NOTES

1.   After a hiatus from the debates over slavery and capitalism that centered on Robert William Fogel and Stanley Engerman's 1974 study *Time on the Cross: The Economics*

of American Negro Slavery, a new wave of scholarship emerged in the late 1990s that added cultural understandings of capitalism onto the earlier era's debate over slave labor efficiency. Beginning with books such as Mark W. Smith's *Mastered by the Clock: Time, Slavery, and Freedom in the American South* (Chapel Hill: University of North Carolina Press, 1997) and Walter Johnson's *Soul By Soul: Life Inside the Antebellum Slave Market* (Cambridge, MA: Harvard University Press, 1999), a vast amount of scholarship, too lengthy to be catalogued herein, has revised historians' understanding of slavery and capitalism. For the most recent examples see Sven Beckert, *Empire of Cotton: A Global History* (New York: Knopf, 2014); Edward E. Baptist, *The Half Has Never Been Told: Slavery and the Making of American Capitalism* (New York: Basic Books, 2014); Walter Johnson, *River of Dark Dreams: Slavery and Empire in the Cotton Kingdom* (Cambridge, MA: Harvard University Press, 2013); Joshua D. Rothman, *Flush Times and Fever Dreams: A Story of Capitalism and Slavery in the Age of Jackson* (Athens: University of Georgia Press, 2012); Bonnie Martin, "Slavery's Invisible Engine: Mortgaging Human Property," *Journal of Southern History* 76 (November 2010): 817–66; Caitlin C. Rosenthal, "From Memory to Mastery: Accounting for Control in America, 1750–1880," *Enterprise and Society* 14 (December 2013): 732–48; Amy Dru Stanley, "Slave Breeding and Free Love: An Antebellum Argument over Slavery, Capitalism, and Personhood," in *Capitalism Takes Command: The Social Transformation of Nineteenth-Century America*, ed. Michael Zakim and Gary J. Kornblith (Chicago: University of Chicago Press, 2012), 119–44; and Michael O'Malley, *Face Value: The Entwined Histories of Money and Race in America* (Chicago: University of Chicago Press, 2012). For recent historiographic discussions of the history of capitalism and slavery's place in it see Sven Beckert et al., "Interchange: The History of Capitalism," *Journal of American History* 101, no. 2 (2014): 503–36; Seth Rockman, "What Makes the History of Capitalism Newsworthy?," *Journal of the Early Republic* 34, no. 3 (2014): 439–66, esp. 444–45; and Anthony E. Kaye, "The Second Slavery: Modernity in the Nineteenth-Century South and the Atlantic World," *Journal of Southern History* 75 (August 2009): 627–50. For a very important challenge to arguments for slavery as an expression of capitalism see Scott P. Marler's contributions in "Interchange" (above) and his book *The Merchants' Capital: New Orleans and the Political Economy of the Nineteenth-Century South* (New York: Cambridge University Press, 2013).

2. Michael O'Brien, *Conjectures of Order: Intellectual Life in the American South, 1810–1860*, 2 vols. (Chapel Hill: University of North Carolina Press, 2004), 1:18; Jonathan Daniel Wells, *The Origins of the Southern Middle Class, 1800–1861* (Chapel Hill: University of North Carolina Press, 2004), 163.

3. Harold S. Wilson, *Confederate Industry: Manufacturers and Quartermasters in the Civil War* (Jackson: University Press of Mississippi, 2002), 291–92; Chad Morgan, *Planters' Progress: Modernizing Confederate Georgia* (Gainesville: University Press of Florida, 2005), 88. Also see Mary A. DeCredico, *Patriotism for Profit: Georgia's Urban Entrepreneurs and the Confederate War Effort* (Chapel Hill: University of North Carolina Press, 1990).

4. Edward A. Pollard, *The Lost Cause: A New Southern History of the War of the Confederates* (New York: E. B. Treat, 1866), 60–61. The best description of the Myth of

the Lost Cause is probably Alan T. Nolan's essay "The Anatomy of the Myth" in *The Myth of the Lost Cause and Civil War History*, ed. Gary W. Gallagher and Alan T. Nolan (Bloomington: Indiana University Press, 2000), 11–34. The two current major works on Civil War memory are David W. Blight, *Race and Reunion: The Civil War in American History* (Cambridge, MA: Harvard University Press, 2001) and Caroline E. Janney, *Remembering the Civil War: Reunion and the Limits of Reconciliation* (Chapel Hill: University of North Carolina Press, 2013).

5. Thomas Nelson Page, *The Old South: Essays Social and Political* (New York: Charles Scribner and Sons, 1892), 111; *I'll Take My Stand: The South and the Agrarian Tradition* (New York: Harper and Bros., 1930), 96.

6. Jack Temple Kirby, *Media Made Dixie: The South in the American Imagination* (Athens: University of Georgia Press, 1986), 158; W. Stuart Towns, *Enduring Legacy: Rhetoric and Ritual of the Lost Cause* (Tuscaloosa: University of Alabama Press, 2012), 126; James C. Cobb, *Away Down South: A History of Southern Identity* (New York: Oxford University Press, 2005), 244–46; Gary W. Gallagher, *Causes Won, Lost, and Forgotten: How Hollywood and Popular Art Shape What We Know about the Civil War* (Chapel Hill: University of North Carolina Press, 2005), 55.

7. For controversies over the flag and other Confederate heritage issues see Towns, *Enduring Legacy*, 139–44; David Goldfield, *Still Fighting the Civil War: The American South and Southern History* (Baton Rouge: Louisiana State University Press, 2002), 311–14. Quotation is in John Avlon, "Georgia Is Celebrating Confederate History and Heritage Month?" The Daily Beast, April 2, 2013, http://www.thedailybeast.com /articles/2013/04/02/georgia-is-celebrating-confederate-heritage-and-history-month -really.html (accessed February 23, 2014).

8. Data collected from National Parks Service Visitor Use Statistics, "Annual Park Ranking Report for Recreation Visitors in 2012," https://irma.nps.gov/Stats/SSRS Reports/National%20Reports/Annual%20Park%20Ranking%20Report%20%281979 %20-%20Last%20Calendar%20Year%29 (accessed February 16, 2014). Because of its place in historical memory in the civil rights movement and its inclusion in the highly trafficked National Mall, where visitors typically view several monuments covering a long span of US history, attendance numbers for the Lincoln Memorial are not included.

9. E. Merton Coulter, *The Confederate States of America, 1861–1865* (Baton Rouge: Louisiana State University Press, 1950), 409; Clement Eaton, *A History of the Southern Confederacy* (New York: Free Press, 1954), 52; Emory M. Thomas, *The Confederate Nation: 1861–1865* (New York: Harper and Row, 1979), 16; William L. Barney, *Battleground for the Union: The Era of the Civil War and Reconstruction, 1848–1877* (Englewood Cliffs, NJ: Prentice-Hall, 1990), 109. Also see David Herbert Donald, Jean Harvey Baker, and Michael F. Holt, *The Civil War and Reconstruction* (New York: Norton, 2001), 30. For an example of the use of the Richmond bread riots as the main example of urban issues in the Confederacy see William C. Davis, *Look Away! A History of the Confederate States of America* (New York: Free Press, 2002), 212–18.

The bread riots have become the focal point for a new wave of studies on gender in the Confederacy, including major works by Drew Faust and Stephanie McCurry. As discussed below, Keith Bohannon in this volume takes another look at those iconic events as well. To be sure these examples of civic unrest remain an important, iconic touchstone for understanding dissent within the Confederacy but for too long they have been treated as the only instance of urban social conflict during the Civil War as witnessed by the inclusion in older studies of the conflict that say little else about Confederate cities beyond the Richmond bread riots.

10. Quotations are from William J. Cooper and Thomas E. Terrill, *The American South: A History*, 4th ed. (Lanham, MD: Rowman and Littlefield, 2009), 355. See Jonathan Daniel Wells, *A House Divided: The Civil War and Mid-Nineteenth Century America* (New York: Routledge, 2012), 18, 192–211; and Christopher Olsen, *The American Civil War: A Hands-On History* (New York: Hill and Wang, 2006). An exception is Scott Nelson and Carol Sheriff, *A People at War: Civilians and Soldiers in America's Civil War* (New York: Oxford University Press, 2007), which discusses the importance of garrison cities to Union occupation on pages 86–88.

11. Howard P. Chudacoff, Judith E. Smith, and Peter C. Baldwin, *The Evolution of American Urban Society*, 7th ed. (New York: Pearson, 2010), 74.

12. For examples see Emily Hazen Reed, *Life of A. P. Dostie: Or, the Conflict of New Orleans* (New York: W. P. Tomlinson, 1868); Charles C. Jones, *The Siege and Evacuation of Savannah, Georgia, in December 1864* (Augusta, GA: Chronicle Publishing Co., 1890); Grenville M. Dodge, *The Battle of Atlanta and Other Campaigns, Addresses, Etc.* (Council Bluffs, IA: Monarch Printing Co., 1910).

13. Patrick W. Rembert, *The Fall of Richmond* (Baton Rouge: Louisiana State University Press, 1960); Alfred Hoyt Bill and Carl H. Pforzheimer, *The Beleaguered City: Richmond, 1861–1865* (New York: Knopf, 1945); Gerald M. Capers, *Occupied City: New Orleans under the Federals, 1862–1865* (Lexington: University of Kentucky Press, 1965).

14. Examples include Gerald M. Capers, *The Biography of a River Town: Memphis: Its Heroic Age* (Chapel Hill: University of North Carolina Press, 1939); Franklin M. Garrett, *Atlanta and Environs: A Chronicle of Its People and Events, 1820s–1870s* (Athens: University of Georgia Press, 1954); Harnett T. Kane and Carl H. Pforzheimer, *Queen New Orleans: City by the River* (New York: W. Morrow, 1949). For the relationship between the Chicago School and urban biography see Carl Abbott, "Thinking about Cities: The Central Tradition in U.S. Urban History," *Journal of Urban History* 22 (September 1996): 692–94.

15. Eric H. Monkkonen, *America Becomes Urban: The Development of American Cities and Towns, 1780–1980* (Berkeley: University of California Press, 1988), 24–30.

16. Leading examples of this scholarship include Richard C. Wade, *Slavery in the Cities: The South, 1820–1860* (New York: Oxford University Press, 1964); John Blassingame, *Black New Orleans, 1860–1880* (Chicago: University of Chicago Press, 1973); Claudia Dale Goldin, *Urban Slavery in the American South, 1820–1860: A Quantitative History* (Chicago: University of Chicago Press, 1976); David R. Goldfield, *Urban Growth in the Age of Sectionalism: Virginia, 1847–1861* (Baton Rouge: Louisiana State University Press, 1977), and *Cotton Fields and Skyscrapers: Southern City and Region, 1607–1980* (Baton Rouge: Louisiana State University Press, 1982); Blaine Brownell and David A. Goldfield, *The City in Southern History: The Growth of Urban Civilization in the South* (Port Washington, NY: Kennikat Press, 1977); Leonard P. Curry,

The Free Black in Urban America, 1800–1850: The Shadow of the Dream (Chicago: University of Chicago Press, 1981); Don H. Doyle, *New Men, New Cities, New South: Atlanta, Nashville, Charleston, Mobile, 1860–1910* (Chapel Hill: University of North Carolina Press, 1990); Kathleen C. Berkeley, *Like a Plague of Locusts: From an Antebellum Town to a New South City, Memphis, Tennessee, 1850–1880* (New York: Garland, 1991).

17. Eugene Genovese, *The Political Economy of Slavery: Studies in the Economy and Society of the Slave South* (New York: Pantheon, 1965), 3, 31. For a recent defense of Genovese's views see Marc Egnal, "What If Genovese Is right? The Premodern Outlook of Southern Planters," in *The Old South's Modern Worlds: Slavery, Region, and Nation in the Age of Progress*, ed. L. Diane Barnes, Brian Schoen, and Frank Towers (New York: Oxford University Press, 2011), 269–87.

18. Wade, *Slavery in the Cities*, 4.

19. Goldfield, *Urban Grow in an Age of Sectionalism* and *Cotton Fields and Sky Scrapers*.

20. Elizabeth Fox-Genovese, *Within the Plantation Household: Black and White Women of the Old South* (Chapel Hill: University of North Carolina Press, 1988), 78; Elizabeth Fox-Genovese and Eugene D. Genovese, *The Mind of the Master Class: History and Faith in the Southern Slaveholders' Worldview* (New York: Cambridge University Press, 2005), 2; Peter Kolchin, *American Slavery, 1619–1877* (New York: Hill and Wang, 1993), 178. Another example is William W. Freehling, *The South vs. The South: How Anti-Confederate Southerners Shaped the Course of the Civil War* (New York: Oxford University Press, 2001) 23.

21. Phillip J. Ethington, *The Public City: The Political Construction of Urban Life in San Francisco, 1850–1900* (New York: Cambridge University Press, 1994); Mary P. Ryan, *Civic Wars: Democracy and Public Life in the American City during the Nineteenth Century* (Berkeley: University of California Press, 1997).

22. Timothy J. Gilfoyle, "White Cities, Linguistic Turns, and Disneylands: The New Paradigms of Urban History," *Reviews in American History* 26 (1998): 176.

23. See the table of contents for *Journal of Urban History*, 2004–2014. The two articles are both on Baltimore. See Mary P. Ryan, "Democracy Rising: The Monuments of Baltimore, 1809–1842," *Journal of Urban History* 36 (March 2010): 127–50; and David Schley, "Tracks in the Streets: Railroads, Infrastructure, and Urban Space in Baltimore, 1828–1840," *Journal of Urban History* 39 (November 2013): 1062–84. Of the thirty-nine books published in the University of Chicago Press's Historical Studies of Urban America since 2000, only two examine the pre–Civil War United States, and both are about New York City. Columbia University Press's Columbia History of Urban Life Series managed to produce one book, also on New York City, on the nineteenth-century United States since 2000. However, their output surpasses the absence of any nineteenth-century studies published by Ashgate's Historical Urban Studies series, the Urban Studies Series of Oxford University Press, and that of Temple University Press. Finally, the programs of the Urban History Association have been heavily tilted toward the twentieth century. To take the 2014 conference as an example, only seven of ninety-six panels considered material prior to 1900.

For more on this trend see Clay McShane, "The State of the Art in North American Urban History," *Journal of Urban History* 32 (May 2006): 589.

24. These numbers are based on a search of WorldCat, a database of more than 10,000 university libraries available at http://www.worldcat.org. For examples of this scholarship see Stephen J. Ochs, *A Black Patriot and a White Priest: Andre Cailloux and Claude Paschal Maistre in Civil War New Orleans* (Baton Rouge: Louisiana State University Press, 2000); Gregg D. Kimball, *American City, South Place: A Cultural History of Antebellum Richmond* (Athens: University of Georgia Press, 2000); Louis S. Gerteis, *Civil War St. Louis* (Lawrence: University of Kansas Press, 2001); Michael W. Fitzgerald, *Urban Emancipation: Popular Politics in Reconstruction Mobile, 1860–1890* (Baton Rouge: Louisiana State University Press, 2002); Nelson Lankford, *Richmond Burning: The Last Days of the Confederate Capital* (New York: Viking, 2002); Judith Kelleher Schafer, *Becoming Free, Remaining Free: Manumission and Enslavement in New Orleans, 1846–1862* (Baton Rouge: Louisiana State University Press, 2003); Elizabeth R. Varon, *Southern Lady, Yankee Spy: The True Story of Elizabeth Van Lew, a Union Agent in the Heart of the Confederacy* (New York: Oxford University Press, 2003); Frank Towers, *The Urban South and the Coming of the Civil War* (Charlottesville: University of Virginia Press, 2004); Alecia P. Long, *The Great Southern Babylon: Sex, Race, and Respectability in New Orleans, 1865–1920* (Baton Rouge: Louisiana State University Press, 2004); Morgan, *Planters' Progress*; A. Wilson Greene, *Civil War Petersburg: A Confederate City in the Crucible of War* (Charlottesville: University of Virginia Press, 2006); James K. Hogue, *Uncivil War: Five New Orleans Street Battles and the Rise and Fall of Radical Reconstruction* (Baton Rouge: Louisiana State University Press, 2006); Robert Tracy McKenzie, *Lincolnites and Rebels: A Divided Town in the American Civil War* (Oxford: New York University Press, 2006); Jacqueline Jones, *Saving Savannah: The City and the Civil War* (New York: Alfred A. Knopf, 2008); Bruce W. Eelman, *Entrepreneurs in the Southern Upcountry: Commercial Culture in Spartanburg, South Carolina, 1845–1880* (Athens: University of Georgia Press, 2008); Michael D. Pierson, *Mutiny at Fort Jackson: The Untold Story of the Fall of New Orleans* (Chapel Hill: University of North Carolina Press, 2008); LeeAnn Whites and Alecia P. Long, eds., *Occupied Women: Gender, Military Occupation, and the American Civil War* (Baton Rouge: Louisiana State University Press, 2009); Justin Nystrom, *New Orleans after the Civil War: Race, Politics, and a New Birth of Freedom* (Baltimore: Johns Hopkins University Press, 2010); Kate Masur, *An Example for All the Land: Emancipation and the Struggle Over Equality in Washington, D.C.* (Chapel Hill: University of North Carolina Press, 2010); Robert Harrison, *Washington during the Civil War and Reconstruction* (New York: Cambridge University Press, 2011); Adam Arenson, *The Great Heart of the Republic: St. Louis and the Cultural Civil War* (Cambridge, MA: Harvard University Press, 2011); Scott P. Marler, *The Merchants' Capital: New Orleans and the Political Economy of the Nineteenth-Century South* (New York: Cambridge University Press, 2013); Kenneth J. Winkle, *Lincoln's Citadel: The Civil War in Washington, DC* (New York: W. W. Norton, 2013); William A. Link, *Atlanta, Cradle of the New South: Race and Remembering in the Civil War's Aftermath* (Chapel Hill: University

of North Carolina Press, 2013); Stephen V. Ash, *A Massacre in Memphis: The Race Riot That Shook the Nation One Year after the Civil War* (New York: Hill and Wang, 2013); Aaron D. Anderson, *Builders of a New South: Merchants, Capital, and the Remaking of Natchez, 1865–1914* (Jackson, Miss.: University Press of Mississippi, 2013); Wendy H. Venet, *A Changing Wind: Commerce and Conflict in Civil War Atlanta* (New Haven, CT: Yale University Press, 2014).

25. See n. 1 above for recent examples of this work.

26. For overviews of this literature see the contributions by Laura Edwards, Peter Kolchin, and Jonathan Daniel Wells to "Forum: Commemorating Seventy-Five Years of *The Journal of Southern History*," *Journal of Southern History* 73 (August 2009): 533–80, 627–62; Barnes, Schoen, and Towers, eds., *The Old South's Modern Worlds*, 3–25; and Jonathan Wells and Jennifer R. Green, eds. *The Southern Middle Class in the Nineteenth Century* (Baton Rouge: Louisiana State University Press, 2011), 1–15.

27. Cobb, *Away Down South*, 336.

28. This very brief statement of defining terms references a deep literature on the topic going back as far as Plato. Among the influential statements are Ferdinand Tönnies, *Community and Society* (Gemeinschaft und Gesellschaft [1887]), trans. Charles P. Loomis (rpt.: Devon, UK: Dover Books, 2002), esp. 226–30; Georg Simmel, *The Metropolis and Mental Life* (1903); Max Weber, *The City* (1921; rpt. Glencoe, IL: Free Press, 1986); Walter Christaller, *Central Places in Southern Germany*, translation by Carlisle Whiteford Baskin of 1933 edition, *Die zentralen Orte in Süddeutschland* (Englewood Cliffs, NJ: Prentice-Hall, 1966); Louis Wirth, "Urbanism as a Way of Life," *American Journal of Sociology* 44, no. 1 (1938): 1–24; Henri Lefebvre, *The Urban Revolution*, translation by Robert Bonono of 1970 edition (rpt.: Minneapolis: University of Minnesota Press, 2002), see esp. ch 1. For an overview see Peter Saunders, *Social Theory and the Urban Question*, 2nd ed. (London: Hutchinson, 1986).

29. For criticisms of this earlier theoretical work see Jan De Vries, "Problems in the Measurement, Description, and Analysis of Historical Urbanization," in *Urbanization in History: A Process of Dynamic Interactions*, ed. Ad van der Woude, Akira Hayami, and Jan De Vries (New York: Oxford University Press, 1995), 43–60; Richard G. Smith, "World City Actor Networks," *Progress in Human Geography* 27, no. 1 (2003): 25–44, 32 (quotation); Ben Derudder, "On Conceptual Confusion in Empirical Analyses of a Transnational Urban Network," *Urban Studies* 43 (October 2006), 2027–46; Peter J. Taylor, "Urban Economics in Thrall to Christaller: A Misguided Search for City Hierarchies in External Urban Relations," *Environment and Planning—Part A* 41 (January 2009): 2550–55; Neil Brenner, "Theses on Urbanization," *Public Culture* 25, no. 1 (2013): 85–114.

30. John W. Cell, *The Highest Stage of White Supremacy: The Origins of Segregation in South Africa and the American South* (New York: Cambridge University Press, 1982), 134.

31. Although they do not refer to the comparison between the South and other regions discussed in this introduction, historians such as Glenda Gilmore have noted that within the interwar South cities and towns could be more cosmopolitan than the surrounding countryside, notwithstanding the presence of segregation. See *Defying Dixie: The Radical Roots of Civil Rights, 1919–1950* (New York: Norton, 2008).

32. For examples see Catherine Clinton and Nina Silber, eds. *Divided House: Gender and the American Civil War* (New York: Oxford University Press, 1992); Stephanie McCurry, *Masters of Small Worlds: Yeoman Households, Gender Relations, and the Political Culture of the Antebellum South Carolina Low Country* (New York: Oxford University Press, 1995); Drew G. Faust, *Mothers of Invention: Women of the Slaveholding South in the American Civil War* (Chapel Hill: University of North Carolina Press, 1996); Michael D. Pierson, *Free Hearts and Free Homes: Gender and American Antislavery Politics* (Chapel Hill: University of North Carolina Press, 2003); Stephen Berry, *All That Makes a Man: Love and Ambition in the Civil War South* (New York: Oxford University Press, 2003); Nina Silber, *Daughters of the Union: Northern Women Fight the Civil War* (Cambridge, MA: Harvard University Press, 2005); Judith Ann Giesberg, *Army at Home: Women and the Civil War on the Northern Home Front* (Chapel Hill: University of North Carolina Press, 2009); Stephanie McCurry, *Confederate Reckoning: Power and Politics in the Civil War South* (Cambridge, MA: Harvard University Press, 2010); Lorien Foote, *The Gentlemen and the Roughs: Manhood, Honor, and Violence in the Union Army* (New York: New York University Press, 2010).
33. McCurry, *Confederate Reckoning*, 203–7.

PART I

The Big Picture

CHAPTER ONE

Regionalism and Urbanism as Problems in Confederate Urban History

J. MATTHEW GALLMAN

Almost a decade ago the folks at the *Journal of Urban History* asked me to write a review essay considering the recent work on Civil War cities and the broader issues raised by that emerging scholarship. I thought it was an interesting task, and I tried to come up with a handful of observations that spanned a diverse array of topics and texts. I suggested that an expanded consideration of Civil War cities might enhance our understanding of the Civil War itself, and also our sense of the experiences of both civilians and Civil War cities in wartime.[1] Of course such a discussion neglects a broader consideration of how the Civil War as a conflict fits into the broad narrative of American urban history. Rather than considering the wartime experience of a particular city (or its denizens), what happens when we ask about the wartime experience of "cities"? How much might such a discussion suggest something about the significance of regional differences? What is the real history of cities and urbanism in the Confederate South, and how is that history fundamentally different from the northern urban narrative?

To put the issue in a slightly different form, consider the much more substantial scholarship on the constitutional history of the Civil War. As Mark Neely Jr., borrowing from Harold Hyman, has observed, much of the scholarship on the Civil War's constitutional history has concentrated on the impact of the war on the Constitution (civil liberties, conscription, emancipation, and so on). In his short book *The Union Divided* Neely proposed "to consider the way the Constitution shaped the war, rather than the other way around."[2] Perhaps there is some value in adopting a similar approach to urban history and the Civil War. Rather than asking how the war affected cities and urban dwellers, what might we learn by asking how cities shaped the Civil War?

I do not propose to offer grand answers here, but I would like to lay out some parameters for discussion. First, what exactly are we talking about when we discuss "cities" as a collective group? The scholarship offers multiple types of definitions, most of which are largely contingent on place and time. Often early cities—or at least towns—emerged around political, legal, and economic functions that drew people together, and sometimes around the military need to protect them behind fortifications. Thus, communities that supported courts, legislative bodies, or established markets emerged as urban places, drawing the diversity of individuals who needed the town's services and those who in turn settled to serve those people. Developments in trade, transportation, and manufacturing played major roles in determining the size and location of urban centers and the relationships among cities. In the early nineteenth century, nearly all US cities had easy access to the Atlantic Ocean. With the development of canals, enhanced river transportation, and eventually railroads, the nation's network of cities expanded and moved into the hinterland, although water routes remained crucial.

We generally define "urban places" by the size of the population and perhaps the overall population density. It is common practice to describe an "urban place" as a town with a population of at least 2,500 people. By that measure, for example, the town of Gettysburg, Pennsylvania, just fell under the bar, with 2,400 people. Gettysburg was the county seat, had a small train station, and stood at the intersection of several fairly substantial roads. It was a bustling town, but hardly an urban center. Vicksburg, Mississippi, the other community that dominated military discussions in the first week of July 1863, was roughly twice as populous as Gettysburg, with about 4,600 people in 1860. So by the traditional measure, Vicksburg would be considered a modest-sized urban place. Less than two weeks after Vicksburg fell and Lee abandoned Gettysburg, all eyes turned to New York City, where draft riots raged over several days. In 1860 New York City was the nation's largest city, boasting a population of 813,669. If the census takers are to be trusted, New York City was about 177 times the size of Vicksburg in 1860. Meanwhile, neighboring Brooklyn ranked as the nation's third-largest city with a population of 266,661. Clearly when we speak of urban places the range is broad.

In 1790 roughly 5 percent of the nation's population lived in towns and cities with populations of 2,500 or larger. Seventy years later, that national figure had risen to 20 percent. In that same period of time the overall population of the country had grown quite rapidly, from just under 4 million people to over 31 million. In 1790 the southern states were roughly 2 percent urbanized, while the entire nation was closer to 7 percent urban. In 1860 the states of the Confederate States of America were nearly 7 percent urban, or roughly comparable to the nation in 1790. The states that would remain in the Union were nearly 25 percent urban. Thus, on the eve of the Civil War, Union states were not only several times more populous than the Confederate states, they were more than three times as urbanized. The overwhelming majority of Americans lived in small towns or rural areas.

Let us, for the sake of discussion, focus on cities with a population of at least 10,000 in 1860.[3] On the eve of the Civil War ninety-three communities in the United States reached that mark.[4] Of the nation's fifty largest cities, only seven—New Orleans, Louisiana; Charleston, South Carolina; Richmond, Virginia; Mobile, Alabama; Memphis, Tennessee; Savannah, Georgia; and Petersburg, Virginia—became part of the Confederate States of America. Five other Confederate cities ranked among the nation's largest ninety-three communities. The total population of these twelve cities was less than a third of the combined population of New York City and Brooklyn. Each of the nine Confederate cities ranked after New Orleans had a population not much more than that of Baltimore, Maryland, the fourth-largest Union city. The Baltimore example raises a further point worth noting. Between Maryland, Missouri, and Kentucky, the border states that remained with the Union had five cities in the top ninety-three, totaling over 470,000 people.

So, if we consider the nation on the eve of the Civil War, some observations seem to be clear. The southern states were certainly growing more urban, both in absolute terms and as a percentage of the entire population, but in 1860 the region's overall level of urbanization was still roughly comparable to the national level seventy years before. In the same period of time the northern states had produced far more cities and had a much more highly urbanized population. Beneath these broad observations there are a few analytic and empirical issues—and debates—to reckon with.

One debate concerns the notion of "modernization." From one perspective, the North was "modernizing" more rapidly than the South in that during the antebellum decades the region experienced a more rapid pace of economic development, as measured by a wide assortment of economic and institutional variables, including industrial output, investment in transportation, the application of technology in agriculture, the state of the banking and finance sector, and so on. A counterargument rejects the term "modernization" as implicitly indicating a preferred evolutionary path. Different economies, working with different variables, might develop in different ways. Who is to judge which is more "modern" at a particular point in time, especially if modern is understood to mean "superior"? The easiest way out of that discussion is to set aside the term "modern" and dismiss any idea that the economic discussion ought to be interested in making value judgments about competing systems.[5] An empirical description of a particular point in time, or an analysis of the pace and pattern of change, need not be freighted with such baggage.

Of course in our particular case, even if we choose to set aside any consideration of which patterns of economic development were "better" and which were "behind" or "inferior," it is reasonable to ask which patterns of development would best serve a nation that would soon be mobilizing for a major military conflict. By that standard, the mid-nineteenth-century nation that is producing more industrial goods, more iron, more miles of railroad tracks (as well as rolling stock and engines), and more ships is likely to have a military advantage, other variables being relatively equal. Thus, the northern states might reasonably be understood to have been "ahead" of the states that would form the Confederacy in their material preparedness to fight a large war, even if in other senses the two worlds might be understood to be developing along different—but equally successful—paths.

A further set of interpretive issues focuses on how we should measure and describe the pace of urban change, and how those measurements might shape our understanding of regional differences. By many measures it seems that the gap in both manufacturing and urbanization was widening with each passing decade, thus expanding the material advantages that the North would enjoy once war began. But if we consider the slave states as a separate region in 1860, they were in the midst of impressive growth and development on many fronts, including urbanization. If we count the number of individuals living in urban places as a percentage of the entire population, that *percentage* (not the absolute number) was actually growing at a rapid rate. That is an intriguing statistic, although it is not entirely clear what it tells us. Between 1800 and 1850 the urban population of the southern states increased from 3 percent to 8.6 percent. Frank Towers has noted that this *rate* of increase (3.59%) is just behind the rate of increase for the northeastern states (3.73%) over the same five decades. But between 1800 and 1850 the Northeast witnessed a net increase of 2,075,092 urban residents, while the urban population in the South experienced a net increase of 823,022. This was the case despite the fact that the two regions were very similar in total population in 1800. Thus, the southern population was urbanizing at a rate comparable to that in the Northeast, but at midcentury the northeastern states were 27 percent urban.[6]

One final observation is crucial. When we speak of the Civil War, we tend to use an imprecise shorthand when we characterize the conflict as between the "Free States" and the "Slave States." Indeed, most of the slave states fought with the Confederacy, and large numbers of slaveholders in those border states that remained in the Union cast their lot with the Confederate states. But when we consider wartime cities, the calculus shifts in important ways. For instance, Towers notes that in the antebellum South urban dwellers clustered in the region's larger urban centers, with nearly two-thirds living in the South's largest ten cities. This is an important observation when compared with the northern states, which actually had bigger cities but also far more smaller cities, producing an ironic result in that a greater percentage of the North's urban dwellers lived in smaller cities. But Towers's list of ten large southern cities includes four slave-holding cities—Baltimore, St. Louis, Louisville, Washington—that remained in the Union. These southern cities proved crucial in framing the South's antebellum political debates, but they did not fall on the Confederate side of the ledger sheet when it came time to mobilize. In both political and military discussions, the distinction between "Confederate cities" and "southern cities" (or "slave-holding cities") becomes crucial.[7]

On the eve of the Civil War, the Confederacy's level of urbanization was both a reflection of the South's distinctive culture and economy, and an important factor shaping its present and future. Most of the more populous urban centers in the Confederacy and in the border states were on the region's periphery, connecting the southern states with the Gulf of Mexico, the Atlantic Ocean, or the northern states, thus reflecting the region's economic emphasis on trade. In the North, far more smaller cities had emerged, fueled by industrial development, massive expansion in canals and railroads, and—especially in the decades of the 1840s and 1850s—major tides of immigration. Southern urban places beneath the level of the region's larger cities tended to grow more slowly, serving multiple urban functions without developing a comparable industrial sector and without attracting European immigrants in similar numbers. The result was, as David R. Goldfield put it more than three decades ago, "urbanization without cities." This was, he explained, "a condition consistent with the relatively few economic functions such cities performed in support of a staple crop economy."[8] In the absence of major industrial development, a fully developed financial sector, or the broader institutional infrastructure emerging in northern cities, southern towns grew into small urban centers without becoming true cities. Goldfield argued further that in many senses these southern cities maintained an agrarian flavor. The rhythms of city life followed agricultural cycles, with many wealthier denizens maintaining both country and city homes. The racial patterns established in planter society were built upon slave labor and shaped southern urban culture, where African Americans were both free and enslaved. Even the southern urban architecture followed agricultural traditions. Goldfield concluded that it was a world that was "modernized without northernizing." Another way to frame the same point would be to say that the urban places that emerged in the antebellum South—and particularly in that portion of the South that would become the Confederacy—met the particular economic and cultural needs of that society.[9]

Certainly these patterns of growth and development owed much to the presence of slavery, as both an economic and cultural force. For decades, investment in slaves as agricultural labor effectively crowded out other forms of investment, as many slave owners and prospective investors put their capital into tobacco and cotton at the expense of alternative investments in industry and transportation. This is not to say that slave labor was incompatible with either industrial work or urban settings (it was not), but only that agriculture provided an attractive option for investment dollars while also allowing many southern planters to remain within a culturally appealing agrarian setting rather than venturing into less familiar economic arenas.

European immigrants play an important role in this narrative, again suggesting how cause and effect become intertwined. The data show that immigrants opted to head for the free states in overwhelmingly disproportionate numbers. To some extent these migratory decisions reflected a moral distaste for the institution of slavery as well as a resistance among poor immigrants to enter a society where they would be competing for work with slave labor and with free blacks. More broadly, poor immigrants gravitated to urban ports and to cities and towns that offered the best options for work, while those migrants with greater resources chose paths that would enable them to purchase land and compete as small farmers. And with the passage of time, immigrants followed where other immigrants had already settled. In sum, the presence of slave labor made the South less appealing to immigrants, while in the North the expansion of immigrant communities and growing work opportunities in factories made those states above the Mason-Dixon Line progressively more appealing.

Once the war began, how might the different levels of urbanization have affected how the conflict unfolded? How did the regional network of cities shape the war? An argument could be made that to the extent that southerners were a more rural and agricultural people, these traits might have given them an advantage on the battlefield, insofar as farm boys and planters' sons had greater familiarity than urban dwellers with horses and firearms. But such advantages—if they existed—would not have lasted long, and the fact remains that the more populous northern states had more rural dwellers than the South as well as far more city residents. So, if farmland grows better soldiers, that should have given an edge to the Union.

Certainly population centers played an important role in the intertwined considerations of military strategy and logistics. In a war in which theaters of operation were often quite large, and entire armies were periodically moved great distances, railroads and rivers played crucial roles in moving men and supplying troops. In this regard, the size of the population center was less important than its proximity to ports, rivers, and railroad lines. Consider the fascinating material in *Hill & Swayze's Confederate States Rail-Road & Steam-Boat Guide*. In the middle of the Civil War, this guide listed over 170 separate "railroad towns" in Alabama, Georgia, Mississippi, North Carolina, South Carolina, Tennessee, and Virginia. (The guide only included one Louisiana town, and none of the railroad towns in Texas, Florida, or Arkansas.)

Some of the more significant railroad hubs were also substantial population centers. Certainly Richmond and Petersburg played vital roles in the economic life of the Confederacy and in providing supplies to the Army of Northern Virginia. Mobile, Alabama, boasted both railroad and steamboat connections to cities and towns in the hinterland, and the guide reported that although the bay access to the city of 30,000 "is blockaded by the Federal fleet . . . the entrance is protected against them by a number of very powerful fortifications."[10] Other railroad towns had logistical importance while supporting only modest populations. Meridian, Mississippi, at the terminus of several lines, had a population of only 1,000. Corinth, Mississippi—a crucial junction on the Memphis-to-Charleston line—had only about 2,500 residents. The guide's authors described Florence, South Carolina, as "situated on the Wilmington & Manchester railroad, and at the point of junction of the North-Eastern and Cheraw & Darlington railroad" and thus "destined to be a place of importance." Yet in 1880 the census only recorded 1,914 people in Florence.

The crucial point here is that the towns and cities that anchored the South's transportation infrastructure, including ocean ports, towns along inland rivers, and railroad hubs, emerged around these transportation and shipping functions, but they did so in an economic context that was quite distinct from cities in the free states to the North. They were indeed growing

urban without "northernizing." With negligible immigration, limited industrialization, and relatively few opportunities for unskilled manual labor, many
of these smaller communities did not grow into cities, even while they served
these urban functions.

We should note that by the eve of the Civil War this distinctive southern
brand of urbanization had already begun to slip away, at least in Virginia. As
William Link, Steven Tripp, and other scholars have demonstrated, in the
decades before the Civil War Virginia's cities had begun to move away from
traditional southern roots and gradually toward a version of urban society
that—more or less—looked like they were becoming "northernized," or at
least increasingly engaged in manufacturing. Virginia cities, including Richmond, Petersburg, and Lynchburg, began to develop an expanding industrial
sector, partially through the expansion of tobacco-processing firms. Slave
labor continued to thrive in these cities, often in industrial settings, but an
increasing number of free African Americans also found wage labor in these
emerging cities, and in many cases the system of slavery evolved to meet
new urban circumstances.[11]

How, then, did the network of Confederate cities frame military strategy? From the Union's perspective, it is not quite accurate to say that there
was a single strategy, but a few observations are useful. Despite vigorous
debates about whether the Civil War was a "total war," the Union's main
military objectives never emphasized targeting citizens and major population centers. If we paint with a broad brush, the Union's military strategy
for the four years of the war was twofold. First, they endeavored to limit the
Confederacy's ability to wage war by blockading ports, cutting rail lines,
controlling river systems, and attempting to destroy sources of food and
supplies. Second, they attempted to capture or destroy the Confederate
armies in the field. The ultimate goal was to achieve these strategic objectives while simultaneously protecting Washington, DC, and other Union
assets. Of course, the Union's strategic goals periodically took a back seat
when Confederate strategic initiatives intervened, including the Army of
Northern Virginia's excursions into the North in 1862 and 1863.

In the first year of the war, the Union's efforts to strangle the Confederate
war effort did target many of the South's leading urban centers. In February
1862, shortly after Grant's victory at Fort Donelson, the highly symbolic—
although perhaps not strategically crucial—capital city of Nashville surrendered. By the end of April, New Orleans, at the mouth of the Mississippi,
was in federal hands. The following month, Union forces had captured the
port of Norfolk, Virginia, in the process robbing the Confederacy of its major

naval yard. In June the combined efforts of the Union Army and Navy captured Memphis, Tennessee, on the Mississippi River. While the Confederate defenses did not fare well in New Orleans and Memphis, a combination of strong coastal batteries and deadly mines helped protect the Confederate coastal cities of Wilmington, Charleston, Savannah, and Mobile, even while the Union blockade successfully constricted the Confederacy's ability to trade through these strategic ports.

Fourteen months into the war, five of the ten largest cities in the Confederacy were in Union hands, and three of the other five were crippled by blockades. In their foundational study of Civil War strategy, Hermann Hattaway and Archer Jones make a similar point about a broader universe of Confederate ports. They note that despite the extensive Confederate coastline, the Union blockade really only had to shut down ten southern ports: Norfolk, New Bern, Wilmington, Charleston, Savannah, Mobile, New Orleans, and a trio of Florida ports—Pensacola, Jacksonville, and Fernadina. By early 1862 six of these were in Union hands.[12]

Once the Union military had captured the key cities around the Confederate periphery, and blockaded those ports that were not easily conquered, the focus on southern cities was largely secondary to other military concerns. Of course, Richmond—as the political, economic, and symbolic center of the Confederacy—was a major objective, and Petersburg, as the crucial conduit into Richmond from the south, remained crucial. And in the final year of the war, the emerging railroad and industrial hub at Atlanta, Georgia, became an irresistible objective to William Tecumseh Sherman and his invading army. These three cities would be extremely significant when they fell, and Sherman's defeat of Atlanta proved crucial in sealing Lincoln's electoral success in 1864. By the time Sherman took the port cities of Charleston and Savannah, and the inland cities of Columbia and Augusta, these successes were not of great strategic importance. And the eventual fall of Petersburg and then of Richmond really illustrated a truth that was already known.

From a purely strategic standpoint it seems evident that Union military operations targeted urban *functions*, largely transportation and supply lines, without particular emphasis on the size of the town or city in question, and they took opportunities to destroy industrial capacity where they found it, and the Confederacy's ability to build naval vessels, which also occasionally led them to urban targets. The fact that southern cities had grown less rapidly than their northern counterparts did not seem to shape strategic decision-making, although the fact that they had not developed the sort of industrial infrastructure that characterized many northern cities surely had an impact on those decisions. That is, if more southern cities had major industrial or naval capacities, they would have attracted more attention.

These observations about grand strategy do not diminish the fact that quite a few Confederate cities endured heavy destruction during the war, and their denizens endured extreme hardships. As historian Megan Kate Nelson notes, Charleston, Atlanta, and Richmond all lost roughly a third of their buildings during the war, from some combination of shelling and fire.[13] Still, this was not a war characterized by much urban fighting. The examples of actual street fighting in Fredericksburg in December 1862 and Gettysburg the following July are well known, but also distinctive. Union and Confederate troops skirmished outside of Winchester, Virginia, on two occasions, and several cities—most notably Vicksburg, Petersburg, and Charleston—faced Union shelling. In his innovative study of the war's destructive impact on the Confederacy, historian Paul Paskoff makes the crucial point that the powerful images of destroyed buildings in Richmond, Charleston, and Atlanta tend to leave us with an exaggerated sense of the war's impact on southern cities. Paskoff argues that of the Confederacy's 297 towns and cities, just over half were in counties that saw any military conflict, and he lists eleven of these communities as "destroyed or severely damaged" by the war, or about 4 percent. In a slightly different measurement, Paskoff finds that about 5 percent of the Confederacy's county courthouses were destroyed by the war.[14] Of the eleven towns and cities that Paskoff ranks as "severely damaged," five—Atlanta, Charleston, Columbia, Petersburg, and Richmond—ranked among the largest twenty-five cities in the Confederacy. Either by strategy or happenstance, Confederate cities did not suffer disproportionate destruction during the Civil War.

To sum up: the social and economic forces that produced the South's limited urban network had a substantial impact on the Confederacy's capacity to wage war, but it also meant that the southern cities did not constitute major strategic targets for the Union war effort. What happens when we move beyond the strategic concerns of the Union war effort, and instead consider the role of Confederate cities in helping the South wage war? How might cities—or urban centers that were not quite cities—have shaped the political culture of two nations at war? Scholars have noted that the cities of mid-nineteenth-century America were a particularly vibrant location for political discourse and engagement. Speaking in the most general terms, urban centers shared various traits that would naturally encourage spirited—and occasionally violent—public discourse. Let me suggest four interwoven traits that seemed to set the city apart from the countryside in potentially relevant ways.

First, cities generally attracted a more diverse population, defined by class, ethnicity, religion, and race, than smaller towns in the hinterland or dispersed agrarian communities. They also tended to attract unmarried young women, who had relatively fewer occupational options in the countryside than young men. And as long as travel was limited by walking or horse-drawn conveyance, urban denizens could not avoid some interaction with each other. Collectively, cities represented a more diverse cacophony of voices than the countryside.

This leads to, second, the "public square"—both literally and symbolically—was much more vibrant a political space in the urban centers. Urban residents came together in the city streets, parks, and squares for a wide array of public speech, both symbolic and more traditional. Differences were voiced, dissent articulated. This is not to suggest that the cities in mid-century America were places of calm political debate, leading to elegant compromise. Minority voices were subject to violent responses in this rough and tumble world of street politics and public theater. But, one need not celebrate the "politics of the streets" as an ideal laboratory for democracy to recognize that political debate was different in urban settings.[15]

In addition to the political interactions in the public square, cities offered greater opportunities for private voluntary societies, providing a further venue for framing and articulating political opinions. By 1860 the nation's cities supported a diverse array of political groups, churches, literary societies, fire companies, voluntary societies, militias, historical societies, ethnic organizations, and fraternal groups. Access to these groups was not universal, and white men had far and away the greatest array of voluntary choices, but it is probably fair to say that urban dwellers had greater organizational options than rural Americans.

Finally, cities and larger towns had a broader sort of political discourse insofar as they supported the publication and distribution of more newspapers, journals, and political pamphlets, and they were the homes of more booksellers, publishers, and private printing presses. This last point is worth making, but perhaps should be considered with care. After all, tiny Gettysburg had two highly partisan daily newspapers; there was also a weekly paper reporting to Adams County. And, thanks to transportation systems and the telegraph, citizens in all communities certainly could acquire various printed materials even if they did not live in cities.

So, painting with the broadest possible brush, on the eve of the Civil War urban centers were distinctive for various ways beyond their size and their economic functions. They had more diverse populations; those populations interacted in various political ways within a relatively confined geographic space; and residents had access to a greater diversity of printed materials than folks in rural areas.

We have established that the Confederacy had fewer cities with smaller populations, which might lead logically to the conclusion that insofar as cities are the center of dynamic political discourse, the South should have experienced less of this sort of political give and take. But of course the differences between northern and southern cities were not entirely a matter of scale. What other regional variables might come into play in considering these four traits?

Most obviously, southern cities had very different demographic compositions than urban centers to the North and Midwest. Northern cities, which had been destinations for European immigrants for decades, had far more ethnically diverse white populations than cities in the Confederacy. This produced an array of interesting regional differences reflecting ethnic and religious diversity. White urban dwellers in the Confederacy were more Anglo and more Protestant than their counterparts in the Union. Of course these are broad patterns, and they do not describe every Confederate city. New Orleans was in most senses *sui generis*, with a complex ethnic makeup and religious diversity that stands apart from most southern cities. David Gleeson has described a substantial Irish community within the Confederacy, although Irish Confederates were nowhere near as numerous as Irish northerners. Similarly, Andrea Mehrläuder has uncovered a vibrant German community in Richmond, Charleston, and New Orleans.[16] But the fact remains that first- and second-generation Americans were far more prevalent in the Union states, leaving us to ponder how this difference might have shaped Confederate political culture.[17]

The more dramatic demographic difference between the Union and the Confederate cities was in their racial makeup. The Union's cities generally had more African American residents than the agrarian areas of the North, but the northern states as a whole were only roughly 2 percent African American. Southern cities were dramatically different. In 1860 the ten largest southern cities had 68,000 slaves as well as large numbers of free black residents.[18] These Confederate cities—and especially those in Virginia—had become the centers for an evolving form of slavery in at least two senses. Slave owners had increasingly set their chattel to work in factory settings, and especially tobacco processing, effectively demonstrating that the

South's peculiar institution did not need new agricultural land to prosper. Meanwhile, an increasing number of urban slaves found themselves in a peculiar labor situation, where they were given the "freedom" to hire their labor out to the highest bidder, with the bulk of their earnings going to their master. This demonstrated that the institution of slavery could and would evolve in response to new economic circumstances.[19]

The demographic composition of Confederate cities also evolved during the war. Some urban areas lost populations as the Union's military actions placed them under siege or naval blockades crippled their economies. In other places the war's refugees streamed into Confederate towns and cities in search of protection and assistance, or they gravitated to those cities that offered employment in war-related industries. In his chapter on Atlanta, for instance, Bill Link describes all of these forces at work turning the Georgia railroad terminus into a booming wartime city.[20]

Did the distinctive demographic composition of Confederate cities produce a unique political culture that in turn shaped the Civil War? I suspect that it did, but I am not entirely sure how. Bill Link's study of antebellum Virginia found, among other things, that enslaved blacks became political actors through their acts of dissent or destruction, which in turn yielded white political responses. The early returns from his work on wartime Atlanta suggests similar patterns, perhaps moving at an accelerated pace, as the war presented African Americans with unfamiliar opportunities and white Atlantans pushed back where they could. And of course where Confederate cities became occupied by Union forces, emancipation dramatically reconfigured the position of African Americans within southern cities.[21] In his study of southern cities and secession, Frank Towers underscored the significance of urban workers in framing a political discourse that ran counter to the dominant southern culture. This urban vision of democracy, influenced by northern sensibilities, helped encourage southern secessionists to push forward with their separate agenda, while defining these southern cities as outside of the Confederate reality. The story is compelling. Even in the slave South, free workers perceived a set of political truths that ran counter to the dominant planter paradigm. Towers's three southern cities—Baltimore, St. Louis, and New Orleans—only spent a total of about twelve months in the Confederacy, but perhaps similar worker sensibilities were at play in other Confederate cities? Or, to reverse the issue, perhaps the overall failure of the South to urbanize more rapidly limited the possibilities for southern urban workers to construct a persuasive case that ran counter to the Confederate narrative?[22]

How might Confederate cities have become a conduit for wartime dissent? Here, too, I have more questions than answers. In her path-breaking study of Confederate politics and society, Stephanie McCurry expanded our understanding of the bread riots that broke out in the spring of 1863. McCurry demonstrates that the celebrated Richmond riot of April 1863 was not an isolated moment, but one event in a carefully constructed train of protests organized by Confederate women and intended as a direct challenge to the path the Confederate government had pursued. She argues that the protesters were the wives of Confederate soldiers, who were making a highly organized and distinctly political set of demands. For our purposes, the key point here is that these bread riots were the product of organized meetings in towns and cities, designed to produce a powerful political message.[23] In his study of Georgia's wartime riots, Keith Bohannon comes to different conclusions, arguing that the rioters were most concerned with speculating merchants rather than a recalcitrant government, and disagreeing with McCurry about the overall effectiveness of the demonstrations. But the core point remains the same: Georgia cities and towns became important centers of political dissent, led by Confederate women. Once again, the question for us is whether these politically disruptive events reflect something specific about Confederate cities. And, moreover, would larger and more numerous cities have yielded a larger result? Here Bohannon's research is particularly interesting in that he suggests that perhaps the women who organized in Atlanta, Augusta, and Columbus began their political discussions in new factories established to support the Confederacy. Thus, rather like Towers's antebellum cities, urban working-class culture became a trigger for political dissent.[24]

What final insights might we gain by comparing the wartime experiences of Confederate cities with Union cities? The most obvious difference is that the bulk of the war's military campaigns were fought in the slave South. The two capitals of Washington and Richmond were so close to each other, and to the seat of war, that both sides were forced to think strategically about protecting their capital city even while challenging the enemy's political center. But that is where the similarity ends. Neither of the invasions by the Army of Northern Virginia represented a serious threat to northern cities. In 1862 Robert E. Lee seemed intent on exploiting northern farmlands, while perhaps recruiting locals to the Confederate cause. Had the Gettysburg campaign gone as planned, Lee's army might have threatened Harrisburg or perhaps Philadelphia, but it is hard to imagine a scenario where any northern city was in serious danger. When we move north of the border states, the actual military damage to the Union was limited. In October 1862 Confederate general J.E.B. Stuart led a raid into Chambersburg, Pennsylvania, destroying much of the town. The following July, Gettysburg, Pennsylvania, witnessed a massive three-day battle, which left considerable damage in its wake, but nothing compared with the sort of destruction experienced by quite a few Confederate towns. Simply put, the Confederacy lacked the resources and the military successes necessary to put pressure on the North's network of cities.

As economic and transportation resources, the northern cities proved extremely valuable, allowing the Union to exploit an array of material advantages, including the construction of ships and railroad rolling stock, and the production of all manner of armaments. In this regard the advantages that the North enjoyed in 1860 only expanded over time. The Union had large advantages in transportation and manufacturing, and their cities reflected these material differences.

How did northern cities, as urban spaces, affect the Civil War in distinctive ways? Certainly the North's cities remained a place for vibrant political discourse in "the public square" of the mid-nineteenth century. On the one hand, the city streets were often the rallying point for northern patriotism. Civilians commonly gathered at newspaper offices to read the latest news telegraphed from the front, military recruiters set up tents in town squares, and regiments home on furlough paraded down city streets in search of new enlistees. Those same public spaces became the scene of a seemingly unending array of parades and fairs supporting voluntary societies raising money for various patriotic causes. The most spectacular of these were the grand Sanitary Fairs that dotted not only the patriotic calendars of the nation's largest cities but also several dozen more modest-sized towns and communities. But the diverse northern cities were also sometimes flashpoints for angry dissent. New York City's violent and destructive draft riots are the most obvious example, but other cities and towns witnessed more moments of violent political conflict. Sometimes these were in response to conscription, but other moments of tension accompanied speeches by leading Copperheads or violent responses to antiwar newspaper editorials. This is too complicated a topic for serious scrutiny here, but suffice it to say that the North was not politically unified, and northern cities were often the location where conflicts erupted into the public arena.

If politics was often played out in the public square, an awful lot of the business of wartime politics was also carried out behind closed doors.

During the Civil War, as in the antebellum decades, the North supported a much denser array of clubs and organizations than the slave states. In response to the crisis, northerners embraced their impulses to organize in all sorts of local voluntary groups, often tied together by national or regional umbrella organizations. Thus, volunteers who worked for the local branch of the Sanitary Commission or the Christian Commission acted locally while becoming part of a national movement. Meantime, patriotic-minded civilians formed local branches of the national Union League, an ostensibly nonpartisan body devoted to promoting the war effort. This again is a complicated story, with fascinating tensions between the local and the national, and also intriguing gendered subplots. For our purposes, the central point is that the North had the inclination and the resources to organize vast networks of voluntary societies that far outstripped southern efforts. And the cities and larger towns were often the center of such efforts.

Finally, there is the matter of the printed word. Here, again, the gap between the North and the South was substantial in 1860. The census that year showed nearly 1,000 printing offices scattered across the northern states, and only 151 in the South. The northern states had 190 bookbinders, while the South had only 17. As historian Alice Fahs has noted, in many senses southern society had been unable to break free of "the North's literary influences."[25] It is true that the antebellum southern states supported a vibrant newspaper publishing industry that would have compared favorably with many nations across the globe, but the South published far fewer newspapers per capita than the North. In 1860 New York State produced three times more newspapers per capita than all the future Confederate states; Pennsylvania's newspaper circulation exceeded those Confederate states; Massachusetts nearly matched the entire southern newspaper output.[26]

As the Civil War progressed, the South continued to publish newspapers, but the Confederacy suffered from shortages of paper, ink, presses, and even the personnel with the skills to produce printed materials.[27] In contrast, the northern homefront witnessed a great explosion in the publication of newspapers, journals, pamphlets, cartoons, song sheets, and patriotic envelopes. Much of this output served to entertain or distract from the carnage on distant battlefields, and a wide array of editors and authors used the printed word to criticize the Lincoln administration or its policies, but the most striking publishing innovations were dedicated to exhort civilians to greater patriotism. Once again, for our purposes the central point is that during the war years the northern states—led by its major cities—produced far more printed public discourse than the Confederacy.[28] It remains to be determined how much such published output affected the war. Did citizens of the Confederacy have less access to information about the war? Did this have an important impact on their war effort?

In sum, what do we know and what can we surmise? The most obvious facts are simply that the southern states that became a part of the Confederacy had fewer and smaller cities than their opponents. Most of those Confederate cities were along the coast or on the periphery of the Confederacy. In the interior, towns had formed around railroads and rivers, but few had grown to be true urban areas. So, how does this speak to our core question: how did the South's urban network affect the course of the war? Perhaps the answer is an ironic one. On the one hand, the relatively limited urbanization of the Confederacy spoke to traits that would inhibit its chances of winning the Civil War. On the other hand, that same absence of major cities—beyond the Richmond-Petersburg artery—helped produce a dispersed Union military strategy. They did their best to shut down those major cities that were ports, and they were quick to capture New Orleans and the Tennessee cities, but then military strategy had little to do with urban centers as urban centers. Perhaps the traits that led the South to secession, and the traits that enabled the South to endure for four years, and the traits that made their ultimate loss on the battlefield almost inevitable, were really all intertwined, and were all intrinsically wrapped up in the status of their cities.

NOTES

1. J. Matthew Gallman, "Urban History and the Civil War," *Journal of Urban History* 32 (May 2006): 631–42.
2. Mark E. Neely Jr., *The Union Divided: Party Conflict in the Civil War North* (Cambridge, MA: Harvard University Press, 2002), ix. Neely notes Hyman's similar observations in *A More Perfect Union: The Impact of the Civil War and Reconstruction* (New York: Knopf, 1973). In his more recent book, *Lincoln and the Triumph of the Nation: Constitutional Conflict in the American Civil War* (Chapel Hill: University of North Carolina Press, 2011), Neely considers a parallel set of questions about the shaping role of the Constitution.
3. What follows are some fairly straightforward observations based on the published census returns. For the classic study of antebellum city systems see Allan Pred, *Urban Growth and City-Systems in the United States, 1840–1860* (Cambridge, MA: Harvard University Press, 1980).
4. Although I chose 10,000 as a nice round number, it is worth noting that this leaves Columbus, Georgia (9,621), Atlanta, Georgia (9,551), and Wilmington, North

Carolina (9,552), just on the outside looking in. In his chapter for this volume, Bill Link notes that Atlanta had reached a population of 10,000 on the eve of the war. William A. Link, "Invasion, Destruction, and the Remaking of Civil War Atlanta" (chapter 10 in this volume).

5. Of course that economic analysis is distinct from any moral or ethical assessment of a system dependent on slave labor.

6. For a valuable overview of this statistical terrain as well as some broader comparative insights, see Frank Towers, "The Southern Path to Modern Cities: Urbanization in the Slave States," in *The Old South's Modern Worlds: Slavery, Region, and Nation in the Age of Progress*, ed. L. Diane Barnes, Brian Schoen, and Frank Towers (New York: Oxford University Press, 2011), 145–50.

7. Ibid., 149. Of course some men from all four cities fought for the Confederacy.

8. David R. Goldfield, "The Urban South: A Regional Framework," *American Historical Review* 86 (December 1981): 1016.

9. Goldfield pursued these themes more fully in *Cotton Fields and Skyscrapers: Southern City and Region: 1607–1980* (Baton Rouge: Louisiana State University Press, 1982). For a useful discussion of this and related work see Carl Abbott, "Frontiers and Sections: Cities and Regions in American Growth," *American Quarterly* 37 (1985): 395–410.

10. *Hill & Swayze's Confederate States Rail-Road & Steam-Boat Guide* (Griffin, GA: Hill and Swayze, Publishers, 1862) The guide is available in an electronic form at Documenting the American South website, http://docsouth.unc.edu/.

11. William A. Link, *Roots of Secession: Slavery and Politics in Antebellum Virginia* (Chapel Hill: University of North Carolina Press, 2007); Steven Tripp, *Yankee Town, Southern City: Race and Class Relations in Civil War Lynchburg* (New York: New York University Press, 1999).

12. Herman Hattaway and Archer Jones, *How the North Won* (Urbana: University of Illinois Press, 1991), 127.

13. Megan Kate Nelson, *Ruin Nation: Destruction and the American Civil War* (Athens: University of Georgia Press, 2012).

14. Paul F. Kaskoff, "Measures of War: A Quantitative Examination of the Civil War's Destructiveness in the Confederacy," *Civil War History* (March 2008): 35–62, table on p. 46. Paskoff's tables note that the overall percentages shift if one excludes Texas and Florida.

15. This is a large topic. My thinking on the public in urban America has been influenced by the work of Mary Ryan, and also by the theoretical work of Habermas. Mary P. Ryan, *Women in Public: Between Banners and Ballots, 1825–1880* (Baltimore, MD: Johns Hopkins University Press, 1990); Ryan, *Civic Wars: Democracy and Public Life in the American City during the Nineteenth Century* (Berkeley: University of California Press, 1997); and Craig Calhoun, ed., *Habermas and the Public Sphere* (Cambridge, MA: MIT Press, 1993).

16. See the fine essays in Susannah J. Ural, ed., *Civil War Citizens: Race, Ethnicity, and Identity in America's Bloodiest Conflicts* (New York: New York University Press, 2010).

17. Frank Towers has pointed out that by 1860 the percentage of immigrants among the white population of larger southern cities (>20,000 people) was comparable to the percentage of immigrants among the white population of northern cities, but of course that figure includes those southern cities that remained in the Union. Towers, "Southern Path to Modern Cities," 154.

18. Howard P. Chudacoff and Judith E. Smith, *The Evolution of American Urban Society* (Englewood Cliffs, NJ: Prentice-Hall, 1994), 57. Frank Towers notes that slaves were a declining percentage of Southern cities; Towers, "Southern Path to Modern Cities," 156.

19. See Link, *Roots of Secession;* Claudia Goldin, *Urban Slavery in the American South, 1820–1860: A Quantitative History* (Chicago: University of Chicago Press, 1976).

20. Link, "Invasion, Destruction, and the Remaking of Civil War Atlanta."

21. See Justin Behrend, "Black Political Mobilization and the Spatial Transformation of Natchez" (chapter 8 of this volume).

22. Frank Towers, *The Urban South and the Coming of the Civil War* (Charlottesville: University of Virginia Press, 2004).

23. Stephanie McCurry, *Confederate Reckoning: Power and Politics in the Civil War South* (Cambridge, MA: Harvard University Press, 2010).

24. Keith Bohannon, " 'More like Amazons than starving people': Women's Urban Riots in Georgia in 1863" (chapter 6 of this volume).

25. Alice Fahs, *The Unwritten War: Popular Literature in the North and South, 1861– 1865* (Chapel Hill: University of North Carolina Press, 2001), especially 5–41. Quote from p. 5.

26. David E. Reynolds, *Editors Make War: Southern Newspapers in the Secession Crisis* (Carbondale, IL: Southern Illinois University Press, 2006).

27. Fahs, *Unwritten War*, 5.

28. In his fascinating study of Confederate intellectuals, Michael T. Bernath argues that southern editors trained their intellectual and publishing resources on constructing a vibrant Confederate identity. See *Confederate Minds: The Struggles for Intellectual Independence in the Civil War South* (Chapel Hill: University of North Carolina Press, 2010). Bernath's book provided the inspiration for David Moltke-Hansen's chapter, "Urban Processes in the Confederacy's Development, Experience, and Consequences" (chapter 2 in this volume).

CHAPTER TWO

Urban Processes in the Confederacy's Development, Experience, and Consequences

DAVID MOLTKE-HANSEN

Cities civilize. They also corrupt. Many educated antebellum southerners simultaneously held both views in the face of their region's accelerating urbanization. This was especially true of writers, who understood
that cities provide the concentrations of colleagues and readers that make
literary pursuits rewarding. Yet this understanding proved unstable. By 1860
some urban centers in the South were receding in literary importance; others were growing. Indeed, a shift toward the interior from the coast was re-
configuring the structure and flows of intellectual life and communications.
That fact was only emerging in 1860. The reasons are important for an understanding of the Civil War era.[1]

That era is usually defined as the thirty years between the Mexican War
in 1847–48 and the end of formal Reconstruction in 1877. Often it is treated
apart. Yet, to grasp many of the developments then, one needs to consider
their antecedents and consequences. This is certainly true for the study of
the roles of both urbanization and cities in the South. At one level, however,
the ambition to put these intertwined topics in longer-term perspective
must be footling. Despite good work, the scholarly base is inadequate.[2] All
one can venture, therefore, are preliminary observations and conclusions.

In that spirit, the argument here is as follows: having lagged behind the
North in the development of urban networks and processes much more
than in the development of urban places, or cities and towns, the South
began to catch up by the 1850s; the Civil War and its aftermath accelerated
some of those developments while undercutting others. The case is in several parts. The first briefly reviews the broadly accepted understanding of
the antebellum South's urbanization: the region was far behind the North in
urban development although experiencing the same rate of increase in the
future Confederate states and exceeding that rate in the border states and,

therefore, also in the South as a whole. Yet, as the second and third sections below contend, this perception is at least partially misleading, as by the late antebellum period even the future Confederacy was urbanizing faster than its cities were growing. That is, in addition to the people who lived in urban settings, conventionally defined in the decades before the Civil War as communities with at least 2,500 inhabitants, more and more southerners were establishing or moving into small towns, engaging in what Louis Kyriakoudes calls "lower-order urbanization."[3]

These small-town dwellers substantially increased the population participating in elements of urban life. The fourth section below focuses on how the Civil War accelerated at least temporarily the rate of urbanization of southern populations in complex ways. The fifth and sixth sections look in greater detail at one aspect of urbanization—print communication—and the changes consequent upon the war. This is because print had become a principal vehicle of urban culture and values, as well as an important networking device for people who lived outside of cities and large towns but nonetheless were involved in urban activities and associations. The conclusion briefly considers postwar urbanization and urban development.

In moving from sweeping consideration of broad patterns of urbanization to more detailed examination of one aspect—the changing role of print communications—the argument shifts from a telescopic toward a microscopic perspective. Matching this shift in the optics of the argument is a rhetorical one. It derives from print cultural and communications studies and examines, from the perspective of participants, the dynamics of core-periphery relations consequent upon the war. The prior, broad review of the South's urban development before and during the Civil War uses the language of systems and networks to evoke the changing patterns of urban processes, relations, and functions. While familiar in other discourses, such as urban and environmental studies and historical geography, the language is less used in southern historical and Civil War studies.[4] This is despite the fact that southern regional sociology drew on such thinking in the 1930s and 1940s, subsequently inspiring the first writers on ecology. In both studies, the regional and the ecological, the need to consider the interplay of multiple factors in a specific setting defined the pursuit and led to the application of systems thinking.[5]

COUNTING

As did the makers and imbibers of the Lost Cause myth, most modern historians think of the Old South as overwhelmingly rural and agrarian and,

so, radically different from the industrializing North. There are many reasons. In 1860 the Confederacy had the same level of urban development
as the North in 1790. Outside of the border states, the South did not have
densely settled metropolitan areas, as did many northern cities. Consequently, cities in the South did not function to the same degree as drivers of
commercial, industrial, political, and cultural development.

In 1860 almost one in four northerners lived in urban places—more than
one in three in the Northeast. In the future Confederacy, however, only
about one in fifteen did. Northerners, therefore, were more than three-and-
a-half times as likely to live in cities at both the end of the Revolution and
the outbreak of the Civil War. By 1860 northeasterners were more than
five times as likely. Yet, also by the close of the antebellum era, northerners overall were only two-and-a-half times as likely to live in urban places
as southerners as a whole. By then the percentage of urban dwellers in the
border states had swelled to three-quarters of the overall northern rate—
more than 50 percent of the northeastern rate. Consequently, one in ten
southerners lived in cities. After Britain and the Northeast, therefore, the
antebellum South was one of the fastest urbanizing areas in the world. That
point as well has failed to gain much interpretive traction.[6]

In part, this failure is because the measures typically used to gauge the
disparity between the North and the South do not account for other developments. These additional factors make urbanization central to the Civil
War's unfolding, experience, and consequences in the South. By the mid-
nineteenth century, the region was urbanizing more rapidly even than it
was becoming urban. This process took place in many areas where urban
development—the growth of communities of 2,500 and more people—
either did not occur or was much less than in the North. Without this rapidly accelerating urbanization, the Civil War becomes almost unthinkable.

Earlier, the westward movement helped flesh out the idea of the South
and extend the interest of King Cotton. Yet for some time frontier conditions or, following in their aftermath, plantation settlements obviated the
necessity of small market towns in much of the expanding region. At that
stage the South was disarticulated both functionally and ideologically. Not
until railroads and other networks connected the parts of the region did the
white southern idea and political interest become a substantially interactive
and integrated social, cultural, and economic reality. In the process, urban
places and functions became meaningful in new ways. While progressive,
the evolution was uneven both geographically across the South and tempo-
rally throughout the antebellum period. It accelerated, as railroad construction quickened dramatically. Finally, in 1857–58, railroads connected such

East Coast centers as Richmond, Virginia, and Charleston, South Carolina, with the Mississippi Valley, heart of the rising South.[7]

This literal linkage facilitated the war to come in many ways. One was the promotion, production, and dissemination of the Confederacy in print. As wartime shortages hampered local media, national media from Richmond and elsewhere created a South-wide readership for new, or newly purposed, periodicals, using the railroads for distribution. While in the past southern views had been widely circulated and concatenated through local media excerpting each other, there had been no widely read South-wide journals. This was despite the heroic efforts of editors of regional literary magazines and quarterly reviews, as well as the southern religious press, which was segregated by denomination.[8] In the new Confederate nation, the railroads and the media together were consolidating a networked South for the first time. Travel, commerce, and communications all accelerated as a result.

URBANIZATION VERSUS URBAN DEVELOPMENT

The sparse historiography on the nineteenth-century urban South has focused primarily on urban places—that is, cities and towns—rather than on urban processes—that is, the ways in which urban functions and activities were developed, distributed, operated, and connected. One reason is that urban historians generally have accepted that city growth, with industrialization, has been a fundamental index of modernization in the nineteenth-century United States. In the standard narrative, the North was modernizing successfully, while the antebellum South lagged.[9] A different index suggests another conclusion. The urbanization affecting the development of the late antebellum and Civil War South had two consequences. On the one hand, it led to the increasingly rapid spread of urban functions—long-distance transportation, commerce, finance, communications, service sector growth, cultural institutions, and government. On the other hand, it incorporated more and more of the population in urban systems and networks—not just the people in growing urban places, but those in multiplying small communities serving the rapidly expanding transportation and commercial systems and the development of local government.

These technological, commercial, and institutional advancements increased the importance of cities but also of connections by rural and small-town inhabitants to urban networks. City dwellers were not the only ones embraced in the emerging urban economy and society. This is not to claim urban status for smaller communities but to argue that places and processes were not the same and had different reaches. Too small to be urban, many towns nevertheless performed an array of urban functions. Now, at last, scholars are finding that those towns rooted a growing middle class of business and professional people.[10]

Yet towns were more than sites of urban activity. They increasingly articulated an emerging transportation and urban system. *Hill and Swazy's Confederate States Rail-Road & Steam-Boat Guide* makes the point effectively. Many of the 170-plus railroad towns listed in eight Confederate states were both small and new. Most had been established just in the decade before the war. Trains needed refueling and watering every dozen or so miles. Clearly, much of the Old South was young in 1860—and burgeoning.[11]

The South also was urbanizing, and many of the secessionist leaders were urbane—that is, people of urban sophistication, regardless of where they lived. But how many were urban? The Confederate government was urban, but were its policies? To reframe that question, drawing on a concept from ecology: to what extent did the Confederacy serve as an integrated environment and system of urban systems? The summary answer of much recent scholarship is: remarkably, but nonetheless unstably and incompletely.[12] The Confederacy struggled to sustain transportation, communications, and commercial, as well as political and military, networks. In the face of the extraordinary obstacles encountered from the outset, many of those urbanizing functions and systems nevertheless worked more or less of the time over more or less of the territory of the new nation. In this way, the Confederacy was an urbanizing influence even as it saw its networks of railroads, media, and urban communities progressively destroyed or occupied and, so, taken offline by the war.

In the conflict's aftermath, the partial, and ever only partly functioning, system of systems collapsed. Cities, however, resumed their growth, and urbanization continued its spread. In the process, the place of places in memory became increasingly distant and distinct from the meaning of places in daily lives. As Randall Miller has observed, "one wonders how the war fed the supposed anti-urban bias of southerners, especially given all the suffering and dislocation experienced in the 'new' urban places."[13] In any event, the New South emerged in stark contrast to the image of the Old being codified by Lost Cause mythmakers. This shift has obscured the processes at work. From the days of the founding of Jamestown in Virginia and Charlestown in Carolina to the days of the founding of Boonesborough in Kentucky and later, towns have been at the leading edge of southern development. This is true even when those towns have failed, as they often have, to grow sufficiently to rank (by the common definition) as urban places.

What the patterns of later colonization and settlement show, in Georgia, Alabama, Mississippi, Tennessee, and then Texas and Florida, is that during and after Native displacement white and black settlement occurred in stages. In the frontier phase, there were many native and sometimes Spanish or French but otherwise few nonnative communities or community institutions. As Anglo-colonizers moved in, farms were hacked out of the woods, and churches began to appear, as did grist mills, ferry services at river crossings, and eventually crossroad taverns, stores, and blacksmiths. In plantation areas, many of these services were staffed and provided or made unprofitable by the plantations, which often had camps and then villages for enslaved workers, whose limited purchasing power did not accelerate urban development.[14] Yet elsewhere, in the majority of the expanding region, clusters of these services became the nuclei of towns. Once a territory was organized, counties established, and county seats designated, registries of deeds, courts, and lawyers became essential even in plantation districts. So did doctors, barbers, and dentists. Post offices were established, as were newspapers.

Towns did not need to be big—that is, urban-sized—to accommodate and aggregate these functions. Other services soon were added: dressmaking, livery stables, hotels, and restaurants. Those are all featured in the one-horse towns in countless cinema Westerns. In 1860 large parts of the South were at this stage of development.[15] Up to that point, the growth of the region, through the westering process, had been more extensive than intensive.

The coming of the railroads, however, began to change that dynamic. One measure was the establishment and growth of an increasing number of communities. More fundamental was the linkage of these towns and cities in a spreading, hierarchized urban network. This next stage of development occurred as towns accumulated still further functions, as centers of shipping, industry, and culture, and as towns' service areas grew. This further elaboration and concentration of networks, however, could not occur until towns also had transportation links.

Before the railroads, that in effect meant that navigable waterways determined largely which towns were connected and what their service areas and relations were. Because most southern railroad tracks were laid only in the ten years before the Civil War, and transregional lines were not completed until the late 1850s, the South was in the midst of developing its urban networks and centers at the same time as it decided to transform itself into a new nation. The Confederacy could not have been created sooner, because in critical ways the South was just coming into being.

ANTEBELLUM ANTECEDENTS

Between the first US census in 1790 and the fourth in 1820, and again between the fourth in 1820 and the eighth in 1860, the South and its urban life
underwent radical restructuring. The French sale of the Louisiana Territory
to the United States suddenly expanded the South to the shores of what
John C. Calhoun later called an "inland sea," the Mississippi River basin.
The ports there—St. Louis, Natchez, and New Orleans chief among them—
joined the Atlantic ports serving the southern United States—notably, Savannah, Georgia; Charleston, South Carolina; Wilmington, North Carolina;
Norfolk, Virginia; and Baltimore, Maryland. As a result, the region changed
character dramatically. It was no longer a strip of lightly developed Atlantic coastal plain bounded on the interior by a strip of backcountry settlements, colonized by first-, second-, or third-generation immigrants coming
down the Great Wagon Road. Instead, it became in effect a region defined
by water-oriented communities around almost its entire rim. Inside that
aqueous and urban circle and its rough-hewn second ring, the region was
dominated by Native Americans in a frontier area of increasing white en-
croachment and Native American resistance and negotiation.[16]

Conflict with the British over impressment of American sailors and the
freedom of trade and the high seas led not only to President Thomas Jefferson's trade embargo, authorized at the end of 1807, but also to virtual ces-
sation of immigration from Europe. The increasingly ineffective embargo
lasted just eighteen months, but immigration did not resume substantially
until after the War of 1812. Then it quite rapidly shifted northward, thanks
to war-fueled industrialization, the subsequent building of the Erie Canal,
and the progressive opening of the Northwest Territory, starting with the
admission of Ohio to statehood in 1803, the same year as the Louisiana
Purchase.[17]

At secession, the Confederacy had less than a fifth of the percentage of
free immigrants that the North had—fewer than one in twenty-two. Despite
the late antebellum influx of potato-famine Irish and Germans into southern ports and at railroad construction sites and despite substantial northern
in-migration, therefore, white and black southerners were the ones who
mostly settled the South—especially the future Confederate states—in the
half century before the Civil War. When immigrants earlier had led in the
region's expansion, the South was not nearly as demographically homogeneous as New England. In the mid-nineteenth century, southern cities
were still diverse—particularly places like New Orleans and Memphis—
but the states that seceded overall were becoming less and less so because

they were increasingly native born. Consequently, many—particularly smaller—cities there were looking and feeling unlike northern ones. The large presence of slaves and slavery was only one reason. The range and nature of enterprises was another.[18]

A significant part of urban population, although a relatively small part of the region's total, the Irish railroad construction crews helped facilitate the shift of the urban and developmental balance in the South. The two decades-plus after Indian removal and before the Civil War saw the dramatic expansion of mostly newer cities and towns, drawing many immigrants and northerners. While the fifth-largest city in the country in 1810, Charleston, South Carolina, fell to twenty-second by 1860. This was despite a 40 percent population increase, stemming in large part from immigration. The cities that grew fastest either were other ports, often with burgeoning rail connections (St. Louis, Missouri; Louisville, Kentucky; Richmond, Virginia; Memphis, Tennessee; Mobile, Alabama; and Covington, Kentucky; as well as New Orleans, Louisiana), or they were state capitals (Richmond; Nashville, Tennessee; Columbia, South Carolina; and Raleigh, North Carolina).

Still, to focus on such cities, in the country's top 100 by population, is to miss the much more impressive growth of smaller towns, especially across the piedmont South. Earlier examples include Huntsville, Alabama (1805); Murfreesboro, Tennessee (1811); and Columbus, Missouri (1821). Other towns emerged in areas of the Indian removals of the 1830s and in the new state of Texas—for instance, Rome, Georgia (1834); Chattanooga, Tennessee (1838); Gadsden, Alabama (1845); Waco, Texas (1849); Corinth, Mississippi (1853); and Orlando, Florida (1857). Atlanta, Georgia, incorporated in 1845, is an even more striking example. By 1854 it was at the intersection of four railroads, so a principal rail center, and by 1860 it had nearly 10,000 inhabitants, up from just thirty individuals occupying a total of six buildings in 1842. Despite the success of Baltimore at one end, and of New Orleans and Houston/Galveston at the other end, of the coastal South, population growth and economic development were shifting to the interior.

This emergence and rapid expansion of the interior South followed the westward movement of whites, especially in the immediate aftermath of the War of 1812, and of enslaved blacks, especially in the 1830s.[19] Only now are studies beginning to delineate the dynamics and functions of the new towns that became either local centers of economic, political, and cultural life or, in instances, regional hubs. As in colonial South Carolina, often the planters rode, or rowed out, from town to their plantations in the Alabama black belt. The cotton belt, like the tobacco belt, grew more urbanized, if not urban, than scholars once understood. Towns also became centers of

middle-class life. Most professional people there—doctors, lawyers, minis-
ters, editors, teachers—owned few, if any, slaves. The Victorianization of
their culture reinforced their town- and class-centered identities. Set against
the backdrop of slavery, this is not to suggest that middle-class lives were
no different than in the North. Yet town culture suffused the South of 1860
in many ways that it had not in 1760.[20]

At that earlier period, fifteen years before the American Revolution and
in the midst of the French and Indian Wars, southern towns were effectively
islands in seas of woods and dispersed farms. Often they had more connections with Atlantic ports in Britain and the Caribbean than with settlements
a few hundred miles away. Yet increasingly, by the end of the antebellum
era, towns were connected through multiple, rapidly expanding, transportation, trade, social, and political, as well as information networks. They also
were strikingly new in their number, scale, and geographic distribution. In
1810 only nine southern cities had populations over 5,000. By 1840 twenty
did. By 1860 twenty-one had populations either approaching or exceeding
10,000. New Orleans and Baltimore each had more inhabitants than the top
ten southern cities together on the eve of the War of 1812.[21]

The means and variety of communications had grown even more dramatically. Land routes, thanks to trains and coaches, were becoming primary rather than supplementary. As a result, communications and commerce increasingly linked towns in different watersheds rather than just
those sharing waterways. Instead of a newspaper or two for a whole colony,
almost every county seat or commercial center had at least one and, often,
two or more. The mails brought the Disciples of Christ *Millennial Harbinger* magazine, printed in little Bethany, Virginia, from the Ohio River port
of Wheeling as readily as they brought the *Southern Literary Messenger*
from Richmond or the Charleston *Mercury* or *De Bow's Review*, published
in New Orleans.[22]

This explosion of correspondence and print communications fostered a
public sphere of polyvocal dialogue, an urban function. It did so, though less
intensively, outside as well as within densely populated cities and towns.
As traditionally defined, therefore, urban places were no longer as necessary
for such urban functions. That the Reverend Alexander Campbell's base-
ment religious press in his home near Buffalo Creek could reach tens of
thousands of Disciples as effectively as periodicals from the biggest and
culturally richest urban centers of the region and the nation meant that urbanism in some sense was being expanded and redefined. In the same years,
mechanized transportation began to extend urbanism's reach beyond cities
and towns.

Originally marked by concentrations of people and face-to-face transactions and amplified by trade within market areas and over the distances traversed by caravans, carts, and ships, towns began to expand geographically after the introduction of omnibuses and streetcars in the 1820s. Thereafter, however, urbanism increasingly took on extralocal meanings. The growth of railroads, steam packets, and coach lines at once symbolized and promoted these trends. Emblematic was the 1857 completion of the Charleston and Memphis Railroad, begun in Charleston thirty years before. Just in advance of that completion, in 1855, the East Tennessee and Georgia Railroad gave East Tennessee rail access to the Atlantic at Savannah and Charleston. By 1858 the East Tennessee and Virginia Railroad also connected Knoxville with Richmond and Norfolk, Virginia, and New York City. Two years later, Meridian, Mississippi, was founded as another hub connecting rail and steamboat services. Only then, on the eve of the Civil War, did the South effectively have in place a regional transportation network, however uneven.[23]

Yet the impact of the railroads already was reshaping cultural production in the region. Although Charleston had functioned as the principal cultural center of the South Atlantic area during the city's pre-Revolutionary and antebellum history, by 1860 its leading cultural journal, *Russell's Magazine*, had ceased production. At the same time, however, other cities and towns were growing in significance as print centers. Augusta, Georgia, an important rail hub as well as river port, is a case in point. Home of the *Southern Cultivator* since 1843, in 1859 it added what Michael Bernath judges to have been "perhaps the best of the literary family papers at the start of the war": *Southern Field and Fireside*. It also was the place of publication for the *Southern Medical and Surgical Journal*. By 1860, too, other rail towns— Atlanta, Columbia, Fayetteville, Greensboro, Montgomery, Nashville, Raleigh, and Richmond among them—had become centers of religious or educational publications serving the whole, or large portions of, the region. These addressed markets that journals out of New York and Philadelphia, Edinburgh and London did not.[24] Soon thereafter the Confederacy had a hierarchy of print communications from the national to the local level at once reflecting and articulating an urbanizing region's emerging shape.

URBAN TRANSFORMATION IN THE CIVIL WAR

The intervention of the Civil War in the midst of these developments had profound consequences. Several things happened with remarkable alacrity. Ports lost many of their communications links and capacities, thanks to implementation of Union general Paul Winfield Scott's plan to strangle the

South's waterborne shipping and trade. As a result, railroads and the nation's interior centers grew even more important as distributors of intellectual output, as well as war materiel and troops.[25] Thanks to the recently completed rail links, the Confederacy developed a national press and publication center in Richmond that served not only to concentrate and ramp up intellectual production, but also to make that production nationalistic in tone and purpose.

Enhancing the role and reach of the media were the concentration of men in the army, of politicians and government officials in Richmond and other administrative centers, and of refugees in numerous cities, towns, and camps. Some members of these audiences may have been readers before, but never had they and others been gathered together in such numbers and for such reasons. Inevitably, these concentrations of people meant enlarged readerships (and auditorships) for the latest word, however unreliable.[26] These concentrations also influenced what authors produced and publishers sold.

Consider one by one the congeries of people created by the war, taking the smallest group first. The Confederate government necessarily included many more than the antebellum South's share of federal officeholders and representatives. Functions that once had been distributed across the whole of the prewar Union or centered in Washington, DC, were suddenly being staffed by southerners in Richmond and elsewhere in the new nation. The Confederacy had just over 40 percent of the Union's population, but by the middle of the war, there may have been seven Confederate for every ten Union civil service employees. Many of the 70,000-plus Confederate civil servants worked outside of Richmond—for instance, most of the 7,000 postmasters (initially former federal postmasters) and also tax collectors and conscription agents.

Yet the Confederacy also employed many others than civil servants in Richmond—for instance, some "5,000 women . . . in the factories or doing piece work." There were as well thousands of African Americans engaged in construction of fortifications, in factories, and elsewhere.[27] Richmond, therefore, had a concentration of leadership, functionaries, and workers dramatically greater than, and different in purpose from, any ever assembled before south of the Potomac. This assemblage, together with new, nationalistic cultural centrality, meant that Richmond had a metropolitan role greater than any southern city had had previously.[28]

But there was another reason that the capital's population nearly doubled during the first year of the war: refugees. Many of those displaced by military movements or occupation and guerrilla depredations moved from rural community to rural community or from city to country, seeking to rent farms and reestablish a semblance of ordinary life. Yet many others—disproportionately women and children—did not have that option. Instead, they went to camps or cities such as Richmond. These latter found themselves not only displaced, but also often living an urban existence that was in greater or lesser degree novel to them and horrible. The relatively large concentrations and variety of people were only part of the reason. Work, when it was to be had, threw many people from different communities together. Often it was unfamiliar as well, whether in the sex trade or in factories. That left a growing number, however, effectively living as urban poor, because they were unable or unwilling either to pay ruinous, predatory prices or to participate in such work and so found themselves scavenging with increasing desperation.[29]

Never had the region's cities and towns seen so many flood in so quickly or in such dire circumstances. The sometimes heroic, if often inefficient, efforts of local authorities and churches to cope fell progressively shorter of the need as the war continued. The political sensitivity to this mushrooming population of poor, on the one hand, and for law and order, on the other hand, grew as a result. Here too the Confederate media played a role that the prewar media had not, at least not nearly to the same degree. Awareness of the tensions that resulted from rapidly growing immiseration became a shaper of editorial policy but also of editorial consumption.[30]

Soldiers were perhaps even more radically urbanized than refugees—for a period. Large-scale military encampments in many respects functioned as and had the attributes of temporary cities and towns. So, in a fashion, did prison camps. The dense populations again were only one reason. Camp economy, the organization and conduct of essential services (from medical and livestock care and cooking to waste management), the centrality of simultaneously hierarchical, multilayered, and broad communications, and large systems thinking and operations were all aspects of what may be characterized as urbanized experiences and expectations. Sex workers and colporteurs both followed military columns because they represented concentrated, relatively large-scale markets, as in cities and towns. The men moved in those columns and acted together on orders reflecting often imperfect but nevertheless relatively dense volumes and flows of information and communication—again, such as towns and cities served to gather and distribute.

Further, even when units were from particular areas, their array, in any large-scale encampment, on the march, or in battle, meant soldiers were often cheek-by-jowl with others from more-or-less distant parts of the

Confederacy or abroad. True, Pickett's Division at the Battle of Gettysburg was made up entirely of Virginia brigades (and a Virginia artillery battalion). Yet all the other Confederate divisions there were from multiple states, and Pickett's famous charge drew on numbers of them as well.[31] Neighborhoods back home also often placed people from different parts of the South, as well as the North, Europe, and Africa, together. Consequently, recruits and camp followers from these more recently settled or expanding communities reflected this diversity too. The more than 40 percent of white South Carolinians who lived outside of their natal state by 1860 were relatively more numerous than the out-migrants from other South Atlantic states, but all these states saw substantial parts of their populations move west or south before the war.

Complicating still further the relations of soldiers was the fact that many units drew recruits from more than one community within an area and did so from the very beginning of the war. Maxcy Gregg's regiment, the First South Carolina Volunteers, is a case in point; its recruits were drawn from all over South Carolina.[32] So, while initial unit cohesion and morale sometimes had an aspect of neighborhood attachment, particularly at the company level, in many instances how and to what degree this mattered are not straightforward questions. At the least, neighborhood attachments were nested and understood, as in towns and cities, in the context of multiple additional kinds, quantities, and frequencies of relations among the soldiers.

Print fostered both these community and other wider interactions. The copy of a local newspaper became a basis for men of that locale to talk, worry, and write home about their experiences, anxieties, and messmates. Amplifying these discussions were private letters between home and distant encampments. To participate in these written communications, some soldiers, as well as family members back home, learned to read and write, although roughly 81 percent of white adults (compared to 93 percent of northern adults) already claimed to be literate to one degree or another.[33] These aspects of nation building helped transform or, at any rate, modify the meaning of local attachments and associations not just in the army but at home. Whether in print or in manuscript, the written word reinforced the military's role as an urbanizing and nationalizing force.

At the same time, such writing necessarily reflected the progressive dislocation of an ever greater percentage of the nation's inhabitants. The making of refugees also rewrote the meaning and functions of many communities—both those from which people fled and those to which people moved. The individuals and families thus uprooted and relocated often literally were lost to view, not just by soldiers, but by other friends and relatives from their home communities. Simultaneously, the refugees of necessity formed new attachments, linking with people from elsewhere in some of the same ways as soldiers did in their encampments, in hospital, on the march, and in battle. Their westering parents and grandparents had done the same earlier.[34] Even in rural settings, such experiences in some senses served to urbanize elements of the relations, if not always the sensibilities, of the people involved.

WARTIME CULTURAL PRODUCERS AND PRODUCTION

These new audiences had new as well as continuing needs of their cultural producers. The writers and editors trying to meet them faced kinds and degrees of challenges that they had not had before. Despite the severity of the challenges and the number of failures, the Confederacy generated and circulated a remarkable range and quantity of printed materials. This development reflected a progressive redistribution of print culture resources. Many small towns lost their voices, their newspapers unable to continue production. Old centers such as Charleston declined further in importance. Other centers, such as Augusta and, above all, Richmond, dramatically expanded their reach and influence. As a consequence, for the first time the South had widely read nonreligious publications that were produced there. The virtual communities of periodical readers, which they generated, extended these urbanizing influences.

This was accomplished—if sometimes only briefly—by one editor or writer at a time. Consider two Charlestonians especially influential before the war. The younger, James D. B. De Bow, edited *De Bow's Review*, one of "the two most prestigious journals in the Confederacy," a standard bearer "for high southern intellectual culture."[35] The elder was William Gilmore Simms. No antebellum man of letters played a larger or more visible role in the South's literary framing and life or in the South's place in the nation's imagination and cultural development. Although both men were Charleston-born and although both were committed promoters of the southern nation in the run-up to the Civil War, Simms had made his reputation in New York, Philadelphia, and London, as well as Germany, beginning in 1832, and De Bow from New Orleans starting fourteen years later. Yet the war, which seemed the fulfillment of their ambitions, changed their outputs, venues, preoccupations, competition, and audiences.

How to answer the need to promote the Confederacy while facing wartime shortages and dislocations? Late in 1861 De Bow commenced combining issues of the *Review* and publishing on a bimonthly instead of a

monthly schedule. As he explained early in the spring of the next year, the
scarcity of paper, labor, and equipment had pushed publication costs up
threefold. Just weeks later, New Orleans fell to federal forces. As a result, he
had to move his Louisiana operations, and did so, to Columbia, SC. He arrived too soon to avail himself there of the huge new plant of the Charleston
printing firm of Evans and Cogswell, built in 1864 and housing "seventy-six
presses, twenty-five ruling and binding machines, and 344 employees" in a
facility that sprawled over two acres.[36]

Earlier, after the start of the war, De Bow had used (and advertised) the
firm's Charleston operation: he issued his journal from the South Carolina
port, as well as New Orleans. Columbia, however, seemed a safer place to
which to remove, as it was not under siege. The state capital also had better
rail connections. From there he published a quadruple issue to catch up as
much as possible and meet subscribers' expectations. But the move had left
over half of his paying readership of perhaps 4,000 behind enemy lines, and
that loss meant that he had to suspend publication again for 1863.

Others did better. After going into a steep decline in size and physical
quality, as well as content, in 1862, in part as a consequence of the same
paper shortages faced by *De Bow's*, *Southern Field and Fireside* began in
a new format and a new series in January 1863. Some of the new series'
dramatic success was the result of the recruitment of established authors
such as Simms. Some was the result of a remarkable circulation increase. It
yielded a subscription list many times that of *De Bow's*.[37] Yet the *Southern
Field and Fireside*'s success paled in comparison to that of the *Southern Illustrated News* and the *Magnolia Weekly*, both begun in the fall of 1862 in
Richmond.

Home of the well-regarded *Southern Literary Messenger*, once edited by
Edgar Allan Poe, the Confederate capital and the South had never produced
such broadly popular cultural journals. As George Bagby, wartime editor of
the *Messenger*, ruefully noted, in just over a month the *Illustrated News* had
four times as many subscribers as his journal had after twenty-seven years—
some 16,000 compared to 4,000.[38] Six months later, the *News* claimed "more
than *one hundred thousand respectable and honorable* residents of the
Southern Confederacy" in its readership. Like *Southern Field and Fireside*,
the *Illustrated News* paid its contributors, although at considerably higher
rates. Moreover, located in the Confederate capital, it had claims to national
stature and audiences beyond any journal issuing from Augusta, Columbia,
or Charleston. Therefore, it too got Simms to contribute.[39]

In the eight years before the war, this patriarch of southern letters had
nursed a selected edition of twenty volumes of his writings through the

press in New York. Earlier, in the 1840s, he and James Fenimore Cooper had sold better than any other historical romancers in America. That reputation meant that Simms's planned 1856 fall lecture tour in New York and New England was heavily subscribed to in advance. Yet, as his first lecture, in Buffalo, showed, his aggressive defense of the South's role in the American Revolution did not sit well with his auditors. After his second lecture, in Rochester, the audiences stayed away in droves.[40] Perhaps it was not so surprising, then, that Justus Starr Redfield, publisher of the selected edition, went bankrupt in 1861.

As New York in greater or lesser degree was being foreclosed to Simms as a place of successful further publication in the increasingly heated years before secession, Charleston also was declining as a southern base for its most noted man of letters. During the war, therefore, Simms turned more and more to other southern venues. He picked up old pieces, both published and unpublished, and reworked or added to them in the interest of promoting patriotism in poems and fictions that he sent not just to the *Charleston Mercury*, but also to *Southern Field and Fireside*, the *Southern Illustrated News*, and the *Magnolia Weekly*. For the last, he also completed a long, multipart drama in an essay, on Benedict Arnold and other northern traitors in the Revolution. He had been working on the drama for decades, publishing portions along and along.[41]

WARTIME PRINT DISSEMINATION AND CONSUMPTION

Such writings gave Simms broader and larger southern audiences than he had ever had. If the war had begun twenty years earlier, this development could not have occurred. The conflict came in the wake of the emergence and subsequent, dramatic expansion, of both railroads and illustrated weeklies and monthlies. Simms already had benefited from this transition, as far as it had gone, in the 1850s. That was when these developments accelerated. His Revolutionary romance "Katherine Walton; or, the Rebel's Daughter: A Tale of the Revolution" appeared in serialized form in 1850 in *Godey's Lady's Book*. This first, and long the most popular, of the large-circulation lady's cultural magazines made this early example of realism the most widely read of all his long fictions during his life time. *Godey's* was precursor to the popular illustrated weeklies and monthlies, such as *Harper's* and *Frank Leslie's*, which served as the lenses through which many people saw the approaching Civil War and its conduct.[42]

On the eve of secession the country produced some 3,000 newspapers in addition to 1,000 magazines. The newspaper circulation was almost

1.5 million or one for roughly every nine literate free adults. Because some dailies had large circulations, most of the rest sold only a few hundred copies each. "The largest . . . , the *New York Herald*, had a daily circulation of about 77,000" in 1860, up from about 29,000 in 1847. In the South "no newspaper . . . had a circulation of more than 10,000." With just over the equivalent of 80 percent of the literate free population of the future Confederacy, the state of New York consumed more newspapers than all eleven seceding states.[43] The popular weeklies and monthlies had the largest circulations—200,000 for the weekly *New York Herald Tribune* and about the same for *Harper's*. In each case, this was nearly a seventh of the newspaper buying public. The literary and other niche monthlies and quarterlies, such as those Simms and DeBow edited at different times, tended to average circulations of no more than about 4,000 each.

Before the war, the audience for the largest weeklies and monthlies was disproportionately northern. Although the future Confederacy had roughly 20 percent of the adult free population in 1860, it had only 18 percent of the self-declared, literate population. On a per capita basis, subscriptions there were lower even than that number might suggest. Those to northern periodicals necessarily ceased soon after the war commenced. Yet the taste for the illustrated weeklies and monthlies remained strong. To meet the demand for this increasingly popular form of media and to do so from a southern point of view, therefore, Confederate entrepreneurs developed similar popular cultural magazines. It was in these periodicals that Simms reached the largest *southern* readerships of his career.

Had Simms been a religious writer, he might have had wider readership both before and during the war. In many respects the broad print market of the Civil War era was developed by the religious press. In 1840 perhaps three-quarters of the journalism read in America was religious. Many of the largest circulation weeklies and monthlies were in this category. Like the *Millennial Harbinger*, they often issued from smaller communities, not metropolitan ones.

Well before the war, every southern state had religious periodicals, with more-or-less large circulations. They benefited from the evangelical Protestant emphasis on the importance of scriptural study and reached far beyond the ministry to lay members and even the unchurched. In the midst of the war, the urgency about sharing instruction in the faith and getting right with God became all the more acute. Consequently, many religious publishers got support to give soldiers thousands of copies of journal issues, tracts, and bibles.[44]

The volumes and kinds of linkages among these distributed networks of print-based missions, production centers, and readerships were substantially greater, more robust, and also different than earlier in the South. This was so even in the face of wartime challenges. The differences were the result of intentional efforts at the intellectual transformation of an American region into a separate nation. The Confederacy was remarkably successful in this pursuit for several reasons. The notion of building on distinct southern interests and associations to promote and fortify a unifying southern identity and nation was not new. Neither was the romantic nationalist impulse behind it. Nor was the commitment to use the media to support that cause, whether in schools, churches, parlors, or military encampments. Nor was the idea that patriotism could be transferred from an old to a new allegiance.

What was new was the extent to which elements of the message were so often repeated and reinforced that they became internalized. The process resulted in the South achieving an emotional and imaginative reality that earlier it had had only for an aspiring, romantic nationalist minority (De Bow and Simms among them). This commitment to southern ethnogenesis, or the flowering of a southern national and ethnic character, culture, and independence, grew as a firm, majority, white self-identity and allegiance through the process of secession, Confederate discourses, and the urbanized interactions created or expanded by the war. The end of hostilities did not stop but rather reinforced the process. Consequently, by the close of the nineteenth century, commonly asserted experiences, attitudes, and beliefs helped transform southern peoplehood from a personal, ideological, and political commitment into a shared, totalizing, and hegemonic social phenomenon. Not only the meaning but also the function of southernness changed profoundly as a result.[45]

THE POSTBELLUM RECONFIGURATION OF URBAN-BASED SOUTHERN CULTURE

The defeat of the Confederacy immediately ended Richmond's national capital role as well as cultural centrality. Yet, despite federal occupation, defeat did not end Confederate discourses in either private or public. Those, however, no longer were dominated by the publications that had shaped them centrally during the war. Many of the Confederate-era prints had trouble continuing. Moreover, those that did found their audiences drastically reduced. There was no longer either the military or the national government to address. Temporarily, it is true, the peace dramatically heightened the number of refugees, as freedmen left the quarters, many returning soldiers found their property devastated, and starving former Confederate civilians sought food and shelter. Such refugees, however, had no money for publications.[46]

Nevertheless, De Bow resumed his *Review*, and Simms edited newspapers in Columbia and Charleston. The two men needed whatever income they could earn, but they also were determined to make defeat the foundation of a perduring South. Of necessity, this would be within rather than without the United States. Yet defeat did not mean for them automatic acceptance of the policies and presence of the victors. De Bow picked up again his old themes of the region's economic development and relations. In doing so, he and his contributors also weighed the impact of federal Reconstruction. Looming above everything for them was the issue of the status of the freedmen.

Simms in time came to anticipate race war. Yet his foci as author nonetheless were different. When he wrote in 1865 of the *Sack and Destruction of Columbia, S.C.*, by the Union army under General Sherman, he was intent on making sure his fellow white southerners remembered what had been lost and why. In part this was to forestall their acceptance of things as they were. As he told the ladies of the Charleston Horticultural Society just before his death in 1870, they needed the commitment to beauty to protect them against the awful, self-serving crassness of the Yankees. He also urged them to persevere in elevation of the memory of the sacrifices of the war and of the world they had lost.[47]

The series on South Carolina's intellectual and literary history that Simms had just concluded in *The XIX Century*, another new and short-lived Charleston cultural journal, illustrated this commitment. Although this preoccupation was hardly designed to gain him broad new northern readerships, Simms nevertheless also worked hard to reclaim for himself and other southerners a national American cultural presence and audience. Some Copperhead periodicals in New York were ready to publish him. So were the new journals in Baltimore, Atlanta, and elsewhere, which claimed dedication to the South's cultural life and future. It was in a collection of Confederate war poetry, published in New York in 1867, that Simms explained part of his motivation:

> Though sectional in its character, and indicative of a temper and a feeling which were in conflict with nationality, yet, now that the States of the Union have been resolved into one nation, this collection is essentially as much the property of the whole as are the captured cannon

which were employed against it during the progress of the late war. It belongs to the national literature . . . just as legitimately to be recognized by the nation as are the rival ballads of the cavaliers and roundheads, by the English, in the great civil conflict of their country.[48]

The effort at cultural reclamation and integration could not obscure how unlike the present was the past. By 1920 Charleston no longer even ranked among the nation's top 100 cities. Most of the places that did had not existed or were just villages in 1820, when Charleston ranked sixth in the United States. Although some southern communities—New Orleans, Baltimore, Washington, Richmond, Norfolk, Savannah, and Louisville— were among the country's biggest cities then, too, there were almost three times as many southern cities among the top 100 in 1920. The pattern of urban growth in the half century after Simms's death suggests some of the reasons.

Between 1860 and 1880—that is, through the course of the war and Reconstruction—many of the South's largest cities grew by 50 to more than 100 percent. Charleston grew by less than 25 and New Orleans by less than 30 percent. The cities that saw the greatest growth were either at the fringes of the war zone, as were Baltimore, St. Louis, Washington, and Louisville, or they were growing rail centers, as were Richmond, Atlanta, Nashville, and Augusta, or they were gateway cities to the West, as were San Antonio and Galveston, Texas, and St. Joseph, Missouri. Except in the border states, there were few industrial cities.

In most urban places in the former Confederacy, the economic driver continued to be the same extractive production that fueled the Old South's growth. A Hampton Roads, Virginia, might boom as a result, but it was at the expense of places like Mobile and Charleston, which could not accom- modate the new, large draft vessels that began to be constructed in quantity in the 1880s. The New South was not built on this old, extractive economy. The textile and other manufacturing industries only began migrating to the southern piedmont and upper South in significant numbers in the late 1880s and 1890s. When they came, it was for cheap labor and cheap access to raw materials. Because railroads carried the finished goods, Atlanta and other hub cities benefited.

Other drivers increasingly moved the economy as well. Eventually the drag of the war no longer retarded growth in places such as New Orleans and Memphis, as they came to handle the dramatically increasing shipping of the Mississippi, Ohio, and Missouri river valleys and the expanding rice and cotton production of the Mississippi and Arkansas deltas. Cities such as

Jacksonville, Florida, and Dallas, El Paso, and Houston, Texas, grew rapidly, too, in areas of large-scale in-migration—often from elsewhere in the South or from the North. The oil industry drew many of the in-migrants to Texas. It was another extractive industry, but a new one for the region.

Knowing this history, scholars not surprisingly have felt justified in talking about the urban-industrial lag in the South as compared with the North. In the process, however, they have obscured much of the vitality and meaning of urbanization in the late antebellum period and for the Confederacy. To say city growth lagged is not to say how the multiplication of urban functions made possible the intellectual and military establishment and conduct of the Confederate states or with what consequences. Too often the assumption has been that the Old South was Jeffersonian and agrarian, not urbanizing and modernizing. Yet the Civil War would not have been fought if the Old South had not been urbanizing and modernizing at least at the rate it had.

NOTES

In addition to the editors of this volume and the anonymous readers for the University of Chicago Press, the following helped me correct errors and refine and clarify my language and argument, even when they did not agree with it: Michael Bernath, Christopher Curtis, Louis Ferleger, William Freehling, Matthew Gallman, Sarah Gardner, Louis Kyriakoudes, John Majewski, John Mayfield, Randall Miller, Alexander Moore, Patricia Poteat, Beth Schweiger, Johanna Shields, Jewel Spangler, and Clyde Wilson.

1. [William Gilmore Simms], "Country Life Incompatible with Literary Labor," *Southern Literary Journal* 3 (1836–37): 297–99. See David Moltke-Hansen, "The Expansion of Intellectual Life: A Prospectus," in *Intellectual Life in Antebellum Charleston*, ed. Michael O'Brien and David Moltke-Hansen (Knoxville: University of Tennessee Press, 1986), 3–44.

2. David R. Goldfield, *Cotton Fields and Skyscrapers: Southern City and Region, 1670–1980* (Baton Rouge: Louisiana State University Press, 1982); J. Matthew Gallman, "Urban History and the Civil War," *Journal of Urban History* 32 (May 2006): 631–42; and Frank Towers, *The Urban South and the Coming of the Civil War* (Charlottesville: University of Virginia Press, 2004).

3. Louis M. Kyriakoudes, "Lower-Order Urbanization and Territorial Monopoly in the Southern Furnishing Trade: Alabama, 1871–1890," *Social Science History* 26, no. 1 (2002): 179–98. Cf. Jan de Vries, "Problems in the Measurement, Description, and Analysis of Historical Urbanization," in *Urbanization in History: A Process of Dynamic Interactions*, ed. A. M. van der Wonde, Akira Hayami, and Jan de Vries (Oxford: Clarendon Press, 1995), 43–60, and Gavin Wright, *The Political Economy*

of the Cotton South: Households, Markets, and Wealth in the Nineteenth Century (New York: W. W. Norton and Co., 1978).

4. J. Robert Cox, *Environmental Communication and the Public Sphere*, 2nd ed. (Thousand Oaks, CA: Sage Publications, 2010); and Rudolph Stichweh, "Systems Theory," in *International Encyclopedia of Political Science*, ed. Bertran Badie et al., 11 vols. (New York: Sage, 2011), 8:2579–82.

5. Following regional sociologist Howard Odum, his sons Eugene P. Odum and Howard T. Odum wrote the first ecology textbook, *Fundamentals of Ecology* (Philadelphia: W. B. Saunders, 1953). On print cultural, or history of the book, studies in relationship to the Civil War South, see especially Beth Barton Schweiger, "The Literate South: Reading before Emancipation," *Journal of the Civil War Era* 3, no. 3 (2013): 331–59.

6. Frank Towers, "The Southern Path to Modern Cities: Urbanization in the Slave States," in *The Old South's Modern Worlds: Slavery, Region, and Nation in the Age of Progress*, ed. L. Diane Barnes, Brian Schoen, and Frank Towers (New York: Oxford University Press, 2011). Also see n. 3 above and Leonard P. Curry, "Urbanization and Urbanism in the Old South: A Comparative View," *Journal of Southern History* 40, no. 1 (1974): 43–60; Lyle W. Dorsett and Arthur H. Shaffer, "Was the Antebellum South Anti-Urban? A Suggestion," *Journal of Southern History* 38, no. 1 (1972): 93–100; table 2 in Roger L. Ransom, "The Economics of the Civil War," *EH.Net Encyclopedia*, posted Mon., 2010–02–01 at 19:12 by backhand, and Edward Pessen, "How Different from Each Other Were the Antebellum North and South," *American Historical Review* 85, no. 5 (1980): 1119–49.

7. Aaron W. Marrs, *Railroads in the Old South: Pursuing Progress in a Slave Society* (Baltimore, MD: Johns Hopkins University Press, 2009), xiii–xvii; William P. Thomas, "'Swerve Me?': The South, the Railroads, and the Rush to Modernity," in *The Old South's Modern Worlds*, ed. Barnes, Schoen, and Towers, 177. Benedict Anderson, *Imagined Communities: Reflections on the Origins and Spread of Nationalism* (London: Verso, 1991), argues for the importance of what Thomas calls "regional networks for shared information, social interactions, and trade" (3). Cf. Allan Pred, *Urban Growth and City-Systems in the United States, 1840–1860* (Cambridge, MA: Harvard University Press, 1980); John D. Majewski, *Modernizing a Slave Economy: The Economic Vision of the Confederate Nation* (Chapel Hill: University of North Carolina Press, 2009); David Moltke-Hansen, "Southern Literary Horizons in Young America: Imaginative Development of a Regional Geography," *Studies in the Literary Imagination* 42, no. 1 (2009): 1–31.

8. Michael T. Bernath, *Confederate Minds: The Struggle for Intellectual Independence in the Civil War South* (Chapel Hill: University of North Carolina Press, 2010). See also n. 31 below and Anne Sarah Rubin, *A Shattered Nation: The Rise and Fall of the Confederacy, 1861–1868* (Chapel Hill: University of North Carolina Press, 2005), 11–42.

9. Walt W. Rostow's *The Stages of Economic Growth: A Non-Communist Manifesto* (Cambridge: Cambridge University Press, 1960), and Daniel Lerner, *The Passing of Traditional Society: Modernizing the Middle East* (Glencoe, IL: Free Press, 1958), culminated thirty years of thinking on modernization. The role of and access to information and its flows and production were central to Lerner's understanding.

Cf. Schweiger, "The Literate South"; Frank Towers, "Partisans, New History, and Modernization: The Historiography of the Civil War's Causes, 1861–2011," *Journal of the Civil War Era* 1 (June 2011): 237–64; and Walter Johnson, *River of Dark Dreams: Slavery and Empire in the Cotton Kingdom* (Cambridge, MA: Harvard University Press, 2013).

10. Jonathan Daniel Wells, *The Origins of the Southern Middle Class, 1800–1861* (Chapel Hill: University of North Carolina Press, 2004); Beth Barton Schweiger, *The Gospel Working Up: Progress and the Pulpit in Nineteenth-Century Virginia* (New York: Oxford University Press, 2000); Jennifer Green, *Military Education and the Emerging Middle Class in the Old South* (New York: Cambridge University Press, 2008); and Johanna Nicol Shields, *Freedom in a Slave Society: Stories from the Antebellum South* (New York: Cambridge University Press, 2012).

11. J. C. Swayze, comp., *Hill and Swayze's Confederate States Rail-Road & Steam-Boat Guide* (Griffin, GA: Hill and Swayze, 1862).

12. Majewski, *Modernizing a Slave Economy*, argues that the Civil War strengthened systems thinking and development in the Confederacy. David R. Goldfield, *Region, Race, and Cities: Interpreting the Urban South* (Baton Rouge: Louisiana State University Press, 1997), 6–8, makes part of the case for using an ecological approach.

13. Private email from Randall Miller to the author, August 7, 2014.

14. Christopher Morris, *Becoming Southern: The Evolution of a Way of Life, Warren County and Vicksburg, Mississippi, 1760–1860* (New York: Oxford University Press, 1995); Wright, *The Political Economy of the Cotton South*; and Kathleen Hilliard, *Masters, Slaves, and Exchange: Power's Purchase in the Old South* (New York: Cambridge University Press, 2013).

15. Kyriakoudes, "Lower-Order Urbanization and Territorial Monopoly," 181; Shields, *Freedom in a Slave Society*; Lacy K. Ford, *Origins of Southern Radicalism: The South Carolina Upcountry* (New York: Oxford University Press, 1988), 215–78, 308–37; and Tom Downey, *Planting a Capitalist South: Masters, Merchants, and Manufacturers in the Southern Interior, 1790–1860* (Baton Rouge: Louisiana State University Press, 2006).

16. Clyde N. Wilson, Shirley B. Cook, and Alexander Moore, eds., *The Papers of John C. Calhoun*, vol. 22 (Columbia: University of South Carolina Press, 1996), 229. On the pre-Revolutionary period, see Carl Bridenbaugh, *Cities in the Wilderness: The First Century of Urban Life in America, 1625–1742* (New York: Oxford University Press, 1938), and *Myths and Realities: Societies of the Colonial South* (Baton Rouge: Louisiana State University Press, 1952); Clarence L. Ver Steeg, *Origins of a Southern Mosaic: Studies of Early Carolina and Georgia* (Athens: University of Georgia Press, 1975); Timothy H. Breen, "The Great Wagon Road," *Southern Cultures* 3, no. 1 (1997): 22–57; S. Max Edelson, *Plantation Enterprise in Colonial South Carolina* (Cambridge, MA: Harvard University Press, 2006); and Daniel H. Usner Jr., *Indians, Settlers, and Slaves in a Frontier Exchange Economy: The Lower Mississippi Valley before 1783* (Chapel Hill: University of North Carolina Press, 1992). On post-Revolutionary urban development, see Allan Pred, *Urban Growth and the Circulation of Information: The United States System of Cities, 1790–1840* (Cambridge, MA: Harvard University Press, 1973); Richard Wade, *The Urban Frontier: The Rise*

of Western Cities, 1790–1830 (Cambridge, MA: Harvard University Press, 1959); and Downey, *Planting a Capitalist South*. On Native Americans in the South in this period, see, for instance, Greg O'Brien, "The Conqueror Meets the Unconquered: Negotiating Cultural Boundaries on the Post-Revolutionary Southern Frontier," *Journal of Southern History* 67, no. 1 (2001): 39–72. Adam Rothman, *Slave Country: American Expansion and the Origins of the Deep South* (Cambridge, MA: Harvard University Press, 2005), examines slavery's westward expansion.

17. In large cities, southern-born whites, while a plurality, often were not a majority (if one separates out in-migrants from the North), and the immigrant population was comparable to that in northern cities. See Towers, "Southern Path to Modern Cities," 154–55; Randall Miller, "The Enemy Within: Some Effects of Foreign Immigrants on Antebellum Southern Cities," *Southern Studies* 24, no. 1 (1985): 30–53, and "Recapitulation of the Tables of Population, Nativity, and Occupation," in the US Bureau of the Census, *Population of the United States in 1860* (Washington, DC: Government Printing Office, 1864), 616–23.

18. See Curry, "Urbanization and Urbanism in the Old South," 58, and Miller, "Enemy Within."

19. Peter D. McClelland and Richard J. Zeckhauser, *Demographic Dimensions of the New Republic: American Interregional Migration, Vital Statistics and Manumissions, 1800–1860* (New York: Cambridge University Press, 1982); also Rothman, *Slave Country*; Miller, *South by Southwest: Planter Emigration and Identity in the Slave South* (Charlottesville: University of Virginia Press, 2002); and David Hackett Fischer and James C. Kelly, *Bound Away: Virginia and the Westward Movement* (Charlottesville: University Press of Virginia, 2000), 135–201, 229–52.

20. See nn. 11 and 16 above; also Robert A. Olwell, *Masters, Slaves, and Subjects: The Culture of Power in the South Carolina Low Country, 1740–1790* (Ithaca, NY: Cornell University Press, 1998), 37; and Shields, *Freedom in a Slave Society*.

21. US Bureau of the Census, "Population of the 100 Largest Cities and Other, Urban Places in the United States: 1790 to 1990," comp. Campbell Gibson, Population Division Working Paper 27 (Washington, DC: US Bureau of the Census, 1998).

22. Richard R. John, *Spreading the News: The American Postal System from Franklin to Morse* (Cambridge, MA: Harvard University Press, 1995), 4, notes a twenty-nine-fold per capita increase in letters and a thirteen-fold per capita increase in newspapers circulated by the Postal Service between 1790 and 1840. On the rise thereafter, see Winnifred Gregory Gerould et al., *American Newspapers, 1821–1936: A Union List of Files Available in the United States and Canada* (New York: H. W. Wilson Co., 1937); Scott E. Casper et al., *The Industrial Book, 1840–1880*, vol. 3 of *A History of the Book in America* (Chapel Hill: University of North Carolina Press, 2007), 178, 193, 224–78, esp. 234; Frank Luther Mott, *A History of American Magazines, 1741–1850* (Cambridge, MA: Harvard University Press, 1938); and Mott, *A History of American Magazines, 1850–1865* (Cambridge, MA: Harvard University Press, 1966). On Campbell, see Beth Barton Schweiger, "Alexander Campbell's Passion for Print: Protestant Sectarians and the Press in the Early United States," *Proceedings of the American Antiquarian Society* 118, no. 1 (2008): 143–76.

23. See n. 8 above.

24. Bernath, *Confederate Minds*, 84–85.

25. David G. Surdam, *Northern Naval Superiority and the Economics of the Civil War* (Columbia: University of South Carolina Press, 2001).

26. One can roughly calculate the numerical impact of the Confederate exposure to urban experiences and settings. At the outset of the Civil War, just over 600,000 people lived in Confederate urban places of 2,500 or more inhabitants, 385,000 of them in the ten biggest cities. Cumulatively the war may have more than quadrupled this urban population. The estimate is based on a rough addition: the over 600,000 prewar urbanites + the portion of the 1,000,000 in the Confederate military from rural places who participated in large-scale formations + the equivalent portion of the +/– 200,000 whites and blacks from the Confederate states in Union service + the portion of the estimated +/– 800,000 Confederate, slave, and white Unionist and free black refugees who fled from rural to urban places and across military lines in the Confederate states + the number of government workers who came from rural places to work in urban settings + the number of rural slaves building fortifications and repairing roads and railroads + the numbers of rural inhabitants recruited to work in factories— multiple inclusions for some individuals. The crude, order-of-magnitude total is 2.4-plus million people, exclusive of small-town dwellers.

27. Harry N. Scheiber, "The Confederate Civil Service," *Journal of Southern History* 25, no. 4 (1959): 448–70; quoted at 459.

28. Emory Thomas, *The Confederate State of Richmond: A Biography of the Capital* (Austin: University of Texas Press, 1971), and Ernest B. Furgurson, *Ashes of Glory: Richmond at War* (New York: Alfred A. Knopf, 1996). George C. Rable, *Civil Wars: Women and the Crisis of Southern Nationalism* (Urbana: University of Illinois Press, 1989), 183, judges that "at least a quarter of a million Southerners left their homes [that is, refugeed] during the war"; Susanna Michele Lee, "Refugees During the Civil War" in the *Encyclopedia Virginia*, ed. Brendan Wolfe (Charlottesville: Virginia Foundation for the Humanities), http://www.EncyclopediaVirginia.org/Refugees_During _the_Civil_War (last modified May 23, 2012, and retrieved November 26, 2012), estimates 200,000—the majority in the Old Dominion. Stephen V. Ash, *When the Yankees Came: Conflict and Chaos in the Occupied South, 1861–1865* (Chapel Hill: University of North Carolina Press, 1995), gives attention not only to Confederate refugees but also to an estimated 80,000 anti-Confederates who fled to Union lines. Yael A. Sternhell, *Routes of War: The World of Movement in the Confederate South* (Cambridge, MA: Harvard University Press, 2012), 5, 94–154, estimates that as many as a half million slaves refugeed behind Union lines by the end of the war and that there were approximately a quarter-million white Confederate refugees. See also Leon F. Litwack, *Been in the Storm So Long: The Aftermath of Slavery* (New York: Alfred A. Knopf, 1979), and Mark Grimsley, *The Hard Hand of War: Union Military Policy toward Southern Civilians, 1861–1865* (Cambridge: Cambridge University Press, 1995).

29. Mary Elizabeth Massey, *Refugee Life in the Confederacy* (Baton Rouge: Louisiana State University Press, 1964); Paul Escott, *After Secession: Confederate Nationalism* (Baton Rouge: Louisiana State University Press, 1978); William Alan Blair, *Virginia's*

Private War: Feeding Body and Soul in the Confederacy, 1861–1865 (New York: Oxford University Press, 2000).

30. Amy R. Minton, "Defining Confederate Respectability: Morality, Patriotism, and Confederate Identity in Richmond's Civil War Public Press," in *Crucible of the Civil War: Virginia from Secession to Commemoration*, ed. Edward L. Ayers, Gary W. Gallagher, and Andrew J. Torget (Charlottesville: University Press of Virginia, 2006), 80–105; Harry S. Stout and Christopher Grasso, "Civil War, Religion, and Communications: The Case of Richmond," in *Religion and the American Civil War*, ed. Randall M. Miller, Harry S. Stout, and Charles Reagan Wilson (New York: Oxford University Press, 1998), 313–59; Kurt A. Berends, "Wholesome Reading Purifies and Elevates the Man: The Religious Military Press in the Confederacy," in *Religion in the American Civil War*, ed. Miller, Stout, and Wilson 131–66; Andrew J. Cutler, *The South Reports the Civil War* (Princeton, NJ: Princeton University Press, 1970); Patricia G. McNeely, Debbra Redden van Tuyll, and Henry H. Schulte, eds., *Knights of the Quill: Confederate Correspondents and Their Civil War Reporting* (West Lafayette, IN: Purdue University Press, 2010).

31. Cf. Sternhell, *Routes of War*, 12–92. See Earl J. Hess, *Pickett's Charge—The Last Attack at Gettysburg* (Chapel Hill: University of North Carolina Press, 1997), 36–81, 405–8.

32. Tommy W. Rogers, "The Great Population Exodus from South Carolina, 1850–1860," *South Carolina Historical Magazine* 68, no. 1 (1967): 14–21. Cf. Alfred Glaze Smith, *Economic Readjustment of an Old Cotton State, South Carolina, 1820–1860* (Columbia: University of South Carolina Press, 1958), 25–26. On Gregg, see Clay Ouzts, "Maxcy Gregg and His Brigade of South Carolinians at the Battle of Fredericksburg," *South Carolina Historical Magazine* 95, no. 1 (1994): 6–26. On soldiers' motivation, see James M. McPherson, *For Cause and Comrades: Why Men Fought in the Civil War* (New York: Oxford University Press, 1997), and Aaron Sheehan-Dean, *Why the Confederates Fought: Family and Nation in Civil War Virginia* (Chapel Hill: University of North Carolina Press, 2007).

33. Calculations of mid-century literacy rates of free people derive from the 1850 census data at ICPSR (http://www.icpsr.umich.edu/icpsrweb/ICPSR). See Schweiger, "The Literate South." She reports that a North Carolina woman, to write to and read letters from her soldier husband, became literate, although she still could not read other hands; see Paul D. Escott, ed., *North Carolina Yeoman: The Diary of J. Basil Armstrong Thomasson, 1853–1862* (Athens: University of Georgia Press, 1996), 124, 129.

34. See Sternhell, *Routes of War*; Joan E. Cashin, *A Family Venture: Men and Women on the Southern Frontier* (Baltimore, MD: Johns Hopkins University Press, 1991); and Miller, *South by Southwest*.

35. Bernath, *Confederate Minds*, 83. See also Jonathan Crider, "De Bow's Revolution: The Memory of the American Revolution in the Politics of the Sectional Crisis, 1850–1861," *American Nineteenth Century History* 10 (September 2009): 317–32; Otis Clark Skipper, *J. D. B. De Bow: Magazinist of the Old South* (Athens: University of Georgia Press, 1958); and William F. Mesner, "*De Bow's Review*, 1846–1880," in

The Conservative Press in Eighteenth- and Nineteenth-Century America, ed. Ronald Lora and William Henry Longton (Westport, CT: Greenwood Press, 1999), 201–9.

36. *De Bow's Review*, o.s. 32 (January–February 1862), n.p.; the note from the "Office of Debow's review" occurs at the end of the backmatter above the date of April 1, 1862. Bernath, *Confederate Minds*, 180. See James Henry Rice, *100 Years of "WECCO": A History of the Walker, Evans & Cogswell Company, Manufacturing Stationers, 1821–1921* (Charleston, SC: Walker, Evans and Cogswell, 1921). Bernath supplemented the 9,457 works recorded in Michael T. Parrish and Robert M. Willingham Jr., *Confederate Imprints: A Bibliography of Southern Publications from Secession to Surrender* (Austin, TX: Jenkins Publishing Co., 1987), and earlier bibliographies compiled by Marjorie Crandall (1955) and Richard Harwell (1957), among others.

37. Bernath, *Confederate Minds*, 173.

38. "Editor's Table," *Southern Literary Messenger* 36 (September and October 1862): 581.

39. "The Drama," *Southern Illustrated News*, April 11, 1863, 8. See Miriam J. Shillingsburg, "Simms in the War-Time Richmond Weeklies," *Southern Literary Journal* 37, no. 1 (2004): 41–52.

40. William Gilmore Simms, *The Letters of William Gilmore Simms*, 6 vols., ed. Mary C. Simms Oliphant et al. (Columbia: University of South Carolina Press, 1952–82), 3:458. See John Hope Franklin, "The North, the South, and the American Revolution," *Journal of American History* 62, no. 1 (1975): 5–23; Miriam J. Shillingsburg, "Simms Failed Lecture Tour of 1856: The Mind of the North," in *"Long Years of Neglect": The Work and Reputation of William Gilmore Simms*, ed. John C. Guilds (Fayetteville: University of Arkansas Press, 1988), 183–201; and Todd Hagstette, "Private vs. Public Honor in Wartime South Carolina: William Gilmore Simms in Lecture, Letter, and History," in *William Gilmore Simms's Unfinished Civil War: Consequences for a Southern Man of Letters*, ed. David Moltke-Hansen (Columbia: University of South Carolina Press, 2013), 48–67.

41. William Gilmore Simms, "Benedict Arnold: The Traitor. A Drama, in an Essay," *Magnolia Weekly* 1 (May 16–August 1, 1863): 165–67, 173–75, 186–87, 194–95, 202–3, 210–11, 218–19, 226–27, 234–35, 250–51, 258–59.

42. David Moltke-Hansen, introduction to *Katherine Walton; or The Rebel of Dorchester*, rev. ed., 1854 (Columbia: University of South Carolina Press, 2013), xxx, xxxviii, xl. On the circulation of *Godey's*, see Fred Lewis Pattee, *The First Century of American Literature, 1770–1870* (New York: Cooper Square Publishers, 1966), 495.

43. Ford Risley, *Civil War Journalism* (Santa Barbara, CA: Praeger, 2012), xv; David W. Bulle and Gregory A. Borehard, *Journalism in the Civil War Era* (New York: Peter Lang, 2010), 26. On magazine publishing and consumption in the late antebellum South, see Jonathan Daniel Wells, *Women Writers and Journalists of the Nineteenth-Century South* (New York: Cambridge University Press, 2011), 65–66.

44. Bernath, *Confederate Minds*, 158–59, 175–79. See also Stout and Grasso, "Civil War, Religion, and Communications," 313–59.

45. Robert Penn Warren observed in *The Legacy of the Civil War: Mediations on the Centennial* (New York: Random House, 1961), 14: "In defeat the Solid South was born—not only the witless automatism of fidelity to the Democratic Party but the mystique of prideful 'difference,' identity, and defensiveness." Also see C. Vann

Woodward: *The Strange Career of Jim Crow* (New York: Oxford University Press, 1955), and *The Burden of Southern History* (Baton Rouge: Louisiana State University Press, 1960).

46. Paul F. Peskoff, "Measures of War: A Quantitative Examination of the Civil War's Destructiveness in the Confederacy," *Civil War History* 54, no. 1 (2008): 35–62. "An Act to establish a Bureau for the Relief of Freedmen and Refugees" passed the US Congress on March 3, 1865.

47. Nicholas G. Meriwether, "Simms's Civil War: History, Healing, and the Sack and Destruction of Columbia, S.C.," *Studies in the Literary Imagination* 42, no. 1 (2009): 97–120. One expression of anticipation of race war is at Simms, *Letters*, 5:131. Also see Ehren Foley, "Isaac Nimmons and the Burning of Woodlands: Power, Paternalism, and the Performance of Manhood in William Gilmore Simms's Civil War South," in *William Gilmore Simms's Unfinished Civil War*, ed. Moltke-Hansen, 89–111. On Simms's final address, see, in the same collection, Sara Georgini, "The Angel and the Animal," 212–23, and John D. Miller, "A Sense of Things to Come: Redefining Gender and Promoting the Lost Cause in *The Sense of the Beautiful*," 224–38. That address is William Gilmore Simms, *The Sense of the Beautiful* (Charleston: Agricultural Society of South Carolina, 1870).

48. The articles appeared in six installments in 1869–70 and have been gathered together and introduced by Jim Scafidel in William Gilmore Simms, *Essays on the Literary and Intellectual History of South Carolina* (Columbia, SC: Southern Studies Program, 1977). The collection of poems is William Gilmore Simms, ed., *War Poetry of the South* (New York: Richardson and Co., 1867). Most of the essays in *William Gilmore Simms's Unfinished Civil War* treat Simms's wartime or postwar writings. See also John C. Guilds, *Simms: A Literary Life* (Fayetteville: University of Arkansas Press, 1992), 304–25. On De Bow and the resumption of *De Bow's Magazine*, see n. 36 above and the letter of J. D. B. De Bow reprinted in the *New York Times* of August 30, 1865.

PART 2

Secession

CHAPTER THREE

To Be the "New York of the South": Urban Boosterism and the Secession Movement

FRANK TOWERS

In February of 1860 a Mississippi correspondent to the *Baltimore Sun* listed the benefits of secession should Maryland leave the Union. Among the most valuable, he contended, would be a boom for Baltimore. "Her great city here is talked of as the New York of the southern country. When the Southern Confederacy is formed, as it most assuredly will be, it will have no generally acknowledged commercial standpoint. Our immediate necessities will demand one or more, and those cities which bid the fairest, by their position and advantage will surely reap the golden harvest."[1] Such predictions were not confined to Baltimore. According to a British observer, "South Carolina's passionate determination to secede does not proceed solely from a sense of injustice or from indignation at the alleged interference of the North with her 'domestic institution.' . . . She fancies also Charleston would then become a sort of New York for the South, the future capital and scepter of its commercial operations."[2] Thomas Ellison, a supporter of the cotton trade, disagreed. "Georgia is considered to be the most go-ahead State of the South," he wrote early in 1861. "Of the seceded States she stands at the head; and in case that the proposed Confederacy is consummated, the general opinion is that she will undoubtedly take the lead; Savannah, and not Charleston, will become the New York of the South."[3] Virginians had more than one prototype in mind. Discussing "the future" in the event of secession, a Richmond editor claimed that "the immense manufacturing profits which have hitherto gone to the North would build up here a Manchester and Sheffield combined, whilst Norfolk, with her magnificent harbor, would become the New York of the South."[4]

As these quotes suggest, during the secession crisis of 1860–61 advocates of a separate southern nation reached out to their section's urbanites by promising that disunion would make their particular city the new Confederacy's equivalent of New York, the great metropolis of the old republic. Unlike the problem in the spring of 1861 confronting Confederates seeking to unify Upper and Lower South, ably described by Lloyd Benson in the next chapter, this aspect of the secession movement had a longer history and targeted the economic dreams of urban dwellers throughout the slave states, but aimed especially at those living in Atlantic seaports whose own increase had stalled while cities in the northeast and the Mississippi Valley boomed. Ignoring comparisons with thriving New Orleans and Memphis, secessionists told southeastern city dwellers that their problems lay in federal policy that had unfairly advantaged free-state cities, particularly New York, and held back urbanization across the South more generally. Secession, they argued, would free southern cities from federal tyranny and break New York's stranglehold on southern commerce, opening the way for unparalleled growth.

This secessionist appeal to the urban South was riddled with contradictions: At times protectionist and at others free trade; anti-urban in its diatribes against New York City while simultaneously promising to recreate it in the South; assuming that the South would have only one New York but that more than one city could wear that crown; and promising a glorious cosmopolitan future for southern cities by entrapping them in an anticosmopolitan nationalist project. These contradictions in the urban case for secession reflected a broader tension between two trends of the nineteenth century, the spread of nationalism and the growth of cities. Those seeking to incorporate cities into the secession movement had to reconcile competing imperial dreams, one for nation builders and another for urban boosters. Although most nineteenth-century thinkers regarded a great metropolis as a requisite element of a great nation, nationalists and city promoters often disagreed about the direction growth should take and the correct balance between national interests and urban ones.

Admittedly, some secessionists opposed urbanization and even those who supported it usually put more emphasis on defending slavery; nonetheless the secessionist appeal to the urban South merits attention for what it reveals about the intersection between nineteenth-century southerners' metropolitan dreams and their nationalist ambitions. The topic also provides an opportunity to bridge the methodological gap between urbanists and Civil War historians by joining scholarship on urban boosters with recent work on Confederate nationalism.

Booster rhetoric, a popular subject for urban historians writing in the late twentieth century, provided a uniquely urban framework for engaging the sectional crisis. In the pages of daily newspapers and at public meetings in Anglophone settlements around the world, boosters promoted their

particular location as a prime spot for future growth. Their promise of collective progress via the market economy gave transient urban populations
a common framework for belonging that emphasized the positive benefits
of capitalism's often-divisive impact on local communities. At its broadest
level of imagination, boosterism advanced "a powerful vision of a new urban world in the process of being created free of the evils of the old."[5]

Beyond specific schemes for town promotion, city builders drew on an
older cultural identity that Richard Wade termed "metropolitan imperialism," or a "struggle for primacy and power" that projected the influence of
the city onto vast hinterlands and dependent towns. Thinking about this
concept across historical epochs, Eugene Moerhing writes, "Athenians, Ro-
mans, Venetians, Parisians, New Yorkers, and San Franciscans all gloried
in the spectacle of their cities' growing power over distant lands. . . . These
cities were not just monuments celebrating the greatness of their residents'
empire or economic system. They were themselves living entities that gave
their citizens a sense of place—a place they were often proud of and emotionally attached to."[6] Although contained within the emerging system of
nation states, London, New York, and other urban giants of the nineteenth
century exerted influence far beyond their national borders.

As members of such transnational collectivities, many city dwellers, especially the well-traveled businessmen and editors who predominated among
the boosters, prized cosmopolitanism, a term Emanuel Kant used to characterize a future of "perpetual peace" and "universal brotherhood" brought by
free trade and Enlightenment rationality. At mid-century, the most influential
propagators of cosmopolitanism were metropolitan capitalists who, starting
with London's Great Exhibition in 1851, staged displays of a new market-
driven utopia that shrank distances of time and space and set the world's
goods and peoples side by side in a baroque but ordered co-existence.[7]

This rising tide of urban cosmopolitanism occurred simultaneously with
the spread of a potential countervailing force, nationalism, which attached
itself to political conflicts all over the world, including the US divide over
slavery. Challenging a long-held interpretation of southern separatists as
reactionary agrarians opposed to northern plans for a centralized state and
industrial economy, a recent wave of studies highlights secessionist advocacy of nation-making strategies that were common on both sides of the Atlantic. For example, John Majewski writes, "Many secessionists envisioned
industrial expansion, economic independence, and government activism as
essential features of the Confederacy. Secessionists imagined that an independent Confederacy would create a modern economy that integrated slavery, commerce, and manufacturing."[8] This "protectionist nationalism," as

Nicholas and Peter Onuf term it, opposed an older Jeffersonian free-trade vision wherein commerce allowed states to complement each other's needs rather than aggrandize themselves by warring against their neighbors. Although sometimes supportive of protectionism, mid-century advocates of cosmopolitanism more often endorsed the Jeffersonian model of free trade and international complementarity.[9]

Those southerners interested in economic self-sufficiency received added support from nationalist thinkers influenced by another transatlantic intellectual movement, romanticism, which defined nationality as a distinctive mix of culture, kinship, and geography. At their most extreme, Robert Bonner argues, the South's romantic nationalists viewed "'society' as an organic entity, with needs, exigencies, and urges distinct from those of its citizens and superior to any set of political principles." Similar to the aspirations of urban boosters to have their particular city dominate vast hinterlands, southern romantic nationalists wanted to spread a proslavery version of American Manifest Destiny to the Pacific and beyond.[10]

Thus, urban boosters and southern nationalists were both attracted to the idea of empire wherein a core city or nation exerted dominion over a much larger range of territory and people. As ideologies of empire relevant to the nineteenth century, nationalism and boosterism fed off of each other. With the days of the medieval city-state long past, nations provided the infrastructure, military protection, and home markets that cities needed to establish far-flung networks. Conversely, because cities were the geographic site for the symbols of modern progress—mass-production industries, markets and high finance, educational and cultural sophistication—nation-makers regarded them as essential items on the checklist of what made a country great. Although the interests of city and state often clashed, city builders and nation-makers could treat each other as allies in their respective drives for imperial glory.

When read in this context, claims that disunion would turn a small southern city into a world-class metropolis like New York support the case for secession as an effort to create a modern nation that, by the standards of the day, included large cities as elements of their success. Furthermore, ambitions to supplant New York as the center of trade fit with a protective nationalist worldview wherein the wealth of rival nations and cities was to be gained at the expense of one's own society. However, urbanism and nationalism were uneasy allies. For all they shared in common, city boosters and nationalists came into conflict over their ultimate ends; metropolitan dominance for the former and, for the latter, the pre-eminence of the collective, national interest over local ones, including those of particular cities. In

this respect, the difficult courtship between secessionists and urban boosters highlights practical as well as theoretical impediments to nationalism's
effectiveness as an organizing principle for the Confederacy.

The history of the "New York of the South" trope shows how nationalists and urbanists could come together but it also illustrates the obstacles
to making that relationship stable over the long term. Although they converged during the secession crisis of 1860–61, for decades the programs of
urban boosters and southern separatists shared little in common. In fact,
when in the 1850s separatists started talking about secession as a way to
make a "New York of the South," they borrowed a metaphor that had a
much longer history among southern city promoters seeking metropolitan
growth within the Union. For those earlier boosters, and for later urbanites
opposed to secession, New York and the government activism that facilitated its rise were examples to imitate rather than symbols of sectional oppression. These arguments dated to the 1820s, when observers recognized
that the Erie Canal, the first transatlantic packet service to England, and
other improvements had vaulted New York ahead of Philadelphia in the
race to become the nation's largest city. Such comparisons were implicitly
pro-Union but more noteworthy for their focus on metropolitan imperial-
ist aspirations that aimed at competition with other cities rather than rival
nations.

To gauge the popularity of New York City as a reference point for southern city promoters I searched digital databases for newspapers published
in the slave states between 1800 and 1861. The phrase "New York of the
South" and related keywords appeared in over 100 separate items, none
of them prior to 1820. Rather than examine the statistical distribution of
New York comparisons across southern newspapers, this chapter considers the discursive meaning of these comparisons via a few representative
examples.[11]

As noted above, the South's earliest booster comparisons to New York
treated it as an example to be copied. In 1826 promoters of Savannah, Georgia, obtained a state charter for a canal connecting the rivers flowing to
the Atlantic with those draining into the Gulf of Mexico, an improvement
that would shorten travel time between the two coasts. In support of the
proposed Mexico Atlantic Canal, a local editor marveled "what we may not
expect for our city! . . . It will realize the prediction of one of the best able to
judge of its natural advantages, and become at no distant day 'the New York
of the South.'" The plan included a federal naval yard and federally funded
harbor improvements. Combined with a water transport system patterned
on the state-financed Erie Canal these public works promised Savannah

the same success achieved by New York City. Acknowledging criticisms of overreaching, the editors of the *Daily Georgian* pointed to their role model; "those who predicted like consequences from like effects, in the state of New York twenty years since . . . were also considered as visionary speculators. If the works already projected, however, in this state, be carried into effect, the importance of Savannah must be increased ten-fold. . . . It will become the New York of the South for which the hand of nature points it out."[12]

As occurred in countless urban rivalries across antebellum America, Savannah's drive for government funds sparked a backlash in competing towns. Businessmen in Darien and St. Mary's resented the Georgia legislature's aid to their more populous neighbor. Urging coastal towns to reach out to the interior, one writer said,

> If spirited, determined, and enlightened exertions had been made, these counties would have long since had a city at their very doors rivaling Savannah. . . . The south west [of Georgia] is, and always has been ready to cooperate with those counties in their views of internal improvement; but have been retarded by the unnatural political union, which some of their leading men have formed with the selfish intriguers of the *"New York of the South."*[13]

Although their attacks on Savannah foreshadowed arguments about intercity inequality and governmental unfairness that secessionists later used to promote their cause, Savannah's urban rivals gave little indication of hostility to state-financed growth policies other than that they had not received their fair share.

In the 1830s railroad promoters in Charleston, South Carolina, followed Savannah in selling their project as a way to emulate New York City. The completion of the South Carolina Canal and Railroad Company's (SCCRR) line between Charleston and Hamburg in 1833 stimulated calls for more tracks. Using the pseudonym "Obadiah Workhard," one supporter said, "a Rail Road to the Tennessee would make Charleston the New York of the South." Workhard wrote at the tail end of South Carolina legislators' unsuccessful five-year campaign to nullify a federal tariff that they believed indirectly sapped the profits of southern agriculture, and which fed into the secession movement of the 1850s. Notwithstanding some nullifiers' support for the SCCRR, Workhard believed that improving Charleston's trade network would undermine their brand of states' rights fanaticism. "Let such a work be completed," he wrote, "and Charleston may bid defiance to the

Tariff, to Nullification, to the 'Chivalry of the State,' and every other cause of her unhappy situation."[14] Three years later, railroad promoters in the South Carolina legislature again claimed that improved transportation, this time to the Ohio River, would "make Charleston the New York of the South."[15]

Significantly, in these New York City comparisons southern city builders were either indifferent or, in Workhard's case, actively hostile toward southern sectionalism. New York served as a model for imitation not only because of its prosperity and size but also because of its successful adoption of government-supported improvements to achieve those ends. If it had any connection to sectional political economy, the rhetoric of southern urban boosters in the era of nullification favored a strong government that would aid their quest for metropolitan growth. Questions about slavery, tariffs, and cotton exports were secondary to boosters' quest for the new markets within the Union that canals and railroads would open up. Because government provided crucial aid to these projects, town builders necessarily wedded their schemes for improvement to those advocating a greater role for the state in economic development.

Booster growth schemes that avoided sectionalism persisted into the 1850s, even as secessionists began to argue that southern cities would only grow if the South was independent. In 1853 Charleston business leaders campaigned for a $500,000 municipal bond for the Blue Ridge Railway that would connect their city to Knoxville, Tennessee. Merchant and hotelier G. A. Neuffer, who wanted to build all the way to the Ohio River, vowed, "This great enterprise carried out will make Charleston the New York of the South."[16] Similarly, supporters of Virginia's troubled James River and Kanawha Canal argued that extending the waterway to the Ohio River would be a catalyst for urban expansion. "Let this canal go through to the Ohio," the *Richmond Whig* pleaded in 1858, "and it follows as a consequence not to be avoided that Richmond and Norfolk will become the Philadelphia and New York of the South." Amid chronic delays and funding shortfalls, the canal's urban advocates turned the comparison into an indictment of their state government. In 1860 Joseph Segar, a Whig legislator from the vicinity of Norfolk, warned that "Baltimore is to become the 'New York of the South' and her dependence for that great result is on the dragging slowness of Virginia!"[17] Missing from these calls to imitate the Empire State's aid to city building were discussions of the evils of free labor and the particular benefits of urban slavery that dominated writing on cities by southern nationalists. As such, these late antebellum urban boosters implicitly adopted a cosmopolitan perspective on city growth. Their objective was greatness for their own city in competition with a diverse array of metropolitan rivals.

This openness to imitating rivals outside the slave South clashed with some elements of the southern separatist agenda. Secessionists tempered their support for urban growth with criticism of cities as they existed in the North. Rather than a model to copy, uncompromising proponents of disunion, often called "fire-eaters" by contemporaries, regarded New York City as home to almost everything they hated about the North: abolitionists, feminists, and property-seizing land reformers; street gangs prone to crime sprees and election riots; throngs of inassimilable immigrants and ungovernable free blacks; the sharp contrast of wealth and poverty; and the merchants and financiers who skimmed the profits of southern agriculture. In an 1860 US Senate debate with New Yorker William Seward over the merits of slavery and free labor, Mississippi's Jefferson Davis asked, "Is there nothing of the balm needed in the Senator's own State that he must needs go abroad to seek objects for his charity and philanthropy? What will he say of those masses in New York now memorializing for something very like an agrarian law? What will he say to the throng of beggars who now crowd the streets of his great commercial emporium?"[18] After listing similar evils in his 1854 book *Sociology for the South*, proslavery polemicist George Fitzhugh concluded that "large cities, like New York and London, are great curses, because they impoverish a world to enrich a neighborhood."[19]

The fire-eaters' attacks on New York were not blanket condemnations of urbanization. Although he thought big cities were evils, Fitzhugh also wrote that "numerous small towns are great blessings, because they prevent the evil effects of centralization of trade, retain wealth and population at home, and diffuse happiness and intelligence, by begetting variety of pursuits, supporting schools, colleges and religious institutions, and affording the means of pleasant and frequent association."[20] His distinction between the free-labor metropolis of New York and smaller southern towns resembled the thesis of *The Interest in Slavery of the Southern Nonslaveholder*, a pamphlet written during the secession crisis by New Orleans editor and statistician J. D. B. De Bow. According to De Bow, slavery made "the cities, towns and villages of the South . . . agencies for converting the product of other labor obtained from abroad. . . . In the absence of every other source of wealth at the South, its mercantile interests are so interwoven with those of slave labor as to be almost identical." Better yet, for De Bow, urban growth would follow secession. "The establishment of a Southern confederation will be a sure refuge from the storm. In such a confederation . . . the wealth being retained at home, to build up our towns and cities, to extend our railroads, and increase our shipping."[21] Fitzhugh and De Bow both advocated economic self-sufficiency for the South as the key to its independence. Cities were essential ingredients in this vision of a self-reliant South, but they needed to conform to the slave-based social order on which the new nation would be built.

Despite their occasional association with preserving traditions, Fitzhugh and De Bow echoed modernizers the world over by arguing for a brand of urbanization that brought the benefits of the city but avoided its ill effects. For southern separatists, this strategy meant using slavery as a check on the excesses of free labor and dispersing towns sufficiently to prevent abuses that they associated with large urban populations. There would be no replica of New York in this version of an independent South. Alluding to economic growth plans that imitated England and the northeastern United States, Obadiah Jennings Wise, editor of the *Richmond Enquirer* and son of Virginia's fire-eating governor Henry Wise, said, "We must cease to be cosmopolitan, imitative, and dependent, and become national, original, and independent."[22] Significantly *Sociology for the South* and *The Interest in Slavery of the Southern Nonslaveholder* aimed at the general population, rather than a distinct urban audience, and fit better with the anticosmopolitan strain of southern culture expressed in the celebration of regional traditions. To the extent that urbanization figured at all in appeals to the general southern population, which was mostly rural, it was presented as a process that would be made safe for slavery through the act of separation.[23]

However, when city dwellers were the intended target of secessionist appeals, this focus on different kinds of cities—big versus small; free versus slave; southern versus northern—disappeared in favor of arguments better suited to the booster growth agenda and the prospect of outshining New York. When fire-eaters explained to city dwellers how the existing Union inhibited southern urbanization, they drew on the old nullification argument that the federal tariff that protected domestic industry, most of which was located in the urban North, inhibited the South's economic potential. In his 1828 "Protest" of the tariff, John C. Calhoun, then US vice president and the state's most prominent politician, said:

> Give us a free and open competition in our own market, and we fear not to encounter like competition in the general market of the world. . . . If this impediment were removed, we would force out all competition; and thus, also, enlarge our market,—not by the oppression of our fellow-citizens of other States, but by our industry, enterprise, and natural advantages.[24]

Calhoun juxtaposed a natural economy of unfettered exchange versus an artificial one of government intervention. The economic case for southern independence assumed that the South had natural advantages in exporting their staples that could be used to build up local resources if not for the unnatural interposition of federal tariff rates that had siphoned wealth northward.[25] As a way to connect with the concerns of urban boosters, the nullifiers' argument that federal tariffs transferred the profits of southern exports into the pockets of northern businessmen managed to address the problem of urban growth without getting into messy details about local politics and cultural homogeneity that put town and country into conflict.

Building on these ideas, late antebellum secessionists promised urbanites that an independent South would either launch its own protective taxes against the North, or that they would abolish tariffs altogether and thereby allow southern cities to exploit their supposed natural advantages in global commerce. For example, in 1860 the *Charleston Mercury*, edited by arch fire-eater Robert Barnwell Rhett, told readers that

> Without the partial interference of government to our disadvantage, Charleston would have flourished and grown as much as New York. How, with the diversion of commerce, New York has expanded and Charleston remained stationary, our readers can carry out the sickening comparison. But just place the cities of each section in their natural position, free from interference of Government, and with free trade. Break up our union with the North—let Charleston and other Southern cities resume their natural commerce . . . and what a mighty change will come over the prospects of our city![26]

Indicating its influence on disunionist thought, the anti-tariff argument also showed up in formal declarations of secession. The Texas secession convention stated that federal officials "have impoverished the slaveholding States by unequal and partial legislation, thereby enriching themselves by draining our subsistence."[27] In a February 1861 letter to Maryland's governor, the Georgia legislature said of Baltimore that "under the oppression and unequal administration of the present Federal Government, she has maintained the third rank in the list of American cities. That she has natural and artificial advantages equal, if not superior to New York and Philadelphia, is plain to the commonest observer. Under a friendly, or even a fair system of government, she would soon take rank among the first cities of the world."[28] When they cited the tariff as a roadblock to urban development, secessionists adapted a longstanding grievance of rural planters to address the concerns of southerners in coastal cities like Charleston and Baltimore who worried about competition with ports in the northeast.

Rhett's argument resembled the late antebellum policy of the southern commercial convention movement, a campaign to promote southern trade and industry that began during the Panic of 1837 with a call for "breaking down the trammels which have so long fettered our commerce and of restoring the South to its natural advantages."[29] Because convention delegates represented urban merchants and manufacturers, their ideas about how to achieve economic self-sufficiency open another window onto the perspective of urban boosters. Over time, the failure of convention self-sufficiency schemes such as buying southern-made goods, promoting internal improvements, and establishing direct shipping lines to Europe, persuaded these gatherings to endorse disunion as the ultimate remedy for what they perceived as predatory federal economic policy. In 1857 convention president James Lyons, a Richmond lawyer and railroad promoter who later served in the Confederate Congress, made the case for secession as the way to end tariff distortions and thereby stimulate urbanization.

> Whilst [the South] has not had the majority to tax, she has had the broad shoulders to bear the burden of protective taxation, and navigation laws, which are building up feudal palaces throughout New England, and sending fleets of merchantmen from her ports. Let the South but assume her stand among the nations, and these palaces and fleets and navies, shall . . . have taken their seats among the mountains of Virginia, Tennessee, and Carolina, or in the harbors of the Chesapeake, of Charleston, Brunswick, Savannah, Mobile, and New Orleans. Great interior towns will spring up as by enchantment and great sea-coast cities and the arteries of communication between them reticulate the whole face of the country.[30]

Rather than copy the success of New York within the Union, as some boosters advocated, Lyons promised that independence itself would make southern cities thrive. For Lyons and Rhett urban growth via separation assumed that the South had natural advantages that would drive prosperity upon the removal of artificial interference by the US government.

Commenting on this shift in tone, John Majewski argues that "the changing nature of southern commercial conventions demonstrates how secession itself became an economic policy."[31] Lyons's claim that secession would expand southern cities "by enchantment" resonated with boasts of "a city sprung up as if by magic" made by urban boosters in other places and times.[32] Although it ignored a host of other factors that had made southern cities smaller than northern ones, the argument that urban growth would follow the South's break with a Union dominated by New York resonated emotionally with city dwellers frustrated by their failure to win the race for urban greatness. In secessionist hands New York and the protective policies that had helped it grow had turned from examples to be emulated to sources of tyranny.

Yet despite their agreement that New York and the old Union's federal tariff were enemies, not all secessionist advocates of urbanization agreed that an end to protective tariffs would help southern cities. Disunionists with connections to the Whig Party and manufacturing wanted to tax northern exports in order to build up southern industry. During the 1850 congressional debates over slavery's expansion into the federal territory conquered from Mexico, North Carolina Whig Thomas Clingman predicted that such a policy would help Maryland, home to the largest city in the South. "She is in advance of most of the Southern States in manufactures," Clingman said, "and a duty on northern imports would give her for the time better prices on such things as are now coming from the North. Baltimore would, perhaps, from its considerable size and capital become the New York of the South." Nor was Baltimore alone. "Charleston and New Orleans would expand rapidly. The like might occur to the cities of Virginia. Even the little towns on the eastern coast of my own State would more than recover the trade which they had prior to the war duties and the tariff of 1816."[33]

Another manifestation of protectionism within the secession movement was the nonintercourse campaign of the 1850s that boycotted northern-made goods as part of a two-sided strategy aimed at pressuring northern businessmen to curb antislavery, on the one hand, while simultaneously stimulating demand for locally made products on the other.[34] In 1860 South Carolina's William Gregg, a textile maker who advocated keeping southern profits at home, denounced New York City's parasitical relationship to southern commerce.

> It is inconceivable how a large city, containing a million people can grow rich. . . . They produce nothing yet they live on the fat of the land; live by their wits in exchanging luxuries produced in other nations for the products of the labor of this country which is tributary to their trade. . . . The patronage of the South has gone there to feed and pamper that monster city, while our Southern importing cities have been left to stagnate and die out.[35]

Clingman hailed from the mountains of western North Carolina where schemes to promote industry through state aid had long been popular, and Gregg was perhaps the antebellum South's leading proponent of industrialization. They resented the influence of New York business interests in the national political economy, but they remained convinced that the Whig program of state aid to economic development was the best way to build a New York within slavery's borders. The protectionist case for secession tracked more closely with what southern urban boosters had advocated since the 1820s, but this position had fewer supporters among southern separatists than did an economic policy of unrestricted commerce, which had long been an article of faith among cotton planters.[36] Thus when Gregg and the nonintercourse movement asked the Confederacy to impose protective taxes on imports they met opposition from free traders who had fought high tariffs since the 1820s.

Some secessionists sought to reconcile free traders and protectionists by proposing a "revenue tariff" that would tax imports only enough to fund the government and avoid the higher rates that had been used to make domestic products competitive in price with cheaper imports. The revenue tariff's duties of 5–25 percent per item were far below the federal tariff's antebellum highs of 40–60 percent. Although low enough to avoid the charge of protectionism, practically the revenue tariff aided southern merchants and manufacturers by raising the price on goods imported from the North. In 1855 Charleston editor Leonidas Spratt used this logic to argue for secession. "With a horizontal duty upon all imposts it would be impossible for foreign products to come to us by way of the cities of the North," Spratt reasoned. "At the South, therefore, must spring up the importing cities for the South. The cities of the South, from which the exports of the continent will go abroad, must stand with metropolitan splendor in the sight of foreign states." Spratt explained that European merchants would trade directly with southern ports to avoid the double customs duties that would be incurred if they first shipped goods to New York, paid a US tariff, and then re-exported to the South and paid another import tax. Applying these ideas to a particular city, Virginia fire-eater Edmund Ruffin predicted that the revenue tariff would turn Norfolk into "the chief seaport and commercial mart on the Atlantic Coast."[37]

The secessionist appeal to southern city dwellers concentrated on their aspirations for metropolitan success by claiming the Confederacy as a superior promoter of their ambitions than the Union. Disunion would make southern cities bigger, more prosperous, and better respected around the world. Unlike trade policy, slavery rarely mattered in these discussions, either as an institution under threat or as the key to making southern cities superior to northern ones. Secessionists' emphasis on urban rivalry and resentment of New York's success suggests their awareness that the issues that preoccupied the planter class were less persuasive to urban audiences than were concerns familiar to townsmen in any number of rapidly urbanizing nineteenth-century societies, both slave and free.

For their part, southern Unionists attacked the idea that separation would bring growth and in doing so highlighted the divergence between the aims of Confederate nation-makers and those of southern urban boosters. Taking on the natural advantages argument of the free traders, Benjamin Johnson Barbour, another prominent Virginia Whig, told Norfolk residents that "Virginia is to be cheated by the promise of great commercial advantages" made by secessionists. "The laws of trade are beyond the control of legislative enactments, or the resolutions of commercial conventions, and to fret over the vast streams of which set towards the great centres of commerce, is as absurd as to quarrel with the blood for flowing to heart. The true course for the South is to assert its independence by industry, energy, and diversified occupation." Contradicting Ruffin, Barbour said "Within the Union I see a bright future for the city of Norfolk—out of it I see nothing but decay and desolation."[38]

Maryland Unionists were equally critical of the logic that secession would enable Baltimore to surpass New York. Attacking what he called "the delusion that . . . the establishment of a Southern Confederacy, embracing Maryland within its limits, would greatly enhance the trade and business of Baltimore," a local Unionist pointed out the disastrous consequences of drawing national boundaries between the states.

> The wealth and trade and commercial advancement of . . . Baltimore, have not only sprung from, but [have] been almost exclusively dependent upon her connection with the North and West. Our city has been in part the great agent, or commission storehouse, for the transfer of these products. Take away this profitable agency, as these sections would naturally do, were we a separate, inimical nation, and our city must sink into insignificance.[39]

John Pendleton Kennedy, a writer, factory owner and longtime Whig activist prior to the party's demise, asked "if it should be discovered . . . that this free trade fancy is but an expensive delusion, and that the old, long tried, universal and inevitable system of duties, known to and practiced by all nations, as the most commendable system of national support, must be substituted by the Confederate States, what then will be the condition of their commerce?" Kennedy predicted a trade war that would devastate local merchants.[40]

Others pointed out the obvious problems of interurban rivalry that would continue after disunion. According to Ashe County, North Carolina's T. N. Crumpler, "South Carolina wishes to get rid of a tariff, throw her port open, and have free trade with all the world, so as to build up a great importing city at Charleston. That may be very advantageous to South Carolina, but how is it to benefit us?"[41] Some wondered how cities would grow if they became battle zones. Nashville Unionist Henry Clay Yeatman, the stepson of Constitutional Union presidential nominee John Bell, warned that secession "will make Missouri and St. Louis chiefly the centre of the worst description of civil war."[42] Whatever the promises of secession for southern cities, plenty of voices within the urban South expressed doubts about the practicality of such grand ambitions, and they strengthened support for the Union among Whigs and businessmen.

The skeptics were proven right. Beginning in October 1860, commerce in the urban South declined as fears of disunion sparked a contraction among New York banks worried about southern repudiation of northern debts.[43] More serious than the recession, which could be explained away as a temporary panic, were conflicts between the fledgling Confederate state and urban business. Worried that the proposed revenue tariff would discourage secession in Tennessee and North Carolina, in February 1861 Charleston merchant William McBurney asked well-connected fire-eater William Porcher Miles, "Why shall those states seek admission to our Confederacy while their cities not only buy cheaper by staying out but gain advantage from our border customs?"[44]

In contrast, secessionist intellectual William Gilmore Simms warned Miles against wooing the Upper South because it would weaken the pro-slavery mission of the cotton states. "We might conciliate Western Virginia and Maryland by adopting the three fifths rule of representation for our slaves but that would be suicidal; would ruin Charleston and Savannah & Mobile & New Orleans as great ports and yield the ascendancy to Norfolk and Baltimore. In a few years we should have the same trouble with those states which we now have with the North." Behind Simms's worries about Upper South political influence was his romantic nationalist conception of the cotton states as the essential core of the South, a core that should only gradually add the more diverse populations of the Upper South to its body politic. "I would rather have a compact empire than a very extensive one," he told Miles, "and our future prospect of safety and success must depend wholly upon the homogeneity of our society and institutions."[45]

For their part, Upper South businesses found the looming imposition of Confederate tariff duties (they were not enacted until May 1861) an added burden to an already collapsing commerce due to the political turmoil of secession. While on a business trip to Memphis in March, Richmond merchant John Steger assessed the tariff's impact. "I do not know what we will do here as Tenn seems determined not to go out [of the Union] and Miss has withdrawn her trade and Arkansas will do the same as soon as she joins the Southern Confederacy." Commenting on a colleague's plans to relocate from Memphis to Charleston, Steger said "I would not be surprised if he moves this fall as the tariff of the Southern Confederacy amounts to almost prohibition of the Mississippi and Alabama merchants trading here. . . . This was up to short time since the most flourishing City in the Union but will go down from this time if Tenn does not join her fortunes to the Southern Confederacy."[46] Meanwhile, a northern friend warned Robert Barnwell Rhett that merchants in Tennessee and North Carolina were organizing smuggling rings to bypass Confederate customs officers.[47] Resistance to the revenue tariff defied secessionists' hope that it would win over urban merchants.

These tensions carried into the war. New Orleans merchants, followed by those in other ports, led the push to embargo cotton exports in order to force European recognition of the Confederacy. When urban merchants, who stood between planters and foreign shippers, supported the disastrous cotton embargo they acted against the interests of planters. This conflict also manifested in the Louisiana legislature's debate over passing stay laws and other forms of debt relief supported by cash-starved planters but opposed by their urban creditors. Finally, New Orleans banks were slow to comply with the Davis administration's demand that they accept Confederate currency at par, a measure that would devalue their credit abroad. As historian Scott Marler observes, "the banks' stubbornly independent course of action during much of 1861 helped perpetuate the costly impression that the Crescent City commercial community was less than united behind the new southern nation."[48]

New Orleans' disputes with other Confederate constituencies were one of several ways that cities troubled the new nation state. In 1861 workers demanded government jobs to offset the effects of the recession. The next year, the same class of city dwellers mobbed conscription officers rather than comply with the Confederate draft. Immigrants, whose numbers were highly concentrated in Confederate cities, thronged consulates for foreign citizenship papers that would enable them to avoid military service, sparking diplomatic headaches for the Davis administration. By 1863 urban women were rioting to protest food shortages. And while domestic manufacturing thrived, foreign exports, the lifeblood of the antebellum South's urban economy, all but died, ruining many of the merchant houses that had dreamt of metropolitan glory under the Southern Cross.[49]

These conflicts affected the course of the war. For example, businessmen's obstinacy likely disinclined Davis to devote extra resources to New Orleans's defense and the disaffection of its immigrant conscripts weakened the garrisons that did little to stop the Union from taking the city in April 1862. A more spirited defense of the forts and redeployment of troops to New Orleans may have saved the city.[50] It is more difficult to assess the impact of ideas on specific outcomes but the divergence between urban and nationalist conceptions of the South's collective purpose surely hampered efforts to mobilize the full resources of the Confederacy for the war effort.

Viewed as an attempt to join proslavery nationalism and urban boosterism, the arguments for secession as a boon to southern cities were less as an integral element of a Confederate master plan than the effort of longtime partisans in the struggle for an independent South to attract city dwellers interested in urban growth. For some southern city builders, secession represented an unprecedented opportunity to catch up in a metropolitan rivalry with the North. For others, it was a disaster that would kill plans for growth within the Union. Noticeably absent in this debate were some of the key issues discussed in other realms of the sectional conflict, such as slavery, states' rights, and the cultural clash between North and South. In their place, urban secessionists promoted the ideal of urban imperialism; their particular city would become a world leader that stood on the platform of a nation, the Confederacy in this case, to compete with other cities for global prominence. Urban boosters who got behind secession wanted to build their cities in the Confederacy but they were agnostic about building a distinctively Confederate city.

That outlook diverged from southern nationalist dreams of a self-sufficient, slave-based society that looked after the interests its rural farmers and planters. As the war progressed, internal conflicts over scarce resources led some Confederates to reconsider their earlier enthusiasm for cities. In the spring of 1862 George Bagby, editor of the *Southern Literary Messenger*, expressed his "fear, that the Old Dominion will become the New York of the South, given more to manufactures and commerce, in the interest of which she will grow greedy and grasping, wresting legislation to her own selfish ends, and little heeding the needs of her sister Confederates." Bagby contrasted the selfishness of Virginia city-builders with the patriotism of fallen soldiers. "God forbid this unhappy day should ever come, but if it shall, the accusing voice of history will point to the plains of Manassas and the dells of Valley Mountain, where lie the bones of the children of North and South Carolina, Georgia, Alabama, Mississippi, Tennessee, Louisiana, Kentucky, Alabama and Texas, who came up to die in Virginia's defence which was indeed the defence of all, but then peculiarly her own."[51] Bagby used the war dead, a venerated symbol of the nation's claims on its subjects, to rebuke urban boosters who put city before country.

Ironically the slave-state cities that fared best after 1865 were in the loyal border region or had been small, interior towns when the war began. Savannah, Norfolk, Charleston, and New Orleans languished in the postwar era for a host of reasons, most of them related to railroad building and changing trade patterns.[52] But ideas also played a role. Ultimately, the Confederate war effort sapped enthusiasm for antebellum city building projects and cast aspersions on cosmopolitan ideals that ebbed and flowed as objects of suspicion in a postwar South tormented by Jim Crow segregation and fears of cultural corruption. Moreover, Confederates explained the Civil War in nationalist terms. Southerners understood their wartime suffering as a sacrifice for the cause of the Confederate nation, a collective identity far greater than one city's dreams of metropolitan greatness. The memory of that failed national cause waxed after 1865 while recollections of a once vibrant antebellum boosterism faded sufficiently to make future city builders' claims to make their town a "New York of the South" seem positively novel.

NOTES

The author thanks Marc Egnal, William Link, Scott Marler, and Paul Quigley for their helpful comments on earlier drafts of this essay.

1. *Baltimore Sun*, February 20, 1860.
2. *Glasgow Herald* (Scotland), January 15, 1861.
3. Thomas Ellison, *Slavery and Secession in America: Historical and Economical* (London: S. Low, Son, and Co., 1861), 234.
4. *Richmond Daily Dispatch*, February 2, 1861.
5. Carl Abbott, *Boosters and Businessmen: Popular Economic Thought and Urban Growth in the Antebellum Middle West* (Westport, CT: Greenwood Press, 1981), 10; Don Harrison Doyle, *The Social Order of a Frontier Community: Jacksonville, Illinois, 1825–1870* (Urbana: University of Illinois Press, 1978), 62–64; David R. Goldfield, *Cotton Fields and Skyscrapers: Southern City and Region* (1982; rpt.,

Baltimore, MD: Johns Hopkins University Press, 1989), 9; David Alan Hamer, *New Towns in the New World: Images and Perceptions of Nineteenth-Century Urban Frontiers* (New York: Columbia University Press, 1990), 58, 62 (quotation).

6. Richard C. Wade, *The Urban Frontier: Pioneer Life in Early Pittsburgh, Cincinnati, Lexington, Louisville, and St. Louis* (Chicago: University of Chicago Press, 1959), 336; Eugene P. Moehring, *Urbanism and Empire in the Far West, 1840–1890* (Reno: University of Nevada Press, 2004), xx.

7. E. J. Hobsbawm, *The Age of Capital, 1848–1875* (1975; rpt., New York: New American Library, 1984), 68; Tanya Agathocloeus, *Urban Realism and Cosmopolitan Imagination in the Nineteenth Century: Visible City, Invisible World* (Cambridge: Cambridge University Press, 2011), 2–3; Pheng Chea, "The Cosmopolitical," in *The Ashgate Research Companion to Cosmopolitanism*, ed. Maria Rovisco and Magdelena Nowicka (Burlington, VT: Ashgate, 2011), 214–15.

8. John Majewski, *Modernizing a Slave Economy: The Economic Vision of the Confederate Nation* (Chapel Hill: University of North Carolina Press, 2009), 3 (quotation), 143–46; Paul Quigley, *Shifting Grounds: Nationalism and the American South, 1848–1865* (New York: Oxford University Press, 2012), 33–34, 37; Brian Schoen, *The Fragile Fabric of Union: Cotton, Federal Politics, and the Global Origins of the Civil War* (Baltimore, MD: Johns Hopkins University Press, 2011), 191, 262; Robert E. Bonner, *Mastering America: Southern Slaveholders and the Crisis of American Nationhood* (New York: Cambridge University Press, 2009), 36.

9. Nicholas Onuf and Peter Onuf, *Nations, Markets, and War: Modern History and the American Civil War* (Charlottesville: University of Virginia Press, 2006), 302, 310, 329. Also see Ernest Gellner, *Nations and Nationalism*, 2nd ed. (Ithaca, NY: Cornell University Press, 2006), 19–37.

10. Robert E. Bonner, "Proslavery Extremism Goes to War: The Counterrevolutionary Confederacy and Reactionary Militarism," *Modern Intellectual History* 6, no. 2 (2009): 270; Quigley, *Shifting Grounds*, 56; Michael O'Brien, *Conjectures of Order: Intellectual Life in the American South, 1810–1860*, vol. 1 (Chapel Hill: University of North Carolina Press, 2004), 21. For the European context see Anthony D. Smith, *Nationalism and Modernity* (New York: Routledge, 1998), 53; Josep Llobera, *The God of Modernity: The Development of Nationalism in Western Europe* (Oxford: Berg, 1994), 171–74.

11. Using keywords "New York of the South" and variations on this phrase for the years 1800–1861, I searched the following digital newspaper collections: GenealogyBank. cm at http://www.genealogybank.com/gbnk/newspapers/; Library of Congress, Chronicling America: Historic American newspapers at http://chroniclingamerica .loc.gov; Readex, American Historical Newspapers ser. 47, 1756–1922.

12. *Savannah Daily Georgian*, February 1 and 14, 1826; Laurence S. Rowland, Alexander Moore, and George C. Rogers Jr., *The History of Beaufort County, South Carolina*, vol. 1, *1514–1861* (Columbia: University of South Carolina Press, 1996), 316.

13. *Georgia Patriot*, April 13, 1826.

14. *Charleston Courier*, May 10, 1833; Tom Downey, *Planting a Capitalist South: Masters, Merchants, and Manufacturers in the Southern Interior, 1790–1860* (Baton Rouge: Louisiana State University Press, 2006), 112–14.

15. Carter Goodrich, "Public Spirit and American Improvements," *Proceedings of the American Philosophical Society* 92, no. 4 (1948): 308.

16. *Charleston Courier*, April 12, 1853; Aaron W. Marrs, *Railroads in the Old South: Pursuing Progress in a Slave Society* (Baltimore, MD: Johns Hopkins University Press, 2009), 29.

17. *Richmond Whig*, February 19, 1858, and March 13, 1860; Daniel W. Crofts, *Reluctant Confederates: Upper South Unionists in the Secession Crisis* (Chapel Hill: University of North Carolina Press, 1989), 309; "Segar, Joseph Eggleston," *Biographical Directory of the United States Congress, 1774–present*. Online at http://bioguide .congress.gov/scripts/biodisplay.pl?index=S000227 (accessed May 3, 2012).

18. Jefferson Davis, "Speech in the Senate," February 29, 1860, in *Jefferson Davis: The Essential Writings*, ed. William J. Cooper Jr. (New York: Modern Library, 2003), 169, 171.

19. George Fitzhugh, *Sociology for the South: Or, the Failure of Free Society* (Richmond, VA: A. Morris, 1854), 139.

20. Ibid.

21. J. D. B. De Bow, "The Interest in Slavery of the Southern Nonslaveholder," *De Bow's Review* 30 (January 1861): 70, 77.

22. *Richmond Enquirer*, quoted in David R. Goldfield, *Urban Growth in the Age of Sectionalism: Virginia, 1847–1861* (Baton Rouge: Louisiana State University Press, 1977), 258.

23. Frank Towers, *The Urban South and the Coming of the Civil War* (Charlottesville: University of Virginia Press, 2004), 15–20.

24. Richard K. Cralle, ed., *Reports and Public Letters of John C. Calhoun* (New York: D. Appleton and Co., 1855), 21–22.

25. Schoen, *Fragile Fabric of the Union*, 121–24.

26. *Charleston Mercury*, October 27, 1860.

27. Delegates of the People of Texas, *A Declaration of the Causes Which Impel the State of Texas to Secede from the Federal Union* (Dallas: Basye Bros., 1861), 5. Also see Georgia Declaration of Secession, January 29, 1861. Online at http://avalon.law.yale .edu/19th_century/csa_geosec.asp (accessed May 1, 2012).

28. A. R. Wright to Thomas Hicks, February 25, 1861, in Georgia Convention, *Journal of the Public and Secret Proceedings of the Convention of the People of Georgia Held in Milledgeville and Savannah in 1861* (Milledgeville, GA: Boughton, Nisbet, and Barnes, 1861), 339.

29. William Watson Davis, *Ante-Bellum Southern Commercial Conventions* (Montgomery: Alabama History Society, 1905), 158.

30. W. Blair Lord and B. B. DeGraffenried, *Official Report of the Debates and Proceedings of the Southern Commercial Convention, Assembled at Knoxville, Tennessee, August 10th, 1857* (Knoxville, TN: Kinsloe and Rice, 1857), 13. For Lyons see Ezra J. Warner and W. Buck Yearns, *Biographical Register of the Confederate Congress* (Baton Rouge: Louisiana State University Press, 1975), 155.

31. Majewski, *Modernizing a Slave Economy*, 105.

32. Hamer, *New Towns in the New World*, 133.

33. Thomas Clingman, *Speech of T. L. Clingman, of North Carolina, in Defence of the*

South against the Aggressive Movement of the North (Washington, DC: Gideon and Co., 1850), 13.

34. Eugene D. Genovese, *The Slaveholders' Dilemma: Freedom and Progress in Southern Conservative Thought, 1820–1860* (Columbia: University of South Carolina Press, 1992), 103.

35. William Gregg, "Southern Patronage to Southern Imports and Southern Industry," *De Bow's Review* 29 (July 1860): 82.

36. Schoen, *Fragile Fabric of the Union*, 178–79.

37. Majewski, *Modernizing a Slave Economy*, 128; Leonidas W. Spratt, *A Series of Articles on the Value of the Union to the South* (Charleston, SC: James, Williams, and Gitsinger, 1855), 4; Jay Carlandar and John Majewski, "'A Great Manufacturing Empire': Virginia and the Possibilities of a Confederate Tariff," *Civil War History* 49 (December 2003): 342. Also see *Macon Telegraph*, March 21, 1860.

38. *Richmond Whig*, October 16, 1860.

39. "Our Baltimore Letter," *Philadelphia Inquirer*, August 2, 1861.

40. John Pendleton Kennedy, *The Great Drama: An Appeal to Maryland* (Baltimore, MD: John D. Toy, 1861), 11.

41. Thomas N. Crumpler, *Speech of T. N. Crumpler, of Ashe, on Federal Relations, Delivered in the House of Commons, Jan. 10, 1861* (Raleigh, NC: Raleigh Register, 1861), 7; Martin Crawford, *Ashe County's Civil War: Community and Society in the Appalachian South* (Charlottesville: University Press of Virginia, 2001), 71–73.

42. Henry Clay Yeatman to Mary Polk Yeatman, June 14, 1861, Polk and Yeatman Family papers, ser. 1.2, Southern Historical Collection, Wilson Library, University of North Carolina–Chapel Hill (hereinafter cited as SHC).

43. Russell McClintock, *Lincoln and the Decision for War: The Northern Response to Secession* (Chapel Hill: University of North Carolina Press, 2008), 22.

44. William McBurney to William Porcher Miles, February 21, 1861, William Porcher Miles Papers, Box 3, SHC.

45. William Gillmore Simms to William Porcher Miles, February 22, 1861, Miles Papers, Box 2, SHC.

46. John R. Steger to Mary J. Steger, March 2, 1861, Carter Family Papers, Virginia Historical Society, Richmond.

47. Pritchard Alston to Robert Barnwell Rhett, n.d. [Feb. 1861], Robert Barnwell Rhett correspondence, South Caroliniana Library, University of South Carolina, Columbia; Majewski, *Modernizing a Slave Economy*, 132.

48. Scott P. Marler, *The Merchants' Capital: New Orleans and the Political Economy of the Nineteenth-Century South* (New York: Cambridge University Press, 2013), 132; Marler, "An Abiding Faith in Cotton," 260, 267, 271.

49. Towers, *Urban South*, 163–64; Jacqueline Jones, *Saving Savannah: The City and the Civil War* (New York: Vintage Books, 2008), 149; Eugene H. Berwanger, *The British Foreign Service and the American Civil War* (Lexington: University of Kentucky Press, 1994), 92–107; Stephanie McCurry, *Confederate Reckoning: Power and Politics in the Civil War South* (Cambridge, MA: Harvard University Press, 2010), 178–80.

50. Marler, "An Abiding Faith in Cotton," 274; Michael D. Pierson, *Mutiny at Fort Jackson: The Untold Story of the Fall of New Orleans* (Chapel Hill: University of North Carolina Press, 2008).

51. George William Bagby, "Editor's Table," *Southern Literary Messenger* 34 (March 1862): 193.

52. Goldfield, *Cotton Fields and Skyscrapers*, 126–27.

CHAPTER FOUR

Gender and Household Metaphors in Mid-Nineteenth-Century Nation-Building Cities

T. LLOYD BENSON

Cities had a contradictory relationship to nation-building in mid-nineteenth-century Europe and the Americas. While nationalists often spoke from the cities, urban cosmopolitanism, complexity, and dynamism challenged nationalist calls for cultural distinctiveness, homogeneity, and tradition. As centers for national unification, cities housed the activists and organizational infrastructure essential for promoting nationalism while symbolizing the energy, progress, and aspiration of imagined national communities. Urban forces could unify diverse and often antagonistic regional identities, allowing formerly weakened and quarrelsome peoples to assume a rightful place in what nationalists often called "the great family of nations."[1] However, cities also contained forms of cultural diversity and foreign attachments, whether to the city, to another country, to foreign commodities and fashions, or to abstract cosmopolitan ideals, which could undermine patriotic appeals to a shared land, language, and blood.[2]

The diversity of urban household structures proved equally disruptive. Multifamily tenements, single-sex boarding houses, and many other more transitory or nonconforming relationships challenged the traditional household ideals around which many ethnocultural nationalist visions were built. For white southerners, especially, a corporatist, patriarchal conception of household values defined the boundaries of the southern way of life. As the appeal to "the great family of nations," and the relentless calls by advocates of national unification for citizens to act as brothers and sisters in shared service to motherland or fatherland suggest, metaphors of family and gender helped reconcile the promise and peril of cities for national unity.[3]

Gender and family language helped these city dwellers connect the urban experience to national character. In this democratizing age, political factions often debated over family law and household control policies, especially as they played out on the city's dynamic stage. Scholars have shown how powerfully family and gender language motivates political discourse and how it reveals cross-cultural differences. Gender and family rhetoric enabled political leaders to purge contamination, punish dissenters, revitalize loyalties, broaden coalitions, sharpen distinctions between themselves and opponents, and maintain boundaries between the familiar and the foreign.[4]

Comparison of gendered rhetoric helps to show deep textures in the movement to unify the Lower and Upper South in spring 1861. Seven slave states, South Carolina and the six slave states bordering the Gulf of Mexico, left the Union after Abraham Lincoln's election in November 1860. By February 1861 they had created a national government, the Confederate States of America. After the April 1861 attack on Fort Sumter and Lincoln's subsequent call for volunteers to suppress the rebellion, four Upper South states—Virginia, Arkansas, North Carolina, and Tennessee—decided to join the Confederacy, but only after fierce debate between unionists and secessionists. The unification of Lower and Upper South was a nation-making process akin to other contemporary movements for regional unification, a process that historians too often neglect in favor of explaining the bigger story of the Union's collapse.[5]

A comparison of such rhetoric in three pairs of Atlantic world cities reveals significant commonalities and contrasts in each country's unification processes. In the nascent Confederacy, Charleston, South Carolina, and Richmond, Virginia, played defining roles in Confederate unification, as seen in 1861 editorials and convention speeches. In Italy the parliamentary and press debates from 1860–61 over Italian unification in the royal capital at Turin and the port city of Genoa manifested monarchical-commercial versus liberal-egalitarian nationalisms. In Canada voices from Toronto and Montréal dominated legislative debates leading to Canadian unification in 1864–67.[6] This comparison shows how Confederates advocated for a more homogenous and authoritarian vision for their nation than the more pluralist and pragmatic cases for unification made elsewhere. The difference came down to slavery. Its presence in the South mandated different rhetorical strategies and nation-building processes than those of comparable Atlantic world cities.

Although opinion leaders in all three countries spoke of urban disorders, such concerns were salient in cities like Richmond and Charleston where proximity, slavery, and the color line uniquely challenged household-level social control. As David Moltke-Hansen and Frank Towers contend in this volume, the South's agrarian consciousness predisposed opinion leaders to fear urban threats and corruptions, even as they embraced the city's vitality and cosmopolitan refinement. While southern commentators expressed many of the same fears and admired many of the same nature ideals that drove the Northeast's suburban exodus, slavery's distinctive place within the household multiplied their concerns. Southern nationalists worried that cities would endanger the purity, integrity, and unity of their region's peculiar households, a malaise that would then debilitate the national family.[7]

In part because of these fears, the Richmond-led urbanization of Virginia made unification with an agrarian-minded and South Carolina–dominated Confederacy by no means certain. Richmond's natural advantages and market hinterlands spurred urban growth, while Tredegar Iron and other manufacturing firms invoked similarities to the industrial Northeast. As others have shown, the tenuousness of the ties between Virginia and the Lower South caused conflict before and after 1861. Across the seaboard South, urban rivalries hampered railroad development and market integration, setting Virginia at odds with its sisters. Though regionally dominant, Richmond and Charleston were dependents and rivals for the capital, information, and markets controlled by larger cities. The urge for autonomy and fear of either dominance or duplicity from each other (and not just northern cities) complicated the Confederate unification process. Political leaders found gender and family rhetoric to be a natural fit for expressing their concerns.[8]

It was political anxiety rather than economic development that ultimately drove Richmond's sense of itself. Declining national influence after the 1820s worried Richmond opinion elites as did growing northern attacks on slavery's sexual depravities. That travel accounts so often emphasized the destruction of slave families in Richmond's slave markets made the topic local and personal. Richmond's elites (women as well as men) responded with aggressive defenses of Virginia's "domestic institutions."[9]

Slavery's opponents, in contrast, had little voice in Richmond. Whereas state censorship in Italy and Canada had lessened on the eve of unification, Richmond's slavery debates heightened suppression. Above all, the exclusion of African Americans from citizenship was what the *Richmond Enquirer*, among others, considered a "supporting pillar" of Virginia's social order. When Richmond's multirace residents demanded citizenship rights in 1854, the *Richmond Whig*'s editors wrote that such insolence in seeking status above poor whites threatened to "provoke the resentment of the most humble in this community." Organized antislavery politics was equally forbidden, though often privately discussed. Nor did the city develop the intense sectarian and ethnic political factionalism so visible in Canada, this despite large immigrant and working-class populations. The weakness of Know-Nothingism in Richmond was revealing. Appeals to the common bond of whiteness neutralized any emergent economic or cultural factionalism. So while the city's economic systems encouraged Whiggish and even "Yankee" economic and social modernity, race provided a trump card that the city's leadership played relentlessly.[10]

In Charleston, too, questions of gender, race, and sexual control shaped the city's southern cosmopolitanism. As a leading port city, Charleston's commerce, manufacturing, economic liberalism, and Atlantic world high culture competed with the pull of the egalitarian agrarianism of the Carolina hinterlands. Although Charleston's elites derived wealth and identity from rural plantations, they embraced urban refinement, emulating English and European manners, architecture, and high-brow commodities, and giving their children European grand tour educations. Charleston, like Richmond, was a manufacturing and commercial center, though the formidable Blue Ridge barrier and limited inland river navigation restricted its hinterland, and it lacked Richmond's nearby coal and iron. Its greater distance from Europe disadvantaged its port in the scheduled shipping trade. Culturally, Charleston was one of the South's most religiously diverse communities. In addition to English-stock Episcopalians, Presbyterians, and Baptists, colonial-era Huguenot settlement created a nucleus for welcoming Haitian planter refugees in the 1790s, people whose first-hand memories of slave rebellion were vivid. Irish immigrants in the 1850s reinforced Charleston's significant Catholic establishment. Charleston also hosted some of America's earliest Jewish congregations. Charlestonians did not have to imagine what an urban, industrial, international, and multiethnic society looked like—they lived it. Unlike in Richmond, however, a true second-party system never emerged. Calhounite repressions spurred a Unionist exodus in the 1830s. Such purges silenced opposition while predisposing Charlestonians to purity-related political metaphors.[11]

As in Richmond, this usage was deeply tied to slavery. Charleston had once dominated the North American slave trade and almost half of Charlestonians in 1860 were black. These men and women worked in the heart of every elite white household in Charleston, notably in tending to white children. That many planter men were literally the fathers of enslaved children further destabilized definitions of family and household. Charleston's narrow and water-bound peninsula further concentrated the city's social and racial tensions. The cramping and crowding of the city's households only intensified the fears of equality expressed by Miles and his compatriots.[12]

Naturally, Charleston's literati expressed more concerns than most about the interplay of family, city, and nation. It was no accident that noted Charleston writer Louisa McCord invoked Shakespeare's indictment of the city in the curse of Timon on Athens to show emancipation's family-level destructiveness. "Matrons turn incontinent! Obedience fails in children . . . ! To general filths convert o' the instant, green virginity. . . . Bound servants steal . . . ! Maid to thy master's bed—Thy mistress is o' the brothel . . . ! And let confusion live!" Emancipation would cause violation of duties and transgression of boundaries between husbands and wives, masters and slaves, parents and children, especially in the city. Corruptions would taint the nation, leading inevitably to the "extinction of civilization."[13] In a similar vein, the *Charleston Mercury* strongly endorsed their reprint from *De Bow's Review* condemning the North's supposed racial "Amalgamationism," "Free-loveism," "Infidelity," and "last, and most fatal, because the most insidious and difficult to overcome, when once rooted, *concubinage or marriage assimilated and desecrated to cohabitation.*" The only thing holding back this tide, *De Bow's* and the *Mercury* agreed, was "the conservative presence of Negro slavery."[14]

Similar fears of "unlimited equality in social privileges and political power" motivated Charlestonian William Porcher Miles's opposition to the liberal nationalism of Hungarian Louis Kossuth. Unchecked, Kossuth's nationalism would produce the "separate, discordant, and conflicting interests" so typical of Europe's overcrowded and aristocratic cities, rather than the concord of interests and action Miles so admired in America. He warned of urban-enabled disruptions. "The truckling in so many of our larger cities to what is openly called '*The Foreign Influence,*' " Miles argued, would serve to "not only denationalize us as a Nation, but to degrade us as a people." He associated the vice of equality with a classic list of urban threats, including the reality and metaphor of contagious disease, the bribery and corruption of urban immigrant machines, and the contentiousness of political discord.[15] Erstwhile Charlestonian William Grayson completed this catalog of degradations in his 1858 novel *The Country*: "Such be our champions, children of the field, Strong with the vigour healthful labours yield. Not the pale growth of cities, of the gloom of cellars, cripples from the mill or loom." The city's distortions of household and family would be physical as well as intellectual.[16]

Despite shared interests and anxieties about slavery, however, political leaders in both cities hesitated during unification. For its part, the *Charleston Mercury* regularly jabbed at Virginia's supposed weakness and infidelity. Complaining that Virginia had not labored enough to defeat Lincoln, the *Mercury* stressed their conflicts. "Virginia may now call," the editors wrote,

"but the South will not answer." Alliance could only yield betrayal and deg-
radation. "She has placed the Union above the rights and institutions of the
South," the editors complained, "and will only seek a conference with the
Southern States in order to bring them down to the level of her fatal Union
policy."[17] In April 1861 the paper even blamed the outbreak of fighting on
Virginia's lack of "manly" resistance. "Had Virginia taken her stand at the
beginning with South Carolina," noted a correspondent, "there would be no
war today."[18]

Virginia Unionists responded with the language of sibling betrayal. Governor John Letcher's January 1861 legislative message condemned South
Carolina for having acted "without consultation with any one of her slaveholding sister states," and accused its governor of seeking the "embarrass-
ment of every slaveholding state on the border, which is not disposed to
follow her lead." South Carolina's recklessness, he concluded, "takes her
southern sisters by surprise."[19]

Yet Confederate nationalists eagerly wooed Virginia. When the state's
secession debates opened in February, Virginia native John Preston pleaded
South Carolina's unification case.[20] Southerners, he said, were not

> canting fanatics, festering in the licentiousness of abolition and amal-
> gamation. Their liberty is not a painted strumpet, straggling through
> the streets. . . . They are . . . fighting for their fathers' graves; stand-
> ing athwart their hearth-stones, and before their chamber doors. In this
> fight, for a time, my little State stood alone. . . . We are no longer alone.
> Our own children from Florida and Alabama answered to the maternal
> call. . . . And, sir, wherever Virginia has a son beyond her borders, his
> voice is known. . . . We believe, and have so acted, that the political
> union is an unnatural and monstrous one, and, therefore, that its off-
> spring must be abortive and fruitless, save of that brood of evils which
> always come from such unnatural unions.[21]

Preston's fears of licentious contamination converted the tolerable messi-
ness of parliamentary bargaining into pure evil. His metaphor of the Union
as a monstrous abortion is uniquely shocking among these debates. That
Preston had just returned from a multiyear stay in Europe for his daughter's
education contextualizes his gendered language, as does his patronage of
sculptor Hiram Powers, whose work *The Greek Slave* was one of the era's
most infamous representations of romantic gendered nationalism. Preston's
gender-personified national aesthetic, vulnerable and subject to violation,
would have been a commonplace to Charleston and Richmond elites.[22]

Italy had its own share of gender-framed nationalist debates and these, too, were shaped by their urban cosmopolitan contexts. Turin and Genoa were crucibles of Italian unification. Along with Milan, the two cities formed the "industrial triangle" of modernizing Italy. Turin's unique fusion of progressive royalism, bourgeois liberalism, and cosmopolitan intellectualism give it dominance in Italy's nation-building process. This ideological consensus, what one Turinese political theorist called *monarchia rappresentativa*, defined the new Italian state. Yet Turin's ideological dominance provoked rivalry and resentment in Genoa and beyond.[23]

Lodged between the Mediterranean and the Alps, Turin headed a borderland and imperial invasion route. Napoleonic occupation at the beginning of the century proved especially enduring and polarizing. Turinese diplomat Joseph de Maistre, for example, reacted by becoming Europe's leading ultra-Catholic conservative ideologue, condemning the French Revolution for its impurity, sexual depravity, and moral corruption. Yet others in Turin embraced French ideals of fraternal nationalism. Recreated as an independent buffer state in 1815, the Turin-based Kingdom of Piedmont-Sardinia developed a tradition of qualified press freedom and religious liberty, attracting many refugees and activists. Piedmontese prime minister Camilo Benso di Cavour aggressively promoted railroads, telegraphs, and manufacturing, using England as his model. At the household level, Napoleonic disruptions weakened traditional patriarchal authority and the power of extended kin. But the city's actual Italianness was complicated. Cavour and the king had been raised in the local Piedmontese dialect and used French officially but spoke Italian awkwardly. As an urban and international crossroads with strong French influences, evolving household structures and cosmopolitan international aspirations, the Turinese contrasted with Italians elsewhere.[24]

Seventy-five miles southeast, Genoa was Italy's busiest international port and a city with proud memories of its former Renaissance glory. Politically subordinated to Turin after the 1790s, Genoa became fount of insurrection. Birthplace of unification prophet Giuseppe Mazzini, it witnessed frequent liberal nationalist revolts by groups such as the *Carbonari* and Young Italy. Like the other cities, Genoa underwent significant industrial, railroad, and communications growth during the nineteenth century, though a mountainous coast limited hinterlands and isolated it from neighboring provinces. Genoa's leaders were acutely aware that Cavour's economic development policies, while often beneficial to Genoa, usually worked out in favor of their Turinese rivals.[25]

The 1848 revolutions transformed both cities. An alliance of Mazzinian egalitarians and moderate aristocrats forced a new constitution, the *Statuto*

Alberto, which synthesized monarchical, ministerial, and parliamentary liberal elements. The kingdom was unique in 1848 for having neither its government toppled nor its revolutionary constitution revoked. Yet the rest of Italy remained under foreign control. The king's successor, Vittorio Emanuele II, not only kept the *Statuto* but also used it to win over radicals such as Garibaldi, whose famous Red Shirts shouted "King and Constitution" as they unified the country. *Monarchia rappresentativa* provided enough royal authority to assuage conservatives while its guarded reforms offered promise to urban liberal modernizing nationalists.[26]

After 1848 Genoa's subordinate status and its egalitarian nationalist leanings were reinforced by worker rights activism. The city's ill-fated uprising of 1857 was a catalyst for pushing moderates into an alliance with Cavour. That a woman, Mazzini collaborator Jessie White Mario, led the outbreak was especially distressing for moderate commentators. National unification loomed. Better that change come from Cavourist modernizing elites than from violent and gender-subverting radicals.[27]

From 1857 to 1859 the *Risorgimento* accelerated and mutated. With their French allies, Piedmont's armies ended Austrian control of most of northern Italy. Fearing, however, that further Piedmontese expansion would destabilize the Papal States, Napoleon concluded a separate peace. Outraged, the Italians bypassed Napoleon's plan for a loose Italian federation by creating a Turin-dominated Italian kingdom. Napoleon reluctantly accepted this in return for Savoy and Nice. Over Cavour's objections and with the king's eyes averted, Garibaldi's Red Shirt "army of brothers" gained control of the remainder of southern Italy except Rome. The new Kingdom of Italy was declared in March 1861, with Vittorio Emanuele II as king and the *Statuto Alberto* as the constitution. Public accounts celebrated the heroic virility of Garibaldi, the king's manly bravery in battle, and the importance of ordinary soldiers as "brothers" who won national independence through shared valor and sacrifice. As in the American South, Italian nationalists used metaphors of family and brotherhood to explain their revolution. The Italians, though, emphasized egalitarian sibling language that recognized the diversity of its constituent regions as strengths rather than liabilities.[28]

The importance of accommodating difference within unification was even more pressing in Canada. Here, anglophone Upper Canada, led by Toronto, stood in ethnic, religious, and economic opposition to francophone Lower Canada and its metropolitan center of Montréal. Compared to Italy and the Confederacy, the tale of Canadian unification was more pragmatic than ideological. Few equivalents of a Mazzini, Garibaldi, or Rhett emerged

to champion the ideal of the Canadian nation. Indeed, Canadian confedera-
tionists shunned the examples of Confederate balkanization and Italian monarchical intrigue. The distinctive histories of Montréal and Toronto help
explain these attitudes and their leaders' choices of particular family and
gender metaphors.[29]

France established Montréal in the 1630s at the head of Saint Lawrence
River navigation. Nearby waterways made it a trading crossroads through
the Great Lakes and south to New York, notably in furs. Along with masses,
missions, and charities, the Catholic Church became an economic force in
Montréal, owning extensive properties, manufacturing, and financial interests. After the painful 1760s British conquest, French Canadians were given
specific, if circumscribed, protections in exchange for subordination. Catholic leaders accommodated, and *habitant* households, overwhelmingly rural,
agrarian, and parish-focused, followed their lead. While many francophone
elites abandoned the colony, others married into the British gentry, served
in the British military, or took official government positions. Although the
British merchants who soon settled in Montréal often resented the protections granted to *canadiens* and chafed at restrictions on their own "rights as
Englishmen," they found the idea of joining the United States unappealing,
viewing the seemingly quarrelsome children of Boston much as Turinese
elites would come to view Genoese insurrections.[30]

After 1815 *Les Montréalais* increasingly competed for power with this
English-speaking business elite, who had superior access to capital, shipping resources, and information. Irish Catholic immigration after the 1830s
added to Montréal's ethnocultural divisions. Both "Orangemen" and "Fe-
nians" developed rival fraternal organizations, with uncertain implications
for French Catholics. Seeking to symbolically unify the city's competing
ethnic groups, Montréal's mayor developed a city seal in the 1830s that
combined a French fleur-de-lis, an English rose, a Scottish thistle, and an
Irish shamrock, subscripted with the motto *Concordia Salus* (Well-being
through harmony). Despite such conciliation, rebellions broke out in 1837
and again in 1849. The government repressed both. These urbanizing, economic, and cultural forces pressured household structures and transformed
household ideologies. Victorian domestic ideals became popular, especially
among English speakers and the mercantile bourgeoisie. Meanwhile, the
Catholic Church sought to position an older agrarian familial ideal of francophone *habitants* as a bulwark against Anglicization on one hand and the
egalitarianism of Quebec's francophone but largely urban *Rouge* liberals on
the other.[31]

Toronto, founded in the 1790s as the colonial center for English Upper Canada, became almost as diverse. Though less of a natural crossroads
than its rival, it had a good harbor and a hinterland suited to farming. Fears
of American expansionism shaped its early history, concerns reinforced by
an influx of US-born settlers after 1820 who demanded democratization.[32]
As the urban center for an exceedingly rural hinterland, Toronto attracted
many families experiencing their first generation of city life. Expansion of
manufacturing, growth in mass consumer goods marketing, the impact of
English Victorian cultural models, and the emergence of new mercantile
and technical classes all transformed household structures. The city's social
fabric was further textured by the presence of black ex-slave refugees, including many from Richmond and Charleston. As in Montréal, city leaders
consciously developed a city identity of "Toronto the Good" to encourage
Victorian self-control, civic concord, and bourgeois deference.[33]

Adapting Canadian policies to the perceived lessons of the American
Revolution, British authorities provided the formality of representation
while retaining control through a web of royal officials and appointed councils, a system critics metaphorically dubbed the "Family Compact." Here,
too, rebellions erupted and were repressed in 1837. As elsewhere, urban
disorders alienated moderates from democratization. Reforms growing out
of a postrebellion report by Crown representative Lord Durham served more
to houseclean than replace the Family Compact. The resulting 1840 Act of
Union temporarily put Upper and Lower Canada under one government,
though the arranged marriage created as many tensions as it resolved.[34]

Durham's criticisms of *habitant* culture and calls for "amalgamation"
with English culture were widely shared by Toronto's English-speaking
elites. Moreover, they were similar to criticisms of the "backwardness" of
the American South offered by northern observers—depictions that writers
such as McCord, Miles, and Grayson were reacting against. Anglicization,
Durham thought, would help *les habitants* overcome dependence on a rural, poor, family-focused, and cottage-scale economy, would remedy their
supposed lack of experience with self-government, and would mute any
"spirit of jealous and resentful nationality." In Durham's view the cities
of Canada concentrated progress through their educational resources, market capitalism, opportunities for political discourse, and energetic mercantile and manufacturing elites. Conceding that urban proximity had caused
conflict and segregation between English and French he still hoped that
the urban environment would create opportunities for intermarriage and
amalgamation. These would solve Canada's political and economic development challenges. Significantly, while Durham's contrast of a weak and

private-oriented French Canada with a vigorous and public-oriented British Canada had obvious gender undertones, Durham never presented the French as a threat to sexual purity or integrity within individual British households. The French race could meld into English families. Secessionists, in contrast, could never imagine the slave race amalgamating into white families.[35]

Nor did French *canadiens* discuss threats within the household, even as they reacted bitterly to Durham's *Report* and the 1840 act. Moderate francophone reformers spoke not of household contamination but rather demanded a return to the bilingual equality and "fraternity" that Durham-inspired policies had betrayed. Even *patriote* Louis-Joseph Papineau, whose nationalism idealized the mutualism and intimacy of family, parish, and community in rural Quebec and who feared that the toil, poverty, luxury, and intemperance of Canada's cities would produce demoralizing "libertine celibacy" rather than healthy marriage and large families, did not warn about the English race as a danger *within* the home.[36]

Over the next generation, Montréal's francophone leaders advocated tirelessly for equal rights and minority religious protections, concessions granted (reluctantly) by anglophone opinion leaders in Toronto and elsewhere. Ethnocultural and class conflicts divided both cities but Reform Party advocates found common ground across ethnocultural divides, as did Conservatives. The resulting crisscross of factions enabled a political instability that made confederation appealing. So did the US Civil War, as London asked Canadians to assume more of their own defense. Catalyzed by discussion of unification among the Maritimes, delegates at the 1864 Quebec Conference formulated a Canada-wide confederation plan. For Toronto and Montréal, unification offered mutual advantages as well as a mutually assured destruction pact. Montréal's bourgeois conservative leader and Grand Trunk Railway officer George Etienne Cartier sought confederation as an economic benefit. Reaction in 1866–67 against the Fenian invasions of Canada organized by Irish-born US veterans furthered momentum. The British government finalized Canadian confederation in spring 1867.[37]

The policy success of confederation, however, provoked sharp debates over the meaning of Canadian identity. Many critics worried that confederation amounted to nothing more than an aggrandizement scheme for Montréal or Toronto capitalists. Others, particularly in Montréal's Catholic press, feared the return of Durham-style assimilation. The editors of the Montréal *L'Ordre* warned that obedience would be bought with patronage. Using the language of familial subordination, the paper claimed that "if these counselors would be good children, then almost all of them would be

named" to official posts. *L'Ordre's* editors worried that Protestant schools
would be mandated in French Canada with nothing comparable for Catholic
schools in Toronto or elsewhere in anglophone Canada, and that marriage
and divorce would become merely civil contracts. Such inequities called
into question the meaning of shared citizenship in the Canadian polity. An-
glophones were equally unsure how confederation would affect the balance
of power in the "Canadian family." Thus pragmatism rather than purity
defined Canadian unification.[38]

In all six cities, local social structures and household traditions shaped
the deployment of gender and family language. How these terms were embraced in some places while strenuously avoided in others underscores the
importance of household and urban factors in shaping unification.

The figure of the mother has been one of the richest sources of political
metaphor. Under modernity, the idea of loving mother as a personification
of the state gave an alternative to king-centered feudal loyalties. As state
identity became increasingly defined by citizenship rather than deference,
mothers birthing children within a specific territory became the literal legal
basis for national identity. This notion easily blended into the metaphor
of nation as "mother." The mother-personified state concept aligned with
emergent notions of women as "mothers of the republic." Mothers, in ideal,
were pure and uncorrupted by the sordid bargaining of male-dominated politics. Political leaders used claims of sanction by mothers as proof that their
policies transcended the merely political plane, while using the absence of
sanction by mothers to condemn policies seen as corrupt, self-serving, or
disgusting.[39]

The paradoxes of the "mother" figure, however, led political leaders to
avoid it as often as they invoked it. For Catholic communities, nationalistic uses of the "mother" metaphor competed with Madonna and child
imagery, thus infusing nationalistic claims with deeply sectarian overtones.
Deployed by the church in the rivalry between secular and sacred, these
Madonna-like symbols potentially undermined the secular state's legitimacy. Apart from Catholicism, for Canadians negotiating a new relationship with England the notions of the "mother country," Queen Victoria,
and the "sister colonies" were equally multivalent. In Toronto, for example,
word of confederation plans in September 1864 generated a revealing series
of letters to the *Toronto Globe* about possible names for the new country.
One writer suggested the name "'Britannica," for the "daughter of our venerated mother 'Britannia,'" something he thought "would serve to remind
us of our allegiance to the parent." A writer using the pseudonym "One of
the Daughters of Canada" suggested "Canadia," to honor the two largest

colonies while welcoming in the others. Another suggested "New Britain," as fair to the sibling provinces of the two Canadas and the Maritimes. "We are proud of our parent Britain. . . . Let not her most faithful children dishonour themselves by changing their name." In the Canadian confederation debates the phrase "mother country" was one of the most common gender and family usages in the text.[40]

It was Virginians who invoked "mother" most, claiming that their state's unique maternal history gave it a special status in secession. All factions in the Virginia convention highlighted Virginia's role as "the mother of Washington," "the mother of the first bill of rights," and the "blessed mother of states and statesmen." Like Preston, they frequently invoked newer states as Virginia's "offspring."[41] This metaphorical mother was burdened with unique but conflicting obligations. Secessionist John Goode, for example, insisted that Virginia could no more leave the "kindred" states of the infant confederacy than a "mother could forget and desert her own offspring." William L. Goggin cautioned that the interests of Richmond and other ports required a broader obligation. "Good mother as she is," Goggin contended, Virginia "embraces all her children. She looks around her, to the East and West, and considers alike the interests and the welfare of all." Maternal invocations peaked after Sumter, as delegates shifted their allegiances to the new confederacy and polarization accelerated. On April 16, for example, Richmonder George Randolph urged aid for Virginia's "sister states" while calling for unity and conciliation within Virginia ("mother of us all") as dangers loomed.[42]

As with motherhood, marriage and divorce metaphors differed among the three unification movements. In Virginia, for example, Unionist John Carlile provided a textbook metaphor of companionate marriage. Convinced that secession meant war, he contrasted the union's bonds with separation's discord. To him, constitutional obligations were as enduring and forgiving as wedding vows:

> Like another of the great relations of private life, it was a marriage that no human authority can dissolve or divorce the parties from; and, if I may be allowed to refer to this same example in private life, let us say what man and wife say to each other: "We have mutual fault; nothing in the form of human beings can be perfect; let us then be kind to each other, forbearing, conceding; let us live in happiness and peace."[43]

Secessionists rejected the vision of familial cooperation. For the *Charleston Mercury*, whose every comment on Virginia invoked gendered language, the avoidance of marital metaphors arose from doubts about Virginia's loyalty. More curious was that most unionists avoided these marital analogies despite their demonstrable force. This choice may have been shaped by the constitutional debates in Virginia in the 1850s that shifted divorce from the legislature to the courts. That divorce debates cut across denominational and rural-urban divisions may also have mattered.[44]

The rarity of marriage metaphor usages in Italy likewise reflected recent events. Key to the *Risorgimento* was Cavour's pragmatic abandonment in 1852 of the center-right aristocratic reform party for an alliance with the center-left. Contemporaries derided this as a *"connubio,"* a synonym suggesting a "marriage of convenience" or shacking up. That Cavour then covertly campaigned against pro-church candidates further contaminated the metaphor. A flood of "Rattazzi-Cavour reforms" followed, including a press freedom law, a controversial religious liberty statute including civil marriage, restrictions on religious orders, and a set of laws asserting supremacy of Turinese-dominated national legislation over the laws of any newly added province. The marriage metaphor was further compromised by the unpopular diplomatic marriage between the king's pious teenage daughter Clotilde and Napoleon III's rakish middle-aged nephew Jerome.[45]

Commenting on unification in spring 1860, the Cavourist-centrist newspaper *L'Opinione* pointedly invoked the term "concord" rather than "marriage." They took special pleasure that the new Italy was being created through a more "just and honest" plebiscite process based on popular suffrage. Calling such annexation referenda the best basis for "a more tranquil and stable Europe," they contrasted it with state-building through "conquest, succession, or matrimony." This was an unmistakable allusion to the Clotilde-Jerome travesty. Notably, all three of the other forms of state growth mentioned by *L'Opinione* also involved women, either as victims of conquest, as mothers of future kings, or as pawns in dynastic games. They preferred a state purified of perceived feminine vulnerability and guile.[46]

Pragmatism guided use of marriage and divorce figures in Canada. Under its dual legal system, Toronto's marriages followed English common law while Montréal's came from the colonial *Coutume de Paris*. The dilemmas of Bishop Bourget on this issue resembled those facing every faction in Canada. Pushed toward ultramontanism and against Cavour-style reforms by a trip to Italy during the 1850s, disturbed by the growth of unconventional households in Montréal, and challenged by Montréal's egalitarian leftist *Rouges*, Bourget sought to revitalize marriage as sacramental and indissoluble. Cavour-style Civil Code reforms and the potential for national rather than provincial determination of family law made Bourget anxious.

Excessive metaphorical deployment of marriage and divorce could undermine the coalitions needed for legal protections while bolstering archenemies. Bourget's *Rougist* opponents in Montréal and Brownist anti-Catholics in Toronto mirrored these concerns.[47]

Not surprisingly, all parties avoided these metaphors in the confederation debates. Discussion remained legalistic. This contrasted with Virginia, where unification threatened few new changes to family law but where perceived threats to the color line forged a cross-factional bond of white unity. It also contrasted with Italy, where the supremacy of Piedmontese family law was settled and where Cavour's ardently anticlerical *connubio* and Rattazzi's reforms had already ruptured church ties. Cavour had considered reforms to family law and religious authority to be integral to the full array of his modernizing reforms. The civil marriage bill was not accidentally one of the first measures he proposed once in power. Bourget, following Pius IX, also understood these reforms as a package. Not surprisingly, a synopsis of the pope's *Syllabus of Errors*, endorsed under Bourget's authority, supplanted otherwise saturation coverage of confederation in the columns of Catholic house organ *L'Ordre*.[48]

Sibling metaphors, in contrast, found wide deployment. As with "mother," these figures replaced an older vocabulary of monarchical dependence. Within the nation, mutual family obligations of siblings bonded them together in equality and distinguished them from outsiders. That siblings could and should take different paths allowed for diversity and sibling rivalry without negating "common birthright citizenship" in the family. Yet, as the Carolina versus Virginia exchanges illustrate, implied duties and obligations suited sibling metaphors for describing betrayal. That siblings were subordinated to parents made siblinghood an apt metaphor for colonial or provincial relationships. Differences in birth order and rivalries for parental attention allowed discussions of fairness, privilege, and hierarchy to overlay implied status equalities. Siblinghood also nicely described city versus city rivalries. Finally, fraternal language proved ideal for describing shared military service in national armies. The concept of a "fraternal" "band of brothers" whose unit cohesion depended on replicating the blood ties of actual siblings fit well with emergent notions of manhood suffrage. Heterosexual marriage, in contrast, often implied the subordination of one partner.[49]

Viewed comparatively, usages across the six cities suggest that gendered metaphors were deployed most by those who had lost faith in the efficacy of legislative debate. Appeal to deep interests and deep fears transcended mere political give and take. But it was high-risk rhetoric. To accuse one's opponents of corrupting fundamental human relationships was to abandon reconciliation, mutual understanding, compromises, or companionate forgiveness. It was the path of ultimatums and separation.

Yet the relationship between gendered language and household structures was inexact. That southerners turned to this language first and most stridently was as rooted in deep uncertainties about loss of control because of the competing elements within southern slaveholding households as it was to patriarchy alone, though the two were intertwined. This was more than simply patriarchal authoritarianism. Equivalent forms of male patriarchal dominance over households could be found in both Italy and the Canadas, but neither had slavery. Moreover, use of gendered language was also common among those on the egalitarian liberal end of the spectrum whose household and gender ideologies were less insistently patriarchal and often more open to companionate or feminist understandings of household relations. Patriarchy, in other words, was inflected by other forms of perceived vulnerability and by the degree of simplicity or fragmentation in politics. As we have seen, the fluidity, concentration, and diversity of family relationships, and their potential for blurring the color line, were greatly intensified in the urban environments of Charleston and Richmond.

Normally, the urban context's plurality of stakeholder interests and imperatives for community stability made this a dangerous strategy. Political leaders could invoke such metaphors as appeals to transcendent interest, but only when the debates were unencumbered with practical discussions of family law and practice or where the array of political alliances could by reduced to only two sides. In the cities of Charleston and Richmond, in contrast, the conjunction of abolitionist threats, slave insurgencies, and the dangers of military coercion posed threats to family control unique to these communities. Household metaphors could forge alliances across factions while rationalizing the suppression of subordinated groups. The uncertainties of the urban environment and the certainties of the southern color line made such polarizing language easier to invoke and more effective in forging unity.

It is intriguing to consider the ways in which gendered rhetoric may have worked to enable Richmonders and Charlestonians to set aside their urbanness in the interest of gaining concord with their hinterlands. Everyone, urban or rural, had a family. Everyone knew slaveholders and slaves. Everyone had brothers and sisters or knew someone who did. Purely municipal policies such as fire protection, street maintenance, and water and sewage infrastructure, in contrast, served often to disharmonize and generate resentment. Gendered language could unite city and country as well as liberal and conservative or upper and lower classes. That Charlestonians, in particular, were very likely to have both rural and urban homes served to further blur the distinctions and open common conversations.

Outside the South, there was no slavery to serve as antipluralist trump card. In Montréal, for example, Bourget and the Catholic establishment adopted "live and let live" cooperation with the bourgeois Catholic elite and their secular and English bedfellows of the sort represented by Cartier. They agreed to trade political power to Toronto, George Brown, and the English majority of the new nation in exchange for patronage favors and noninterference. Likewise, Cavour manufactured consensus in Italian unification by creating a policy center that could absorb moderate liberal aristocrats and constitutional monarchists into a coalition with the more pragmatic Mazzinian liberal republicans. Clever use of royal prestige could win over those such as Garibaldi whose admiration for the throne's sanctity outweighed their contempt for Cavour's secret schemes. Because the boundaries between coalitions were constantly evolving, the absolutism of household metaphors made them unproductive in Italy and Canada. Turin's factions and allegiances were further complicated by the ongoing shifts of great power diplomacy. Genoa's bifurcation between aristocratic and working-class Mazzinian forces made it most similar to the racially simplified South but, here too, the third pole of the Catholic Church, the imperatives of international trade, and the implications of subordination to Turin made the rhetorical options for the city's coalition-builders less clearcut. Nor did the era's public policy changes and dislocating modernities cut so clearly into the heart of existing family structures as did the threat of abolitionism in the South.

This look at comparative histories and language usages reveals surprising interconnections and parallels among Canada, Italy, and the Southern Confederacy in their paths to unification, as well as several puzzles. The American Confederacy experienced sharp internal divisions despite commonalities of language, religion, history, and economic activities. Canada's nation-building process involved a great deal of grumbling but comparatively little political violence—this despite religious, linguistic, ethnic, and economic divisions in British North America that exceeded anything in the Confederacy except the color line. Canada's relative stability is surprising, if not miraculous. Italy's processes were somewhere in between, with the unification process involving both coercion and hegemonic persuasion, especially as the Turin-based Sardinian monarchy sought to impose its systems on Genoa and other communities that had very different histories and structures.[50]

The nation-building processes in these six cities were much more inter-
connected than historians have often appreciated. As we have seen, their
shared usages of gender, family, and household metaphors speak to a common conversation rooted in shared national unification and urban development. Yet variations mattered, too. The crisscrossed fragmentations of
Canadian cities, and the stark ideological, cultural, and religious conflicts
so important to shaping Italian unification, might pit city against city,
neighborhood against neighborhood, and household against household. But
unlike slavery, they did not potentially place households themselves into
conflict. Slavery, in contrast, defined an internal conflict within the household that could not be removed without ending slavery itself. The intensity
with which southern nationalists invoked gendered metaphors of purity
and vulnerability were a reflection of this household civil war. The urban
context weakened the household by generating a diversity and fluidity of
household structures. Slavery's potential for civil war within the plantation
"family" made the notion of a "house divided within itself" literal rather
than figurative. Slavery's urban context made the gender and family rhetoric deployed by Confederates unique among its sister cities.

NOTES

1. For "great family of nations," see for example, "Speech of Henry Wise," March 27,
    1861, in *Proceedings of the Virginia State Convention: February 13–May 1*, ed.
    George H. Reese, 4 vols. (Richmond: Virginia State Library, 1963), 2:437; Robert R.
    Rowison, "History of the War," *Southern Literary Messenger* 34 (September/October
    1862): 524; Jefferson Davis, "Message of President Davis," April 29, 1861, *Rich-
    mond Daily Dispatch*, May 4, 1861; Giuseppe Mazzini, "Istruzione generale per gli
    affratellati nella Giovine Italia," in *Scritti editi ed inediti di Giuseppe Mazzini*
    (Imola: Cooperativa Tipografico-editrice P. Galeati, 1907); "Giuseppe Garibaldi
    alla cara populazione di Napoli," September 7, 1860, in *Scritti politici e militari:
    Ricordi e pensieri inediti*, ed. Domenico Ciampoli (Rome: Enrico Voghera, n.d.),
    177; speeches of Christopher Dunkin and Arthur Rankin, in Eighth Parliament of
    Canada, *Parliamentary Debates on the Subject of the Confederation of the British
    North American Provinces* (Quebec: Hunter, Rose and Co., 1865), 524–29, 916–22.
2. Alan Smart and Josephine Smart, "Urbanization and the Global Perspective," *Annual
    Review of Anthropology* 32 (2003): 276–77; Peter J. Taylor, *Modernities: A Geohis-
    torical Interpretation* (Minneapolis: University of Minnesota Press, 1999), esp. 75–76,
    98–103, 107–8.
3. A. Gordon Darroch and Michael Ornstein, "Family and Household in Nineteenth-

Century Canada: Regional Patterns and Regional Economies," *Journal of Family History* 9 (June 1984): 158–77; John Modell and Tamara K. Haraven, "Urbanization and the Malleable Household: An Examination of Boarding and Lodging in American Families," *Journal of Marriage and Family* 35 (August 1973): 467–79; Christine Jacobson Carter, *Southern Single Blessedness: Unmarried Women in the Urban South: 1800–1865* (Urbana: University of Illinois Press, 2006), 22–40; and David I. Kertzer, "Living with Kin," in *Family Life in the Long Nineteenth Century, 1789–1913*, ed. Kertzer and Marzio Barbagli (New Haven, CT: Yale University Press, 2002), 62–72; Paul Quigley, *Shifting Grounds: Nationalism and the American South, 1848–1865* (New York: Oxford University Press, 2012), esp. 95–103; Stephanie McCurry, *Masters of Small Worlds: Yeoman Households, Gender Relations, and the Political Culture of the Antebellum South Carolina Low Country* (New York: Oxford University Press, 1995) esp. 56–61, 72, 85–91; Aaron Sheehan-Dean, *Why Confederates Fought: Family and Nation in Civil War Virginia* (Chapel Hill: University of North Carolina Press, 2007), xvi, 20–27; Elizabeth Fox Genovese, *Within the Plantation Household: Black and White Women of the Old South* (Chapel Hill: University of North Carolina Press, 1988), esp. 64–82.

4. Floya Anthias and Yuval-Davis, *Woman-Nation-State* (New York: St. Martin's Press, 1989), 3–14; Joan Landes, *Visualizing the Nation: Gender, Representation, and Revolution in Eighteenth-Century France* (Ithaca, NY: Cornell University Press, 2003), *passim*, esp. 17–23, 102–34; Michael Broers, "Sexual Politics and Political Ideology under the Savoyard Monarchy, 1814–1821," *English Historical Review* 114 (June 1999): 607–35; Cynthia R. Comacchio, *The Infinite Bonds of Family: Domesticity in Canada, 1850–1940* (Toronto: University of Toronto Press, 1999), 19–25; James Jasinski, "The Feminization of Liberty, Domesticated Virtue, and the Reconstitution of Power and Authority in Early American Political Discourse," *Quarterly Journal of Speech* 79 (1993): 146–64; George Lakoff, *The Political Mind* (New York: Viking, 2008), 75–87.

5. Daniel W. Crofts, *Reluctant Confederates: Upper South Unionists in the Secession Crisis* (Chapel Hill: University of North Carolina Press, 1993); For the broader context see also Andrew M. Fleche, *The Revolution of 1861: The American Civil War in the Age of Nationalist Conflict* (Chapel Hill: University of North Carolina Press, 2012).

6. This chapter uses qualitative rather than quantitative approaches, due to the challenges of comparing different languages and the uneven digitization of the sources used in this study. Where digital editions exist, however, a close traditional reading was supplemented with a systematic scan for keywords related to household, gender, family, and city. Initial vocabulary lists were developed using Princeton University's Wordnet lexical databases for English, French, and Italian (English version at http://wordnet.princeton.edu/), and Harvard's General Enquirer database (http://www.wjh.harvard.edu/~inquirer/), supplemented by other keywords that emerged in the study. Among the newspapers and legislative proceedings cited below, every available issue was read and/or scanned for the indicated periods. Periods were December 1860 through April 1861 for the South, March 1860 through June 1861 for Italy, and September 1864 through March 1865 for Canada.

7. For the suburban exodus see John Stilgoe, *Borderland: Origins of the American Sub-urb, 1820–1939* (New Haven, CT: Yale University Press, 1988), and Delores Hayden, *Building Suburbia: Green Fields and Urban Growth, 1820–2000* (New York: Vintage, 2003). Moltke-Hansen, chapter 2 (this volume); David Goldfield, *Cotton Fields and Skyscrapers: Southern City and Region* (Baton Rouge: Louisiana State University Press, 1982), esp. 28–39. The provisional, elastic, and sometimes cross-racial or fictive kinship dynamics of Charleston families, clearly intensified by its urban set-ting, are depicted in John Murray, "Poor Mothers, Stepmother, and Foster Mothers in the Early Republic and Antebellum Charleston," *Journal of the Early Republic* 32 (Fall 2012): 463–92.

8. Scott Reynolds Nelson, *Iron Confederacies: Southern Railways, Klan Violence, and Reconstruction* (Chapel Hill: University of North Carolina Press, 1999), esp. 11–26; John Majewski, *A House Dividing: Economic Development in Antebellum Pennsyl-vania and Virginia before the Civil War* (Cambridge: Cambridge University Press, 2006), 161–72; William A. Link, *Roots of Secession: Slavery and Politics in Antebel-lum Virginia* (Chapel Hill: University of North Carolina Press, 2007).

9. Greg D. Kimball, *American City, Southern Place: A Cultural History of Antebellum Richmond* (Athens: University of Georgia Press, 2000), esp. chaps. 1, 3, and 5; Majew-ski, *A House Dividing*; Link, *Roots of Secession*; and Virginius Dabney, *Richmond: The Story of a City*, rev. ed. (Charlottesville: University of Virginia Press, 1990), 129–39. For representative travel accounts see "A Slave Auction in Virginia," *The Liberator*, March 25, 1853; William Chambers, *Things as They Are in America* (Lon-don: William and Robert Chambers, 1854), 269–86; and James Redpath, *The Roving Editor: Or Talks with Slaves in the Southern States* (New York: A. B. Burdick, 1859), 245–54; Elizabeth R. Varon, *We Mean to Be Counted: White Women and Politics in Antebellum Virginia* (Chapel Hill: University of North Carolina Press, 1998), 107–14.

10. *Richmond Enquirer*, March 10, 1857; *Richmond Whig*, December 24, 1854. The count of nativities is derived from Ancestry.com: *1860 United States Federal Census*, manuscript returns for Henrico County, free population schedules. John David Blalock, " 'Virginia Is Middle Ground': The Know Nothing Party and the Virginia Gubernatorial Election of 1855," *Virginia Magazine of History and Biography* 106 (Winter 1998): 35–70; Daniel W. Crofts, "Late Antebellum Virginia Reconsidered," *Virginia Magazine of History and Biography* 108 (Summer 1999): 253–86.

11. Robert Rosen, *A Short History of Charleston* (1982; rpt., Columbia: University of South Carolina Press, 1997), esp. 67–106; Maurie Dee McInnis, *The Politics of Taste in Antebellum Charleston* (Chapel Hill: University of North Carolina Press, 2005), *passim*, esp. 23–5, 60, 141; manufacturing value added, University of Virginia Library Historical Census Data Browser (http://mapserver.lib.virginia.edu/index.html); "Drayton, William (1776–1846), *Biographical Directory of the American Congress*, http://bioguide.congress.gov/scripts/biodisplay.pl?index=D000490; Richard E. Ellis, *The Union at Risk: Jacksonian Democracy, State Rights and the Nullification Crisis* (New York: Oxford University Press, 1987), 180–93.

12. Rosen, *Short History of Charleston*; Bernard Powers, *Black Charlestonians: A Social History* (Fayetteville: University of Arkansas Press, 1994), esp. 1–35; Powers, " 'The

Worst of All Barbarism': Racial Anxiety and the Approach of Secession in the Pal-metto State," *South Carolina Historical Magazine* 112 (July–October 2011): 139–56; Michael A. Gomez, *Exchanging Our Country Marks: The Transformation of African Identities in the Colonial and Antebellum South* (Chapel Hill: University of North Carolina Press, 1998), 20–24; William Freehling, *Road to Disunion: Secessionists at Bay*, 2 vols. (New York: Oxford University Press, 1990), esp. 2:30–37.

13. *Timon of Athens*, act 4, scene 1, quoted in Louisa S. McCord, "Negro and White Slavery—Wherein Do They Differ?," *Southern Quarterly Review* (July 1851): 125 (ellipsis added). For discussion of these within-household tensions and social control systems, see Thavolia Glymph, *Out of the House of Bondage: The Transformation of the Plantation Household* (Cambridge: Cambridge University Press, 2008).

14. *Charleston Mercury*, March 28, 1857.

15. William Porcher Miles, *Republican Government not everywhere and always the best; and Liberty not the Birthright of Mankind. An Address delivered before the Alumni Society of the College of Charleston* (Charleston. SC: Press of Walker and James, 1852), 10–11, 22–23.

16. William Grayson, *The Country* (Charleston, SC: Russell and Jones, 1858), 15.

17. *Charleston Mercury*, November 21, 1860.

18. Ibid., April 15, 1861.

19. "Message of Governor John Letcher," in State of Virginia, *Journal of the House of Delegates of the State of Virginia, for the Extra Session, 1861* (Richmond: William F. Ritchie, Public Printer, 1861), doc. 1, iii–xxvii.

20. Charles B. Dew, *Apostles of Disunion: Southern Secession Commissioners and the Causes of the Civil War* (Charlottesville: University Press of Virginia, 2001), 60–61, 68–72.

21. Speech of John S. Preston, February 19, 1861, in *Proceedings*, ed. Reese, 1:87, 90.

22. William Kauffman Scarborough, *Masters of the Big House: Elite Slaveholders of the Mid-Nineteenth Century South* (Baton Rouge: Louisiana State University Press, 2006), 40–41; Brian Meggitt, "Hiram Powers," in *American National Biography*, ed. John A. Garraty and Mark C. Carnes (New York: Oxford University Press, 2004) 17:793–94.

23. Geoffrey W. Symcox and Anthony L. Cardoza, *History of Turin* (Torino: Einaudi, 2006), 151–94; Franco Bolgiani, et al., eds., *Storia di Torino*, 9 vols. (Torino: Einaudi, 1997–2002), esp. vol. 6, *La città nel Risorgimento (1798–1864)*; Emanuele Menietti, ed., *Il Risorgimento nelle vie di Torino* (Torino: Punto-Torino, 2010); Cesare Balbo, *Della monarchia rappresentativa in Italia* (Firenze: Felice Le Monnier, 1857).

24. Cardoza and Symcox, *History of Turin*, 151–64; Broers, "Sexual Politics and Political Ideology"; Kertzer, "Living with Kin"; Gian Mario Bravo, "L'Evoluzione di Torino dalla Scienza all'Utopia, Ovvero, l'etica del Lavoro e lo Spirit del Socialismo," in *Città e pensiero politico italiano dal Risorgimento alla Repubblica*, ed. Robertino Ghiringhelli (Milano: V&P, 2007), esp. 29–32; Joseph de Maistre, *Considerations sur la France* (Lyon: Louis Lesne, 1843), 60–63.

25. Bianca Montale, *Mito e realtà di Genova nel Risorgimento* (Milan: Franco Angeli, 1999), passim; Ennio Poleggi e Paolo Cevini, *Genova: Le città nella storia d'Italia* (Roma: Editori Laterza, 1981), 211–18.

26. John A. Davis, *Italy in the Nineteenth Century* (New York: Oxford University Press, 2000), 92–96.

27. Torino, Italy, *l'Opinione*, July 2 and 10, 1857; John M. Daniel to Lewis Case, July 25, 1857, National Archives, M-90 reel 7; Jessie White Mario, *The Birth of Modern Italy: Posthumous Papers of Jessie White Mario* (London: T. Fisher Unwin, 1909), 256–71.

28. Davis, *Italy in the Nineteenth Century*, 92–96; Don H. Doyle, *Nations Divided: America, Italy, and the Southern Question* (Athens: University of Georgia Press, 2002), 68–71; Paolo Colombo, "Il consenso spezzato; La legittimazione militare di Vittorio Emanuele II," in *Vittorio Emanuele II: Il Re Galantuomo*, ed. Elena Fontanella (Milan: Fabbrica delle Idee, 2010), 66–73; Lucy Riall, "Martyr Cults in Nineteenth-Century Italy," *Journal of Modern History* 82 (June 2010): esp. 263–64.

29. Overviews include Donald G. Creighton, *The Road to Confederation: The Emergence of Canada, 1863–1867* (Boston: Houghton-Mifflin, 1965), and Christopher Moore, *1867: How the Fathers Made a Deal* (Toronto: McClelland and Stewart, 1997).

30. Paul-André Linteau, *Brève histoire de Montréal* (Montréal: Boréal, 1992), 51–73; Susan Mann, *The Dream of a Nation: A Social and Intellectual History of Quebec*, 2nd ed. (Montréal: McGill-Queen's University Press, 2003), 26–40; Mark R. Anderson, *The Battle for the Fourteenth Colony: America's War of Liberation in Canada, 1774–1776* (Hanover, NH: University of New England Press, 2013), esp. 31–36; John Hare, *La pensée socio-politique au Québec, 1784–1812: Analyse sémantique* (Ottawa: Éditions de l'Université d'Ottawa, 1977), esp. 32–33.

31. Comacchio, *Infinite Bonds of Family*, esp. 22–23; Bettina Bradbury, *Working Families: Age, Gender, and Daily Survival in Industrializing Montréal* (Toronto: McClelland and Stewart, 1993), esp. chap. 2; Sherry Olson and Patricia Thornton, *Peopling the North American City: Montréal, 1840–1900* (Montréal: McGill-Queens University Press, 2011), 131–81; Allan Greer, *The Patriots and the People: The Rebellion of 1837 in Lower Canada* (Toronto: University of Toronto Press, 1993), 189–218.

32. D. C. Masters, *The Rise of Toronto* (Toronto: University of Toronto Press, 1947); Ann M. Carlos and Patricia Fulton, "Chance or Destiny? The Dominance of Toronto Over the Urban Landscape, 1797–1850," *Social Science History* 15 (Spring 1991): 35–66; J. I. Little, *Loyalties in Conflict: A Canadian Borderland in War and Rebellion, 1812–1840* (Toronto: University of Toronto Press, 2008).

33. G. P. de T. Glazebrook, *The Story of Toronto* (Toronto: University of Toronto Press, 1971); Victor L. Russell, ed., *Forging a Consensus: Historical Essays on Toronto* (Toronto: University of Toronto Press, 1984), esp. part 1; Masters, *Rise of Toronto*; Cynthia Comacchio, "'The History of Us': Social Science, History, and the Relations of Family in Canada," *Labour/Le Travail* 46 (Fall 2000): 167–220; Sandwell, "The Limits of Liberalism: The Liberal Reconnaissance and the History of the Family in Canada," *Canadian Historical Review* 84 (September 2003): 423–50; Benjamin Drew, *The Refugee: or the Narratives of Fugitive Slaves in Canada* (Boston: John P. Jewett, 1856), 94–117.

34. Colin Read and Ronald J. Stagg, introduction to *The Rebellion of 1837 in Upper Canada* (Toronto: Canadian Historical Association, 1988); Glazebrook, *Story of Toronto*, 70–84; Paul Romney, "The Struggle for Authority," in *Forging a Consensus*, ed. Russell; "MacKenzie, William Lyon," in Library and Archives Canada, *Dictionary*

of Canadian Biography Online (http://www.biographi.ca/009004–119.01-e.php?&id
_nbr=4562&& PHPSESSID=ychzfqkvzape).

35. C. P. Lucas, ed., *Lord Durham's Report on the Affairs of British North America*,
3 vols. (Oxford: Clarendon Press, 1912), 2:17–28; Moore, *1867*, esp. 4–15.

36. Mann, *Dream of a Nation*, 82–91; Louis-Hippolyte Lafontaine, "Aux Électeurs
du Comté de Terrebonne," *L'Aurore des Canadas*, August 28, 1840; Louis-Joseph
Papineau, "Discours À L'Assemblée du Marché Bonsecours," in *Cette fatale union:
Adresses, discours et manifestes, 1847–1848*, ed. Georges Aubin (Montréal: Lux,
2003), 105–7.

37. Moore, *1867*; Mann, *Dream of a Nation*, 83–113.

38. *Montréal Herald*, January 23, 1865; Montréal, *L'Ordre* (Catholic Union), February 24,
1865. For concern about schools, marriage, and family, see, for example, *L'Ordre*,
February 20 and March 13, 1865.

39. See n. 10 above.

40. Riall, "Martyr Cults"; Andrew E. Kim, "The Absence of Pan-Canadian Civil Religion: Plurality, Duality, and Conflict in Symbols of Canadian Culture," *Sociology of
Religion* 54 (Autumn 1993): esp. 261–65; Wade Andrew Henry, "Royal Representation, Ceremony, and Cultural Identity in the Building of the Canadian Nation, 1860–
1911" (PhD diss., University of British Columbia, 2001), 98–101; *Toronto Globe*,
October 21 and November 11, 1864. *Parliamentary Debates on the Subject of the
Confederation*, ASCII text version accessed and proofed for typographical errors from
the Internet Archive, https://archive.org/stream/parliamentarydeb00canarich
/parliamentarydeb00canarich_djvu.txt.

41. Reese, ed., *Proceedings of the Virginia State Convention*, 1:695, 2:466, 601.

42. Ibid., 1:197, 225; 4:9. Word count timeline from the University of Richmond's digital
edition (http://dlxs.richmond.edu/d/ddr/).

43. *Virginia State Convention*, 3:414.

44. Glenda Riley, "Legislative Divorce in Virginia, 1803–1850," *Journal of the Early
Republic* 11 (Spring 1991): 51–67; Thomas E. Buckley, *The Great Catastrophe of
My Life: Divorce in the Old Dominion* (Chapel Hill: University of North Carolina
Press, 2001).

45. Cardoza and Symcox, *History of Turin*, 188–94; Denis Mack Smith, *Cavour* (New
York: Knopf, 1985), 61–85.

46. Turin, Italy, *L'Opinione*, March 10, 1860; Silvana Patriarca, "Indolence and Regenera-
tion: Tropes and Tensions of Risorgimento Patriotism," *American Historical Review*
85 (Summer–Autumn 2005): 403–5. For the use of "concordia," see especially "Con-
dizioni Dell'Italia," *L'Opinione*, March 22 and 27, 1860, and September 26, 1860, as
well as discussion of Mario, July 2, 1857.

47. For Canada, see Bradbury, *Working Families*, 49–57.

48. *Parliamentary Debates*, Montreal, *L'Ordre*, February 27, 1865. A full condemnation
of Cavourist unification can be seen in Ignace Bourget, "Lettre aux directeurs du
Pays, 14 Février 1862," in *Le rouge et le bleu*, ed. Yvan Lamonde and Claude Corbo
(Montréal: Presses de l'Université de Montréal, 1999), 187–92.

49. Frank J. Sulloway, *Born to Rebel: Birth Order, Family Dynamics, and Creative Lives*
(New York: Vintage, 1997), pts. 1 and 2, esp. 55–82.

50. David Forgacs and Eric Hobsbawm, eds., *The Antonio Gramsci Reader: Selected Writings* (New York: New York University Press, 2000), esp. 247–59; Lucy Riall, *Risorgimento: The History of Italy from Napoleon to Nation State* (New York: Palgrave-Macmillan, 2009); Patriarcha, "Tropes and Tensions," 380–408; and Alberto Mario Banti, *La Nazione del Risorgimento: Parentela, Santità e Onore alle Origini dell'Italia Unita* (Torino: Einaudi, 2000).

PART 3

Gender

CHAPTER FIVE

Stephen Spalding's Fourth of July
in New Orleans

MICHAEL PIERSON

U nion lieutenant Stephen Spalding spent an exciting Fourth of July in
New Orleans in 1862. By the time the sun came up on the fifth, he had
gone AWOL, spent an astonishing fifty-seven dollars, drunk just about every
kind of booze a person might get his hands on, and attempted to dance. His
inebriated dancing resulted in torn dresses and physical harm to his neighbors on the dance floor. He had also gotten into a brawl, helping to throw
two British naval officers out of a party and into the middle of the street.
He had found his way into at least one brothel, and probably two. Finally,
he managed to stagger back to camp. In all of this, he had been joined by another young Union lieutenant, Daniel Foster. Despite the city's reputation
as a hotbed of Confederate sympathies, Spalding and Foster never seemed
to be in any danger. In fact, Spalding never seemed in any doubt about his
place, either culturally or personally. He seemed at home, even though he
was a native of Vermont. There are hints in his story about new ways to
think about the role of southern cites during the war years.

Historians have only Lieutenant Spalding's own word for how he spent
Independence Day. Spalding's one surviving letter is dated July 8, 1862;
Spalding wrote it in Algiers, Louisiana, a working-class town located just
across the Mississippi River from New Orleans. Spalding's regiment, the
8th Vermont, had occupied Algiers since early June, protecting the western
flank of Union-controlled New Orleans. His letter responded to one from his
friend, James Peck, who had recently written him a letter so full of Greek,
Latin, and literary allusions that Spalding claims to have taken days (and a
small library of reference works) to make his way through it. Despite the
fact that Spalding was twenty-two and blessed with good health, a degree
from the University of Vermont, an officer's paycheck, and an earlier stint
in the famous 7th New York State Militia, we might still feel a bit sorry for

him. We might pity him for his unit's inactivity and his lack of war news.
The best he could do for important news was to guess about the future and
speculate about the extent of Unionist sentiment in New Orleans and Algiers. He had seen no combat and earned no glory. "I am sorry that I cannot
make my letter more interesting," he concluded to his senior year roommate at UVM, "but give us some fighting & I will. As it is, take nothing
from nothing & nothing remains."[1] Spalding's lack of war news, however, is
good news for historians. For anyone interested in the interaction between
Union soldiers and southern cities, Spalding's need to fill up his letter with
personal news means that he wrote of himself, not of the war more broadly.
And Spalding, it turns out, was a sparkling writer, and he filled his letter with humor, unusual details, emotion, and revelations about himself
and his actions that rarely appear in historical sources. Through his words,
we gain insights into the gender ideologies of a conservative man who felt
remarkably at home in both northern and southern cities. Spalding's masculinity, as we will see, encompassed many privileges, including sexual
license and public alcohol abuse.

Spalding's letter runs a full seven pages, but it hits its stride with his description of how he spent the Fourth of July in New Orleans. With quite a
story to tell, he rattled off two big pages of text. The story fills readers' imagi-
nations with action and characters, none the least of whom is Spalding himself. Spalding clearly wanted James Peck to know that he had had a good time
on the Fourth, and he told his tale with verve and humor. For historians, the
letter serves as a reminder that Union soldiers and officers interacted with
southern civilians in a variety of ways. As we will see, both Spalding and his
men visited New Orleans for what modern American soldiers would refer
to as R&R. Cities serve as commercial centers, and the Vermonters came to
rely on the Crescent City for food, drink, and amusements of many kinds.
By July Spalding and his men could easily find their way to the pleasures of
the city, having spent May patrolling its streets. Fighting crime more than
the Rebel army, they learned about the city's least reputable neighborhoods.
That may well have helped Spalding carouse as successfully as he did when
it came time to celebrate his nation's birthday in July.

But familiarity with the location of the city's streets, bars, and brothels would have helped Spalding navigate New Orleans only so well. What
mattered more, this chapter argues, was Spalding's deeper understanding
of shared urban cultures, particularly in regard to how gender roles were
enacted. Spalding felt at home in New Orleans because he could enact the
same masculine roles that he had performed as an undergraduate in Burlington, Vermont, as a young law student in New York City in 1860 and

1861, and as a soldier stationed in New Orleans and Algiers for about two months before he wrote his letter. Spalding had spent most of his life since he was sixteen in urban centers. Obviously, New Orleans did not perfectly resemble any northern city, especially Burlington, which after all was quite a bit smaller than the Crescent City. This chapter suggests, however, that Spalding's formative experiences in Burlington and New York City made him acquainted with immigrant populations, wage labor, commercialization, and marked gradations of wealth.[2] More to the point, he would have been familiar with bars and the sex trade.

New Orleans, in other words, provided Spalding and other Union soldiers with commercialized rest and relaxation, particularly leisure moments that allowed them to continue to occupy gender roles with which they had grown familiar during their lives in the North. The urban South offered a northern soldier like Stephen Spalding the relief and natural ease that comes to a person living amid an otherwise alien landscape and people when they finally discover themselves on familiar cultural ground. A forgotten part of the history of southern cities in the Civil War is how recognizable their commercial roles, gender ideologies, and ethnic or working-class neighborhoods were for many Union soldiers who now lived in their midst.[3] For Stephen Spalding and many northern soldiers, New Orleans and other southern cities could be home away from home.

The soldiers' familiarity with urban southern gender ideologies may have been especially true for northern men affiliated with the Democratic Party, the more conservative of the two political parties in the North. Most soldiers who served in the Union's Department of the Gulf in 1862 had such Democratic leanings. Spalding's regiment, the 8th Vermont Volunteers, had been recruited by Maj. Gen. Benjamin F. Butler late in 1861. Lincoln hoped that Butler, a former Democratic state senator from Massachusetts, could spur enlistments among New England Democrats. Butler convinced Republican governors to appoint prominent Democratic politicians to command his new regiments, and the 8th Vermont was no exception. These new colonels then selected recruiting officers, and the regiments took on a distinctly conservative air.[4] This was true, for example, in racial matters. Spalding opens his letter with a joke about throwing a stool at his newly hired African American servant, Jim. Many other members of his regiment voiced grave doubts about emancipation. Democratic resistance to change took many other forms in the antebellum decades and the war years, including objections to newly enlarged roles for the federal government in matters pertaining to economic development, monetary policy, and federal powers relative to the states.

The Democratic Party's devotion to the status quo continued into family ideology and gender practices. Starting as early as the 1820s, Democrats
(including Andrew Jackson) campaigned on the idea that women should
occupy no position that placed them in the public eye. While their Whig
opponents felt more comfortable with women appearing in public as social
reformers, as participants in political campaign events, and as authors and
opinion-makers, Democrats almost unanimously condemned such women
as morally degraded, out of their proper social place, and threats to male
privileges.[5] Democratic resistance to female involvement in anything political became particularly vicious in the aftermath of the Seneca Falls Convention in 1848, when women publicly demanded a wide range of political,
legal, economic, and social rights that Democrats held as the special pre-
serves of men. Such political positions on gender and family issues often appealed to the all-male electorate, and served as a common ground on which
northern and southern Democrats could stand.[6]

At much the same time that Democrats and their opponents debated
whether women should play public roles in society, the parties also took
positions, at least informally, on prostitution and male sexual rights and
liberties. As we will see later, Democratic political culture celebrated male
sexual rights, especially in the North's growing cities, while Whig and Republican politicians and their male and female allies in social reform movements tried to establish new limits on male sexual activity in and out of
marriage. In an era in which sexual customs were changing, the traditional,
patriarchal order found its defenders in the Democratic ranks, while people
who sought to curb sexual activity outside of marriage and also within it, by
granting wives more authority in sexual matters, enrolled in the Whig and
then Republican parties.[7] Like other Democrats, the men in the 8th Vermont embraced patriarchal ideas about masculinity, including the right of
men to drink alcohol openly and to enjoy masculine privileges regarding
sex.[8] The Vermonters seized what physical pleasures they could without
any expressions of guilt or ambivalence. Coming from an urban culture that
fostered alcohol consumption and commercialized sex, Spalding found in
New Orleans many places that catered to his interests. This chapter argues
that the masculinity practiced in New Orleans and found in the Democratic
cultures of the urban North was so similar that Spalding and many of his
fellow soldiers knew how to act without even thinking about it.

Lieutenant Spalding had his own way of articulating this thesis: "New
Orleans is a great place for fun."[9] Even though the city now has a pro-
Confederate reputation that celebrates some white women's opposition to
the Union military, the city's voters in 1860 had given more votes to both of

the moderate Unionists, John Bell and Stephen Douglas, than to the radical John Breckinridge. When secession came on the ballot in January, secession won the city by only two percentage points.[10] The people's willingness to cooperate with the Union government after May 1862 merely continued that moderate trend. Most of the city's people, even in its white population, grew accustomed to the Union army by early July, and many had welcomed it upon its arrival. By the time Spalding visited on July 4, the Union blockade had been lifted, the United States had restored a stable currency, and the city had fed and employed many residents. By June at the latest, northern soldiers safely explored the city even alone. New Orleans unions showed their control over the city by staging four Independence Day events, including a ceremonial breakfast, a speech by a local orator, and a parade during which three local women presented a home-sewn flag to the 13th Connecticut. So it is not surprising that Lieutenants Spalding and Foster, as well as other members of their regiment, felt safe enough to venture into the city on the Fourth. The four men who left records of their day in the city seem to have skipped the formal ceremonies, all of which seem to have been staged largely for the benefit of the city's natives. William Smith and Jonathan Allen crossed through New Orleans on their way to the shore of Lake Pontchartrain, but complained that "there was no celebration, here and I think it was the dullest Fourth I ever spent." Spalding and Foster may have been the only ones to enjoy themselves the whole day. Justus Gale left the only other account of Independence Day in the 8th Vermont, and he spent it in a railroad car in Algiers, suffering from "dierea," writing letters, and watching it rain "very pleasantly." He told his brother that he knew this made for a dull letter, but life had its compensations: "I guess I had the best musketoe bar last night."[11] While Gale had a slow day, Union troops were often seen in the city's stores, theaters, and bars.[12]

Spalding probably had more fun than his fellow Vermonters on the Fourth because he could afford to find his pleasures in the city. As officers, he and Lieutenant Foster had more money at their command. The fifty-seven dollars Spalding spent equaled about four months of pay for a private, but only about two weeks of pay for a lieutenant. This was one of the privileges that Spalding enjoyed, but only one of them. His family's status, his rank, his paycheck, his new servant, and his race placed him near the top of the social hierarchy.[13] But his trip into New Orleans illustrates a further aspect of his social privilege: he was a man in a culture that granted men many liberties. Masculinity counted for a lot in New Orleans, as it did elsewhere in the United States during Spalding's life.[14] That was never more apparent than when Spalding and Foster hopped the ferry in Algiers and landed in the Crescent City.

The men in the 8th Vermont revered the public drinking of alcohol as one of the emblems of masculinity. Spalding and Foster, both in their early twenties, relished their alcoholic freedom, but they were not alone.[15] Their regimental culture seemed awash in hard liquor. The regiment's fondness for drink emerged even in Vermont. While still in training camp, Col. Stephen Thomas marched a company of men (who presumably joined him only reluctantly) into nearby Brattleboro to demand that merchants stop selling liquor to his soldiers.[16] Throughout their time in Louisiana, the soldiers (like Spalding and Foster) found many opportunities to skirt Thomas's policing. Many Civil War soldiers took to drink, and one recent study has found men assigned to the "loneliness and boredom" of garrison duty to be especially susceptible to temptation.[17] Such was the case with the Vermonters stuck in Algiers. The 8th Vermont's embrace of alcohol as a potent sign and source of their masculinity can be seen in the reaction of Pvt. Justus Gale to New Orleans and its drinking culture. Gale served in Company A, the most Republican unit in the regiment, and he bemoaned the extent of alcohol consumption in the Pelican State. While they might differ on whether men should drink alcohol or not, he and his Democratic comrades would have agreed on Gale's denunciation of drunken women: "This State is the worst place for drinking of any place I ever heard of," he wrote. "Liquor is just as common here as water is in Vt; you can hardly go by a door in this City without seeing the glass and bottle siting on the bar. there is about as many women here that get drunk as there is men in the north that get drunk."[18] Gale's horror at the thought of inebriated women reminds modern readers of the extent to which public drinking remained a male preserve in the 1860s. Conservative men drank proudly, and jealously guarded their right to do so. The significance of alcohol emerges when they reminisced and joked about the war after it ended.

To an extent, the men's blend of liquor and masculinity transcended any urban/rural dichotomy. They would, in short, drink anywhere. So, while Algiers and New Orleans gave them more opportunities to forage for alcohol, rural Louisiana had its share of liquor to be found. In 1896 Moses McFarland, a former captain in the 8th, wrote *Some Experiences of the Eighth Vermont West of the Mississippi*. His memoirs take up less than twenty pages, but include four drinking stories, two of which go on at length. His tales of rural binges sound like college memories, fondly remembered for their comradery and humor. McFarland's first drinking tale follows him and a scouting party as they enjoy "a friendly introduction" to a newly discovered barrel of whiskey. Shortly after drinking his fill, McFarland mounts a troublesome mule (is there another kind?) that he has confiscated. Warned by some blacks about the mule's idiosyncrasies, McFarland jokes that he was "not far enough from the whiskey barrel to be easily frightened by rebels or kicking mules." Predictably, he soon lands "flat on my back in the road."[19] Another of McFarland's scouting parties ends with the captain paying for an open bar at a saloon for his twenty exhausted men. The barkeeper comes to regret charging McFarland only three dollars for his twenty soldiers, whom he claims drank an astonishing eight gallons of whiskey. McFarland advises him, jokingly, that before he agrees to host thirsty soldiers again, "he would do well to inquire if the men belonged to the Eighth Vermont."[20] Comic encounters with drunk pickets and looters also appear, rounding out a picture of men at liberty and feeling their oats (and other distilled grains).

Drinking takes on an overtly gendered aspect when McFarland tells more serious tales of hard liquor. If the funny stories of the 8th Vermont sound like fraternity escapades remembered fondly in old age (with hangovers and stomach upset forgotten), the introduction of women into the stories means that events take on the serious tone of the parlor. McFarland tells two stories in which he receives liquor from planters' wives, and the rules of polite society dictate both of the proceedings. In one instance, he enjoys the hospitality of a Confederate officer's wife, though he adds approvingly that she "was not a fanatic." He tells her, seriously, that he is sick and has been advised to drink brandy, but cannot find any. She gives him an entire bottle and refuses all of his efforts to pay her. He respects her for her hospitality, but he really admires her for her femininity. She occupies her (circumscribed) female role as host, does credit to her husband, and stays clear of politics. To make her femininity the focus of the story, he concludes by contrasting "such women and the women of New Orleans," who had disgraced their sex by spitting on Union soldiers and called down upon themselves Butler's Woman Order, "denouncing them as women of the town plying their vocation."[21] He praises her loyalty to her Confederate husband, which is presented as right because it is wholly personal. Her loyalty is a familial one, not a political one to the Confederacy. McFarland recognizes and values her obedience to her patriarch.

In a second story, women, whiskey, and good manners bridge even the divide separating the Confederates from Moses McFarland and his men. Nina Silber has found that many northern men longed for an emotive re-attachment of the North and South in the 1890s, when McFarland wrote his memoir. They imagined (or reimagined) decorous southern ladies as the agents through which the re-union could occur.[22] McFarland tells just such a story when he recounts how he and his men approached the plantation of Captain Ranseau, who commanded a nearby Confederate cavalry company.

With the handful of Confederates fleeing on their arrival, McFarland finds himself negotiating with Mrs. Ranseau, the only white resident left on the plantation. All goes well, the wheels of society greased by whiskey and etiquette, at least as McFarland chose to remember the scene. He remembers having "suggested" that his "men would appreciate a little good whiskey." When Mrs. Ranseau "very promptly and courteously set out what proved to be a very excellent article," McFarland's "men paid their hearty respects" to both her and the alcohol.[23] The Union troops then searched the Ranseau house, but they allowed Mrs. Ranseau to "show us over the house," a gesture that eliminated the threat of unlicensed plunder.[24] So far this is pretty normal, but McFarland's adventure takes an odd turn, enabled by the woman's hospitality, properly gendered, and the plying of alcohol.

Getting ready to leave, McFarland, in the role of gracious guest, "requested [Mrs. Ranseau] to give my compliments to Captain Ranseau on his return and say to him that on such a day I desired to meet him at Boote [Boutte] Station, and that on the honor of a gentleman no advantage should be taken of him." Everything here is as it should be in a society united by manners, not divided by war. Mrs. Ranseau hosts McFarland, an officer, and even extends her generosity to his men. They get a tour of the house from her. McFarland states that he hopes to meet her husband, and pledges his "honor" as a "gentleman" to treat her husband well if they do. Better still, Captain Ranseau accepts McFarland's invitation, and the two men have "a friendly chat."[25] A fly gets in the ointment during the chat when Ranseau asks McFarland to retrieve two of his "valuable negroes" and the Union officer refuses, but the existence of slavery as the only cause of disagreement between McFarland and the properly mannered Ranseau household merely accentuates that all should be right between them in the 1890s, with slavery ended (and white supremacist rule restored in another guise). With slavery off the table, women should be able to go back to serving alcohol to men, who will then get along splendidly.

One suspects, however, that Algiers and New Orleans offered the average soldier greater opportunities for drinking heavily than did life in the countryside. Certainly this was true for men in the ranks who drank illicitly; Moses McFarland, an officer, supervises most of his men's drinking during his stories. Stephen Spalding's turn as a judge at a court-martial in July 1862 offers proof that Lieutenants Spalding and Foster shared their unauthorized thirst for certain aspects of urban life with their men. Spalding may well have felt hypocritical to sit in judgment on men who had only acted as he had done twenty-four days before, but if he did we have no record of it. Whatever he felt, the court record shows that Vermont soldiers managed to get very drunk when stationed near New Orleans.[26] After one such binge, Pvt. A. J. Stickney found himself stuck in the regiment's guard-house, accused of drunkenness. He had not gone quietly, however. He was charged with "disorderly conduct" on account of his "continual swearing and cursing, and by his refusing to keep quiet." Stickney's accusers, perhaps employing some understatement, said of his lengthy, profane, and drink-fueled outbursts that they "kept the camp in an uproar the principal part of the night, contrary to military order." Stickney pleaded guilty and forfeited one month's pay. Another defendant, Pvt. Thomas Ferrin of Company E, was accused of "running the Guard and getting drunk" on July 4. In other words, he was accused of doing exactly what Spalding, one of his judges, had bragged of doing on the same day. Predictably, his commanders found that "on his return [Ferrin] was very much intoxicated." Ferrin pleaded guilty.[27]

After that awkward case, the judges turned their attention to four members of Spalding's own company. Three of the cases involved excessive drinking. Private John O'Mere was found guilty of "getting drunk on duty," in particular "while standing guard as sentry." The next private, Andrew McIver, left his post as guard for "hours," returning "drunk and wholly unfit for the duty of a Guard." In the third case, Pvt. Francis Hagan left camp and got drunk. We cannot know how Spalding viewed these men's actions. Lorien Foote has suggested that there could be a double standard in the army, whereby officers could routinely get away with conduct that would be criminal for ordinary soldiers. Alternatively, we can sense an ambiguity in how Spalding felt about punishing men who felt the lure of the city as much as he did; Foote points out that officers could summarily punish soldiers whom they felt were guilty; as the ranking officer of Company B, Spalding chose instead to have these men's actions judged by a larger panel.[28] Perhaps that allowed him not to take full responsibility for issuing punishments that he did not feel comfortable handing down on his own. Whatever Spalding thought, his soldiers obviously wanted to get into the city and drink just as much as he did. In that sense, most of the 8th Vermont—including the soldier-historian Moses McFarland, Lieutenant Foster, McFarland's men, Stephen Spalding, and the guilty privates—shared a (perhaps blurred) vision of masculinity enhanced by alcohol.

Seen in the context of McFarland's joyous binges and the convicted soldiers' guilty pleasures with alcohol, Spalding's drunken carouse through the city on Independence Day should not come as a surprise. Neither should the flurry of jokes about alcohol that dot Spalding's letter, including references to drinking so much upon his future return to Vermont that he would not be able to stand up, even though he very much wanted to, in order to denounce his current superiors. He also wrote that he drank "700 to 800 times a day to keep my spirits up." We might hope that Spalding exaggerated for comic effect when he stated that on the Fourth of July he and Foster "drank gin, whiskey, brandy, rum, beer, gin coctails modesty prevents me from putting in the K., Eleven other different kinds of coctails, Cobblers of all kinds, julips d[itt]o, smashes d[itt]o."[29] Spalding shows no remorse about indulging in all of this, even when his resulting lack of coordination leads to mishaps on the dance floor. Presented as comedy, the havoc caused by his drunken dizziness damages neighboring shins, noses, toes, and dresses. All comes right, he tells Peck, with the help of his just-visible pistol and the need to keep the business of the party moving along. For Spalding, as for other men, drinking nearly topped the list of what made being a man such a happy and privileged status in these years.[30]

But men held another social right. Spalding hinted at a second prerogative held by men when he jokingly inserted "modesty prevents me from putting in the K" after he had written "coctail" (instead of "cocktail"). Readers might be tempted to read this as a throw-away joke at which Peck could snort before moving on to the rest of his friend's staggering bar tab. But there is more to Spalding's "coctail" joke than meets the eye. It serves to flag an alert reader's attention that Spalding did more than drink at "the hospitable retreat of Miss Bianca Robbins." By claiming that "modesty" prevents him from writing out the word "cock," Spalding lets Peck know that the same (sexual) modesty will inhibit him from going into even more provocative details. Spalding continues, including more telltale jokes along the same lines as his "cock" joke, and Peck would not have had to stretch too far to figure out what we can learn from the historical record; Miss Bianca Robbins ran a prosperous brothel. Her death in a steamship accident in 1866 earned her a brief notoriety, and lists of people killed in the accident sometimes identified her by her profession. The Monroe, Louisiana, *Ouachita Telegraph* described her as "a woman who kept a fashionable Bagnio in New Orleans." She left an estate of $100,000.[31] Her death triggered an unseemly court case over control of her estate and the valuable jewels that went with it.[32]

Knowing that Bianca Robbins kept a brothel suddenly makes Spalding's fifty-seven-dollar expense account for the day more understandable. It also clarifies his jokes. Robbins may have been "a lady of northern parentage," but one now doubts whether Spalding's description of her as "friendly to the Union" concerned the North and the South as much as it did men and women. Spalding's line about his "close investigation into the theory of Spiritual rappings" prior to his departure for a party at Miss Burdell's now also requires a reinterpretation. Spiritualism, or spirit rapping, flourished in the mid-nineteenth century, and many people accepted the idea that the dead could communicate with the living through mediums and by producing noises in answer to stated questions. Spalding and Peck, however, probably had nothing to do with the people who believed this claim. Spiritualism shared a social and political circle with a host of other liberal reformers, including abolitionists, feminists, temperance advocates, vegetarians, and pacifists, all of whom Democrats held in contempt.[33] Spalding's line about closely investigating spirit rapping was meant to mock spiritualists, but more than that it served as a euphemism for sex. In this case, the knocking on the furniture that spiritualists would have heard was not from the dead, but from a prostitute and her client loudly fornicating upstairs. Spalding, in other words, told Peck he had left the "k" out of "cocktail" to let him know that modesty forced him to put the true account of his afternoon's affairs into a thinly veiled, humorous code that Peck could easily decipher.

After leaving Miss Robbins's brothel, Spalding went to Miss Burdell's for a "grand masquerade ball." Burdell cannot be firmly identified in the records. Spalding's description of her event, however, sounds like the masquerade balls staged with increasing frequency by well-capitalized urban brothels as the century progressed.[34] As Spalding described it, "the scene viewed with the naked eye was truly splendid. The quintessence of beauty in the City were collected together dressed in the various costumes of the last 19 centuries."[35] Spalding's suggestion that he and Peck should view the scene with "the naked eye" again points to a sexualized understanding of the event, and the name "Burdell" sounds like a possible personalized code for "Bordello." Other factors point to an economically developed form of prostitution that would have been familiar to some city-goers, but not to those in the countryside. Miss Burdell's fancy historical costumes and the expensive ten-dollar cover charge almost guarantee that this was no ordinary brothel or any kind of private party. The presence of so many military officers of different nationalities (US, British, and French officers are mentioned) also suggests that Miss Burdell invited men who were in the city temporarily, not her personal friends. That Spalding had "during the day" (perhaps at Miss Robbins's business?) "received a kind invitation to attend" that evening's festivities also suggests that men were invited on short notice. More to the point, it shows how readily Spalding navigated the city's commercialized recreation industry.

New Orleans has long held a reputation for relaxed moral codes of conduct, and the city earned this distinction in the middle decades of the nineteenth century. Both before and after the war, the city did little to police prostitution. Historian Judith Kelleher Schafer has concluded that "evidence abounds in the New Orleans newspapers and court records that prostitution in the city flourished virtually unchecked throughout the antebellum period."[36] The sex trade, in full swing as the war started, faced no opposition from the Butler administration once Union troops arrived. While the Union administrators of the city receive high marks in terms for their fair enforcement of laws in 1862, prostitution nevertheless continued unabated. One historian, who has found little evidence that the Union army actively curtailed the sex trade anywhere during the war, notes that Benjamin Butler did "little to control the brothels" in New Orleans.[37] Caring about prostitution would arguably be out of character for a Democratic politician-turned-soldier, and Butler seems to have allowed other matters to claim his attention during his administration. The *New Orleans Daily Picayune* wrote very shortly after Union troops arrived that "street-walking by abandoned women" had been noticed for the first time "of late."[38] Butler was not alone in allowing prostitution to flourish. Looking beyond New Orleans, historian Catherine Clinton has found a steady increase in prostitution during the war, citing evidence from Nashville, Richmond, and other places to make the case for a "boom in prostitution from 1861 to 1865."[39] In that sense, it matters little whether New Orleans was Union-controlled or its old antebellum self. Regardless of who controlled City Hall, Spalding would have had abundant opportunities to go into a brothel if he so desired. But would he have wanted to? Was brothel-going likely to have been part of his experience in Burlington and New York City, his home between his graduation from UVM in 1860 and his enlistment in the 7th New York State Militia in 1861?

Several factors point toward the likelihood that Spalding would have been familiar, and comfortable, with brothel culture by 1862. Spalding's youth, his status as a single man, his relative wealth, and his likely identification with the Democratic Party pointed him to the brothel life. Starting in the 1830s and 1840s, Democratic politicians in New York allowed prostitution to flourish. The party's newspapers, especially William Gordon Bennett's *New York Herald*, covered the sex trade with more fascination than disapproval. Starting with their exploitive and profitable coverage of the murder of well-known prostitute Helen Jewett in 1836, the *Herald* and other "penny papers" ran up large circulations with glamorized coverage of brothels and crime. The murder in 1841 of Mary Rogers, a second famous woman involved in sexualized advertising and illicit sexual relationships, only fueled an already raging fire.[40]

New Yorkers coined the term "sporting culture" to identify the boister-
ous male culture then on display on the city's streets. The young men living
in sporting culture favored outward expressions of masculinity, especially
sports ranging from horse racing to boxing. But they did more than try one
another's athletic prowess. Historian Amy Srebnick finds them involved
in both politics and prostitution. Politically, she sees the young men as a
merger of "older workingmen's politics with the newer club house politics
of Tammany Hall," which puts them firmly in the Democratic Party camp
by the 1840s. She also locates "their advocacy of prostitution and brothel
culture" as an important part of the construction of American masculinity.[41] Brothel culture involved paying for sex, but also included participation
in a world of men who attended brothels together, drank there, discussed individual prostitutes, and generally used brothels as social gathering places.
Visiting a brothel need not embarrass a man in this culture; rather, the trip
gained a young man admission into a group of like-minded men. Brothel-
going could be a social as well as a sexual enterprise, as much something to
be proud of as hidden. This openness was a distinctly urban phenomenon in
both the North and the South.

The surest proof that the sporting life could be boasted of comes from
the pages of the city's so-called flash press. With titles like *The Libertine*, *The Whip*, and the *Weekly Rake*, these illustrated newspapers covered
the brothel scene, using only the thinnest veneer of moral disapprobation
in an often-futile attempt to skirt the city's censorship laws. Circulations
soared, giving publishers ample reason to try to squeeze out issues despite
their legal difficulties. Similar papers sprang up in Philadelphia, Baltimore,
and Boston, while copies of these papers found their way throughout the
North via the mail.[42] In other words, people in New York and other northern cities in these years lived in a culture where sex could be discussed, and
bought, relatively openly; we should not imagine a strict Victorian taboo on
sexual topics during the antebellum decades.

The men of the sporting culture did not occupy the field alone, however.
They were part of what Helen Lefkowitz Horowitz calls a "lively, multivalent conversation about sex in their time."[43] Moral reformers, both men and
women, did what they could to curb prostitution, to help women to leave
the trade, and to embarrass men who visited brothels. The largest antiprostitution group, the Female Moral Reform Society, started in New York City
in 1836 and quickly spread to cities and towns throughout the North. The
FMRS's newspaper published the names of brothel clients in the hopes of
embarrassing men into cutting off their trade, but at least with the single

men in sporting culture that may not have been much of a deterrent.[44] By the 1850s, political parties in the North took sides on sexual issues, with Democrats supporting male sexual privileges and Republicans calling for greater self-restraint and a crackdown on illicit sex. All of this debate meant that when Spalding set foot in Gotham in 1860, he knew about prostitution and its ready availability. Visiting brothels would reinforce his identity as a Democrat, as a conservative on matters of male sexual privilege, and as a man. All he would lose by brothel-going was his money (and maybe his health). We see this literally shameless attitude in his letter, which lets Peck know exactly what he had done on Independence Day. He did not have to reveal that information at all, obviously, and the fact that he did so tells us about the freedom with which he and Peck could brag about their exploits with, and exploitation of, prostitutes.

Spalding and Peck may have, in fact, visited brothels together during their Burlington years, though this is undoubtedly only a guess. The main hint in this direction comes from the close of Spalding's letter, when he urges Peck to remember him to a host of other men that they must both have known. In the midst of this male world, Spalding writes, "If you go to Burlington please tell the young ladies of my acquaintance to hop up and bite without salt." The meaning of Spalding's phrase, "hop up and bite without salt," has unfortunately been lost over time. Two slang dictionaries published at the time do not include the phrase in any form.[45] The tone, however, does not appear genteel. Ladies of the period did not, as a rule, hop up and bite anything, even less so without the encouragement of salt. If Spalding and Peck knew women to whom they could give orders, as Spalding's sentence is grammatically, then what kinds of young ladies were they? While admittedly conjectural, speculation that Peck and Spalding shared a common history with prostitution would explain Spalding's willingness to discuss the subject, and his apparent assurance that Peck would both get the jokes and see the adventure in the same positive light in which Spalding saw it. If true, the common bond of brothel-going between the two men would have cemented their friendship and served as a basis for their shared sense of themselves as men.

Stephen Spalding, in other words, wanted to share his brothel experience with his former roommate, now absent. The adventure, arguably, improved with the sharing, creating a bond between the two men of greater permanence than that between Spalding and Bianca Robbins's employee. Nor was Spalding alone in writing such letters, even among the ranks of the 8th Vermont. Private William T. Church also wrote a comic letter to a friend, Ed, about his sexual exploitation of women in Louisiana. Only one letter of what must have been an exchange of at least three letters between William and Ed survives. In the first two, both now missing, William Church must have told Ed about the woman he had hired to do his laundry and how much he paid her. Ed, replying, seems to have asked him what services, exactly, he received for that pay, implying perhaps that the laundress also worked as a prostitute. Church's reply, which is extant, comically pretends to be shocked (shocked!) at the implications of Ed's letter. He then launches into a rant of over a page, in which he ridicules the Female Moral Reform Society for its antiprostitution efforts. Throughout his sarcastic digression he mocks those who oppose the sexual exploitation of female employees:

> Now Ed I have one very serious charge against you and that is being to inquisitive. when I consider the import of that question you proposed to me my mind becomes seriously affected: *What* inquire of me if my wash womman did anything more than to wash and mend for me: What why it beats all I ever heard in my mortal career. Now you know that I have all- ways ben a contribeter to the Ladies Moral Reform Society in Boston & New York and various other virtuous Societys. why Ed I have in my posession a large Silver *Medal* given to me by [small tear in the paper] [a com?]mitee of the different societies and inscribed on it a token of dis- respect for protecting those that their steps lead to *Hell*. if you wish for any more proofs of my virtuous abilities I refer you to Ben Graves, Hiram Coloney Now I hope that will be all that is nessary to convince you.[46]

Perhaps the most important word in Church's letter is "disrespect." He has been given a medal as "a token of disrespect for protecting those that their steps lead to *Hell*." Of course, the Female Moral Reform Society commit- tee would have honored his "respect" for prostitutes, not his disrespect of them. But for Church, as for Spalding, disrespecting prostitutes was all just part of the joke.

Another member of Spalding's regiment joked about male sexual privi- leges, daring to do so with his own wife. In October 1862 Deming Fairbanks wrote to Mary Spencer Fairbanks, his wife, about all of the "pretty darned nice looking gals" in Gretna, a town close to New Orleans. Would Mary have seen the humor of Deming's next thought, which was to tell her that these local beauties were "all after me as fast as blood hounds"? Perhaps it was a private joke, and she saw it as part and parcel of a friendly letter in which he also expressed his desire to send her "great nice oranges."[47] Or perhaps Deming Fairbanks let his wife know that the sexual license afforded to, and enjoyed by, other men in the 8th Vermont could carry over to him as well. Whether or not Mary was in on the joke or not, Deming's letter shows that men could boast about their opportunities for illicit sex whether they were married or not. Living when and where they did, the Vermonters knew that their rights as men included sexual freedom as well as the right to hard liquor.

What of the women involved? Then, as now, the degree to which an individual prostitute is victimized by masculine privilege varies. Historical studies of prostitution demonstrate a wide variety of backgrounds and experiences among women in the trade. Studies of antebellum New York City's commercialized sex industry emphasize the diversity of sex workers; women could work temporarily or make careers of it. They could be street-walkers or work in brothels. Some—really only a rare few—became famous and could chose for whom they would work. But historian Timothy Gilfoyle and others suggest that, for most prostitutes, their work was neither lucrative nor truly voluntary. The work was usually taken on as a last resort to destitution. As Gilfoyle concludes, "The major factor inducing young women to sell their bodies was the low wages for [other] female labor." Women faced with low pay and bouts of joblessness had few options when confronted with homelessness and starvation. Gilfoyle adds that "when work was slow or money slack, milliners, servants, and peddlers alike resorted to prostitution." Girls in their teens often worked in the industry.[48] Historian Christine Stansell sees the same dynamic frequently causing women to undertake sex work on a short-term basis. Drawing on William Sanger's survey of New York prostitutes done on the eve of the Civil War, Stansell finds that many women who sold their bodies lacked a male income in their household at a time when "women on their own earned such low wages that in order to survive, they often supplemented waged employment with casual prostitution." While she also finds other reasons for why women turned to prostitution, Stansell's picture of the sex trade is only marginally more empowering than Gilfoyle's.[49] Sexualized commerce, in other words, included a range of women, motivations, and situations. But most interpretations of antebellum and Civil War prostitution start with the exclusion of women from highly paid careers and the sweatshop wages paid for most women's work. For Stephen Spalding in New York and New Orleans, many of the women he would have found in brothels had very few options but to have sex with him.

Not all men lived and thought as Stephen Spalding, Daniel Foster, and William Church did. The most outspoken abolitionist in the 8th Vermont, Rufus Kinsley, can also serve as the regiment's unofficial spokesman for an evangelical, sentimental vision of women. Though he was vastly outnumbered in the 8th by those who lived by patriarchal rules of masculinity, Kinsley would have found more company in most other northern units.

Recuperating from a long illness, Kinsley wrote to a friend that when he was sick, "I lay and thought of my mother, and my Aunt Elvira, and a number of other mothers in Fletcher, and of some who are not mothers yet, but who hope to be by and by; and how ardently I wished I might fall into their hands, during sickness, at least, if not longer." Perhaps wondering if he had implied too much sexual desire, Kinsley added that "there is no care like mother-care; no love like mother-love, eh Charley?"[50] One suspects that many of his fellow soldiers in the Democratic 8th Vermont would have sought other kinds of love first.

Which brings us back to the fact that Stephen Spalding, like almost all white men in this period, experienced power and privileges that almost no women ever had the thrill of feeling. Some Republican-leaning men might refuse to abuse those powers, but Spalding and his fellow conservatives drank their way through New Orleans and Louisiana, perhaps enjoying that right even more frequently than they had in their hometowns. Spalding never seems to have doubted his right to enter a brothel and pay for sex. Finding a brothel and navigating its rules and cultures seemed easy for him, at least as he describes it, despite his being far from home. Spalding gives no evidence of having considered how the women involved in the transaction may have felt. His social power was to be exercised and, perhaps equally important, bragged about later in the interests of building a gender-based friendship with Jim Peck. Being a man involved not just honor or restraint, as some gender historians have hypothesized. Masculinity revolved around the practice of gaining sexual access to as many desirable women as one could pay for or cajole. The sex act itself, and the later sharing of one's conquests and adventures, proved a significant part of masculinity among the conservative Vermonters. New Orleans provided the 8th Vermont with alcohol, and Stephen Spalding and others with commercial sex. As such, southern cities need to be reconsidered as places of recreation, in which the people welcomed US dollars and opportunities for exchange. That exchange happened readily and comfortably, and speaks to a culture of masculinity shared by many people in both northern and southern cities.

. NOTES

1. Stephen Spalding to James Peck, July 8, 1862, Spalding Letter, Vermont Historical Society (hereafter cited as VtHS). For college educated volunteers as Union officers,

see Kanisorn Wongsrichanalai, "Leadership Class: College-Educated New Englanders in the Civil War," *Massachusetts Historical Review* 13 (2011): 67–96.

2. Over one-quarter of the population of New Orleans had been born in Ireland or the German states in 1860. At that time, the city's overall population was about 168,000. See Ella Lonn, *Foreigners in the Confederacy* (Chapel Hill: University of North Carolina Press, 1940), 417. For New Orleans compared to Philadelphia, see Dell Upton, *Another City: Urban Life and Urban Spaces in the New American Republic* (New Haven, CT: Yale University Press, 2008). Spalding himself wrote of Burlington's "French village" and would have been familiar with that city's range of poverty and comfort. For "French village," see Stephen Spalding to James Peck, July 8, 1862, Spalding Letter, VtHS.

3. For the history of southern cities behind Union lines, see especially Stephen V. Ash, *When the Yankees Came: Conflict and Chaos in the Occupied South, 1861–1865* (Chapel Hill: University of North Carolina Press, 1995), 76–92; Walter T. Durham, *Nashville, the Occupied City, 1862–1863* (1985; rpt., Knoxville: University of Tennessee Press, 2008); and Walter T. Durham, *Reluctant Partners: Nashville and the Union, July 1, 1863 to June 30, 1865* (1987; rpt., Knoxville: University of Tennessee Press, 2008).

4. Benjamin F. Butler, *Butler's Book: Autobiography and Personal Reminiscences of Major-General Benj. F. Butler* (Boston: A. M. Thayer, 1892), 294–336; George N. Carpenter, *History of the Eighth Regiment Vermont Volunteers, 1861–1865* (Boston: Deland and Barta, 1886), 1–16.

5. Norma Basch, "Marriage, Morals, and Politics in the Election of 1828," *Journal of American History* 80 (December 1993): 890–918; Catherine Allgor, *Parlor Politics: In Which the Ladies of Washington Help Build a City and a Government* (Charlottesville: University Press of Virginia, 2000), 147–246; Ronald J. Zboray and Mary Saracino Zboray, *Voices without Votes: Women and Politics in Antebellum New England* (Hanover, NH: University Press of New England, 2010), 1–162; Elizabeth R. Varon, *We Mean to Be Counted: White Women and Politics in Antebellum Virginia* (Chapel Hill: University of North Carolina Press, 1998), 71–102; Daniel Walker Howe, *What Hath God Wrought: The Transformation of America, 1815–1848* (New York: Oxford University Press, 2007), 605–9. During the early years of the Second Party System, radical northern Democrats sometimes prove to be an exception to this rule, as with their brief cooperation with feminist speaker Frances Wright.

6. For the Democratic Party's reaction to the women's rights movement in the aftermath of Seneca Falls, see Michael D. Pierson, *Free Hearts and Free Homes: Gender and American Antislavery Politics* (Chapel Hill: University of North Carolina Press, 2003), 97–114. Women stopped actively campaigning for candidates in Tennessee after 1848. See Jayne Crumpler DeFiore, " 'COME, and Bring the Ladies': Tennessee Women and the Politics of Opportunity during the Presidential Campaigns of 1840 and 1844," *Tennessee Historical Quarterly* 51 (Winter 1992): 197–212. For Seneca Falls, see Judith Wellman, *The Road to Seneca Falls: Elizabeth Cady Stanton and the First Woman's Rights Convention* (Urbana: University of Illinois Press, 2004); Sally G. McMillen, *Seneca Falls and the Origins of the Women's Rights Movement* (New York: Oxford University Press, 2008), 3–103.

7. The links between antislavery activism, which would eventually lead many northern-
    ers to Republican Party ranks, and unease about male sexual license have been well
    established. See, for example, Lewis Perry, *Childhood, Marriage, and Reform: Henry
    Clarke Wright, 1797–1870* (Chicago: University of Chicago Press, 1980); Ronald G.
    Walters, *The Antislavery Appeal: American Abolitionism after 1830* (Baltimore, MD:
    Johns Hopkins University Press, 1978), 70–87; Chris Dixon, *Perfecting the Fam-
    ily: Antislavery Marriage in Nineteenth-Century America* (Amherst: University of
    Massachusetts Press, 1997), 203–33; Stacey M. Robertson, *Parker Pillsbury: Radical
    Abolitionist, Male Feminist* (Ithaca, NY: Cornell University Press, 2000), 47–62; and
    Michael D. Pierson, "'Slavery Cannot Be Covered Up with Broadcloth or a Bandanna':
    The Evolution of Radical Abolitionist Gender Ideologies, 1830–1860," *Journal of
    the Early Republic* 25 (Fall 2005): 383–415. Nancy A. Hewitt has demonstrated that
    Democratic couples in Rochester, New York, had more children than Whig and Re-
    publican families, while abolitionist households had the fewest. See Nancy A. Hewitt,
    Women's Activism and Social Change: Rochester, New York, 1822–1872 (Ithaca, NY:
    Cornell University Press, 1984), 154, 156.
8. Whigs and Republicans tended to support temperance legislation, while Democrats
    opposed such laws. See, for example, Michael F. Holt, *The Rise and Fall of the
    American Whig Party* (New York: Oxford University Press, 1999); Bruce Laurie,
    Beyond Garrison: Antislavery and Social Reform (New York: Cambridge University
    Press, 2005), 62–63, 168–70, 225–30; John W. Quist, *Restless Visionaries: The Social
    Roots of Antebellum Reform in Alabama and Michigan* (Baton Rouge: Louisiana
    State University Press, 1998), 294–99; Eric Foner, *Free Soil, Free Labor, Free Men: The
    Ideology of the Republican Party before the Civil War* (New York: Oxford University
    Press, 1970), 237–42; and William E. Gienapp, *The Origins of the Republican Party,
    1852–1856* (New York: Oxford University Press, 1987), which argues for the central-
    ity of temperance legislation in the politics of the early 1850s.
9. Stephen Spalding to James Peck, July 8, 1862, Spalding Letter, VtHS.
10. Frank Towers, *The Urban South and the Coming of the Civil War* (Charlottesville:
    University Press of Virginia, 2004), 196–98; John D. Winters, *The Civil War in Loui-
    siana* (Baton Rouge: Louisiana State University Press, 1963), 3–13; Jefferson Davis
    Bragg, *Louisiana in the Confederacy* (Baton Rouge: Louisiana State University Press,
    1941), 1–33.
11. Jonathan Allen to Dear Sister, July 9, 1862, Allen Family Papers, VtHS; Justus F. Gale
    to Dear Brother, July 4, 1862, Gale-Morse Collection, VtHS. Ceremonies described in
    Letter to the Editor, dated July 5, 1862, in *New York Times*, July 21, 1862. The 1862
    ceremonies, organized by both local Unionists and Brig. Gen. George Shepley, the
    commander in New Orleans, exhibited none of the reservations found in some July 4
    celebrations in southern cities. See Paul Quigley, "Independence Day Dilemmas in
    the American South, 1848–1865," *Journal of Southern History* 75 (May 2009): 235–66.
12. Michael D. Pierson, *Mutiny at Fort Jackson: The Untold Story of the Fall of New
    Orleans* (Chapel Hill: University of North Carolina Press, 2008), 129–84.
13. Stephen Spalding's racial entitlement is considered in Michael D. Pierson, "The
    Meaning of a Union Soldier's Racial Joke," *Civil War History* 61, no. 1 (March 2015).

14. Michael Kimmel, *Manhood in America: A Cultural History* (New York: Free Press, 1996), 43–50; Charles E. Rosenberg, "Sexuality, Class and Role in Nineteenth-Century America," in *The American Man*, ed. Elizabeth H. Pleck and Joseph H. Pleck (Englewood Cliffs, NJ: Prentice-Hall, 1980), 223–29; E. Anthony Rotundo, "Learning about Manhood: Gender Ideals and the Middle-Class Family in Nineteenth-Century America," in *Manliness and Morality: Middle-Class Masculinity in Britain and America*, ed. J. A. Mangan and James Walvin (New York: St. Martin's Press, 1987), 35–51; On southern masculinity, see Lorri Glover, *Southern Sons: Becoming Men in the New Nation* (Baltimore, MD: Johns Hopkins University Press, 2010).

15. "Daniel S. Foster," Compiled Service Records, 8th Vermont Volunteers, National Archives and Records Administration. Foster was twenty-two when he joined the regiment on February 18, 1862. He had been elected first lieutenant immediately. He made captain in the summer of 1863 and was mustered out in June 1864.

16. *Burlington Weekly Sentinel*, February 7, 1862.

17. Judkin Browning, "'I Am Not So Patriotic as I Once Was': The Effects of Military Occupation on the Occupying Union Soldiers during the Civil War," *Civil War History* 55 (June 2009): 234.

18. Nina Silber and Mary Beth Sievens, eds., *Yankee Correspondence: Civil War Letters between New England Soldiers and the Home Front* (Charlottesville: University Press of Virginia, 1996), 99.

19. Moses McFarland, *Some Experiences of the Eighth Vermont West of the Mississippi* (Morrisville, VT: News and Citizen, 1896), first two quotations, 4, last quotation, 5.

20. Ibid., 8, 9.

21. Ibid., 17; last quotation, 18.

22. Nina Silber, *The Romance of Reunion: Northerners and the South, 1865–1900* (Chapel Hill: University of North Carolina Press, 1993), 159–96.

23. McFarland, *Some Experiences of the Eighth Vermont*, 7

24. Ibid., 8.

25. Ibid.

26. A judge from a nearby Connecticut regiment would later assert that every soldier he had convicted had been drunk. The 12th Connecticut Volunteers' court-martial happened across the Mississippi from Spalding's court at much the same time. John William De Forest, *A Volunteer's Adventures: A Union Captain's Record of the Civil War* (1946; rpt., Baton Rouge: Louisiana State University Press, 1996), 29–30.

27. General Order no. 13: court-martial transcript, dated July 25, 1862, Algiers, Louisiana. Eighth Vermont Regimental Books, vol. 3, National Archives and Records Administration.

28. Foote, *The Gentlemen and the Roughs*, on double standard, 37; on courts, 10–11.

29. Stephen Spalding to James Peck, July 8, 1862, Spalding Letter, VtHS.

30. On alcohol, see W. J. Rorabaugh, *The Alcoholic Republic: An American Tradition* (New York: Oxford University Press, 1979).

31. Monroe, Louisiana, *Ouachita Telegraph*, October 18, 1866; see also *New York Times*, October 9, 1866. The ill-fated ship was traveling from New York to New Orleans.

32. Case of Mrs. M. Johnson v. Succession of B. Robbins, in *Reports of Cases Argued and Determined in the Supreme Court of Louisiana, Volume XX, for the Year 1868*, ed. J. Hawkins (New Orleans: Caxton Press, 1868), 569–71.

33. Ann Braude, *Radical Spirits: Spiritualism and Women's Rights in Nineteenth-Century America* (Boston: Beacon Press, 1989).

34. Timothy J. Gilfoyle, *City of Eros: New York City, Prostitution, and the Commercialization of Sex, 1790–1920* (New York: W. W. Norton, 1992), 130, 232–34.

35. Stephen Spalding to James Peck, July 8, 1862, Spalding Letter, VtHS.

36. Judith Kelleher Schafer, *Brothels, Depravity, and Abandoned Women: Illegal Sex in Antebellum New Orleans* (Baton Rouge: Louisiana State University Press, 2009), especially 140–55, quotation on 155. For the postwar period, see Alecia P. Long, *The Great Southern Babylon: Sex, Race, and Respectability in New Orleans, 1865–1920* (Baton Rouge: Louisiana State University Press, 2004). See also Dell Upton, *Madaline: Love and Survival in Antebellum New Orleans* (Athens: University of Georgia Press, 1996).

37. Steven J. Ramold, *Baring the Iron Hand: Discipline in the Union Army* (DeKalb: Northern Illinois University Press, 2010), 79–80, 110–18, quotation on 118; Joy J. Jackson, "Keeping Law and Order in New Orleans under General Butler, 1862," *Louisiana History* 34, no. 1 (1993): 51–67.

38. *New Orleans Daily Picayune*, May 7, 1862.

39. Catherine Clinton, *Public Women and the Confederacy* (Milwaukee, WI: Marquette University Press, 1999), 9.

40. Patricia Cline Cohen, *The Murder of Helen Jewett* (New York: Vintage Books, 1998); Amy Gilman Srebnick, *The Mysterious Death of Mary Rogers: Sex and Culture in Nineteenth-Century New York* (New York: Oxford University Press, 1995); Daniel Stashower, *The Beautiful Cigar Girl: Mary Rogers, Edgar Allen Poe, and the Invention of Murder* (New York: Dutton, 2006).

41. Srebnick, *Mysterious Death of Mary Rogers*, 53. For sporting culture, see also Richard Stott, *Jolly Fellows: Male Milieus in Nineteenth-Century America* (Baltimore: Johns Hopkins University Press, 2009), 97–128, 214–24.

42. Patricia Cline Cohen, Timothy J. Gilfoyle, and Helen Lefkowitz Horowitz, *The Flash Press: Sporting Male Weeklies in 1840s New York* (Chicago: University of Chicago Press, 2008), 10, 23–25.

43. Helen Lefkowitz Horowitz, *Rereading Sex: Battles over Sexual Knowledge and Suppression in Nineteenth-Century America* (New York: Alfred A. Knopf, 2002), 11. For examples of this dialogue, see Helen Lefkowitz Horowitz, ed., *Attitudes toward Sex in Antebellum America: A Brief History with Documents* (Boston: Bedford/St. Martin's, 2006). See also Donna Dennis, *Licentious Gotham: Erotic Publishing and Its Prosecution in Nineteenth-Century New York* (Cambridge, MA: Harvard University Press, 2009).

44. Carroll Smith-Rosenberg, "Beauty the Beast and the Militant Woman," *American Quarterly* 23 (1971): 562–84; Daniel S. Wright, *The First of Causes to Our Sex: The Female Moral Reform Movement in the Antebellum Northeast, 1834–1848* (New York: Routledge, 2006).

45. George W. Matsell, *Vocabulum: or, the Rogue's Lexicon* (New York: George W. Matsell, 1859); and Ned Buntline, *The Mysteries and Miseries of New York: A Story of Real Life* (New York: Bedford, 1847), glossary on 113–16.

46. William T. Church to friend Ed, May 14, 1863, William T. Church Civil War Letters, Bailey-Howe Library, Special Collections, University of Vermont.

47. Deming Fairbanks to Mary Spencer Fairbanks, May 12, 1862, Deming Dexter Fairbanks Letters, VtHS.

48. Gilfoyle, *City of Eros*, 59, 60; for juvenile sex workers, see 63–70. For New York City prostitution, see also Marilyn Wood Hill, *Their Sisters' Keepers: Prostitution in New York City, 1830–1870* (Berkeley: University of California Press, 1993).

49. Christine Stansell, *City of Women: Sex and Class in New York, 1789–1860* (New York: Alfred A. Knopf, 1982), 176, 179.

50. Rufus Kinsley to Charlie Bingham, July 23, 1863, Rufus Kinsley Papers, VtHS.

CHAPTER SIX

"More like Amazons than starving people": Women's Urban Riots in Georgia in 1863

KEITH S. BOHANNON

The spring of 1863 was a time of unrest in cities across the Southern Confederacy. Over the course of several weeks in March and April, women in Richmond and Petersburg, Virginia; Salisbury, North Carolina; Mobile, Alabama; and Atlanta, Columbus, Milledgeville, Augusta, and Macon, Georgia, participated in "bread riots." These riots took place in cities that had undergone dramatic change in the first two years of the Civil War. In Georgia an influx of refugees from Union-occupied regions of the Upper South had filled cities with refugees. The growth of war industries had also drawn large numbers of rural women into urban centers seeking work. These women's employment in government clothing depots and textile mills provided locales where they could discuss shared grievances, learn about demonstrations taking place in other cities, and decide when and where to stage their own marches.[1]

When desperate and impoverished women living in cities and the surrounding countryside planned and executed demonstrations in March and April 1863, many did so with knowledge of urban streets, alleys, shops, and public buildings. As Darrett Rutman points out, the urban South in the late antebellum era did not stand apart from the countryside, but was "integral to the structure of this agriculturally based society." Farmers and their families traveled regularly into cities to buy and sell stock and make purchases of supplies. Englishman James S. Buckingham witnessed this firsthand when he visited Macon, Georgia, before the Civil War. "We saw many country people coming into town," noted Buckingham, "some on horseback, some in wagons, and some on foot."[2]

These country folks undoubtedly strolled through stores such as one in Milledgeville owned by Jacob Gans. While Gans offered items such as parasols and silks that only the planter class could likely afford, his newspaper advertisements reveal that he also carried brogans, osnaburg shirting, and striped homespun that could have been purchased by yeoman and possibly even poor white households. What then prompted dozens of women, some of them likely former customers, to storm into the store of Jacob Gans in the second week of April 1863 and plunder his shelves?[3]

Although it is likely impossible to determine the origins of animosity directed toward specific merchants like Gans, scholars such as Frank Byrne, Ted Ownby, and Jonathan Daniel Wells explore what Byrne terms "the Janus face" of the antebellum southern merchant. On the one hand, merchants contributed to community growth and prosperity. They were the linchpins, writes Darrett Rutman, "connecting the countryside with the larger national and international economy." At the same time, there existed a stereotype of merchants as greedy outsiders embracing "Yankee values" in an agrarian society.[4]

Under the pressures of war, the negative images of urban merchants, particularly those who were foreign-born, loomed even larger in people's consciousness. Five of the six known merchants targeted by women in Georgia's 1863 riots had been born outside the United States, four in German states and one in Ireland. At least two of the Germans were also Jewish, one of them being Jacob Gans. Even before the Civil War, Jewish store operators in the South had struggled with only partial success to throw off the venerable stereotype of being selfish and untrustworthy creditors.[5]

By the spring of 1863, the southern populace had started to view many established urban merchants as speculators, charging inflated prices for luxury items as well as necessities such as bread or cloth. This resulted in their being targeted by angry women. The stores of city shopkeepers such as Jacob Gans also probably had larger stocks than the fewer similar establishments located in smaller crossroads settlements or county seats. Some desperate rural women also undoubtedly hoped to remain anonymous while threatening and plundering the stores of urban merchants. The likelihood of being identified by authorities was less than it would have been if these women had targeted stores in closer proximity to their homes.

Historians in recent years have offered conflicting interpretations of what motivated female rioters to target merchants in southern cities in 1863. Drew Faust argues that women did so out of a belief in "the justness of pre-market values and the illegality . . . of the prices they now had to pay for life's necessities." The riots, Faust claimed, provided clear examples of what E. P. Thompson called "the moral economy of the crowd" challenging "the new political economy of the free market." Stephanie McCurry provides an alternate political reading of the riots, arguing that the demonstrations were a "highly public expression of soldiers' wives' mass politics of subsistence." Soldiers' wives, McCurry states, "helped transform the content and direction of social policy in the C.S.A." by successfully demanding that politicians expand public welfare. In the wake of the riots, McCurry claims that throughout the Confederacy "the response was the same: immediate public acknowledgement of the claims of social justice and legitimacy of the women's demands."[6]

McCurry further argues, as do David and Teresa Crisp Williams, that public officials in the Confederacy had been largely unwilling to address poverty prior to the 1863 riots. The Williamses claim, without offering substantive supporting evidence, that the women's riots in Georgia occurred in part because thousands of indigent women had begged for assistance from state government officials "to no avail." Measures taken by the state legislature in its fall 1862 and spring 1863 sessions, along with public and private statements by Georgia's governor, Joseph E. Brown, refute this argument. State government actions likewise partially challenge McCurry's claim that government welfare in Georgia was "a direct product of poor white women's mass politics and direct actions." Instead, the governor, legislators, city councils, and county officials were well aware of food and cloth shortages prior to the spring 1863 riots. Georgia's public officials had taken considerable measures to address the crisis before women took to the streets, even though these efforts and continued assistance following the riots did not meet fully the acute needs of struggling households across the Empire State of the South.[7]

Governor Brown's annual address in the November 1862 legislative session acknowledged the hardships encountered by soldiers' families. The wages of privates and noncommissioned officers, even if all sent home, afforded loved ones "a most meager subsistence at the present prices of provisions and clothing." Brown recommended that the legislature appropriate a bounty of $100 for each family or widow of a Georgia soldier whose property was worth less than $1,000 as measured by the most recent tax records. The whole net proceeds of the state-owned Western and Atlantic Railroad for the ensuing year, Brown proposed, should be appropriated to pay the bounty. Soldiers' families "should be supplied . . . at the public expenses," Brown exclaimed, "with such of the necessaries of life as their labor will not afford them, cost the State what it may."[8]

The Georgia legislature responded to Brown's request for aid to soldiers' families, as well as to petitions for increased relief received from city councils and county governments, by appropriating $2.5 million to support the indigent widows or families of Confederate soldiers. This was the largest-single appropriation in the state budget for 1862. Legislators requested county inferior courts to compile lists of needy households and forward them to the state comptroller general by February 1, 1863. While the comptroller general put together a master list of households, the legislature voted to provide immediate relief in the form of $400,000 to justices of inferior courts.[9]

Other laws also provided relief to needy families. Legislators appropriated $500,000 to purchase salt. The state outlawed distillation of alcohol in order to conserve corn and fruits. Last, the legislature provided $100,000 to procure machinery and materials to manufacture wool and cotton cards, the distribution of which would facilitate home production of textiles.[10]

On March 11, 1863, Governor Brown called on the state legislature to convene on March 25. This was earlier than it had been scheduled to start its regular session. In a private letter to Confederate vice president Alexander Stephens dated March 16, 1863, Brown justified convening the legislature early by claiming that it was vital "that we look to the production of provisions to the exclusion of everything else . . . our ultimate success depends on the bread supply."[11]

While Brown called for an early legislative session, Georgia comptroller general Peterson Thweatt started the process of providing relief funds to county inferior courts. By March 3, the state had advanced over $200,000 to counties that had applied for funds and Thweatt had permission from the governor to distribute more of the $2.5 million appropriation. Thweatt estimated that each beneficiary would receive "not quite $29.72," the equivalent of almost three months' pay for a private soldier, but an amount less than Brown had recommended in his 1862 annual address.[12]

Determining the impact an additional $29.72 would have on household budgets in the spring of 1863 is difficult, but prices in Augusta, Columbus, Atlanta, and Macon markets show bacon selling for between 85 cents and $1.25 a pound. Corn being sold from stores and wagons cost $2.25 to $3.00 a bushel, with the supply in Atlanta reported as light with "good demand." Since the average adult southerner consumed about thirteen bushels of corn and 138 pounds of pork a year, state assistance alone would not have sustained families with several children for more than a few months. Fortunately, many households also had wages from war work, soldiers' pay sent home, and assistance from relatives, friends, city officials, and charities.[13]

The unmet needs of struggling women resulted in the first of Georgia's urban riots taking place in Atlanta on March 18, 1863. Between twelve and twenty women targeted a store on Whitehall Street in one of the main commercial districts. Upon entering the business, the group's tall female "boss," "on whose countenance rested care and determination," asked the proprietor the price of bacon. When he replied that it was $1.10 a pound, the woman stated that "it was impossible for females in their condition to pay such prices for this necessity of life."[14]

A refusal by the merchant to lower his price resulted in the woman drawing from her bosom a "long navy repeater" and telling the other women to "help themselves to whatever they liked." After taking some $200 in goods, primarily bacon, the women departed. According to the *Atlanta Intelligencer*, the group of women then dispersed. The editor of the *Southern Confederacy* claimed that the women visited several stores, seizing not only bacon but also meal and vegetables. Police arrested the man who "planned, instigated, and perfected" the raid and he remained in jail several weeks after the riots.

Newspaper accounts of the Atlanta riot, some sympathetic and others hostile to the demonstrators, offer conflicting details of the women's motives and identities. The *Atlanta Intelligencer* editor claimed that the demonstrators were the "wives and daughters of soldiers' families" who had eaten nothing for several days except for "a portion of corn bread." Editor J. Henley Smith of the *Southern Confederacy* reported that there was but one soldier's wife in the crowd and three Atlanta residents. One of the three Atlanta women was apparently the group's tall leader, who the city marshal later claimed was the wife of a shoemaker who had not served in the army and earned "very high wages."[15]

The rest of the "very ignorant and wicked" women hailed from four surrounding counties. These women, Smith continued, were "all decently and some well dressed—wearing earbobs and breast-pins," had money, and worked "making clothes for the government." The presence of earbobs and breast pins suggests that these women had not always been poor and had probably entered into government work out of economic necessity. Demonstrators had money with them, claimed Smith, but "refused to give the common prices for the articles they wanted."[16]

Despite the hostile editor's claims that the rioting women had money, numerous sources attest to the impoverished condition of "needlewomen" who sewed uniforms for the Confederate and US governments. Judith Giesberg notes that sewing work was a "poorly paid and crowded field of labor" in northern cities, the wages often being inadequate to support households with children, especially when one considers inflation and shortages of necessities. Such was also the case in Georgia cities like Atlanta, where diarist Cyrena Stone encountered a woman who walked several miles into the city to get piecework, worried about the rising prices of meal and calico, and supposedly confessed that she wished the Yankees would arrive before her family starved to death.[17]

A week after the Atlanta riot, the Georgia state legislature met in Milledgeville. Governor Brown's message to the assembly emphasized the need to restrict further the amount of cotton that could be grown per hand and outlaw the distillation of grain. Brown pointed out how the enemy had overrun a large part of the most productive lands in the Confederacy, resulting in refugees from these regions moving behind southern lines and further taxing resources. Since so many of the white farm laborers in Georgia were in the army, "fields are left uncultivated," while the women and children must still be supported. Showing an awareness of the problems facing plain folk, Brown noted that "at the present prices of all the necessaries of life, it is impossible for the women and children to support themselves." The governor predicted that it would "take every acre of land, and every day's productive labor which we can command this year, to make our necessary support."[18]

Comptroller General Thweatt's report in the same legislative session revealed that by the end of March 1863, $869,137.50 had been distributed to county inferior courts of the $2.5 million appropriated to indigent soldiers' families in the previous legislative session. A table accompanying Thweatt's report shows that the total number of beneficiaries in Georgia's cities: 1,466 in Fulton County (Atlanta); 1,206 in Bibb County (Macon); 1,137 in Muscogee County (Columbus); 953 in Richmond County (Augusta); and 429 in Baldwin (Milledgeville). While these figures reflected only a portion of needy urban residents, they still represented a commitment on the part of the state to help the families of soldiers.[19]

In most cases, state aid supplemented ongoing efforts by businessmen, city councils, county governments, and private organizations to assist those in need. The Augusta Purveying Association, for example, had been founded in the fall of 1862 by Augusta's mayor and city council. As LeeAnn Whites points out, the Purveying Association regularized and standardized the "improvised and sporadic" assistance already offered by men of wealth to the city's poor women. By the spring of 1863 the association had identified and assisted many indigent families in the city, in part by opening a store where these households could purchase goods at reduced rates by presenting ration tickets. According to the editor of the *Augusta Chronicle and Sentinel*, a woman sent out in mid-April 1863 by the president of the Augusta Factory to identify those in need had found "but few who have not been relieved through the [Purveying] Association or some kindred agency."

Such efforts, notes William Blair in an examination of charity efforts in wartime Virginia, sent a message that elites understood the problems of less fortunate citizens and that antebellum paternalistic efforts to assist the poor would not cease.[20]

Governor Brown's correspondence with the legislature and others reveals state efforts in the spring of 1863 to produce cotton and wool cards. The state had at least eight machines for making cards set up in a factory connected with the state penitentiary in Milledgeville, but shortages of card components such as wire and leather had severely limited production. Despite such obstacles, Brown assured the state senate that he would do all in his power to increase production, being "fully sensible of the great importance of running our machines every day and increasing the number of machines as fast as possible."[21]

The governor's desire to provide families with cotton cards reveals an awareness of the increasing difficulties civilians had in acquiring cloth. All of the women's riots in the spring and summer of 1863 with the exception of the one in Atlanta involved the seizure of cloth, particularly calico. Calico, a printed fabric used for everything from dresses to shirting and linings, had been shipped to southern merchants from the North before the Civil War and became scarce in the Confederacy after the advent of hostilities. Rising prices of clothing by the spring of 1863 had caused "a great deal of anxiety and excitement among the masses," noted a Macon newspaper editor, with calico selling for $2.50 and $3 a yard. Other types of cloth, including sheeting, shirting and osnaburgs, sold for between $1.00 to $1.45 a yard, with prices in Augusta markets described as stiff and supplies as scarce. Jeans, a cloth made of cotton and wool, sold in Augusta for $4.00 to $5.00 a yard.

Women who turned to household production of textiles still needed yarn. In the Augusta, Columbus, and Atlanta markets, cotton yarn sold for between $9.00 and $15.00 a bunch, a price many households could not pay. When cotton factories in Newton County outside Atlanta had yarn available to the public, the rush of rich and poor women from miles around was "immense and painful to behold." The factory proprietors appeared "anxious to accommodate all," noted an observer, either giving away yarn or selling it at $5.00 a bunch.[22]

On April 1, 1863, a small group of women in Macon, some armed with revolvers and bowie knives, entered a dry goods store on Second Street operated by Bavarian-born, twenty-nine-year-old merchant Edward Rosenwald and his brother. When the women forcibly took several bolts of calico, the proprietor rushed upon one of them with a bowie knife, recapturing two out of three pieces of goods. Although a Macon newspaper editor claimed the incident was "quite exciting for the time it was in progress," the women shortly thereafter scattered and "usual quiet . . . resumed."[23]

Nine days after the riot in Macon, women living in the countryside around the Georgia state capital of Milledgeville gathered in the city, some on foot and some with carts. Onlookers heard the ladies announce that "they had come to supply their wants" as they were "suffering and must have provisions & clothes." Around 11 a.m. about seventy-five women, numbers of them carrying pistols, descended upon the "fancy" dry goods store of Jacob Gans, a thirty-eight-year-old, Prussian-born, Jewish merchant. Marching into the store in double file, the women helped themselves to muslins, calicos, silks, ribbons, parasols, handkerchiefs, cotton thread, "& anything else." A frightened Gans tried to appease the women by giving them "a bale of yarns he had on hand, and then let other merchants give them something also." Another report says Gans offered "several shoes" to the women. The offerings had little effect and the women continued emptying the store.

After departing Gans's Store, the women headed toward the business of locally prominent, German-born, Jewish merchants Leopold and Solomon Waitzfelder. In addition to their own business, the Waitzfelders had connections with the Milledgeville Manufacturing Company, a producer of woolen cloth for Confederate uniforms. The Waitzfelders had bundles of cotton yarn that the rioting women hoped to take. At this point the crowd encountered Judge Iverson L. Harris of the Baldwin County Superior Court. Harris appealed to the women to desist, promising that their needs would be met, but denouncing those who had instigated the outbreak. Members of the Georgia House of Representatives, which had adjourned in the nearby capital building and witnessed the demonstrations, were undoubtedly fearful of what course the demonstration might take. These public servants and other male bystanders took up a subscription of some $2,000 to furnish the needy women with goods.[24]

State government officials, finding city authorities "either unable or indisposed" to disperse the crowd, sent the state penitentiary guards into the streets "with unequivocal orders" to quell the women's "lawless proceedings at any cost." Given that the penitentiary was only a few blocks from Milledgeville's small business district, it likely took only minutes for the guards to arrive at the demonstration. Governor Brown, informed of the riot by an inferior court judge, also instructed Adjutant General Henry C. Wayne to order the local militia regiment commander to muster his men, drawing arms and ammunition from the state arsenal. The presence of the penitentiary guards and probably the militia, combined perhaps with the speech of Judge Harris, resulted in the crowd dispersing. While some rioters returned plunder to Jacob Gans, others carried off their booty.[25]

Ebenezer Fain, a member of the state legislature, related some of the protestors' comments in a letter to his daughter. Fain found it distressing to hear the women explain how their husbands were "poor men in the army fiting for their property & their liberty." The ladies contrasted their husbands with heartless merchants enriching themselves at the expense of poor families and bragging that soldiers "fight better & do better on half rations." If the women's wants were not met, they claimed, their soldier husbands "would not lay down their arms & come home but would come with gun in hand & their would be more blood shed than was at Bunker Hill." While acknowledging the dual loyalties of their soldier husbands as protectors of the nation and family, these women warned of possible violence at home (directed against merchants?) if husbands deserted and returned to fulfill familial obligations.[26]

Speculating merchants, the women claimed, "could go to the legislature & call on them for pay for searvants that have died while working on the public works but would not propose paying widows anything whose husbands have died or fallen." The women were wrong about the legislature not providing relief for soldiers' widows, although county governments might not have started distributing aid in the weeks immediately prior to the riot. Rioters' anger over legislative attempts to reimburse slave owners for servants who died while laboring on public works undoubtedly referred to a suggestion made in Governor Brown's March 25, 1863, message to the legislature. Georgia's government had impressed hundreds of slaves to construct fortifications around Savannah and Brown believed that the state should compensate owners of "negroes who have died in service." State senators responded by introducing a bill to provide compensation for such losses, but the acts of this legislative session suggest it did not pass.[27]

The rioters' comments to legislators suggest that the Milledgeville demonstration was a political event as well as an attempt to plunder businesses. Some women had clearly followed the proceedings of the state legislature and possibly planned their demonstration to coincide with the legislative session. At least a few of the women had assumed what Stephanie McCurry calls a "new, war-born political identity." Like the northern women described by Judith Giesberg who sought aid from the state, the women in Milledgeville "understood relief as a debt that was owed them when they were denied their husband's support."[28]

Newspaper accounts of the Milledgeville riot failed to describe the women as soldiers' wives and left out, perhaps on purpose, the elements of class tension and threats of soldier desertion present in Fain's account. Instead, the papers claimed that the women had been motivated by "a spirit of revenge" against "a Jew who had made himself obnoxious." Jews, another editor claimed, "as a class, are more or less under public ban," hence Jacob Gans had been selected as the women's target. While the rioting women and general population harbored anti-Semitic sentiments, the looting of stores did not result in an exodus of Jewish merchants from the state capital. Gans and the Waitzfelders remained in business in Milledgeville at least through the end of the Civil War, the Waitzfelder brothers having close ties to the governor and other local and state leaders. This situation reinforces Mark Greenberg's argument that "the scapegoating of Jews in the Southern mind was tempered, even at the height of wartime tension and anxiety, by the recognition . . . that Jewish merchants played an essential role in economic life" in cities and small towns.[29]

While breaking up the Milledgeville demonstration, officials arrested three women and two men. These five individuals, a correspondent claimed, were "enemies of social order and the government," having "easily duped" the "ignorant and rude" creatures in the crowd into acts of lawlessness. The ringleaders appeared before a grand jury during the August 1863 term of the Baldwin County Superior Court. The grand jury found the state's evidence against the accused compelling, returning a true bill that endorsed the state's bill of indictment and opened the way for a trial by jury.[30]

The five people arrested in connection with the riot might not be representative of the mob as a whole, but the residences of two of them reinforce newspaper assertions that the crowd included people from rural counties adjacent to Milledgeville. Mary Ward was a thirty-four- or thirty-five-year-old wife of Jones County farmer John W. Ward and mother of seven children. David Milton Beck was a forty-seven-year-old farmer in Wilkinson County with a wife and at least five children.[31]

The other three individuals charged with inciting the crowd were all from Baldwin County, where Milledgeville is located. They include siblings William W. Boutwell and America Dennis, both Milledgeville residents. William W. Boutwell appears in the 1860 census as a thirty-year-old peddler with $420 in personal and real estate. America Dennis was the twenty-five-year-old wife of carpenter William L. Dennis. The Dennises, who had three children and owned $100 in personal estate, were living in the household of America's father. Eliza Moran, the final person arrested, was probably a thirty-three-year-old Milledgeville widow with four children under the age of ten.[32]

Baldwin Superior Court records do not indicate the ultimate disposition of the cases against Boutwell and Beck. Beck's presence in Wilkinson County in an 1864 militia census suggests that his case had been dropped by then. The cases of the three women apparently languished until the August 1864 term of the superior court, when the prosecutor indicated he would no longer pursue the charges against them.[33]

The same day as the Milledgeville riot, a small number of women assembled in the upper part of Augusta. They proceeded to the store of Julius Reinhart, a Prussian-born merchant, asking him "if he had shoes for a dollar a pair, and calico at fifty cents per yard, as those were the prices they intended to pay." Reinhart, worried that violence might ensue, "recollected that he had pressing business at one of the banks." He hastily locked the doors of his business and left.

Next the women visited a grocery store near the Upper Market operated by Irish-born Edward Gallaher. While Gallaher made "some show of resistance," the mayor and two policemen arrived and the crowd dispersed in every direction. Before scattering, a bystander asked one of the women why they had demonstrated. "We heard that they had raised the red flag all over the country," the woman replied, "and people only had to go and take what they wanted." Although the editor of the *Augusta Constitutionalist* claimed not to understand the reference to a red flag, it likely suggested a declaration of war against speculating merchants. The police arrested one individual in connection with the riot, a man who had told the women "they did perfectly right." The editor of the *Augusta Chronicle and Sentinel* claimed that there had been only a single soldier's wife in the party, while the *Augusta Constitutionalist* editor said that several of the women were not citizens of Augusta.[34]

The final urban demonstration in Georgia that spring occurred in Columbus. Early on the morning of April 11, approximately sixty-five women from Columbus and the town of Girard, Alabama, located directly across the Chattahoochee River, congregated on the western end of the upper bridge over the Chattahoochee and "organized themselves into a seizing party." After "choosing a Captain and Lieutenants," the women crossed the bridge into Columbus and turned down Broad Street. Some of the women, armed with pistols, knives, shovels and axes, were "cursing . . . and threatening what they intended to do in case the 'speculators' or merchants refused to grant their reasonable requests." Upon arriving at a dry-goods store specializing in women's dress goods operated by an established and respected merchant named George A. Norris, the women entered and helped themselves to the stock. A man identified in the *Columbus Sun* as a "graceless vagabond" named Shanghai Brooks stood outside the store "encouraging the Amazons in their seizures."[35]

Mayor F. G. Wilkins arrived and spoke to the women, who dispersed after hearing him order the police to arrest any woman who didn't "behave herself," presumably meaning that the women needed to stop brandishing weapons and stealing and go home. As the women left, police arrested and put in jail two men, William E. Brooks and Adoniram Williams. Williams, a thirty-three-year-old illiterate harness-maker born in Georgia but living in Girard, Alabama, was married with several children. Brooks, a Massachusetts-born farmer and merchant born in 1800, was hardly a vagabond, as the editor of the *Sun* described him. Brooks had moved to Columbus in 1840, where he had served at various times as a city marshal, alderman, and health officer. Former Columbus mayor John G. Winter, who had been an antebellum business partner of Brooks, described the Massachusetts native in an 1864 list of Columbus Unionists as a "true friend of the Union."[36]

When the Muscogee County Superior Court met a few weeks after the arrest of Brooks and Williams, a grand jury returned a decision in their case of "no bill," indicating that it would not proceed to trial. Unfortunately the reasons for this decision are not in the court records. In the case of Brooks, previous involvement in city government and the likelihood that he didn't participate in the looting might have spared him a trial.[37]

The three known demonstrations outside of cities by Georgia women in the spring and summer of 1863 were similar in several respects. Two of the events involved armed groups of women, one gang accompanied by a man with a shotgun, seizing bolts of cloth from wagons traveling from mills to towns located on railroads. The only occupants of the ambushed wagons were African American drivers, one described as a "trusty old negro" named Jim who offered no resistance. Jim claimed to recognize a number of the women who stopped his wagon between the Seven Islands Factory in Butts County and the town of Forsyth. He also supposedly opined that few of these women could plead "poverty or necessity" as they were generally able to clothe themselves.[38]

The rural sites of these ambushes possibly emboldened the women as there would have been few if any eyewitnesses and little risk of being arrested by law enforcement officials. The women might also have assumed that older slaves like "Jim" would not have offered much if any resistance to the seizures. City merchants, on the other hand, were more likely to be armed and confrontational, as was the case in several of the urban riots.

Another rural riot involved twelve women in Pickens County raiding a tanyard in August 1863, helping themselves to "as much leather as they could well carry off." Unlike the Milledgeville protestors, who displayed conditional loyalties to the Confederacy, the Pickens women were staunch Unionists, a situation not unusual in their mountainous region. The women in Pickens told tanyard employees that they "longed to see the day when the Yankee army would take possession of this country." Two of the women had husbands at home who had been there since the start of the war.[39]

The 1863 women's riots in urban and rural Georgia reveal a willingness on the part of some poor and desperate women to challenge traditional gender expectations. By publicly brandishing weapons, marching through city streets, entering stores to threaten male merchants, ransacking shelves, and demanding that state legislators respond to their needs, women not only broke laws and disturbed the peace. They also "unsexed themselves," in the words of one angry newspaper editor, or, as another editor exclaimed, engaged in "unladylike demonstrations." The mob actions unleashed a torrent of abuse from several of the state's newspaper editors, who denounced the rioters as "viragos" and "amazons," as well as "prostitutes, professional thieves, and jail birds hailing from different sections of the country." The editor of the *Central Georgian* claimed that if a few lawbreakers received severe punishment, "we should hear no more of such conduct." The remedy for the rising of women, suggested another editor, was "the vigorous application of the Hydropathic principle from the noozle of a Fire Engine."[40]

Hostile editors also claimed that the unruly women were well dressed and well fed. Most rioters robbed stores not of foodstuffs, but finery. Denying that women had the ability to plan and carry out such raids, the editors claimed that they had been incited by male Unionists, "mischief makers," and "loafers and vagrants" to "give a stab at the vitals of our government and society." Captain George S. Jones, stationed in Virginia, agreed with the editors, claiming that it was generally thought the women who were "playing the devil in Macon, Augusta, Atlanta and Georgia" had been motivated by "Northern emissaries in our midst" hoping to "injure our cause at home and abroad."[41]

Some civilians and soldiers expressed sympathy for the rioting women. Daniel W. Snell, a soldier in Virginia, wrote his wife that he was not surprised by news of the riots in Columbus and Augusta. "What will become of the women and children with the food situation . . . if they cannot get it one way, then another." Huldah Fain said that the "patriotic ladies" who had staged the demonstration in Milledgeville "are right if they realy are suffering." Fain didn't believe in government impressment, but if there is suffering then "take if it is to be had." The editor of the Macon *Confederate* implored authorities to supply food and clothing to destitute women who could not find "employment that will yield sufficient remuneration."[42]

"A citizen," writing in response to one of the rural seizures of cloth, said that "anarchy and disorder" should not be blamed on the "poor, unclad women of Monroe County." The writer instead criticized the cotton factories that practiced extortion by pocketing "500 and 1,000 per cent profits" in the sale of cards and the railroads that failed to protect freight from being plundered. "There is a point when not only unclad women, but the good and virtuous will rise up," warned the citizen, "and arrest your nefarious practices."[43]

An Upson County soldier encamped outside Savannah pointed to the difficulty of controlling extortion through legislation. He gave the example of a cotton manufacturer selling yarn at a reasonable price to a man who then sold the same yarn for the inflated price of $8.00 to $10.00 a bunch. This soldier even charged the rioters with extortion, making the unlikely but possible claim that some women had taken the goods given them by nervous proprietors and turned around to sell them "for large profits."[44]

Several newspaper editors claimed that the rioters were only emulating the examples set by Governor Brown and the Jefferson Davis administration in implementing policies of impressment. Is it any wonder, asked the *Southern Confederacy* editor, that the "ignorant and vicious" would follow the "lawless example of the Governor of this State and the Secretary of War of the Confederate States"? The editor of the *Columbus Weekly Sun* said that the women's actions were "some of the legitimate fruits of what Gov. Brown is pleased to call 'impressments' for the benefit of the people," citing as an example the state's seizure of salt.[45]

Civilians who watched urban riots, as well as city and state leaders, reacted in various ways to the demonstrations. Male bystanders witnessing the Atlanta and Milledgeville riots, looking to uphold in public their role as protectors of the fairer sex and probably provide examples of Christian benevolence, took up immediate subscriptions to assist needy women. Some of the Atlanta witnesses, described by the *Atlanta Intelligencer* editor as "gentlemen of moderate means with families," asked the rioting women "what they meant" by their actions. The women responded by describing their suffering condition. The bystanders subsequently formed a committee composed of three men who worked in Atlanta's Government Clothing Depot to disburse the collected funds. The committee subsequently gave the money to the editor of the *Intelligencer* to distribute to needy women and encourage others to contribute.[46]

Five days after the Milledgeville riot, the state legislature authorized the governor to take a portion of the money set aside at the previous legislative session for indigent families and use it to purchase yarn from various factories in the state. The legislature added that the factories should furnish the yarn to the state "at supply, not speculative prices." This yarn would then be turned over to inferior courts for distribution to families of destitute soldiers. While the abortive efforts of the rioting women in Milledgeville to seize yarn might have influenced the legislators in making this decision, the lawmakers were also responding to a situation that had been a source of anxiety for many months.[47]

Local leaders in several cities, including Atlanta, Savannah, Columbus, and Milledgeville, also established stores in late March and early April 1863 specifically to benefit the poor and maintain social stability. A meeting held in the city council chamber of Milledgeville on the day before the riot took place there suggested the establishment of an association to raise money to purchase "the necessaries of life at the lowest possible price" and then sell them to the poor "at such prices as will barely cover costs and expenses." In Savannah banks loaned $50,000 without interest as trading capital for a similar endeavor, while other cities financed stores by individual subscriptions and donations. The Columbus Relief Association, whose store commenced business on April 25, 1863, had as its object "to buy provisions, and sell them at cost to the families of absent soldiers and others whose means are not sufficient to enable them to pay war prices." Industrial laborers in Columbus, who also suffered from the inability to buy provisions at inflated prices, could provide for their families by trading at this store.[48]

The establishment by city governments of stores for the poor shows that not only poor women believed in a "just price" for necessities, at least in the midst of a war. Such actions suggest that while rioting women hoped to force their moral economy on unwilling merchants with threats, urban leaders instead tried to create sources for necessities other than private businessmen. At the same time, the willingness of rioting women in several cities to explain their motives to bystanders, including members of the state legislature in Milledgeville, suggests that Stephanie McCurry is partially right in describing women as political actors.

While scattered acts of lawlessness perpetrated by women continued in Georgia for the rest of the Civil War, the state's cities did not again experience multiple riots in a short span of time as happened in the spring of 1863. There are likely numerous reasons for this. Many women surely knew that city officials and police would arrive quickly on the scene of a disturbance, given the small size of urban business districts. Women also likely feared being arrested, given that police, mayors, and judges had resorted to this measure or threatened it during at least four of the five riots. The increased presence of Confederate provost marshals and soldiers in cities by 1864 also likely dissuaded further demonstrations.[49]

Finally, some women might have been discouraged in part from further demonstrations by continuing and increased assistance from city councils, county and state governments, and private businesses and associations. In Columbus, as was probably the case in other urban centers, the city council expended more money on indigent relief than anything else, eventually exhausting the city's treasury by the winter of 1864–65. The editor of the *Macon Journal and Messenger* noted in January 1864 that had it not been for the efforts of the city council, "our poor would have suffered immensely." Total state spending on civilian welfare in the final two years of the Civil War amounted to only "slightly less than aggregate wartime military expenditures," claims Peter Wallenstein.

Many Georgia citizens in the two years following the women's riots undoubtedly felt what Paul Escott argues in an essay on poverty in the Confederacy. Governor Joseph E. Brown "sensed what people were feeling," writes Escott, and responded to their problems, attacking poverty with "speed and vigor." Even though life remained extremely difficult in many wartime households and relief often provided a bare subsistence, state, county and city efforts to provide corn, cotton cards, cloth and thread demonstrated to civilians that public officials were aware of their needs and attempting to address them.[50]

<hr />

NOTES

The author thanks the following individuals for assistance with this chapter: Nancy Bray, Angie and Myers Brown, Lee Ann Caldwell, Ken Denney, Elizabeth Dunn, J. Matt Gallman, Mark I. Greenberg, Kristen Griffin, Hugh Harrington, Phil Hatcher, Keith Hebert, Caroline Janney, Gordon Jones, Eileen McAdams, James Ogden III, Tim Schroer, Andrew Slap, Ken H. Thomas Jr., Frank Towers, and Rosemary Turner.

1. On riots outside of Georgia, see Christopher A. Graham, "Women's Revolt in Rowan County," *Columbiad* 3, no. 1 (Spring 1999): 131–37; Harriet E. Amos, "'All-Absorbing Topics': Food and Clothing in Confederate Mobile," *Atlanta Historical Journal* 22, nos. 3–4 (Fall–Winter 1978): 17–28; Michael B. Chesson, "Harlots or Heroines? A New Look at the Richmond Bread Riot," *Virginia Magazine of History and Biography* 92, no. 2 (April 1984): 131–75; George C. Rable, *Civil Wars: Women and the Crisis of Southern Nationalism* (Urbana: University of Illinois Press, 1989), 108–

11; Drew G. Faust, *The Creation of Confederate Nationalism: Ideology and Identity in the Civil War South* (Baton Rouge: Louisiana State University Press, 1988), 52–54; Frank J. Byrne, *Becoming Bourgeois: Merchant Culture in the South, 1820–1865* (Lexington: University Press of Kentucky, 2006), 188; E. P. Thompson, "The Moral Economy of the English Crowd in the Eighteenth Century," *Past and Present* 50 (February 1971): 78–79; E. Merton Coulter, *The Confederate States of America, 1861–1865* (Baton Rouge: Louisiana State University Press, 1950), 424.

2. Darrett B. Rutman and Anita H. Rutman, *Small Worlds, Large Questions: Explorations in Early American Social History, 1600–1850* (Charlottesville: University Press of Virginia, 1994), 233; James S. Buckingham, *The Slave States of America* (London: Fisher, Son and Co., 1842), 1:210.

3. "Georgia Made Black, Russetts . . . ," *Milledgeville Confederate Union*, December 2, 1862.

4. Byrne, *Becoming Bourgeois*, 65–69; Ted Ownby, *American Dreams in Mississippi: Consumers, Poverty, and Culture, 1830–1998* (Chapel Hill: University of North Carolina Press, 1999), 19–24; Jonathan Daniel Wells, *The Origins of the Southern Middle Class, 1800–1861* (Chapel Hill: University of North Carolina Press, 2004), 204–5; Rutman and Rutman, *Small Worlds, Large Questions*, 255.

5. Ownby, *American Dreams in Mississippi*, 23–24.

6. "Crinolin Imitations of the Habits of Certain Officials," *Atlanta Southern Confederacy*, March 19, 1863; "More of Joe Brown's Work," *Columbus Weekly Sun*, April 21, 1863; Faust, *Creation of Confederate Nationalism*, 52; Stephanie McCurry, *Confederate Reckoning: Power and Politics in the Civil War South* (Cambridge, MA: Harvard University Press, 2010), 179, 4, 135, 169, 192.

7. Teresa Crisp Williams and David Williams, " 'The Women Rising': Cotton, Class, and Confederate Georgia's Rioting Women," *Georgia Historical Quarterly* 86, no. 1 (Spring 2002): 59; McCurry, *Confederate Reckoning*, 192; Diffee W. Standard, *Columbus, Georgia, in the Confederacy* (New York: The William Frederick Press, 1954), 48.

8. Brown justified increasing freight rates on the Western and Atlantic to pay for the bounty by claiming that a large part of the freight is owned by "speculators of this and other States, who, if their commodities were shipped for nothing, would still charge the highest prices for all they sell." Allen D. Candler, ed., *The Confederate Records of the State of Georgia*, 3 vols. (Atlanta: Charles P. Byrd, State Printer, 1910), 2:263–64.

9. The Inferior Court of Fulton County, where Atlanta is located, began placing notices in newspapers in the first week of January 1863 requesting that women entitled to benefits register in person for them at a store on Decatur Street. These notices continued to appear throughout the month of January. *Acts of the General Assembly of the State of Georgia . . . at an Annual Session in November and December 1862; also Extra Session of 1863* (Milledgeville, GA: Boughton, Nisbet & Barnes, State Printers, 1863), 13, 49; "To The Soldiers' Families of Fulton County," *Atlanta Southern Confederacy*, January 14, 1863.

10. *Acts of the General Assembly . . . at an Annual Session in November and December 1862*, 6, 8, 25–26.

11. Over the course of several weeks in late February and early March 1863, the governor

opened corn cribs and barns on his plantation near Canton to distribute surplus corn
to needy families in Cherokee County. "Governor Brown at His Farm," *Augusta
Chronicle and Sentinel*, March 4, 1863; "Governor Brown's Donations to Soldiers'
Families," *Milledgeville Confederate Union*, March 3, 1863; Candler, ed., *Confederate Records of the State of Georgia*, 2:366; U. B. Phillips, ed., *The Correspondence of
Robert Toombs, Alexander H. Stephens, and Howell Cobb* (Washington DC: American Historical Association, 1913), 614.

12. Peterson Thweatt to Alexander H. Stephens, Milledgeville, GA, March 3, 1863, Alexander H. Stephens Papers, vols. 31–32, General Correspondence, Library of Congress.

13. On the networks of support and survival strategies utilized by poor northern women,
see Judith Giesberg, *Army at Home: Women and the Civil War on the Northern
Home Front* (Chapel Hill: University of North Carolina Press, 2009), 29; "Augusta
Market," *Augusta Chronicle and Sentinel*, March 25, 1863; "Columbus Market" and
"Macon Market," *Augusta Chronicle and Sentinel*, April 23, 1863; "Atlanta Mar-
ket," *Augusta Chronicle*, May 26, 1863; "Augusta Prices Current," *Augusta Daily
Constitutionalist*, May 13, 1863; "Atlanta Market," *Augusta Daily Constitutionalist*,
April 15, 1863; "Columbus—April 27," *Augusta Daily Constitutionalist*, April 29,
1863; Sam B. Hilliard, *Hog Meat and Hoecake: Food Supply in the Old South, 1840–
1860* (Carbondale: Southern Illinois University Press, 1972), 105, 157.

14. "Relieve the Distressed," *Macon Journal and Messenger*, March 25, 1863 (citing
the March 19, 1863, issue of the *Atlanta Intelligencer*). For evidence that distribution of state aid had started in Atlanta prior to the riot, see "The Needy Women of
Atlanta," *Atlanta Southern Confederacy*, March 25, 1863.

15. Unfortunately, the *Confederacy*'s editor failed to give the arrested man's name and
it does not appear in the Fulton County court records. "Relieve the Distressed";
"Crinolin Imitations of the Habits of Certain Officials"; "Needy Women of
Atlanta,"; "Rioting Women," *Atlanta Southern Confederacy*, April 16, 1863.

16. Major George W. Cunningham, in charge of the Confederate Clothing Depot in
Atlanta, said that the several thousand employees sewing uniforms for him were
"women whose male supporters are absent with the army." "Relieve the Distressed";
"Crinolin Imitations of the Habits of Certain Officials"; "Rioting Women"; US War
Department, *The War of the Rebellion: A Compilation of the Official Records of the
Union and Confederate Armies*, 127 vols., index, and atlas (Washington, DC: Gov-
ernment Printing Office, 1880–1901) ser. 1, vol. 23, pt. 2, 767.

17. Giesberg, *Army at Home*, 120; Thomas G. Dyer, ed., *Secret Yankees: The Union
Circle in Confederate Atlanta* (Baltimore, MD: Johns Hopkins University Press,
1999), 286–87.

18. Candler, ed., *Confederate Records of the State of Georgia*, 2:367–70.

19. Ibid., 2:399–406; Standard, *Columbus, Georgia, in the Confederacy*, 35.

20. "Praiseworthy Liberality," *Augusta Chronicle and Sentinel*, April 17, 1863; LeeAnn
Whites, *The Civil War as a Crisis in Gender: Augusta, Georgia, 1860–1890* (Athens:
University of Georgia Press, 2000), 78; Florence F. Corley, *Confederate City: Augusta,
Georgia, 1860–1865* (Columbia: University of South Carolina Press, 1960), 72; Wil-
liam Blair, *Virginia's Private War: Feeding Body and Soul in the Confederacy, 1861–
1865* (New York: Oxford University Press, 1998), 76.

21. Candler, ed., *Confederate Records of the State of Georgia*, 2:395–97; Joseph E. Brown to H. J. Johnson, May 15, 1863, Joseph E. Brown Papers, Ms. 95, Georgia Special Collections, University of Georgia, Athens.

22. "Editorial Correspondence," *Macon Journal and Messenger*, April 22, 1863; "Augusta Market"; "Columbus Market"; "Augusta Prices Current"; "Calico vs. Homespun," *Savannah Morning News*," March 27, 1863.

23. "Unauthorized Seizures," *Macon Daily Telegraph*, April 2, 1863; "The Women Rising," *Columbus Weekly Sun*, April 7, 1863. Rosenwald and Bros, antebellum merchants in Albany, Georgia, moved to Macon sometime after February 1861. 1860 Dougherty County, GA, Census, 539; *Albany Patriot*, February 21, 1861; US Passport Applications, 1795–1905, M 1372, US National Archives, Washington, DC.

24. James Bonner claims, apparently based on an article in the May 19, 1875, issue of the *Milledgeville Union Recorder* that this author could not locate, that the riot had been instigated by Judge Iverson L. Harris's emotional denunciation to a grand jury of "speculators and extortioners" robbing destitute wives and children of Confederate soldiers. "Georgia Legislature," *Macon Daily Telegraph*, April 14, 1863; "Women Riot in Milledgeville," *Columbus Weekly Sun*, April 21, 1863, "Mobocracy," *Columbus Weekly Sun*, April 21, 1863; "Our Milledgeville Letter," *Augusta Chronicle and Sentinel*, April 15, 1863; Huldah Fain to Murphy C. Briant, Santa Lucah, GA, April 14, 1863, Huldah Fain Briant Papers (hereafter Briant Papers), Special Collections, Duke University, Durham, NC; 1860 Baldwin County, GA, Census, 139; Candler, ed., *Confederate Records of the State of Georgia*, 2:239–40; James C. Bonner, *Milledgeville Georgia's Antebellum Capital* (rpt., Macon, GA: Mercer University Press, 1985), 162–63.

25. Adjutant General Henry C. Wayne to "Commander of the 33rd Regiment G.M.," April 10, 1863, Georgia Adjutant General's Letter Book, No. 15 (ts.), Georgia Department of Archives and History, Morrow, GA; "Mobocracy."

26. Drew Faust and others who cite this letter state that the riot targeting Jewish merchants took place in Santa Lucah, GA. When the letter is read within the context of accompanying correspondence, it is clear that Huldah Fain is relating events described by her father, a state legislator in Milledgeville. Huldah Fain to Murphy C. Briant, Santa Lucah, GA, April 14, 1863, Briant Papers; Faust, *Creation of Confederate Nationalism*, 52.

27. Huldah Fain to Murphy C. Briant, Santa Lucah, GA, April 14, 1863, Briant Papers; "Governor's Message," *Milledgeville Southern Recorder*, March 31, 1863; "Georgia Legislature," *Milledgeville Southern Recorder*, April 7, 1863.

28. McCurry, *Confederate Reckoning*, 135; Giesberg, *Army at Home*, 33.

29. The printer's devil of *The Countryman* made a joke out of the Milledgeville women targeting Jewish merchants, asking readers, "In what did the riotous women in Milledgeville differ from Abraham?" The answer was that "Abraham was going to sacrifice Isaac, but these women undertook to sacrifice Jacob." *The Countryman*, April 21, 1863. "Georgia Legislature," *Macon Daily Telegraph*, April 14, 1863; "Mobocracy"; "Our Milledgeville Letter"; Nancy J. Cornell, *1864 Census for Re-Organizing the Georgia Militia* (Baltimore, MD: Genealogical Publishing Company, 2000), 10, 11; Candler, ed., *Confederate Records of the State of Georgia*, 2:879–83;

Mark I. Greenberg, "Ambivalent Relations: Acceptance and Anti-Semitism in Confederate Thomasville," *American Jewish Archives* 45 (1993): 13; Robert N. Rosen, *The Jewish Confederates* (Columbia: University of South Carolina Press, 2000), 268–75.

30. The *Augusta Chronicle* correspondent claimed that the Milledgeville demonstration had been "concocted under the advice and sanction" of a local unnamed man "of questionable loyalty." "Our Milledgeville Letter"; Baldwin County, GA, Superior Court Minutes, Book A, 209, Drawer 140, Box 58 (microfilm), Georgia Department of Archives and History, GA.

31. 1860 Jones County, GA, Census, 712; 1860 Wilkinson County, GA, Census, 28.

32. William W. Boutwell and America Dennis were the children of Chappell Boutwell, a longtime Milledgeville butcher who had been the city's mayor in 1857–58. 1860 Baldwin County, GA, Census, 155, 159; "Interesting History of Mayors of this City," *Milledgeville News*, February 28, 1913.

33. Baldwin County, GA, Superior Court Minutes, Book A, 209, 244, Drawer 140, Box 58 (microfilm), Georgia Department of Archives and History, GA.

34. A search of the Richmond County, Georgia, Superior Court records reveals no obvious candidate arrested in connection with this riot. "An Exciting Time," *Augusta Chronicle and Sentinel*, April 11, 1863; "Amazonian Display," *Augusta Daily Constitutionalist*, April 11, 1863; Cornell, *1864 Census for Re-Organizing the Georgia Militia*, 544, 549; 1860 Richmond County, GA, Census, 769.

35. Calico or Bust," *Mobile Advertiser and Register*, April 16, 1863; "A Mob in Columbus," *Columbus Weekly Sun*, April 14, 1863; Standard, *Columbus, Georgia, in the Confederacy*, 48; "Spring Goods! George A. Norris," *Columbus Daily Enquirer*, April 6, 1860; "Death of Mr. George A. Norris," *Columbus Daily Enquirer*, January 15, 1887.

36. "Calico or Bust"; "A Mob in Columbus"; Muscogee County, GA, Superior Court Minutes, vol. K, 1859–1863, 602, Drawer 80 (microfilm), Box 67, Georgia Department of Archives and History, Georgia; 1870 Russell County, AL, Census, 25; 1860 Muscogee County, GA, Census, 255; "Death of William Brooks," *Columbus Weekly Enquirer*, February 6, 1872; "Manufacturing in Columbus and Vicinity," *Macon Journal and Messenger*, June 13, 1849; LeRoy P. Graf and Ralph W. Haskins, eds., "The Letters of a Georgia Unionist: John G. Winter and the Restoration of the Union," *Georgia Historical Quarterly* 46, no. 1 (March 1962): 50.

37. Muscogee County, GA, Superior Court Minutes, vol. K, 1859–1863, 602, Drawer 80 (microfilm), Box 67), Georgia Department of Archives and History, Georgia.

38. "Sustain Law and Order," *Macon Daily Telegraph*, April 22, 1863; "Robbery—It Must Be Stopped," *Atlanta Southern Confederacy*, April 24, 1863. Mary D. Pettite, "*The Women Will Howl": The Union Army Capture of Roswell and New Manchester, Georgia, and the Forced Relocation of Mill Workers* (Jefferson, NC: McFarland and Co., 2008), 107, mentions several occasions, dates not given, where armed citizens robbed wagons filled with factory goods bound for Atlanta.

39. A. J. Glenn to Joseph E. Brown, "Talking Rock, Pickens Co Ga Aug 7th 1863," in Georgia Governor's Papers, Joseph E. Brown, Telamon Cuyler Collection, Ms. 1170, Special Collections, University of Georgia, Athens.

40. Outside of newspapers, it is difficult to find Georgia civilians or soldiers commenting on the 1863 women's riots. A survey of over forty diaries and letter collections
covering March and April 1863 reveal only two mentions of the riots. This sample
includes seven diaries and memoirs (mainly from planter households or merchants)
from Atlanta, Columbus, Augusta, and Milledgeville civilians. "A Mob in Columbus"; "Amazonian Display"; "Riots—Who Compose Them?" *Columbus Weekly
Sun*, April 14, 1863; untitled editorial in *Sandersville Central Georgian*, April 15,
1863; "A Contagious Disease," *Milledgeville Confederate Union*, April 28, 1863.

41. "Riot," *The Countryman*, April 21, 1863; "Rioting Women"; "Our Milledgeville
Letter"; "Riots—Who Compose Them?"; Captain George S. Jones, Camp Anderson's
Division, April 8, 1863, to Mr. A. McCallie, Macon, GA, Notes taken by author from
original letter owned in 2009 by John Steele, Walterboro, SC.

42. Louise C. Barfield, *History of Harris County* (Columbus: Columbus Supply Co.,
1961), 757–58; Huldah Fain to Murphy C. Briant, Santa Lucah, GA, April 14, 1863,
Briant Papers; "Women Rising."

43. "A Citizen," *Macon Telegraph*, April 23, 1863.

44. "A Word upon the Times," *Macon Telegraph*, April 30, 1863.

45. "Robbery—It Must Be Stopped"; "A Mob in Columbus."

46. "Relieve the Distressed"; "Women Riot in Milledgeville."

47. *Acts of the General Assembly . . . at an Annual Session in November and December 1862*, 235. For press publicity of this legislative action, see "To Cotton Yarn Spin-
ners of Georgia," *Macon Daily Telegraph*, May 4, 1863.

48. "Protection of the Poor," *Macon Daily Telegraph*, April 2, 1863; "Columbus Relief
Association," *Columbus Daily Sun*, April 25, 1863; "Relief for the Poor," *Macon
Georgia Journal and Messenger*, April 8, 1863; "Public Meeting, "*Milledgeville
Southern Recorder*, April 1, 1863; "Help to the Poor," *Milledgeville Confederate
Union*, March 31, 1863. For the actions of individual planters selling meal to soldiers'
families at low prices, see "Commendable Examples—Prospects of Crops," *Colum-
bus Weekly Sun*, April 21, 1863.

49. David and Teresa Crisp Williams document a number of later rural disturbances
involving women, but only one in a city (Savannah). Williams and Williams, "The
Women Rising," 75–83.

50. Standard, *Columbus, Georgia, in the Confederacy*, 49; "The Old Year and the New,"
Macon Journal and Messenger, January 13, 1864; Paul D. Escott, "Joseph E. Brown,
Jefferson Davis, and the Problem of Poverty in the Confederacy," *Georgia Historical
Quarterly* 61, no. 1 (Spring 1977): 60. On the efforts of state government in Georgia
to provide for civilians, see Peter Wallenstein, *From Slave South to New South: Pub-
lic Policy in Nineteenth-Century Georgia* (Chapel Hill: University of North Carolina
Press, 1987), 102–5.

PART 4

Emancipation

African American Veterans, the Memphis Region, and the Urbanization of the Postwar South

ANDREW L. SLAP

George A. Crutchfield probably knew as much as anyone about Union Civil War veterans in the Memphis urban region, Tennessee. As special examiner for the US Pension Bureau in the Memphis area, Crutchfield spent his days tracking down veterans—as well as their families, neighbors, and former comrades—to determine whether a soldier or his surviving dependent met the qualifications for a pension. He investigated such things as the original cause of a veteran's injury or whether a woman was the legal widow of a soldier. He already had twelve years of experience in 1899 when he was assigned the case of the widow Mary Johnson. She had filed a pension claim for her husband Robert Johnson, and Crutchfield needed to determine if he was identical to either of the men by that name who had served in either the Third US Colored Heavy Artillery (3 USCHA) or the Eighty-Eighth US Colored Infantry (88 USCI). Fortunately for Crutchfield, both units had been raised and stationed in Memphis, and approximately half of the soldiers from the 88 USCI had been transferred to the 3 USCHA at the end of 1865. After examining the official records and deposing fourteen witnesses, he reported to the commissioner of pensions, "from the description given of claimants husband and of the Robert Johnson who served in Co H 3 USCHA and the Robert Johnson who served in Co G 88 USCI I am convinced the claimants husband is not identical with either of said soldiers." For Crutchfield, though, "the most convincing fact to indicate that claimant's husband did not serve in either of said companies is that there are hundreds of those two regiments in Memphis Tenn and it is hardly conceivable that he would live here from discharge to 1887 without being known to many of them and without talking of them to his wife and having them at his house." George Jones of the 88 USCI corroborated Crutchfield's assessment, testifying in 1899 that "I think there are in the neighborhood of

15 or 20 members of my company here in Memphis Tenn and I know them all and have seen them every once in a while since the war."[1]

The description of hundreds of African American veterans in Memphis was no exaggeration. In 1890 430 African American veterans lived in Memphis and, extrapolating from mortality rates, as many as 1,600 resided there in the decade after the Civil War. To put that in perspective, in 1870 veterans constituted 3.3 percent of the national black population but accounted for approximately 10 percent of Memphis's black population. The number of African American veterans in Memphis after the Civil War was significant and was one of the ways that the conflict irreversibly altered the city's demographic development. Just as important, strong social networks among former comrades were both a cause and a consequence of African American veterans being so influential in shaping the urbanization of Memphis and other southern cities in the decades after the Civil War.[2]

Founded in 1826 on a bluff above the Mississippi River, Memphis quickly grew from a small town of 300 to the nation's thirty-eighth largest city in 1860 with a population of over 22,000. Memphis had added more urban elements in the 1850s, such as establishing a city high school and covering the mud on two major streets with wooden planks. Most important, the Memphis and Charleston Railroad was completed in 1857, connecting the Mississippi River and the Atlantic Ocean—and reinforcing the city's importance as a regional trading center. Foreign-born immigrants flocked to Memphis from the beginning, with the Irish creating the Pinch neighborhood in the city's first few years, and helping to make the city different than much of the South with almost a third of its population foreign born. African Americans meanwhile were underrepresented in Memphis, representing only 17.1 percent of the population. Some of this was intentional, as the city leaders took special steps to control both free and enslaved African Americans living in and traveling through Memphis. For instance, the aldermen passed an ordinance that any African American, slave or free, discovered on city streets after 10:00 p.m. was automatically thrown in jail until morning, when slaves would be given ten lashes and free blacks fined $10. African Americans had been part of the city's explosive growth in the 1850s—their numbers increased by 56 percent—but their increase was vastly overshadowed by the flood of whites, many of them European immigrants, whose numbers tripled between 1850 and 1860.[3]

The city's demographics changed drastically during the Civil War, though, and black soldiers played a leading role. When the Union captured Memphis in June of 1862, whites fled the city and runaway slaves sought shelter within the Union lines. The influx of African Americans became even more pronounced in early 1863, when Abraham Lincoln's final Emancipation Proclamation authorized the use of black troops. Memphis quickly became a central recruiting point for black soldiers and at one point its garrison had at least five African American regiments totaling approximately 5,000 soldiers. Families either accompanied or followed the soldiers to Memphis, and shortly after the end of the war one Union officer estimated that three-quarters of the black soldiers had families depending upon them for support. Racial violence and economic dislocation in the countryside after the Civil War, according to historian Stephen Ash, also "led many freed people to see Memphis as a beacon and a haven," largely because "the presence of the army garrison and the Freedmen's Bureau subdistrict headquarters seemed to offer more security against despotic white power than blacks enjoyed in the hinterlands." Thus in a number of ways black soldiers were instrumental in causing the African American population to almost quintuple. In August 1865 the Freedmen's Bureau counted over 16,000 African Americans in Memphis, comprising over 60 percent of the city's population. The sharp increase in African American population caused tensions in the city, such as the Memphis Race Riot of 1866, which left forty-six African Americans dead but which does not seem to have led many blacks to leave the city. While whites returned to Memphis in the late 1860s and once again became the majority, the war had irreversibly altered the city's demographic development. This was exacerbated by a series of yellow fever epidemics in the 1870s that led many whites to flee the city; over 25,000 left just in 1878, while poorer black residents often had little option but to remain. Throughout the rest of the nineteenth century the white percentage of the population steadily declined as Memphis's black population increased to almost 50 percent by 1900. African American veterans took the lead in continuing the growth of the African American population that had started during the Civil War, increasingly making Memphis an African American city.[4]

Memphis was not unique, for African American veterans were central figures in the migration of African Americans to southern cities in the decades after the Civil War. Before the war African Americans had constituted a tiny percentage of the South's urban population, but by 1890 a slightly higher percentage of the black population was urban compared to the urban share of the white population. African American veterans were significantly more urbanized than other African Americans. In 1890 nearly a quarter of African American veterans in the Upper South lived in cities of at least 25,000 people, compared to only 14 percent of the overall black population. Analyzing the crucial role of African American veterans in urbanizing the

South after the Civil War can simultaneously explicate both the process of urbanization in the South and the lives of African American veterans.[5]

Much of the historical literature on African American urbanization focuses on the Great Migration, traditionally considered the movement of millions of African Americans from the rural South to northern cities in the decades after World War I. Increasingly, though, historians have seen African American southern urbanization and trickles of northward migration in the decades after the Civil War as antecedents of the Great Migration. These new perspectives suggest both that a significant portion of the migration may have been urban to urban, and that the migrants in the twentieth century were following previously established paths. Steven Hahn cautions that "we must remember that a northernward shift in the black migration was already in evidence in the 1890s, and that it was closely connected to a substantial trend, beginning in the 1880s, that took growing numbers— sometimes temporarily, sometimes permanently—from the rural districts to the towns and cities of the South." Private George A. Johnson from Company H seems to be such an example. At the time of the Civil War he was living in St. Charles, Missouri, a town with a population a little over 3,000. After enlisting in St. Louis and serving in Memphis, however, he quickly moved to Chicago, one of the meccas of the Great Migration, by 1872.

Tellingly, though, Howard N. Rabinowitz's 1978 *Race Relations in the Urban South, 1865–1890*, remains the standard work on African American urbanization in the South during the decades immediately after the Civil War. Rabinowitz and historians of southern urbanization lump veterans in with the general southern black population, whose rush to the cities they attribute to a combination of dislocation in the countryside and a desire for economic opportunity. Most of the scholarship on African American veterans, conversely, rarely even mentions that so many former soldiers soon headed toward southern cities, let alone broader issues of urbanization. Making African American veterans part of the story of southern urbanization in the decades after the Civil War can help provide more background for the Great Migration and changes in African American life in the twentieth century.[6]

Numbers only partially explain the role of black soldiers and veterans in urbanization. As Jan de Vries has warned, "Urbanization is not a uniform, linear process. A single statistic cannot take its measure." Instead, urbanization bundles many processes together and black veterans served a vital role as networkers, both among themselves and among the larger African American urban community. As already seen, black soldiers helped to cause much of the initial migration to Memphis. In addition, a strong correlation seems to exist between urbanization and extensive social networks of black veterans. While this relationship could certainly be a result of black veterans choosing to live in the city for other reasons or the result of greater access to community organizations, it was indisputably a tangible benefit particularly for veterans and could help explain why they chose to live in cities at a much higher rate than whites or other African Americans. Richard M. Reid has found clustering of black veterans in postwar North Carolina, arguing that "such grouping allowed many black veterans to remain in close contact with old comrades whom they could see on a weekly basis and from whom they could draw various forms of assistance." The assistance was not limited to veterans, as their families directly benefited from these social networks, such as helping widows get pensions or providing temporary places to live. Even beyond their families, Kevin Hardwick has found that "black soldiers, whose uniform conferred upon them the authority of the victorious Union army, occupied a particularly strategic and powerful position within the larger community of black people living in Memphis, and were prominent in the efforts of the former slaves to redefine their position within southern society." Thus at a number of levels black veterans were key nodes in the African American urban communities that formed after the Civil War. This fits with Hahn's analysis of the experience of the larger African American community with urbanization and migration in the 1870s and 1880s. He contends that, like the Great Migration, "from the outset, African Americans widely imagined their moves as family and community strategies, and, even when departing as individuals, they laid out links in a developing chain of kin, neighbors and friends that would guide and support those who followed." The bonds the veterans forged during the Civil War continued to link them and other African Americans for decades, from working together to going to the same church to helping each other get pensions.[7]

The veterans of Company H showed both a preference for living in cities and strong social networks. Over a third of the forty-three soldiers from the company who applied for pensions lived in cities with a population of over 25,000 for a significant period of time. Nine lived in Memphis. One spent much of his postwar life in Lexington, Kentucky. Another six lived for years in major midwestern cities, such as Chicago and Cincinnati. Company H may appear to be a small sample size, but it is a randomly selected cluster sample of the 3 USCHA which had over 3,000 soldiers. Analyzing the pension applications for soldiers from Company H of the 3 USCHA provides both quantitative and qualitative evidence that veterans who lived in urban areas, and in this instance particularly the Memphis urban region, had a more extensive network of former comrades than those who did not live in or around cities.[8]

The presence of so many of the veterans in northern cities is consistent with the overall demographics patterns of black veterans, for 27 percent of all black veterans were living in the North in 1890. In addition to the six veterans in large northern cities, four of whom lived in either Cincinnati or Columbus, Ohio, another six lived in small towns in Ohio mostly around those two Ohio cities. The cluster of veterans in Ohio appears to have been a fairly self-contained network in the regiment with antebellum origins. While 58 percent of the veterans were born in either Tennessee or the Lower South, none of those who lived in Ohio after the war was born in one of those states. The veterans living in Ohio were all born in Ohio, Kentucky, Missouri, or Virginia, constituting over half of all veterans born in those states. The place of enlistment provides the best and most consistent clue to where soldiers lived before the war, and makes the Ohio cluster even clearer. All nine of the soldiers who enlisted in Ohio returned to the state after the war. All but one were part of a large group of fifty-eight soldiers who enlisted in Ohio during the first few months of 1865 and ended up in either Company G or H.[9]

Milton E. Mallory is a good representative of the Ohio cluster. Born in Culpeper, Virginia, around 1820, by 1856 Mallory was living in the town of Wilmington, Ohio, about halfway between Cincinnati and Columbus. Many of Wilmington's early residents were also from the South, with enough coming from North Carolina alone that the new community was named after Wilmington, North Carolina. Mallory joined the army in early 1865 with his brother Alfred Mallory and other acquaintances to head back to the South, but this time wearing an army uniform. As Willis Jones of Richland, Ohio, recalled in 1900, "I knew the claimant Milton E. Mallory before he or I enlisted. We both enlisted about the same time but were assigned to different companies of the regiment, he to Co. H and his brother and myself to Co. G. While in camp in the Fort the two companies were situated near each other. We could halloo across the street separating the companies easily to be heard and we saw each other almost daily." Milton and Alfred Mallory returned to Wilmington after the war and were neighbors for at least several years. In addition to it being their antebellum home, the Mallory brothers may have found Wilmington more hospitable to African Americans than many midwest towns, at least if the founding of the racial inclusive Wilmington College by local Quakers in 1871 was any indication.[10]

When Milton Mallory applied for a pension in 1881 and sought increases over the next two decades, he was able to rely upon seven different former comrades to testify for him. Significantly, Mallory and the other two Company H veterans who applied for pensions from Ohio only had testimony from former comrades who also lived in Ohio and served in either Company G or H. The pension applications and testimony show that there were at least sixteen soldiers from those two companies living in Ohio, mostly in the southwest part of the state. Some veterans did not see each other often. One veteran who lived about eighty miles north of Wilmington commented that he had not met Milton Mallory "but once since our discharge." On the other hand Moses Trimble, who had served in Company H and lived about twenty miles from Wilmington, had maintained connections with the Mallorys. When he applied for a pension in 1889, Alfred Mallory testified he had been "intimately acquainted" with him for thirty-five years and despite living a few dozen miles away "have seen said claimant on an average of two or three times a year." The network of veterans from the Third US Colored Heavy Artillery certainly paid dividends. While one historian has found that only 75 percent of black veterans were successful in getting a pension, nine of the ten veterans from Company H living in Ohio succeeded in getting a pension, and the only unsuccessful one left the Buckeye State for Philadelphia in the mid-1880s.[11]

The cluster of Company H veterans living around Memphis was more extensive than the one in southwest Ohio. Some scholars have found that the commercial hinterland of Memphis by 1870 stretched in a circle radiating approximately 175 miles. Based on accounts in Memphis newspapers and the movement and interactions of the veterans, the social radius of Memphis appears to have been about fifty miles. The *Memphis Argus*, for example, had a regular section titled "Letter from the Country," with missives from places within a fifty-mile radius of the city. Many of the letters in just a one-week period in the summer of 1865 came from places where some of the veterans soon moved, such as Covington, Tennessee, and Holly Springs, Mississippi. The Holly Springs correspondent started a letter: "Dear Argus: Your kindly face greets us every evening. The only drawback is your agent is too conservative—don't get enough papers to supply demand. Your market report is much sought after." The letters also often explained the social, economic, and political conditions in the countryside, such as the behavior of Union soldiers or the price of fresh butter. The regular exchange of people and information between the city and the surrounding countryside helps to show how social networks expanded beyond the official city limits. Five of the nine veterans who lived in Memphis and applied for pensions moved either in or out of the city at some point after the war, but the majority of those moves were within fifty miles of Memphis. Veterans themselves explicitly referred to a greater Memphis area, such as when one was asked in 1903 where he had been living since his discharge and replied, "All the time round or about Memphis, Tenn." The "around" part of the Memphis cluster is important for understanding both the veterans' social network and the nature of southern urbanization. This reinforces David Goldfield's contention that an active rural-urban interchange was central to defining southern cities in the nineteenth century.[12]

Veterans from the regiment who lived outside Memphis often testified about regularly coming into the city and meeting former comrades, further helping to make Memphis the center of a cluster for members of the 3 USCHA. Counties in Tennessee and Mississippi bordering Memphis, including Fayette, Tipton, DeSoto, and Marshall counties, all formed part of the city's social hinterland. Alex Jones recounted, "I lived most of my time in DeSoto Co Miss after the war until 1884 when I moved to Memphis but I was in and out of Memphis every three or four months during that period." Similarly, Tony Jordan reported in 1899, "I lived in Fayette Co Tenn from muster out to 1882 when I moved back to Memphis. The first two years after muster out I made frequent trips to Memphis Tenn and then it was that I saw Robert Johnson." Lovey Jordan, another veteran from the regiment who lived in Fayette County for a while, was asked in 1900 whether he had seen a former comrade named Manuel Horn. Jordan explained, "After muster out I went to Fayette Co. Tenn where I lived for about ten years. I never saw Manuel Horn but once after muster out and that about 3 or 4 years after muster out. I come down to Memphis to buy some groceries and things and met up with him on the street and we took a drink together and talked over old times." Coming into the city regularly, buying groceries, meeting a former comrade for a drink may seem prosaic, but they point to the social interconnection between Memphis and the surrounding countryside.[13]

The Memphis cluster from Company H comprised almost a third of the company pensioners. Unlike with the Columbus cluster, there appears to be few antebellum connections among the veterans living in the Memphis area. One thing the Memphis area veterans had in common is the lack of evidence any lived in the city before the war, and few seem to have even lived in the surrounding countryside. They were disproportionately born in slave states along the Eastern Seaboard, being almost twice as likely as others in the regiment to be natives of Georgia, North Carolina, Virginia, or South Carolina. While the decades before the Civil War saw a movement of slaves westward, most of the veterans who eventually settled in Memphis had not made it that far west by the outbreak of the war. A majority of the Memphis-area veterans enlisted at Corinth, Mississippi, a rail junction and center of Union recruiting almost 100 miles east of Memphis. It is unlikely African Americans around Memphis would have risked traveling that far through the southern countryside when they could just as easily enlist in the city. The personal histories in the pension records support this theory. Six of the Memphis-area veterans mentioned in their pension files where they had lived at the outbreak of the war, and the five who lived in counties almost 100 miles east of Memphis all enlisted at Corinth. Only Albert Daniel, who was born and raised in nearby Marshall County, Mississippi, enlisted in Memphis.[14]

The pension files confirm that many of the veterans who eventually settled in and around Memphis had lived outside the area in the antebellum period. Some parts of their antebellum social networks accompanied them to the Memphis area, though they do not appear as extensive as the antebellum connections of the soldiers from Ohio. Henry Craig, for instance, was born a slave in Tippah County, Mississippi, about ninety miles southeast of Memphis. His owner, John C. Craig, lived in Sand Hill, Tippah County, Mississippi, in 1860 and was wealthy, with twenty-three slaves and a personal estate valued at $40,000. Henry Craig somehow made it the twenty-five miles to Corinth, Mississippi, by early July 1863 and, just like his uncle Roger Craig a month earlier, enlisted there in Company H. After being mustered out at Memphis in 1866, Henry Craig moved to Brunswick, Tennessee, north of Memphis and less than ten miles from his uncle in Raleigh. Though he lived almost twenty miles outside of Memphis, the city was still listed as Henry Craig's post office in the 1870 census. A few years later Henry Craig and his wife, Julia, moved to Covington, Tennessee, about fifty miles north of Memphis and near the Mississippi River. Perhaps not coincidentally, they moved at the same time that the Memphis and Paducah Railroad completed its tracks to Covington. In addition, Henry Craig knew at least one person in his new town, for he suggested the pension office contact Mr. Smith "of Covington, Tenn. a grandson of my old master [who] knew me well before the war." There is no evidence that the pension office ever contacted Mr. Smith, but Henry Craig did have seven former comrades testify for him. Robert Craig swore, "I have known him from a baby and always lived near him before the war and afterwards up to the time he moved to Covington, Tenn." Another letter of testimony came from John Spight, who had shared some similarities with Henry Craig. Both had been born in Tippah County, enlisted at Corinth in the summer of 1863 at the age of eighteen, and served in Company H. The difference was that Spight returned to Sand Hill, Mississippi, while Henry Craig stayed around Memphis. Significantly, Spight's letter was the only one out of the seven that Henry Craig got from someone who lived outside of the Memphis area.[15]

Henry Jones came from further away than Henry Craig and apparently maintained fewer antebellum connections, though at least some of the reason for that was probably bad luck. He reported that he was born a slave on March 22, 1832, in Decatur County, Tennessee, about 125 miles northeast of Memphis. Technically the area bordering the Tennessee River was not incorporated as Decatur County until 1846, but for decades its rich farmland had been attracting settlers anxious to grow cotton and corn. Jones recounted in 1893,

> I belonged as a slave to Dr. Tory Jones of the village of Decaturville, Decatur Co. Tenn and I lived on his farm two miles west of town when the war come on. In Aug of 1863 I went off with Col Harris a US recruiting officer who came through and with a hundred or more colored men they had gathered up joined the army at Corinth, Miss. We were here but a short time when we went to Memphis Tenn.[16]

The service records give some indication of the sweep Colonel Harris made through Decatur County. All thirteen soldiers in the regiment who listed Decatur County as their place of birth enlisted on August 18, 1863, in Corinth, Mississippi. Jones was the only one of the thirteen native Decatur countians not placed in Company I, but there were plenty of other soldiers who had lived in Decatur County who joined the army with him. Years later Garret Fisher testified, "I was raised in Decatur Co Tenn and have known this clt [claimant] Henry Jones now present since we were boys. He belonged to Dr. Jones and I belonged to Billy Fisher, neighbors. This clt and I run off with the Yankees together and joined the army at Corinth Miss in 1863 and were made up as the 3rd US Col Hvy Arty." Forty-four soldiers enlisted at Corinth from August 16 through August 20, and comparing service records and census data suggests that many probably came from Decatur County. For instance, six other soldiers had the same last name as Garret Fisher, and a few people named Fisher in Decatur County owned slaves, including one who had thirty-four slaves in 1860. Similarly, three of the soldiers had the surname Yarber, the same as that of Jones's first wife before the war. Military service, though, was not kind to the soldiers of Decatur County. Of the twelve other than Jones born in the county six died in the army and another four deserted. It was not much better for the forty-four who enlisted in the five-day span at Corinth, for sixteen died, eight deserted, and only one left the service as a noncommissioned officer.[17]

Henry Jones survived and stayed in Memphis for a few years after being mustered out on April 30, 1866, the day before the Memphis Race Riot started. He soon moved to Barretville, Tennessee, about twenty miles north of Memphis and near to where comrades like Henry and Robert Craig lived, the latter of whom testified for Jones in 1901. Boyhood friend Garret Fisher appears to be the only person from Decatur with whom Jones stayed in contact. Fisher testified, "We served together in said regiment at Memphis Tenn till muster out is 1866. I then worked up in the neighborhood of Brunswick in the north part of Shelby Co and have been there ever since. A few years later he also came into that part of the county and we have never lived over 5 miles apart since." Jones did not show much interest in Decatur or its residents when he was asked about his marriage history in 1901. He replied, "I had been twice married in slavery times. My first wife Mary Yarber was carried away from me by her owners and my 2nd wife Bettie Johnson was left by me on her master Ellick Johnson's place in Decatur Co Tenn. when I went off to join the army. I have never been back to that part of the country and have never seen or heard of her since." Jones spent the rest of his life in the vicinity of Barretville, where he married twice more and had at least fourteen children. He died three days before Christmas in 1925.[18]

Henry Hart's experience shows the importance of antebellum connections in the urbanization of veterans from a couple of perspectives. Hart was born and raised in Henderson County, immediately to the west of Jones's Decatur County, where he still lived on a plantation during the first years of the war. Similar to Jones, Hart enlisted at Corinth in the summer of 1863, but does not appear to have been part of a large group of volunteers from his county. He enlisted on June 9, 1863, with a group of thirty-nine soldiers, all of whom joined Company H. Only three of the soldiers were born in Henderson County, however, compared to sixteen natives of McNairy County, which was just a few miles from Corinth and the border with Mississippi. Many other soldiers not born in McNairy County seem to have been living there before the war. For instance, forty-nine-year-old Eli Weatherly was born in North Carolina, but enlisted at the same place and time as McNairy natives twenty-year-old Richard and nineteen-year-old Barton Weatherly. All three match the ages of slaves owned by the Weatherly family, who were originally from North Carolina. Similarly, David and Jessie Lipford were born in Virginia, but match the ages of slaves owned in McNairy County by Virginia native Amos Lipford. The group that enlisted on June 9 primarily from McNairy County fared better in the military than the one mainly from Decatur County, which enlisted two months later with Henry Jones. Thirteen of the thirty-nine who enlisted on June 9 died in the army, but only one deserted while seven were mustered out as noncommissioned officers. Perhaps the combination of strong antebellum connections and a good military experience affected where the soldiers went after being mustered out in 1866. After the war many of the soldiers returned home, as over half of the veterans who enlisted that day and filed for pensions decades later were living in a six- or seven-mile radius of the small town of Selmer, the county seat of McNairy County.[19]

Henry Hart, meanwhile, spent the rest of his active life in Memphis. While the twenty-five-year-old Hart left Henderson County in August of 1863 with seemingly few ties, he quickly met Henrietta, who worked in the hospital where he recovered from smallpox. By February of 1864 Henry and Henrietta Hart were married in a ceremony, and they eventually had at least five children. Henry Hart certainly kept busy. Sometime in the 1870s he learned how to read and write and he tried his hand at several different occupations, keeping a grocery store in 1867 and being listed on the census as a laborer in 1870, before becoming a candy-maker. He was soon joined in the business by his son and namesake, who explained, "I worked with my said father during the last nine years of his life. We both worked as candy-makers for Frost. Afterwards changed to the American Biscuit Co." Henry Hart's son appears to have remained in the business, for in 1908 a Henry Hart was listed as one of twenty-one African American candy-makers in Memphis, working for the Novelty Candy Company.[20]

While Henry Hart and at least one of his sons maintained a good relationship, the pension file suggests that Henry and Henrietta Hart had a fractious relationship and separated in 1885. Four years later he married Annie Smith without officially divorcing his first wife. He also regularly changed residences, living in at least five different places over thirty years, but generally living in predominantly African American areas of the city. For instance, in 1880 he lived on Beale Street, at the same time the wealthy African American businessman Robert Church was buying up land around the street. By the early 1900s Beale Street was one of the centers of African American culture in the country and synonymous with blues music. Hart maintained enough contacts with comrades from the regiment in the city, though, that he could get testimony from four of them for a pension increase in 1899. By 1891 he had moved five blocks north of Beale Street to 13 Jefferson Avenue, which was near the homes of two former comrades, being just five blocks from Henry Mitchell and less than 350 feet from Robert Piles.

Piles recounted how Hart had helped take care of him while he was in the hospital for smallpox during the winter of 1863–64 and that "he was well acquainted with Henry Hart after the war, as he could be with any man." Interestingly, Hart's former comrades apparently did not like Henrietta Hart, for upon his death they overwhelming gave testimony to support Annie Hart when the two widows contested the veteran's pension. Piles, who was in the hospital when Henry and Henrietta Hart met and married, swore Hart was never married to anyone other than Annie Hart. John Abernathy of Company K drove the ambulances for the hospital, but likewise insisted Henry Hart was not married at the time, though he suggested Henrietta Hart may have been a concubine. The Pension Office eventually decided that Henrietta Hart was the lawful widow and awarded her the pension.[21]

It should be relatively easy to have a snapshot of where all the veterans lived in 1890, as the 1890 Veterans Census was supposed to have provided a detailed list of addresses for every veteran living in Memphis that year. Unfortunately, there is no information for over half of all the veterans in the city. The census was so incomplete that the census-taker felt compelled to note on one of the pages, "I have done my utmost to give a full and complete census of the soldiers as possible. But as you will see it is quite imperfect after all. It is owing to their inability to give the particular information requested of them by the census law." Still, the combination of the Veterans Census and the Company H pension files provides exact addresses for thirty veterans or widows from the regiment living in Memphis in the 1890s. Significantly, almost half of the veterans or widows at some point lived within a few blocks of each other.[22]

Most of the veterans and widows from the regiment in Memphis lived within a few blocks radius of the intersection of Pontotoc Street and Hadden Avenue. This was a section on the south side of the city just a few blocks from the Mississippi River and about ten blocks north from where the veterans had been stationed at Fort Pickering. The five-block-long Hadden Avenue started at Beale Street, with its diverse mixture of African Americans and foreign immigrants. As Hadden ran southward, though, African American tenements increasingly dominated the avenue and halfway down was the Hadden Avenue Colored Church. The lower half of the avenue stretching to Calhoun Street was predominantly African American tenements and businesses, such as the city stables and several wood and coal yards. It was in this area that the veterans and widows of the 3 USCHA were concentrated. Henry Bankel of Company K lived at 44 Hadden Avenue, next door to two regimental widows. A few blocks east on DeSoto Street Joseph Ferguson lived next door to Emily Morton, the widow of John Morton from

Company H. Three blocks south Robert Jones of Company H and Alex Jones of Company I lived together at the rear of 281 Calhoun Street, while George Washington of Company C and Stephen Bowman of Company I lived within a few hundred feet of them.[23]

About ten blocks southwest of Hadden Avenue Colored Church there appears to be another small cluster of the regiment's veterans and widows around the intersection of Georgia Street and Pennsylvania Avenue. The northern section of Fort Pickering had occupied this area until 1866, when resentful white Memphians destroyed any evidence of the hated fort ever existing. On the southern edge of the city near the river, this area of Memphis was at the intersection of two major railroads and a major industrial area. For instance, the Milburn Gin and Machine Company was only 700 feet away from Merchants' Cotton Press and Storage, and each occupied an entire block. Still, there were some African American churches, including the large Salem Baptist Church, and a public school for African Americans. Mary Anne Weston, the widow of Richard Weston of Company H, shows the connections between the different areas even as people moved about the city. She was living down in the southwest cluster area when her husband died of yellow fever during the epidemic of 1878. By early 1890 she was living much further north in the city, on the same block as Robert Piles. Later that year she moved back to her old neighborhood, living next door to Henry Beaumont of Company I on Pennsylvania Avenue and two blocks from Simon Lewis of Company H. A decade later Simon Lewis tried to help Mary Weston get a widow's pension. The odds of thirty people coincidently living so closely together in a city of almost 65,000 is remote.[24]

While the proximity of veterans near each other suggests a social network, many of them made this explicitly clear in their testimony for pensions, some of which is quoted above. Of course, in many instances veterans may have had an incentive to emphasize their closeness to help a comrade get a pension. In some instances, though, veterans testified they did not remember a soldier, such as with the Robert Johnson case. In addition, much of the testimony is so specific and personal that it rings true. John James recounted in 1897 that "he served as a comrade in the same company and regiment with the applicant Simon Lewis and has been very intimately acquainted with him ever since they were serving as comrades in the above command and that he has been a neighbor of the applicant since he has been discharged from the above command and is well acquainted with his condition and habits seeing him almost as much as once and twice each and every week."[25]

Some of the most evocative accounts come from Benjamin Franklin's pension file. After muster out, Franklin and some of his regimental comrades moved to Pleasant Hill, Mississippi. They spent the rest of their lives in the small town about twenty-five miles south of Memphis. When Franklin died Henry Buffit and Louis Hull made out depositions in 1914 to help his widow get a pension. Buffit explained, "I knew him well from the time we became acquainted in the army till he died, and we have talked over our army life." Hull recounted. "I would go to preaching with them sometimes. . . . I visited them at their home and was well acquainted with them." Like Buffit, he said, "He and I were good friends and often talked about the war times." It does not take much imagination to picture these three old friends sitting around together on the eve of World War I and reminiscing about their service during the Civil War, fifty years earlier.[26]

Analyzing the testimony in pension applications from former comrades provides some quantitative measure of the strength and importance of the social network among 3 USCHA veterans around Memphis. The Company H veterans who lived more than fifty miles outside of Memphis after the war, including the smaller clusters in Ohio and Selmer, succeeded in getting a pension 79 percent of the time, which is close to the average 75 percent success rate for all black veterans. Only 31 percent of the veterans had testimony from former comrades, though, and there was an average of 0.8 testimonies in each application. In stark contrast, 64 percent of the veterans living within fifty miles of Memphis had testimony from former comrades to support their pension applications, with an average of 1.9 testimonies per application. The social network of veterans in the Memphis area seems to have paid off, for 93 percent of them successfully got a pension. The testimony from the pension records shows not only that there was a more extensive social network of Company H veterans around Memphis, but also that it correlated with tangible benefits for the veterans.

The choices of Company H veterans suggest a complex interaction of social networks and urbanization. The veterans who had started with and maintained strong antebellum connections tended to return home after the war, living in small towns or the countryside more than fifty miles from Memphis. Meanwhile, the veterans who either entered the army with few antebellum connections or lost them while in the service tended to stay in the Memphis area. Ironically, through sheer numbers and by movement in and out of the city, the veterans who stayed in Memphis possibly because of weak social connections ended up creating a strong, useful, and vibrant social network. The Memphis social network was probably both a cause and a consequence of the high rates of urban residence for African American veterans in the city, and the South more broadly. During the Civil War African American soldiers had taken the lead in changing the South by bringing about the end of slavery. In the decades afterward African American veterans continued transforming the region by helping to lead the urbanization of the South and laying the groundwork for the Great Migration.

NOTES

1. The 88 USCI had a total of 1,264 men on its rolls throughout the course of its existence and on December 16, 1865, the last 608 were consolidated into the 3 USCHA. George A. Crutchfield to Green B. Raum, November 4, 1889, Robert Johnson, Civil War Pension File, Record Group 15, National Archives, Washington, DC (hereafter pension files will be cited as CWPF).

2. The estimate of the number of African Americans living in Memphis in 1870 comes from calculating the number of veterans who would have needed to live in the city in 1870 so that a mortality rate of 72 percent would leave 430 in 1890. This is a very rough approximation, as it is clear that veterans regularly moved in and out of the city. The estimate for the number of African American veterans nationally comes from dividing the approximately 160,000 soldiers and sailors who survived the war by the 4,880,000 black population in the 1870 census. *Report on Population of the United States at the Eleventh Census: 1890* (Washington, DC: GPO, 1897), 815–16; Donald Shaffer, *After the Glory: The Struggles of Black Civil War Veterans* (Lawrence: University Press of Kansas, 2004), 206.

3. *Seventh Census of the United States: 1850* (Washington, DC: Robert Armstrong, 1853), 575; G. Wayne Dowdy, *A Brief History of Memphis* (Charleston, SC: The History Press, 2011), 17–18, 21; Joseph C. G. Kennedy, *Population of the United States in 1860: Complied from the Original Returns of the Eight Census* (Washington, DC: GPO, 1864), 467.

4. Kevin R. Hardwick, "'Your Old Father Abe Lincoln is Dead and Damned': Black Soldiers and the Memphis Race Riot of 1866," *Journal of Social History* 27, no. 1 (Autumn 1993): 112–13; Stephen V. Ash, *A Massacre in Memphis: The Race Riot that Shook the Nation One Year after the Civil War* (New York: Hill and Wang, 2013), 72; Dowdy, *A Brief History of Memphis*, 52; Jeanette Keith, *Fever Season: The Story of a Terrifying Epidemic and the People Who Saved a City* (New York: Bloomsbury Press, 2012). For recent work on African American politics in Memphis during the Civil War era and the late nineteenth century, see Elizabeth Gritter, *River of Hope: Black Politics and the Memphis Freedom Movement, 1865–1954* (Lexington: University Press of Kentucky, 2014), and Brian D. Page, "Local Matters: Race, Place, and Community Politics after the Civil War" (PhD diss., Ohio State University, 2010).

5. *Negro Population, 1790–1915* (Washington, DC: GPO, 1918), 90; Shaffer, *After the Glory*, 50; Daniel O. Pierce, "Urbanization of the Blacks," *Milbank Memorial Fund Quarterly* 48, no. 2, pt. 2: Demographic Aspects of the Black Community. Proceedings of the Forty-Third Conference of the Milbank Memorial Fund Held at the Carnegie Endowment International Center, New York City, October 28–30, 1869 (April 1970), 48.

6. Steven Hahn, *A Nation under Our Feet: Black Political Struggles in the Rural South from Slavery to the Great Migration* (Cambridge, MA: Harvard University Press, 2003), 466; see 590 n. 1 for a list a discussion of literature on the Great Migration. George A. Johnson, CWPF. For examples of how historians of nineteenth-century southern cities have dealt with African American veterans see Jacqueline Jones, *Saving Savannah: The City and the Civil War* (New York: Knopf, 2008), 398–99; Michael W. Fitzgerald, *Urban Emancipation: Popular Politics in Reconstruction Mobile, 1860–1890* (Baton Rouge: Louisiana State University Press, 2008), 75, 87; Lawrence H. Larsen, *The Rise of the Urban South* (Lexington: University Press of Kentucky, 1985); and Don H. Doyle, *New Men, New Cities, New South: Atlanta, Nashville, Charleston, Mobile, 1860–1910* (Chapel Hill: University of North Carolina Press, 1990). Black soldiers are mentioned once in Howard N. Rabinowitz, *Race Relations in the Urban South, 1865–1890* (New York: Oxford University Press, 1978), 23. Donald Shaffer provides the best discussion of African American veterans and urbanization in *After the Glory*.

7. Jan de Vries, "Problems in the Measurement, Description, and Analysis of Historical Urbanization," in *Urbanization in History: A Process of Dynamic Interactions*, ed. Ad Van Der Qoude, Akira Hayami, and Jan de Vries (New York: Oxford University Press, 1990), 59; Hardwick, "Your Old Father Abe Lincoln," 110; *Hahn, A Nation under Our Feet*, 467; Richard M. Reid, *Freedom for Themselves: North Carolina's Black Soldiers in the Civil War Era* (Chapel Hill: University of North Carolina Press, 2008), 306. Kathleen C. Berkeley argues that the African American community in Memphis was divided after the Civil War, but that it was mainly along class lines and that lower- and working-class blacks did form vital self-help networks. Berkeley, *"Like a Plague of Locust": From an Antebellum Town to a New South City, Memphis, Tennessee, 1850–1880* (New York: Garland, 1991).

8. Shaffer contends that "pension files suggest that by the 1870s, about a quarter of black veterans lived in towns with more than 8,000 people; by the 1890s, the figure was over a third." The problem is that he bases these percentages on the "former soldiers whose residence was known" from his random sample, but there may be a selection bias in knowing a soldier's residence. For instance, if there is a correlation between veterans living in cities and applying for a pension, then the locations of ex-soldiers living in cities are probably more likely to be known. *After the Glory*, 51, 219n21. There are ninety-nine pension applications for Company H, 3 USCHA, and for a couple of reasons I used the forty-three applications from soldiers for the statistical analysis in this essay. First, the 1890 Veterans Census counted veterans, so this makes comparing numbers easier. Second, while I use some of the thirty-eight dependent applications as qualitative material, the much higher rate of fraudulent application and inconsistent information for the soldiers among dependent applications makes it problematic to

include them in the analysis. I also excluded soldier pension applications from two white soldiers, two that were almost certainly fraudulent, twelve that could not be found in the archives, and two that are in the Veterans Administration.

9.   The veterans from Company H who applied for pensions from Ohio were Marion Ingraham, Milton Mallory, Mack Morgan, William Sears, John Simpson, Henderson Stewart, Thomas Smith, Moses Trimble, George B. Washington, and Frank White. The information on place of birth and enlistment comes from service records. While Leslie A. Schwalm's book on emancipation and Reconstruction in the upper Midwest does not cover Ohio, it does provide useful background for considering the veterans from Ohio. Schwalm, *Emancipation's Diaspora: Race and Reconstruction in the Upper Midwest* (Chapel Hill: University of North Carolina Press, 2009).

10. Milton E. Mallory, CWPF.

11. Ibid.; 1870 Census, Wilmington, Ohio, page 43; Moses Trimble, CWPF; Shaffer, *After the Glory*, 122, 209.

12. Lynette Boney Wren, *Crisis and Commission Government in Memphis: Elite City Rule in a Gilded Age City* (Knoxville: University of Tennessee Press, 1998), 4; *Memphis Argus*, July 7, 9, 12, 1865; Simon Lewis, CWPF. For instance, after his discharge in 1866 Simon Lewis moved to Raleigh, Tennessee, about ten miles from downtown Memphis and now just outside the city's beltway, along with several other members of the regiment. After five years he moved eight miles north for a few years before moving across the Mississippi River to Marion, Arkansas, which was just twelve miles from Memphis and the home of Franklin Daniels, a comrade from Company H. Lewis moved to Memphis in 1879. When he applied for a pension in 1889 his witnesses included Daniels, who would eventually also move to Memphis, and a comrade living in Raleigh. Porter Marsh, CWPF; David R. Goldfield, *Cotton Fields and Skyscrapers: Southern City and Region, 1607–1980* (Baton Rouge: Louisiana State University Press, 1982), 3. Dylan C. Penningroth also discusses how after the war a black family in Memphis "brought some of the practices of the plantation right into the city," in *The Claims of Kinfolk: African American Property and Community in the Nineteenth-Century South* (Chapel Hill: University of North Carolina Press, 2003), 146.

13. Robert Johnson, CWPF; Manuel Horn, CWPF.

14. Fourteen of the forty-three veterans who applied for pensions lived for a significant amount of time in either the city or the surrounding countryside. Two-thirds of the Memphis cluster had been born in Georgia, North Carolina, Virginia, or South Carolina, while only 37 percent of the veterans in the company who applied for pensions were born in those states. Eight of the fourteen Memphis area veterans enlisted at Corinth, MS.

15. Henry Craig, CWPF; 1860 Federal Census; 1860 Federal Census, Slave Schedules; 1870 Federal Census; 1900 Federal Census. Henry Craig identified John C. Craig as his owner and the 1860 Slave Schedule shows that John C. Craig owned a male slave the same age as Henry Craig. The Sand Hill that John C. Craig and John Spight lived in was not the current Sand Hill, which is far to the south in Rankin County, Mississippi. The Sand Hill referred to here was in Tippah County, near Tilpersville, but was merged with another township in the early twentieth century. The 1900 census shows that Henry and Julia Craig rented a farm in Covington and seven children

lived with them, ranging from eleven to twenty-six. While Henry and Julia Craig were still illiterate, all of their children could read and write.

16. It is difficult to be certain exactly who Colonel Harris was, but there is a good probability that it was Lieutenant–Colonel. Thomas H. Harris, who served as assistant adjutant-general for the Sixteenth Corps in Memphis and acting mayor of Memphis in 1864. He is most famous for writing the report of the Battle of Fort Pillow. Henry Jones, CWPF.

17. Henry Jones, CWPF; 1860 Federal Census, Slave Schedules. The service records differ from Garret Fisher's account, showing him enlisting November 18, 1863, at Fort Pickering.

18. Henry Jones, CWPF; 1900, 1910, and 1920 Federal Census.

19. Henry Hart, CWPF; 1860 Federal Census and 1860 Federal Census, Slave Schedules. The two other soldiers who were born in Henderson County and enlisted on June 9, 1863, did not make it to the end of their service—one died and the other deserted. Five other soldiers were enlisted in the regiment at Corinth the week surrounding the group of thirty-nine on June 9, 1863, but did not seem to have any connection to the larger group and were not included in the analysis. Amos Lipford was the only slave owner in McNairy County with that surname. David and Jessie Lipford were born in Pittsylvania County, Virginia, and the 1840 Federal Census shows an Amos Lipford living in the same county. There was an H. F. Lipford in neighboring Tippah County, Mississippi, who owned five slaves, but only one was close to being the right age and he is listed as a mulatto on the census, while all three Lipfords who enlisted are listed on their service records as black. A Nathan Lipford also enlisted at the same time. He was born in Bedford County, Tennessee. Ten of the thirty-nine soldiers who enlisted at Corinth on June 9, 1863, eventually filed for pensions. Of those, only seven could be found at the National Archives and four of those were from veterans around Selmer, Tennessee: Lewis Hurst, Isham Knight, David Lipford, and Peter McCullough. Their pension applications include testimony from James Pharr, who was also part of the group that enlisted on June 9, 1863, and was living in Selmer in the 1890s. Selmer became the county seat in 1890.

20. Henry Hart, CWPF; 1870 and 1880 Federal Census; Green Polonius Hamilton, *The Bright Side of Memphis: A Compendium of Information Concerning the Colored People of Memphis, Tennessee, Showing their Achievements in Business, Industrial and Professional Life and Including Articles of General Interest on the Race* (Memphis, TN, 1908), 124.

21. Henry Hart, CWPF.

22. 1890 Veterans Census Schedules.

23. Ibid.; Robert Johnson and Simon Lewis, CWPF. The locations of addresses were found on the 1888 Sanborn Map of Memphis.

24. 1888 Sanborn Fire Maps; Mary Anne Weston, CWPF; 1890 Veterans Census Schedules.

25. Simon Lewis, CWPF.

26. Benjamin Franklin, CWPF.

CHAPTER EIGHT

Black Political Mobilization and the Spatial Transformation of Natchez

JUSTIN BEHREND

In the early morning hours of July 4, 1867, thousands of freedpeople in southwestern Mississippi altered their normal routines. They did not make their way to the cotton fields or to the shops and storefronts as they usually did on Thursday mornings. Instead, they converged on one place—taking "the roads . . . , the ferry-boat, and all avenues of approach," heading toward Natchez. They gathered at the end of Main Street, along the bluff that overlooked the Mississippi River. And they gathered in unprecedented numbers and for an unprecedented purpose. The local newspaper estimated that as many as 8,000 black men and women had congregated for the day's parade and celebration, nearly double the existing number of black residents in the small city of Natchez. And they gathered to launch a massive voter registration campaign, in which black men were eligible, for the first time, to vote.[1]

Prior to 1867, black people marching through the city were more likely to be part of a slave coffle, not a parade. Joseph Ingraham, a traveler through the Deep South, witnessed groups of slaves "in straggling procession," each burdened with "a polished iron ball," shuffling through the streets of downtown Natchez in the 1830s. In other instances, a hundred or more slaves disembarked at the river docks and were marched through the city under the watchful eye of traders and slave-conductors, on their way to the infamous Forks of the Road slave mart, located on the eastern outskirts of the city.[2] By contrast the 1867 procession was a parade of freedpeople who were not burdened by the chains of bondage but who celebrated their emancipation by marching as members of the Union League, as members of fraternal orders, such as the Good Samaritans, or merely as spectators lining the streets waving flags and cheering on the marchers. The parade advanced east through the center of the city passing merchant stores, banks, St. Mary

Basilica, and other institutions that embodied the power of local whites. As the parade made its way toward the edge of the city (a distance of half a mile), marchers saluted American flags to signify their loyalty to the nation. The crowd then proceeded along Woodville Road about two miles to the picnic grounds on a nearby plantation, where they convened for an afternoon of dining and political speech-making.[3]

The Fourth of July procession was a stunning example of the changes unleashed by emancipation—changes that had transformed individuals and changes that were beginning to transform the city of Natchez. The political mobilization of ex-slaves did not so much alter the physical structure of the city as it redefined the meaning that residents attached to existing public spaces. The relational space of the city—the way individuals ascribe meaning to a place—shifted from one designed to enforce the enslavement of its black residents to one dedicated to incorporating people of color into the governance and development of the city.[4]

In recent years, urban historians have drawn attention to the physical environment of cities and the interactions between urban residents in the making of a democratic polity. Through struggles in the streets and in contestations over civic spaces, nineteenth-century urbanites struggled to lay claim to citizenship in an increasingly pluralistic society.[5] But these studies tend to ignore the most disruptive event of the nineteenth century—the Civil War—and in their focus on place and space they devote much more attention to the vast metropolises in the northeastern United States, rather than to the more common smaller cities, such as Natchez.[6] Because of its size and its hybridity—in the way that the surrounding cotton plantations shaped the urban environment—Natchez and other similar "agrarian cities" do not fit in the narrow urbanization frameworks that give preference to industrial metropolises.[7]

Although dwarfed by the likes of New York and Philadelphia, Natchez, with its population of 6,612 residents in 1860, was the largest city in the state of Mississippi and the largest urban center within a 170-mile radius.[8] Surrounding Natchez on either side of the Mississippi River was a vast and wealthy cotton plantation region—the Natchez District—that gave shape to the character and development of the city.[9] The overflow from the river's seasonal floods spread nutrient-rich silt across the Louisiana bottomlands, which attracted scores of farmers, slaveholders, and fortune-seekers. But even on the Mississippi side, though spared from floods due to its elevated landscape, the brown loam soil produced abundant returns for the enterprising farmer. Large plantations extended out from the banks of the Mississippi River and tens of thousands of slaves were imported into the region to coax the fibrous cotton boll from the ground.[10] Slave labor produced enormous wealth, so much so that it was believed that more millionaires lived in Natchez than any other city in the nation.[11] As a major commercial center in the lower Mississippi River valley, Natchez boasted the second-largest slave market in the South, a commercial district that included a market square and numerous merchant stores, cultural activities such as the theater and horse racing, and even a few manufacturing shops.[12] In addition to Natchez's wealthy planters and commercial centrality, the other distinctive feature of the city was that it was surrounding by one of the largest concentrations of black people in the South. As far back as census records are available, African Americans, nearly all of whom were enslaved before the Civil War, outnumbered whites by substantial margins. By 1870 four out of every five residents in the District were black.[13]

While urban historians have paid scant attention to small cities such as Natchez, Civil War historians have neglected urbanization, particularly as it relates to political mobilization. Historians over the past thirty years have produced many rich studies on southern cities such as Memphis, Atlanta, New Orleans, and Richmond. These works have been broadly attuned to the ramifications of war and emancipation in the lives of freedpeople, producing subtle and nuanced studies on the struggle to define freedom in the postwar era. Yet the city is often characterized as a setting in which events take place and ideas are contested, not as a place in which people interacted with the urban environment and developed new governing structures and institutions to address the problems of density and representation.[14] Other studies have examined how antebellum cities became "New South" cities, or how race relations evolved in the postemancipation era, and these works have helped to explain how southern cities modernized and how black people gained access to previously excluded public spaces.[15] But the discussions over space and segregation in the postwar city are often disconnected from municipal politics, as if the realm of partisanship had little bearing on the incorporation of a formerly enslaved population into the fabric of urban life.[16] If the postemancipation history of Natchez is indicative of changes in other southern cities, then we have yet to fully conceptualize how political mobilizations altered urban spaces and institutions.

Nearly four years after the Fourth of July parade made its way through downtown Natchez, the reigns of municipal governance had been handed to a coterie of Republicans that included the only black mayor in nineteenth-century Mississippi, two freeborn black aldermen, and two ex-slave aldermen.[17] What did it mean for the city to now be led by men who only a few years before had not been considered citizens? How did the enfranchisement of black men reshape urban politics in a city where half the residents were black? In what ways did urban spaces take on new meanings among city residents? How did a city that owed its existence to the slave plantation economy transition to an emancipated city in which, as one correspondent noted, the "planters . . . have no political influence"?[18]

An analysis of the impact of the Civil War in a small southern city like Natchez suggests that it was not emancipation, per se, that fundamentally altered urban life; it was the political mobilization of ex-slaves. Once black men became voters and began to elect Republican municipal governments, the existing public spaces took on new meanings and the policies of the emancipated electorate reshaped the character of the city. In other words, the way residents related to one another and gave meaning to particular physical structures and other relational spaces shifted dramatically. Civic spaces became more welcoming to African Americans, but more far-reaching changes were evident in the way that black residents politicized the urban environment and used their political power to bend the city toward a more egalitarian ethic while simultaneously adapting the agrarian city to the demands of a postwar industrial economy. This change in the spatial meaning of the city came as a result of freedpeople's vision for a free and democratic society, and it was also a vision that was vigorously contested by many of the white residents in Natchez.

EMANCIPATION

One week after Confederate forces surrendered to Maj. Gen. Ulysses S. Grant in Vicksburg, Union forces landed at Natchez, about sixty miles to the south. The meager Confederate forces were quickly captured, allowing Gen. Thomas E. G. Ransom to take control of the city without a fight on July 13, 1863.[19] The peaceful and orderly conquest was soon replaced by a scene of tepid celebrations that only hinted at the transformations that were about to take place. When young Ben Lewis saw the Yankee soldiers land at the Under-the-Hill docks near where his father worked chopping wood, he remembered that "de colored folks was glad to see 'em . . . [and] some of 'em even shouted out loud."[20] Deborah Smith, a free black woman who managed a boardinghouse along with her husband, recalled that she and her daughter presented General Ransom with a poundcake upon his arrival, one of many gifts that they would bestow on Union soldiers during the war.[21]

Almost immediately after federal troops took possession of the city, slaves began to run away to Natchez, seeking protection and freedom. General Ransom complained to his superiors that black people were "flock[ing] in by thousands (about 1 able-bodied man to 6 women and children)."[22] "On every road they came in crowds, mothers carrying their babes, with every size and age streaming along behind," remembered a white resident of Natchez; "The day of jubilee had come."[23] Two weeks after his landing, Ransom reported that runaway slaves were still coming "in daily by the hundreds," increasing the city population by as much as 60 percent.[24] In a place that only a few months before had hosted a series of ad hoc trials and witnessed the execution of at least 200 slaves for rebellious activities, Natchez had now become a magnet for black freedom.[25]

The city that had once been known for its wealthy nabobs, its broad, tree-lined streets, and its elegant mansions was now home to an occupying army of northern soldiers and a mass assembly of desperate, yet newly emancipated slaves. Both the physical environment and the social spaces of the city began to change in profound ways. Responding to white residents' fears that the large numbers of black refugees would "breed a pestilence," Ransom ordered a series of camps to be built in Under-the-Hill—a seedy district below the city bluffs—to house the growing population of runaway slaves.[26] The city proper escaped an outbreak of disease, but the camp residents were not so lucky. Nearly 4,000 people crowded into leaky tents and hastily constructed shacks that offered little protection from the elements but proved to be a deadly incubator for sickness and death. Hundreds of the newly freed perished in destitute conditions.[27]

Above the contraband camps, at the top of the bluff on the northern edge of the city, a different sort of physical and spatial transformation was taking place. The army began construction of a new fort. Part of the land to be cleared away included the home of Francis Surget, a nabob of extraordinary wealth who had owned 456 slaves in the region.[28] The symbolism of the Surget mansion, which was destroyed by fire, was not lost on one of his former slaves, who noted that "a little while ago it was massa Susett's time . . . now it is God's time. Praise de Lo'd, he's here to-day for sure."[29] Not only was the economic power of this planter dealt a telling blow through emancipation, but his and his class's status were further diminished when upon the land that Surget had anchored his slave-produced wealth a federal fort arose. It was a fort built by employed former slaves to house other ex-slaves who had become Union soldiers.[30] Black soldiers formed the backbone of a new occupying army that allowed the soldiers in General Ransom's regiments to continue their march through the Confederate heartland, while retaining these new black soldiers, who knew the lay of the land, to root out bands of Confederate insurgents. Fort McPherson, which sat on Surget's land, did not merely serve as a physical imprint of federal control; rather, it quickly became a social space for liberation, in which former slaves became educated (both formally and politically) and established their domestic autonomy. Within its walls, the American Missionary Association (AMA) set up schools, operating "4 hours, 6 days in the week," and performed over 300 marriage ceremonies.[31]

The impact of emancipation was registered in other subtle yet significant ways. Throughout the city what had once been private became public, and what was public was opened to the excluded. Union soldiers, who camped near the bluff park on the western edge of the city that overlooks the Mississippi River, opened the park to black people for the first time.[32] When the blue-uniformed troops passed through downtown, an elderly enslaved woman rushed "at the passing soldiers, hugging them, and making a tremendous ado over them," reported the *Natchez Courier*. As she waited for each company to pass by, she danced "in the middle of the street . . . with bare legs and feet . . . keeping time to some music of her own," and in this way used the thoroughfare of commerce as a place to celebrate emancipation and federal power.[33] Newly enlisted black soldiers drilled in town squares and crisscrossed the city from one encampment to the other.[34] More telling, Annie Harper, the white daughter of a Natchez merchant, lamented the fact that her home was no longer the private refuge that it was before emancipation. "We were almost afraid to speak at home," she wrote, lest one of her black servants, whom Harper referred to as "spies," overhear their "disrespectful" conversations and report back to the military authorities, who showed little hesitation in jailing white men and women of wealth and status.[35] As if to signal that a new era had begun in Natchez, painters whitewashed the numerous slave sale advertisements across the city, a small alteration to the physical landscape but a visible reminder of the revolutionary changes.[36] In the year before the war began, $2 million worth of human property had exchanged hands in Natchez.[37]

Under the protection of the US government and with the establishment of a major military post, commerce and trade flourished, but the outlines of this economic activity looked different. The city attracted outside aid from northern missionary societies, as well as capital investments from merchants and entrepreneurs hoping to turn a profit on the rich-lowland fields abandoned by their Confederate owners. For the young and skilled, employment abounded. Future congressman John R. Lynch abandoned his plantation in Concordia Parish and found ready employment in Natchez as a dining-room waiter at a boardinghouse, as a cook for a company of Illinois soldiers, and as a pantryman on a naval transport vessel.[38] "Dealers in fruit, coffee, lemonade, and similar articles, could be found in abundance," reported a northern journalist. In addition, freedpeople in Natchez and other urban environs took up washing, "wood-sawing, house-cleaning, or any other kind of work requiring strength."[39] Draymen took particular advantage of the military's presence, for there was no shortage of supplies that needed to be hauled from ship to shore and back again.[40] Freed from the burden of giving a cut of their earnings to their masters, ex-slave draymen prospered as clients of the federal government. Even more lucrative—and dangerous—draymen took part in excursions into the plantation hinterlands to confiscate hidden Confederate cotton.[41] If he could avoid rebel guerrillas, a drayman could make from $25 to $50 per cotton bale, whereas before the war a successful drayman could only expect to make $15 a month.[42]

As the newly emancipated tested out their freedom and began to inhabit civic and social spaces as equals, they turned to existing religious institutions in an effort to lay claim to the buildings as spaces for collective worship and organizing. Under the auspices of federal authority, the black congregants of Wall Street Baptist Church took possession of the church building, largely because the white members had abandoned it after Union occupation. Over the next three years the black members struggled to continue their mission of spiritual assistance and community support while fighting off white members' claims to the church and its property. It was an audacious claim—that the legal title was invalid and that ownership should be granted on the basis of national loyalty—but not unusual, since many farm laborers made similar claims in relation to plantation lands.[43] Although they ultimately failed to maintain possession of the church property, the struggle helped to establish a thriving black religious community that went on to build the Pine Street Baptist Church, "the first Negro Baptist church erected in Mississippi after freedom was declared," boasted a late-nineteenth-century church historian.[44]

Black Methodists, much like their Baptist brethren, also struggled to establish a church home in the city. Former members of the Methodist Episcopal Church, South created a new church body, the African Methodist Episcopal (AME) Church, and occupied a Methodist building during the war. After a series of contests over property ownership, they purchased a church and lot from the Presbyterians and named their new church Zion Chapel. With 350 members by 1867 and 200 schoolchildren, Zion Chapel became the "central point" in a mission that extended from Natchez "in a circumference of sixty miles in every direction," asserted one minister. Integral to this mission was the Daughters of Zion, a female benevolent association that held fairs and festivals in the city to raise funds for building construction.[45]

One of the most important uses for these new, black-operated church buildings was for education. There was great demand for schools almost immediately after Union troops arrived and many creative places were utilized for schoolrooms such as the upper floor of a fire "engine house" and a temperance hall, but most classes for black children were held in churches, particularly at the Wall Street Baptist Church and the Rose Hill Baptist Church. Other spaces in the city were adapted to the needs for education, particularly for adult education. A night school of thirty men and women met at the military hospital. The AMA set up an "industrial school" for freedwomen and a "free night school," presumably for working adults. Housed on the second floor of a building that was also occupied by a school for children and a Freedmen's Store, which sold low-cost clothing, the industrial school taught fifty "poor women" how to sew, make garments, and repair tattered clothing.[46]

Within these buildings, former slaves learned a practical education—a trade and the basics of reading, writing, and arithmetic—as well as a political education. They had been denied access to formal schooling while enslaved, and now as they were taught in classrooms they also began to discuss the obligations of citizenship and how "to defend their rights."[47] The manifestation of these collaborative ventures (both religious and educational) began to be expressed in more assertive and public ways on the streets. An assortment of black Sabbath schools from across the city came together on New Year's Day 1865, reported an AMA official, for a daylong celebration of emancipation that included "singing, prayer, recitations, Reading the Emancipation Proclamation, a declamation and oration, short speeches +c." The Wall Street Baptist Church hosted the morning exercises, and then the celebrants moved to the Methodist church for the afternoon program. Nearly 600 black children crowded into the house of worship—the largest building in the city—along with hundreds of other family members and onlookers. Before perhaps the largest black audience to ever voluntarily assemble in Natchez, various black speakers gave testimony to the "past and present condition of the slaves," and the participants celebrated their liberation in song—songs that produced "an intense stillness in the house." While it could be argued, as an AMA official did, that Lincoln's proclamation created "a nation born in a day," the real work of nation building was made in moments like this, when different groups came together to celebrate a common experience and to affirm their claims both to the discursive space and the relational space of the city.[48]

Collective efforts in the churches and schools laid the foundation for an unprecedented venture in the public life of the city—the construction of a public school building for black children, the first building designed primarily for the advancement of black people.[49] The local black community, in conjunction with the missionary societies and the Freedmen's Bureau shared the costs of construction (including "gratis" lumber), and the Union School opened its doors to nearly 200 students on February 1, 1866.[50] Although the school would later become a focal point for black and Republican political activism, the initial objective of the school, while narrower, was no less political. It attracted the "most advanced pupils" from "the best classes" in the city to train a new cadre of black teachers to fill the earnest demands for education in the rural hinterland.[51] "A large number of pupils in our school are now qualified to teach others," wrote one teacher at the Union School in the spring of 1866; "They will undoubtedly secure schools on plantations, as planters are frequently asking our Supt. to furnish them teachers; colored teachers . . . seem to have the preference."[52]

A different form of hybridity emerged in postemancipation Natchez. Cotton production resumed in the hinterlands surrounding the city—although on a smaller scale—and cotton bales flowed into Natchez, but now the city was spreading out to the countryside. Urban churches and schools helped to spread an emancipated vision of a democratic society to the rural regions where the vast majority of freedpeople lived. It was an important and necessary precursor to the coming electoral mobilizations.

POLITICAL MOBILIZATION

In the years after emancipation while freedpeople were building social institutions, transforming the terms of labor in the cotton economy, expanding communication networks, and redefining public spaces, they were simultaneously chipping away at the wall that separated people of color from the formal arena of politics. Freedpeople discussed the "rights and privileges" of citizenship in "secret societies" that had formed in Adams County (where Natchez was located), and black Natchezians participated in a national debate through the pages of the *Christian Recorder* on the merits of universal manhood suffrage.[53] Beyond clandestine meetings and informal political discussions, there were few other outlets for formal black political mobilization.[54] Only with the passage of the Military Reconstruction Acts in the spring of 1867 would freedpeople have an opportunity to openly and widely engage in the democratic practices that their white neighbors had enjoyed for decades.

Republican leaders in Congress crafted a new reconstruction policy that sought to rebalance the framework of political power in the South. The new laws dissolved civil governance in ten of the eleven former Confederate states, placed Union army generals in charge, demanded that elections be opened to black men, and that each state must craft new constitutions that dispensed with the Black Codes and incorporated the principles of the Four-teenth Amendment. The revolutionary implications of this legislation gave pause to most Americans, but few had any idea what this radical template for political reform would mean in practice.[55]

Although congressional legislation mandated universal manhood suf-frage, the work of organizing, mobilizing, registering, and voting was a de-cidedly local affair. To that end, the Union League provided invaluable instruction on the political issues of the day.[56] Natchez quickly became the center of League operations in the region, and black institutions were the focal point of partisan gatherings in the city. Not long after the passage of the first Reconstruction Act, "the freedmen of Natchez and vicinity" met in a political meeting at the AME Church, reported the local paper. "Two or three black speakers" addressed a biracial audience of 413 men. They also discussed the implications of the new reconstruction law and selected a committee of twelve freedmen to "meet and confer" with Mississippi's mil-itary commander.[57] Over the next few weeks, freedpeople met at least once a week at different locations throughout the city: one week at the Union schoolhouse, another at the Rose Hill schoolhouse, and still another at an undisclosed spot.[58] Black institutions were a godsend for Union League and Republican activists because they provided a space where political issues could be aired without interference from employers or political opponents. It was quite a contrast from the early years of the war, when any assembly of black people could lead to arrest and possible execution.[59]

Despite freedmen's lack of formal political experience, they immersed themselves in the procedures and rules of nineteenth-century partisan meetings and rapidly created a biracial space for politics. At a Union League meeting at the AME church, the attendees elected "a colored chairman and secretary," while at another meeting, this one at the Rose Hill school, "not less than two hundred members (colored), were admitted to the [Union] League." Each member received a certificate of membership, signed by the League president, E. J. Castello—a former Union army officer from Missouri—and the League secretary, Wilson Wood—a twenty-four-year-old, literate freedman.[60]

One of the main tasks of the Union League was to prepare its members for voter registration. Over the spring and summer of 1867, local chapters of the Union League educated freedpeople on the electoral process, and within a short time Leagues began to function like any other nineteenth-century political organization: selecting leaders, debating party platforms, nominating delegates, and incorporating the aspirations of its members into a political framework. Invariably voter registration, supervised by federal officials, took place in an urban environment. Military officers, who often were also Freedmen's Bureau agents, set up offices in county seats and other substantial towns for freedmen to register. Throughout the late spring and early summer, hundreds of freedmen traveled to the bureau offices to sign up for the first biracial vote in the region's history. Many risked their employment and their homes as planters used all sorts of subterfuges to prevent voter registration. On the first day of registration in the town of Vidalia, four-fifths of those registered were black men, setting a pattern that would continue throughout the Reconstruction years as freedmen greatly outnumbered white voters in the Natchez District.[61]

Much of the registration and many of the partisan meetings took place in the county courthouses. Standing at the center of town, the courthouse cast an imposing presence over the political life of rural communities, for within its walls politicians administered municipal and county governments and ordinary citizens adjudicated judicial disputes before magistrates. Moreover, the courthouse was a desirable meeting place for political parties—an easily accessible public facility with ample space for gatherings.[62] Often political meetings would be announced by ringing the courthouse bell, signaling to the entire town that a major event was about to take place.[63] For freedpeople, however, meeting at the courthouse symbolized the revolutionary implications of emancipation and enfranchisement. When they met one summer night to listen to political speeches at the Natchez courthouse, they met as citizens, not subjects.[64] They came not as slaves waiting to be auctioned off, but as free women and men at a democratic gathering. They came not as individuals seeking justice through the courts, but as a community yearning to influence political events and to learn about their political leaders.[65]

To drum up support for the voter registration campaign in Natchez, Union League and Republican leaders planned a massive parade through downtown. The Fourth of July parade and picnic was intended not just to rally black Natchezians to vote, but also to blend together the tens of thousands of freedpeople in the countryside into a large political movement. One of the 8,000 black people to participate that day was a young freedwoman named Keziah Mably. The day before the grand event, Mably took the afternoon off from her work on a Concordia Parish plantation to do "some washing for herself," so that "she might have clean clothing to wear, to the celebration," reported a Freedmen's Bureau official. The next day Mably crossed the Mississippi River, met her brother in Natchez, and took part in the festivities.[66] Increasingly, these partisan gatherings served as a means for ordinary people to renew kin relationships and expand social networks. Even though Keziah Mably's primary motive in attending the Republican celebration may not have been partisan, grassroots activists, in attracting freedwomen like Mably, extended their political network into the interstices of everyday life. To be sure, there is little to suggest that Mably was opposed to the Republican Party, but her eager participation underscores the kind of political community that local activists hoped to nurture: a community of women, men, and children—not just voters.[67]

Celebrations and parades of this kind were essential to the work of mobilization for they made politics a communal experience. By marching in a parade, black Union League members stepped forward from their secret meetings and gave public testimony to their political loyalties. For the parade-watchers and picnic-goers, public identification with a Republican event brought them closer into the political fold by similarly making a public statement about their political leanings. It was an opportunity for women and men to celebrate and to dissociate oneself from the harsh labor and strict rules of the plantation. And in the process participants came away from these events with a heightened political knowledge and a greater sense of their personal involvement in a movement to radically change the prevailing social structure. The procession on the Fourth was likely the largest gathering of black people in the history of the Natchez District and perhaps one of the largest partisan gatherings in the region.

At the conclusion of the registration period, the success of the Republican mobilization campaign became apparent to all, and it foretold the radical changes that were to come. Approximately, 1,582 new black voters were registered in Natchez, which bested the white vote by three to one.[68] Out of nearly 17,000 registered voters in the Natchez District, 82 percent of the electorate was black, and 88 percent of eligible male citizens were now registered. Where once white men had sole power to select elected officials and enact public policy, now blacks had an 11,000-vote majority.[69] The political culture of the region would never be the same again.

PUBLIC SPACES AND VOTING

The voter registration process and the partisan demonstrations transformed not just how residents used the civic spaces but also how they interacted with one another. The "Cotton Square" in Natchez had traditionally been one of the focal points of the cotton economy, a space where small planters and farmers from the hinterlands sold bales of cotton to city merchants and then purchased food and supplies.[70] But in the heady days of Radical Reconstruction, the square attracted political organizers and stump speakers looking for a broad audience. David Young, a thirty-one-year-old ex-slave, farm laborer who would later be elected to the Louisiana state legislature, made a name for himself in Natchez by, as the antagonistic local paper reported, "haranguing negroes upon the beauties of Radicalism . . . every day on Cotton Square."[71] At another civic space, the courthouse, Republicans held political meetings that included "a large attendance of negroes, including women and children," thereby, transforming the space that had exemplified the patriarchal elite's power into a more public space, open to the many groups that the law had excluded from citizenship.[72] At the Natchez bluff, a space that had once been off-limits to slaves and other black people, nearly 150 freedmen and women attended a "grand mass meeting" in 1868 to hear from Republican nominees for the state ticket. Their presence at this rally not only underscored black claims to this public park but also indicated that public spaces across the city had become politicized as a result of black political mobilization.[73]

The streets themselves also served as settings for new kinds of public and political contestations. As more and more freedmen made a public declaration of allegiance to the Republican Party, there seemed to be more instances of freedpeople openly expressing their true feelings toward white adversaries. During the first voter registration campaign in 1867, a Jefferson County resident was stunned when on a visit to Natchez her former slave confronted her on the streets and "cursed her for everything," wishing that the entire "family was in the hottest spot."[74] Responding to black assertiveness in public spaces, the local Ku Klux Klan posted handbills on street corners, "warning Union men to be aware of their vengeance," reported the *Natchez Democrat*. But when a couple of Klansmen tried "to frighten" two black Union League members in the spring of 1868, "the colored men halted them in regular military style—forced them to uncover their faces and disclose their names, and chastised one of them so severely that he kept his bed for some days."[75] In another instance of partisan conflict in the streets, about "seven or eight Radical negroes," surrounded a black Democrat from Franklin County during his visit to Natchez and "abused and insulted [him], and threatened if he did not disown the Democratic conduct with which he was charged, they would mob him on the spot."[76]

As black people identified with national organizations such as the Union League and the Republican Party, and as they gained a new sense of their power through election victories, the struggle over who would control the streets became a proxy battle for who would control the city. One year after the massive Fourth of July parade of freedpeople, Democrats responded with a procession of their own to celebrate the defeat of the Radical constitution and to launch a mobilization campaign for the fall presidential campaign.[77] As the parade wound its way through downtown Natchez, a group of "negro boys" and a few freedmen began to throw rocks at "the Seymour and Blair banner extended across the street," and later as the beginning of the procession passed by the Commercial Bank, they pelted the Democratic club officers' carriages with other "missiles."[78] It was a rare outburst of black violence against whites, but not the last of the contestations and displays of power in the streets.

In the years after Republicans gained control of city government, black militias frequently paraded through the streets of Natchez in the weeks before elections. Black militias "on drill or parade," noted the Natchez *Democrat* in 1872, stopped in front of City Hall and "gave three cheers" for the Republican candidate for mayor (a native white Mississippian).[79] Colonel George F. Bowles, a freeborn black lawyer and landowner who also held numerous municipal offices in the 1870s, regularly drilled Natchez's well-armed black militia in the streets.[80] In 1873 black militiamen joined black "fire companies" in a Fourth of July parade through downtown Natchez.[81]

When it came time for elections, the placement of and symbolic meaning of polling places reflected the altered civic space that black politicization had unleashed. Indicative of local African American power, two of Natchez's four polling places were located at black institutions—the engine house of Good Will Fire Company no. 2 and the AME Zion Church—furthering the transformation of these places from private, exclusive associations to civic spaces at the heart of the city's public and political life.[82]

When the men entered the polling places on Election Day, they entered one of the most unusual spaces in nineteenth-century America—a decidedly masculine space in which black and white men took part in the most honored ritual of citizenship, and they did so as equals. There was no other space in the city in which white and black men assumed the same status, beyond the usual mitigating factors of race, class, residency, and occupation. While polling places were ephemeral, since they only operated as electoral sites at certain times, the intensity of the partisanship and the presumption of equality gave these spaces meaning far beyond the results of the specific elections.[83]

It is not surprising, then, that voters acted militantly, and that public confrontations in the streets became commonplace during elections. It was not unusual for black Republicans from the countryside, in preparation for a tense vote, to ride "about the streets with swords and banners."[84] It was more "customary," however, for black voters "to assemble at the voting-place at an early hour in the morning," a Republican political operative testified, and many often remained at the polling place throughout the day.[85] In the crowds that developed outside of polling places, party agents distributed tickets, groups harangued dissenters and recalcitrant neighbors, men discussed the implications of the election, police officers and marshals scanned the crowds for signs of organized disturbances, and others just enjoyed the day off from work.[86] "The courthouse yard and square," recalled a resident of Woodville, Mississippi, "were crowded with negroes, as was the case at all elections."[87]

At the end of a long day of voting, William J. Davis, a white Republican and Treasury agent, described the scene at the 1872 Natchez city election with notable hyperbole: "The Streets are like a perfect *pandemonium*. Drunkards in every direction. Oaths so thick in the air you have to dodge them. Shouting, yelling, shooting fire crackers and worse." As an election official, Davis was charged with counting the ballots, but in attempting to remove the ballot box for counting, he was stopped by "10 Revolvers chucked into my face." A mob of defenders rushed to Davis's defense and "bore down" on his assailants. "For a time," he recalled in a letter to Sen. Adelbert Ames, "I stood ballot box clutched in my right [hand,] umbrella in my left hand so thoroughly scared that I suppose my face would have been a good model for a picture of Daniel in the *Lions Den* with the marginal note to the effect that Daniel 'may be recognized' by the blue cotton umbrella under his arm."[88]

To be sure, the rough-and-tumble nature of nineteenth-century electoral politics was evident in the towns and cities across the nation where two-party competition was intense. But Natchez, before the war, was not one of those places. Elections in the antebellum era were decidedly dull affairs, reflected in the fact that no more than one-third of the eligible white men bothered to vote and none of the black men were permitted to vote.[89] While Democrats competed against Whigs and Know-Nothings, the level of partisan conflict paled in comparison with Reconstruction politics. It was not just the increasing levels of participation, particularly among the black population, that spurred the changes but also the issues that were in play. The meaning of citizenship, equality, and freedom hung in the balance, as did more tangible issues such as the taxation rate, the status of public schools, and the outlines of the justice system. In addition, the type of politics that freedpeople lashed onto—an emphasis on grassroots democratic participation—lent itself to a more vigorously contested and public display of politics than had ever been seen in Natchez before.

The results of black political mobilization had an immediate impact on representation in municipal and county government. Before the war, the ranks of local government were filled by middle-class white men, often from the merchant class. By 1871 half of the city's aldermen were black. Of the four men of color, two were former slaves and each came from an artisanal or working class background with minimal connection to the merchant class.[90] At the head of the board was Robert H. Wood, the new mayor, a freeborn photographer's assistant and the only elected black mayor in nineteenth-century Mississippi.[91] The transformation at the county level was no less stunning. Wood (whose white father was a former mayor of Natchez) was also elected to the board of supervisors, one of four black members on the five-member board.[92] In the office of sheriff, one of the most powerful offices in nineteenth-century America, William McCary, a freeborn barber and former alderman, was elected.[93]

The new black-dominated government embarked on a dual task: to demonstrate the legitimacy of black leadership and to alter city policies to better conform to the values of the city's Republican majority. For the most part, the black officeholders did not attempt to fundamentally alter the structure of the city but rather to change the way citizens related to one another within the city. They did this by restructuring the judicial system and by outlawing racial discrimination in certain public buildings. But they also embarked on an ambitious plan to revive the economy of the small river city by constructing a railroad. And in this venture they were joined by the white commercial elite who recognized that the city's future in a new industrial age depended upon a rail link to distant markets. A biracial and bipartisan alliance quickly took shape, and local black voters agreed to finance the construction of a trunk line through county bonds. In the end, the railroad took far longer than anyone in Natchez had predicted and it only tempered the postwar economic decline of the city and region, but the collaborative campaign to boost the city's economic position had the effect of moderating racial and partisan antagonisms that afflicted other cities. Compared to places such as New Orleans, Memphis, and Vicksburg, in which large outbreaks of racial violence accompanied black political mobilization, Natchez remained relatively unscathed.[94] What may account for the more peaceful acceptance of black power and Republican leadership in Natchez was the changed relational space coupled with the universal desire to improve the city's economic prospects.[95]

CONCLUSION

Looking back ten years to the time when Confederates governed Natchez, James K. Hyman recalled, "it was against the law for three colored men to converse together." Hyman was extremely cautious, as an enslaved drayman, in how he interacted with other black draymen in the streets, since "there was people always watching . . . and listening." And those who were suspected of talking in groups or discussing the Union army were "hung and whipped."[96] By 1872 Natchez had changed dramatically. Where once slaves had feared to congregate in public, now freed men and women celebrated their freedom and political power in the streets. Where once free blacks and slaves had to hold their tongues, now black people could openly express their opinions, whether in church, at school, in a public square, or at the ballot box. Where once "a single word indicative of my feelings," recalled Robert W. Fitzhugh (a freeborn carpenter), "known upon the street would have no doubt caused my death," now Fitzhugh walked the streets proudly as a member of the all-black Good Will Fire Company, and entered city hall to take his seat as a member of the board of aldermen.[97]

Emancipation and black political mobilization had transformed the relational space of Natchez. The concerted efforts of freed women and men to build civic institutions and to mobilize for electoral power produced an urban environment conducive to open access and biracial cooperation. It was a city, however, that had not resolved the racial, class, and national tensions that gripped the Reconstruction era, as the small outbursts of violence indicate. But it was a city that had negotiated many of the postwar traumas and produced a lived environment more conducive to the aspirations of *all* its residents.

But just as black political mobilization had transformed the city, the growing power of the white supremacist insurgency after 1875 sparked another transformation in Natchez. The combination of paramilitary violence and the disfranchisement of black voters severely narrowed the opportunities for black politics, leading to the segregation of public spaces at the turn of the twentieth century. It was not a reversion back to the preemancipation days, but the city that had once been known for its open and egalitarian relations became a city where the relational space was designed to compel black people into a second-class status.[98] Although the spatial transformation that freedpeople implemented after emancipation did not persist, their efforts are a reminder of the power of politics to shape the meaning of urban life.

NOTES

1. *Natchez Democrat*, July 8, 1867.

2. Joseph Holt Ingraham, *The South-West, by a Yankee*, vol. 2 (New York: Harper and Brothers, 1835), 185, 235–36.

3. *Natchez Democrat*, July 8, 1867.

4. For more on the meaning of space and place, see Henri Lefebvre, *The Production of Space* (Oxford: Blackwell, 1992); Margaret Kohn, *Radical Space: Building the House of the People* (Ithaca, NY: Cornell University Press, 2003); David Harvey, *Cosmopolitanism and the Geographies of Freedom* (New York: Columbia University Press, 2009).

5. See, for example, Thomas Bender, *Toward an Urban Vision: Ideas and Institutions in Nineteenth-Century America* (Lexington: University Press of Kentucky, 1975); Gunther P. Barth, *City People: The Rise of Modern City Culture in Nineteenth-Century America* (New York: Oxford University Press, 1980); Mary P. Ryan, *Civic Wars: Democracy and Public Life in the American City during the Nineteenth Century* (Berkeley: University of California Press, 1997); Dell Upton, *Another City: Urban Life and Urban Spaces in the New American Republic* (New Haven, CT: Yale University Press, 2008); Richardson Dilworth, ed., *The City in American Political Development* (New York: Routledge, 2009); Dorceta E. Taylor, *The Environment and the People in American Cities, 1600–1900s: Disorder, Inequality, and Social Change* (Durham, NC: Duke University Press, 2009); Lisa Keller, *Triumph of Order: Democracy and Public Space in New York and London* (New York: Columbia University Press, 2009).

6. On the typically small southern city, see David R. Goldfield, *Region, Race, and Cities: Interpreting the Urban South* (Baton Rouge: Louisiana State University Press, 1997), 46. Mary Ryan, in *Civic Wars*, is an exception to the trend in that she interprets the Civil War as a turning point in urban history. But her framework leaves little room for black political mobilization in the postwar era.

7. For more on the agrarian city, see David R. Goldfield, *Cotton Fields and Skyscrapers: Southern City and Region, 1607–1980* (Baton Rouge: Louisiana State University Press, 1982), 28–33. On the narrow framework that historians of urbanization often employ, see Jan de Vries, "Problems in the Measurement, Description, and Analysis of Historical Urbanization," in *Urbanization in History: A Process of Dynamic Interactions*, ed. Ad van der Woude, Akira Hayami, and Jan de Vries (Oxford: Clarendon Press, 1990), 43–60; Frank Towers, "The Southern Path to Modern Cities: Urbanization in the Slave States," in *The Old South's Modern Worlds: Slavery, Region, and Nation in the Age of Progress*, ed. L. Diane Barnes, Brian Schoen, and Frank Towers (New York: Oxford University Press, 2011), 145–65.

8. Joseph C. G. Kennedy, *Population of the United States in 1860* (Washington, DC, 1864), 271. In ten years, Natchez's black population more than doubled and grew from one-third to nearly two-thirds of city residents. Approximately 5,323 black people resided in Natchez in 1870 out of 9,057 total residents. US Bureau of Census, *A Compendium of the Ninth Census* (Washington, DC: GPO, 1872), 236.

9. There is no fixed geographical boundary for the Natchez District either in the historical record or in contemporary scholarship. In this analysis, the Natchez District is comprised of Claiborne County, Jefferson County, Adams County, Wilkinson County, Tensas Parish, and Concordia Parish.

10. In terms of the value of farms, the Natchez District was one of the major centers of wealth. See D. Clayton James, *Antebellum Natchez* (Baton Rouge: Louisiana State University Press, 1968), 136–61; Michael Wayne, *Reshaping the Plantation South: The Natchez District, 1860–1880* (Baton Rouge: Louisiana State University Press, 1982), 6–15; Sam Bowers Hilliard, *Atlas of Antebellum Southern Agriculture* (Baton Rouge: Louisiana State University Press, 1984), 8–11, 36–44, 68–71.

11. Winthrop D. Jordan, *Tumult and Silence at Second Creek: An Inquiry into a Civil War Slave Conspiracy*, rev. ed. (Baton Rouge: Louisiana State University Press, 1995), 33.

12. On Natchez and its immediate surroundings, see James, *Antebellum Natchez*; Ronald L. F. Davis, *The Black Experience in Natchez, 1720–1880* (Natchez National Historical Park, MS: Eastern National Park and Monument Association, 1994); Jordan, *Tumult and Silence at Second Creek.*

13. Historical Census Browser, http://fisher.lib.virginia.edu/collections/stats/histcensus /index.html. In 1870 Concordia Parish had the highest percentage of black population in the nation (93%). Tensas ranked fourth, Wilkinson eighteenth, Jefferson twenty-third, Adams thirty-fourth, and Claiborne thirty-sixth. On regions of high black population concentrations, see Hilliard, *Atlas of Antebellum Southern Agriculture*, 34.

14. On this point, see Peter Maslowski, *Treason Must Be Made Odious: Military Occupation and Wartime Reconstruction in Nashville, Tennessee, 1862–65* (Millwood, NY: KTO Press, 1978); Arthur Bergeron, *Confederate Mobile* (Jackson: University of Mississippi Press, 1991); Bernard Edward Powers, *Black Charlestonians: A Social History, 1822–1885* (Fayetteville: University of Arkansas Press, 1994); Steven Elliott Trip, *Yankee Town, Southern City: Race and Class Relations in Civil War Lynchburg* (New York: New York University Press, 1997); Michael W. Fitzgerald, *Urban Emancipation: Popular Politics in Reconstruction Mobile, 1860–1890* (Baton Rouge: Louisiana State University Press, 2002); Jim Weeks, *Gettysburg: Memory, Market, and an American Shrine* (Princeton, NJ: Princeton University Press, 2003); James K. Hogue, *Uncivil War: Five New Orleans Street Battles and the Rise and Fall of Radical Reconstruction* (Baton Rouge: Louisiana State University Press, 2006); A. Wilson Greene, *Civil War Petersburg: Confederate City in the Crucible of War* (Charlottesville: University of Virginia Press, 2006); Jacqueline Jones, *Saving Savannah: The City and the Civil War* (New York: Alfred A. Knopf, 2008); Justin A. Nystrom, *New Orleans after the Civil War: Race, Politics, and a New Birth of Freedom* (Baltimore, MD: Johns Hopkins University Press, 2010).

15. Don H. Doyle, *New Men, New Cities, New South: Atlanta, Nashville, Charleston, Mobile, 1860–1910* (Chapel Hill: University of North Carolina Press, 1990); Howard N. Rabinowitz, *Race Relations in the Urban South, 1865–1890* (New York: Oxford University Press, 1978).

16. Urban histories also tend to neglect urban politics or conceptualize politics as a variation on the Daley machine in Chicago. A case in point is Dilworth, ed., *City in*

American Political Development. Important exceptions include Peter Rachleff, *Black Labor in the South: Richmond, Virginia, 1865–1890* (Philadelphia: Temple University Press, 1984); James M. Russell, *Atlanta, 1847–1890: City Building in the Old South and the New* (Baton Rouge: Louisiana State University Press, 1988); Phillip J. Ethington, *The Public City: The Political Construction of Urban Life in San Francisco, 1850–1900* (New York: Cambridge University Press, 1994); Kate Masur, *An Example for All the Land: Emancipation and the Struggle over Equality in Washington, D.C.* (Chapel Hill: University of North Carolina Press, 2010).

17. *Natchez Democrat,* January 3, 1871; Vernon Lane Wharton, *The Negro in Mississippi, 1865–1890* (Chapel Hill: University of North Carolina Press, 1947; rpt., New York: Harper and Row, 1965), 167. The black aldermen were William McCary, Robert W. Fitzhugh, S. S. Meekins, and William H. Lynch. McCary was a freeborn barber. Fitzhugh was a freeborn carpenter. Meekins's free status is unknown, but since he was born in Virginia he was likely transported to Natchez as a slave. Lynch was born enslaved and worked as a photography assistant. Biographical information can be found in my database of black politicians, accessible at http://go.geneseo.edu/Black PoliticiansDB.

18. Edward King, *The Great South* (Hartford, CT: American Publishing Company, 1875), 295.

19. Brig. Gen. Thomas E. G. Ransom to Lt. Col. W. T. Clark, July 16, 1863, *The War of the Rebellion: A Compilation of the Official Records of the Union and Confederate Armies,* 128 vols. (Washington, DC, 1880–1901), ser. 1, vol. 14, pt. 2, 681.

20. Ben Lewis interviewed by Edith Wyatt Moore, in George P. Rawick, ed., *American Slave: A Composite Autobiography,* suppl. 1, vol. 8 (Miss. Narrs.), pt. 3 (Westport, CT: Greenwood Press, 1977), 1310.

21. Deborah Smith claim, case 14,868, Adams County, Report 3, Office 647, Microfiche 728, Disallowed Claims, Southern Claims Commission, Records of the United States House of Representatives, Record Group 233, National Archives, Washington, DC.

22. Ransom to Clark, July 16, 1863, *War of the Rebellion.*

23. Jeannie Dean, ed., *Annie Harper's Journal* (Denton, MS: Flower Mound Writing Company, 1983), 31. Annie Coulson Harper, the daughter of a clothing merchant, was born in Natchez in 1840. She lived in that city during the early years of the Civil War, and later moved to Jefferson County in 1864 when she married William L. Harper. Residing at Secluseval, near Fayette, she wrote this journal, probably in 1879 (as there is a reference to the Kansas exodus), to her daughter Lurline, born in 1873, to explain the tumultuous events of the Civil War era.

24. Brig. Gen. Thomas E. G. Ransom to Lt. Col. W. T. Clark, July 21, 1863, no. 546, Box 3, US Army Collection, 1835–1869, Louisiana and Lower Mississippi Valley Collections, Louisiana State University (LSU) Libraries, Baton Rouge.

25. Justin Behrend, "Rebellious Talk and Conspiratorial Plots: The Making of a Slave Insurrection in Civil War Natchez," *Journal of Southern History* 77, no. 1 (February 2011): 17–52.

26. Ransom to Clark, July 21, 1863.

27. James E. Yeatman, *A Report on the Condition of the Freedmen of the Mississippi; presented to the Western Sanitary Commission, December 17, 1863* (St. Louis, 1864),

13–14; Laura S. Haviland, *A Woman's Life-Work: Labors and Experiences of Laura S. Haviland* (by the author, 1881; rpt., Salem, NH, 1984), 285; Matilda Gresham, *Life of Walter Quintin Gresham, 1832–1895*, vol. 1 (Chicago: Rand McNally, 1919), 256–57; Davis, *Black Experience in Natchez*, 158–59. For more on the impact of disease on emancipation, see Jim Downs, *Sick from Freedom: African-American Illness and Suffering during the Civil War and Emancipation* (New York: Oxford University Press, 2012).

28. William Kauffman Scarborough, *Masters of the Big House: Elite Slaveholders of the Mid-Nineteenth-Century South* (Baton Rouge: Louisiana State University Press, 2003), 12, 469.

29. Haviland, *Woman's Life-Work*, 299.

30. Davis, *Black Experience in Natchez*, 147–57.

31. S. G. Wright to Rev. Geo Whipple, January 4, 1865, American Missionary Association Papers (AMA), Mississippi, roll 1, Amistad Research Center, New Orleans, LA.

32. Thomas W. Knox, *Camp-fire and Cotton-field: Southern Adventure in Time of War* (New York: Blelock and Co., 1865), 328.

33. *Natchez Courier*, September 25, 1863.

34. Davis, *Black Experience in Natchez*, 153–54.

35. Dean, ed., *Annie Harper's Journal*, 21. For an example of military officials incarcerating former slaveholders, see *Natchez Courier*, October 20, 1863.

36. Haviland, *Woman's Life-Work*, 299.

37. Steven Deyle, *Carry Me Back: The Domestic Slave Trade in American Life* (New York: Oxford University Press, 2005), 155.

38. John R. Lynch, *Reminiscences of an Active Life: The Autobiography of John Roy Lynch*, ed. by John Hope Franklin (Chicago: University of Chicago Press, 1970), 35–36.

39. Knox, *Camp-fire and Cotton-field*, 436–37.

40. Enclosure, Geo. W. Young to General Lorenzo Thomas, March 31, 1864, entry 202A, in Ira Berlin, Thavolia Glymph, Steven, F. Miller, Joseph P. Reidy, Leslie S. Rowland, and Julie Saville, eds., *Freedom: A Documentary History of Emancipation, 1861–1867*, ser. 1, vol. 3, *The Wartime Genesis of Free Labor: The Lower South* (Cambridge: Cambridge University Press, 1990), 814–17.

41. Many of the black claimants in the SCC files derive from draymen who lost wagons and mules to Confederate attacks while on cotton-hunting expeditions. Most of these claims were rejected because the draymen expected compensation from town merchants, thereby, according to the SCC, negating assertions that they were part of a legitimate military operation. For representative case files, see James. K. Hyman claim, Adams County, Mississippi, Congressional Jurisdiction Case Files, Records of the US Court of Claims, Record Group 123, National Archives, Washington, DC (hereinafter cited as RG 123); Richard Dorsey claim, case 4337, Adams County, Mississippi case files, Settled Case Files for Claims Approved by the Southern Claims Commission, Ser. 732, Southern Claims Commission, Records of the Office of the Third Auditor, Records of the Accounting Officers of the Department of the Treasury, Record Group 217, National Archives, Washington, DC (hereinafter cited as RG 217).

42. Testimony of Richard Dorsey and Lewis Thompson, Amanda Jones claim, Adams County, RG 217; testimony of James K. Hyman, James K. Hyman claim, Adams County, RG 123.

43. Edward Clayton and three others, Deacons from the Wall St. Baptist Church, to Hon. A. Johnson, Pres. of the US, July 3, 1865, Bureau of Refugees, Freedmen, and Abandoned Lands (BRFAL), Commissioner, Letters received, m752, roll 13, RG 105, National Archives, Washington, DC; J. H. Bolden (Elder) and four others to O. O. Howard, July 1, 1865, BRFAL, Mississippi Assistant Commissioner, m826, Letters Received, roll 8; Edward Clayton (Cold) and three other Deacons to Hon. Chief Justice S. P. Chase, July 6, 1865, BRFAL, Miss. Asst. Comr., roll 8.

44. Patrick H. Thompson, *The History of Negro Baptists in Mississippi* (Jackson, MS: R. W. Bailey Printing Co., 1898), 29. On the rejection of the claims to the Wall St. church see *Natchez Democrat*, August 20, 1866.

45. *Christian Recorder*, August 30, 1865, May 25, 1867, December 23, 1865, and February 10, 1866; *Natchez Democrat*, March 9 and 12, 1869.

46. P. Mixer to Rev. G. Whipple, June 24, 1864, no. 71,660; Mattie W. Childs to Rev. Whipple, April 1864, no. 71,639; S. G. Wright to Rev. Henry Coules, March 15, 1864, no. 71,613; and Mixer to Whipple, June 24, 1864, AMA, Mississippi, roll 1

47. S. G. Wright to Geo. Whipple, March 28, 1865, no. 71,748, in ibid.

48. J. P. Bardwell to M. E. Strieby, January 5, 1865, no. 71,719, in ibid. An emancipation celebration likely became an annual event. *Natchez Democrat*, January 8, 1866.

49. The Forks of the Road slave market, although outside the city limits due to an ordinance banning interstate trade within city limits, was arguably the only other space devoted almost exclusively to black people, but notably not for their advancement. For more on the Forks of the Road slave market, see Davis, *Black Experience in Natchez*, 61–84; Jim Barnett and H. Clark Burkett, "The Forks of the Road Slave Market at Natchez," *Journal of Mississippi History* 63, no. 3 (September 2001): 168–87; Deyle, *Carry Me Back*, 227, 229–30.

50. J. P. Bardwell to M. E. Strieby, November 20, 1865, no. 71,842; Blanche Harris to [unknown recipient], March 10, 1866, no. 71,971; Emma M. Stickney to Mr. Hunt, March 14, 1866, no. 71,980; Palmer Litts to Samuel Hunt, March 15, 1866, no. 71,983, AMA. Maj. Gen. T. J. Wood to Gen. O. O. Howard, October 31, 1866, BRFAL, Comr., Letters Received, roll 38.

51. Litts to Hunt, March 15, 1866, and Stickney to Hunt, March 14, 1866.

52. Stickney to Hunt, March 14, 1866. Likewise the Freedmen's Bureau used schools in towns and cities as launching points for educational ventures into the hinterlands. See the testimony of Maj. Gen. Lorenzo Thomas, US House, *Report of the Joint Committee on Reconstruction*, 39th Cong., 1st sess. (Washington, DC, 1866), House Report no. 30, pt. 4, p. 144.

53. Wright to Whipple, March 28, 1865; P. Houston Murray to the editor, *Christian Recorder*, July 1, 1865.

54. In other regions of the South, black people formed political organizations prior to military reconstruction. See Susan E. O'Donovan, *Becoming Free in the Cotton South* (Cambridge, MA: Harvard University Press, 2007), 213–14, 225–31.

55. Edward McPherson, *A Handbook of Politics for 1868* (Washington DC: Philp and Solomons, 1868), 191–94. For more on the Reconstruction Acts, see Eric Foner, *Reconstruction: America's Unfinished Revolution, 1863–1877* (New York: Harper and Row, 1988), 271–80.

56. For more on the Union League, see Michael W. Fitzgerald, *The Union League Movement in the Deep South: Politics and Agricultural Change During Reconstruction* (Baton Rouge: Louisiana State University Press, 1989); Steven Hahn, *A Nation under Our Feet: Black Political Struggles in the Rural South from Slavery to the Great Migration* (Cambridge, MA: The Belknap Press of Harvard University Press, 2003), 177–89.

57. *Natchez Courier*, quoted in the *Daily Picayune*, April 9, 1867; *Natchez Democrat*, April 8, 1867.

58. *Natchez Democrat*, April 15 and 22, and May 27, 1867.

59. Behrend, "Rebellious Talk and Conspiratorial Plots," 45–46.

60. *Natchez Democrat*, April 15 and May 27, 1867; US Bureau of Census, *Ninth Census of the United States: Population, 1870* (Adams County, Mississippi).

61. *Natchez Democrat*, May 6, 1867.

62. For more on how black people used civic spaces to create an inclusive public sphere during Reconstruction, see Hannah Rosen, *Terror in the Heart of Freedom: Citizenship, Sexual Violence and the Meaning of Race in the Postemancipation South* (Chapel Hill: University of North Carolina Press, 2009).

63. *Natchez Democrat*, June 21, 1869, and July 31 and August 14, 1872.

64. *Natchez Democrat*, June 10, 1867.

65. On slave auctions at the Natchez courthouse, see Davis, *Black Experience in Natchez*, 71–74.

66. Tri-Monthly Report, Geo. H. Dunford, August 10, 1867, BRFAL, Records of the Assistant Commissioner for the State of Louisiana, m1027, Registered Letters and Telegrams Received, roll 14, RG 105, NA.

67. For other ways that freedpeople forged urban social networks, see Andrew L. Slap, "African American Veterans, the Memphis Regional, and the Urbanization of the Postwar South" in this volume.

68. *Natchez Democrat*, November 18, 1867. White men registered in much lower numbers (565) than their population would indicate because many rejected the legitimacy of the radical Reconstruction.

69. *Natchez Democrat*, October 7, 1867; Joe Louis Caldwell, "A Social, Economic, and Political Study of Blacks in the Louisiana Delta, 1865–1880" (PhD diss., Tulane University, 1988), 257. Although heavily skewed toward the freedmen, these registration numbers did not diverge substantially from the population figures, but they do suggest that freedpeople were better mobilized. In 1870 whites made up just 20 percent of the residents. 1867 Voter Registration figures: Concordia: 2,195 black (91%), 199 white (8%), 2,394 total; Tensas: 2,413 black (94%), 149 white (6%), 2,562 total; Wilkinson: 2,274 black (81%), 547 white (19%), 2,821 total; Adams: 3,210 black (82%), 729 white (18%), 3,937 total; Jefferson: 1,916 black (78%), 541 white (22%), 2,457 total; Claiborne: 1,977 black (78%), 549 white (22%), 2,526 total.

Using the data from the Historical Census Browser, I determined the 1870 voting age population (male citizens twenty-one years of age and over) and divided it by the registration figures for 1867. There are anomalies in the results. For example, there were more Wilkinson County registered voters in 1867 than there were eligible voters in 1870. The figures are: Adams: 83%; Claiborne: 84%; Jefferson: 88%; Wilkinson: 110%; Concordia: 84%; Tensas: 77%. Historical Census Browser (2004), from the University of Virginia, Geospatial and Statistical Data Center: http://fisher.lib .virginia.edu/collections/stats/histcensus/index.html.

70. Whitelaw Reid, *After the War: A Tour of the Southern States, 1865–1866* (1866; rpt., New York: Harper and Row, 1965), 482.

71. *Natchez Democrat*, March 21, 1869. Young was charged with stealing in 1869, and in a report on this accusation the *Democrat* reminded its readers that he was the one who spoke in Cotton Square every day the year before on the "beauties of Radicalism." On Young's work on a Concordia Parish cotton plantation, see Tri-Monthly Report, Dunford, August 10, 1867.

72. *Natchez Democrat*, June 10, 1867. For a similar mass meeting in which women and children attended, see *Woodville Republican*, November 27, 1869. For more on citizenship and exclusion, see Barbara Young Welke, *Law and the Borders of Belonging in the Long Nineteenth Century United States* (Cambridge: Cambridge University Press, 2010).

73. *Natchez Democrat*, June 4, 1868.

74. Susan Sillers Darden Diary, July 13, 1867, Mississippi Department of Archives and History (MDAH), Jackson, MS.

75. *Natchez Democrat*, May 14, 1868.

76. *Natchez Democrat*, July 18, 1868; Subscription List in Sumner to Howard, January 30, 1868, BRFAL, Comr., Letters Received, roll 55.

77. *Natchez Democrat*, July 7 and 18, 1868.

78. *Natchez Democrat*, July 18 and 21, 1868.

79. *Natchez Democrat*, July 22 and October 7, 1874.

80. Bowles held the offices of city attorney, city weigher, city solicitor, city school board member, and city marshal during Reconstruction. After 1877 he served as chief of police and state legislator. On Bowles militia duties, see *Natchez Democrat*, July 3, 1873, and July 15 and 22, 1874.

81. Del to Blanche, July 4, 1873, in Blanche Butler Ames, ed., *Chronicles from the Nineteenth Century: Family Letters of Blanche Butler and Adelbert Ames*, vol. 1 (Privately issued; Clinton, MA: Colonial Press, 1957), 473–74.

82. *Natchez Democrat*, October 7, 1876. The Good Will Fire House was on Commerce Street between Main and State streets in Ward 4. The AME church was at the southwest corner of Pine and Jefferson in the Second Ward. City Hall was in the Third Ward, and the First Ward polling place was at the corner of Franklin and Canal.

83. For more on the meaning of voting, see Richard Franklin Bensel, *The American Ballot Box in the Mid-Nineteenth Century* (New York: Cambridge University Press, 2004).

84. *Natchez Democrat*, January 3, 1871.

85. Testimony of Wilson Wood, US House, *Testimony in the Contested Election Case of John R. Lynch vs. James R. Chalmers, From the Sixth Congressional District of Mississippi,* 47th Cong., 1st sess., Misc. Doc. No. 12, p. 118 (cited hereafter as *Lynch vs. Chalmers*). Thomas Quarterman, a white painter and Natchez city clerk, noted an uncharacteristic occurrence at the 1880 election: "white voters crowded at the door before the polls opened," whereas in past elections the early crowd was "principally colored men." Testimony of Thomas R. Quarterman, *Lynch vs. Chalmers,* 70.

86. For more on the culture of polling places, see Bensel, *American Ballot Box,* 26–85.

87. J. H. Jones, "Reconstruction in Wilkinson County," *Publications of the Mississippi Historical Society* 8 (Oxford, MS, 1904), 159.

88. William J. Davis to Ames, December 25, 1872, Folder 134, Box 15, Gov. Ames correspondence, MDAH. On the nature of nineteenth-century elections, see Mark Brewin, "Bonfires, Fistfights, and Roaring Cannons: Election Day and the Creation of Social Capital in the City of Philadelphia," in *Social Capital in the City: Community and Civic Life in Philadelphia,* ed. Richardson Dilworth (Philadelphia: Temple University Press, 2006), 40–55.

89. James, *Antebellum Natchez,* 92.

90. *Natchez Democrat,* January 3, 1871. The black aldermen were William McCary, Robert W. Fitzhugh, S. S. Meekins, and William H. Lynch.

91. *Natchez Democrat,* January 3, 1871; Wharton, *The Negro in Mississippi,* 167.

92. Minutes of the Circuit Court, 1870–1873, Adams County, April Term, 1872, p. 265, Adams County Circuit Court Case Files, Historic Natchez Foundation (HNF), Natchez, MS; *Natchez Democrat,* October 11, 1871, and January 26, 1873; James, *Antebellum Natchez,* 96.

93. *Natchez Democrat,* January 10, 1872; Minutes of the Circuit Court, 1870–1873; Wharton, *The Negro in Mississippi,* 169.

94. Hogue, *Uncivil War,* 31–52; Rosen, *Terror in the Heart of Freedom,* 23–84; Christopher Waldrep, *Roots of Disorder: Race and Criminal Justice in the American South, 1817–80* (Urbana: University of Illinois Press, 1998), 151–69.

95. For more on railroad construction and on electoral violence in the Natchez District, see Justin Behrend, *Reconstructing Democracy: Grassroots Black Politics in the Deep South after the Civil War* (Athens: University of Georgia Press,2015).

96. Testimony of James K. Hyman, Richard Dorsey claim, case 4337, Adams County, RG 217.

97. Testimony of Robert W. Fitzhugh, Jeanetta Carter claim, case 21,053, Adams County, Report 4, Office 456, Microfiche 1206, Disallowed Claims, Southern Claims Commission, Records of the US House of Representatives, Record Group 233, National Archives, Washington, DC; *Natchez Democrat,* January 3 and April 5, 1871, April 10, 1872.

98. Allison Davis, Burleigh B. Gardner, and Mary R. Gardner, *Deep South: A Social Anthropological Study of Caste and Class* (Chicago: University of Chicago, 1941; rpt., Los Angeles: The Center for Afro-American Studies, UCLA, 1988); Jack E. Davis, *Race against Time: Culture and Separation in Natchez since 1930* (Baton Rouge: Louisiana State University Press, 2001).

CHAPTER NINE

African Americans' Struggle for Education, Citizenship, and Freedom in Mobile Alabama, 1865–1868

HILARY N. GREEN

U pon concluding its charge to draft a new state constitution in late 1867, delegates to the constitutional convention presented Alabamians with a document that reflected the new postwar reality. Article 11, section 6 demonstrated the greatest change as state officials were now required to provide "schools at which all the children of the State, between the ages of five and twenty-one years, may attend free of charge."[1] Only a few months earlier, Lawrence S. Berry and other prominent black Mobilians called for the creation of a state-funded public school system to serve all citizens regardless of race in an open letter to the *Nationalist*. In eradicating a "consequence of our long servitude," they implored "every member of the Republican party to demand the establishment of a thorough system of common schools throughout the State."[2] Public schools would allow future generations of children, white and black, to become productive citizens, to promote the common good across Alabama, and to erase the state's slave past.

Representing Mobile, John Carraway and Ovide Gregory actively fought for the statewide extension of the educational gains made in Mobile at the 1867 constitutional convention. Carraway, the former slave, and Gregory, a free Creole of Color, drew strength from their respective community's recent past. Despite the concerted efforts of a hostile white community, black Mobilians and Creoles of Color laid the foundation for an enduring system. Neither Dr. Josiah Nott nor arsonists deterred black Mobilians and their allies in their pursuit of education. Inspired by this recent past, Carraway and Gregory refused to accept failure in their struggle for the statewide extension of the model Mobile system.[3] Establishing schools for all children, regardless of race, class, caste or former servitude, was a revolutionary prospect. Article 11 demonstrated how the Civil War fundamentally changed

African American education from illegal to concrete symbols of the new definitions of freedom and citizenship in postwar Alabama. In some respects, though, article 11 was the product of black Mobilians and their allies seizing the opportunities afforded to them when Union troops captured the city on April 12, 1865, and their refusal to accept antebellum notions of education.[4]

Occurring three days after Gen. Robert E. Lee's surrender, emancipation brought new behaviors, new relationships, and new institutions in Mobile. In many respects, black Mobilians' efforts mirrored the activism of African Americans across the urban South. Urban African Americans capitalized on Confederate defeat by making school attendance and acquiring an education at the core of their postwar definitions of freedom, citizenship, and education. School-aged children and adults demonstrated their new freedom by attending day, night, and Sabbath schools in African American churches. Wartime confiscated buildings and old symbols of slavery became spaces for learning, such as the Fitz and Frazier slave auction mart in Montgomery and Chimborazo School on the grounds on a former Confederate hospital.[5] Immense desire to become an educated people by urban African Americans and rural migrants facilitated the construction of new structures, such as the Beach Institute in Savannah, Avery Institute in Charleston, and the Storrs School in Atlanta.[6] Even unconventional spaces, such as a railroad car and hotel dining rooms, were transformed into sites of learning until new permanent structures were secured in Atlanta and Raleigh respectively. Urban African Americans served as the vanguard in postwar African American education across the postwar South.

As demonstrated by the Savannah Education Association (SEA), they spearheaded the creation of African American schools. From late 1864 to 1866, the SEA successfully established, staffed, and financially sustained schools for the newly emancipated throughout the city. Seeking to expand its efforts to include freedpeople in Savannah, the American Missionary Association (AMA) opened schools and eventually co-opted the black-operated SEA schools.[7] Instead of being the objects of educational efforts, the SEA and other urban African Americans demonstrated that they were active agents in the educational movement. Moreover, their initiative often predated the efforts of outside agencies, in which individuals such as Hannah E. Stevenson, Lucy Chase, and Rev. S. W. Magill often noted the existence of schools before their arrivals.[8] Their agency often defied the intentions of northern white agencies who participated and contributed to often uneasy biracial alliances in the struggle to legitimate the African American schoolhouse.

Most significantly, urban African Americans were essential in forging beneficial alliances that crossed class, race, region, and even national boundaries. Antebellum antiliteracy campaigns, laws, and racial exclusions of common school movement heightened urban African Americans' awareness of their lack of freedom and noncitizenship status in the society. Nevertheless, these efforts did not diminish the communal value of education nor did obstacles deter urban African Americans from seizing education and literacy as tools of liberation.[9] Urban African Americans, regardless of status, viewed literacy and education as a means to better their social status and as a benefit of freedom. Carried over into the initial years of freedom, this desire enabled them to forge strategic partnerships with the Freedmen's Bureau, to compromise with northern organizations over the administration of the schools, and to secure funding from regional, national, and even international circles.[10] These alliances aided their struggle against a hostile white community who did not want the postwar educational efforts to succeed. Arson, vandalism, race riots, physical violence directed toward educators, and other manifestations of the opposition forced urban African Americans and their respective educational partners to overcome any internal division for the sake of the survival of the nascent school system.[11] In southern cities, a strong public front proved essential in combating the opposition. Without the efforts of these urban African Americans, postwar educational efforts throughout the former Confederacy would have been stalled.

While African American education became the cornerstone of the postwar realities in the urban South, black Mobilians undertook a different path. Their efforts, as compared to their southern counterparts, bring into sharper relief the uniqueness of Mobile in terms of the educational revolution. As demonstrated by historian Michael F. Fitzgerald, internal divisions among black Mobilians created an environment in which intense rivalries between urban African Americans, rural migrants, and Creoles of Color with mixed African and European ancestry, as well as white hostilities, posed major obstacles to both popular politics and postwar educational advances.[12] Despite these obstacles, black Mobilians and their allies still achieved legitimacy of their expressions of freedom and citizenship through the African American schoolhouse.

Through an examination of the advances in African American education from 1865 to 1868, this chapter seeks to illustrate the transformative nature of the Civil War through the ways that black Mobilians defined the meaning of freedom and citizenship in the postwar urban South. It also explores the ways in which internal strife between the educational partners, local white opposition, and relations with Creoles of Color shaped the quest for schools, access, and legitimacy. Black Mobilians and their educational partners began the process of legitimizing African American education that culminated in a statewide right promulgated in article 11. By emphasizing the educational relationships formed by black Mobilians and their struggle, this chapter offers new insights into a well-established historiography on the initial postwar African American schools while simultaneously providing a detailed view of how the quest for education manifested itself on the ground. In short, it reveals how black Mobilians and their educational partners influenced the first major institutional development of the postwar urban landscape—the Freedmen's Schools. Whether acting alone or with their network of partners, this chapter argues that black Mobilians neither lost sight of their desire to become an educated people nor forgot the role that Confederate defeat played in allowing their assertions of freedom and citizenship through education in postwar Mobile. Both enabled them to persevere and overcome the violence and rhetorical animosity encountered in their early struggle for education. As a result, the landscape of Mobile and Alabama permanently changed.[13]

While schools existed within days of Union victory, the Freedmen's School system formally commenced operations on May 11, 1865, at the State Street Methodist Episcopal Colored Church. Dr. C. H. Roe and E. C. Branch, white Northwestern Freedmen's Aid Society of Chicago missionaries, served as the school's principal teachers. The State Street School quickly expanded from 121 students on the first day to 510 students by the tenth day of operations. Schools also existed at the Stone Street Colored Baptist Church, the St. Louis Street School, and the Medical College. These schools operated until the end of June 1865 and then resumed in the fall.[14]

For black Mobilians, Roe, and Branch, the city of Mobile, located on Mobile Bay, served as the ideal venue for postwar experimentation. Mobile's importance as an urban center began with its establishment in 1702 as a trading post initially for the French. Starting in the 1820s, the cotton industry catapulted Mobile into an international and national trading center. By 1860 the commodity typically comprised 99 percent of the total value of exports from the city to northern and foreign textile mills. While only New York and New Orleans surpassed Mobile in the total value of exports nationally, both domestic and international textile industries highly valued the steady cotton trade with the city. Aptly described as "Cotton City," the city of Mobile influenced the entire state, especially in terms of public school education.[15] At the forefront of the common school movement in Alabama, Mobile established a system of public schools prior to the Civil War.[16] Although the antebellum movement brought little change to African

American education, black Mobilians, Dr. Roe, and E. C. Branch fully expected the city to build on its lead in public education by occupying the vanguard of African American education for the entire state.[17]

At the beginning of the 1865–66 academic year, Mobile's nascent educational system received a new partner. The Bureau of Refugees, Freedmen and Abandoned Lands or the Freedmen's Bureau developed slowly in the state. The organization concentrated its initial efforts primarily in Mobile and Montgomery in order to develop a strong base for a statewide system. Both the pace and use of urban centers typified the federal agency's operations across the region. Bureau agents fully expected Mobile to serve as a model for the eventual expansion to rural Alabama. Headquartered in Montgomery, Maj. Gen. Wager Swayne served as the assistant commissioner for the state's educational and noneducational operations. Swayne made justice for Alabama's African Americans his top priority. He worked directly with Rev. Charles W. Buckley, the state's first superintendent of education, in order to ensure the creation of African American schools in Mobile with hopes of statewide expansion.[18]

More important, Swayne preferred utilizing individuals directly involved in local African American educational movements as local school superintendents. These individuals often had a greater knowledge of local conditions and concerns than federal officials. These individuals, furthermore, often had the trust of the communities in which they served unlike the former white elites who had supported the Confederacy. By hiring individuals directly involved in local efforts, Swayne hoped that it would instill widespread trust in the Freedmen's Bureau as an organization. Hence, Swayne hired E. C. Branch as the superintendent of schools for the District of Mobile in March 1866. Branch reported directly to Superintendent Buckley rather than to the Freedmen's Bureau agent in Mobile. As a result, black Mobilians and their educational partners often deferred to the agency's headquarters whenever problems arose.[19]

The symbiotic relationship proved essential in the development of the African American public schoolhouse in the state. It offered legitimacy to black Mobilians' efforts for education and convincing the broader white community of its merits. It also afforded federal protection. Likewise, the federal agency benefited. As one of the earliest educational systems in Alabama, Montgomery often looked to Mobile as a model for its operations elsewhere. Success in Mobile allowed for the spread of the Freedmen's School system to rural Alabama. By September 1866, the bureau had established the basic organizational structure and cemented relationships with several northern agencies. This foundation permitted the statewide expansion of the Freedmen's School system. Mobile's schools demonstrated that African American education was a worthy endeavor to white naysayers. As a result, the Freedmen's School system expanded beyond Mobile.[20]

Unlike other southern cities, Mobile attracted few northern organizations. During the first year, the school system consisted of the schools operated by the Northwestern Commission of the American Freedmen's Aid Commission at the confiscated Medical College as well as at several independent schools located in various African American churches. Location, restoration of transportation networks, local efforts, and other factors played a role.[21] The lack of northern organizational attention did not reflect a lack of support by black Mobilians. The school system was truly integrated into the fabric of the community. The school system raised money for benevolent and educational purposes. In addition to its own operational expenses, the nascent school system regularly made financial contributions to burial societies, an orphan asylum, almshouses, and other relief societies. Through its philanthropic and educational efforts, the African American schools quickly developed into important cultural institutions. By January 1866, E. C. Branch reported to the *Nationalist* that the city's schools had 1,700 students enrolled and seventeen teachers employed. At the end of the 1865–66 academic year, the school system boasted day, night, and Sabbath schools with 728 enrolled students as well as several private schools operated solely by African Americans.[22]

According to Branch, the initial schools thrived for several reasons. First, he cited the school system's admittance of any interested student, regardless of class or financial circumstances. Branch proudly proclaimed to the *Nationalist* that "no one is debarred the privileges of the school on account of *color or poverty.*" Students paid tuition on a sliding scale in relation to what they could afford. As a result, tuition charged to students ranged from 25 cents to $1.25 per enrolled student.[23] Second, the school system provided structure to the students' daily routine. The six-hour daily session began precisely at "fifteen minutes before nine o'clock" for religious services, and then "the departments return[ed] to their respective rooms in military order." By January 1866 the school system boasted classes using readers ranging from the *Pictorial Primer* to the *Rhetorical Fifth Reader of the Saunders' New Union Series.* Classes also existed in more advanced mathematics and grammar courses.[24] The school system, according to Branch, provided the students with a curriculum and a rigorous schedule comparable to any other common school, regardless of race. Furthermore, white and African American teachers' ability to harness their students' desire to become educated resulted in progress made by the majority of the students within nine months that Branch described as "truly surprising."[25] Branch's surprise was similarly being reported across the urban South. Countless educators and Freedmen's Bureau agents noted that African Americans' desire for education contributed to such high levels of success.[26] Both legitimated the project of using the schoolhouse as a vehicle for postwar assertions of freedom and citizenship. It quickly became a project worthy of continuation but also protection for future generations.

Despite initial success, some of the white educational partners disapproved of black Mobilians' active involvement. Racial assumptions colored these educational partners' attitudes. They viewed the schools operated by African Americans as inferior and staffed by incompetent educators. State Superintendent Buckley voiced this opinion in a report to Swayne. He wrote: "There are in Mobile several colored schools taught mostly by colored teachers. Some of these teachers are not competent for the position they fill. They need suggestions from experienced teachers." Buckley considered the educated class of African Americans as too inexperienced for teaching. He could not overcome the racial assumptions regarding slavery. He saw African Americans as holding inferior capacity and teaching ability. For these reasons, Buckley viewed guidance and supervision by experienced white educators, such as Branch, as necessary during the initial years of the Freedmen's Schools. As a result, he discouraged schools operated by African Americans and encouraged schools administered by white missionaries.[27]

For black Mobilians, the question over schools operated without white assistance never elicited such anxieties. Some preferred independent schools as evidenced by the students attending these schools. However, pragmatism influenced their acceptance of schools operated at the Medical College, too. Individuals often considered factors such as location, costs, and a teacher's experience. Thus, they gave their support to any sincere person who was devoted to African American education. By the end of the academic year, Superintendent Branch's "constant and faithful labors in this community" had received the appreciation of "every loyal citizen."[28] The *Nationalist* afforded the same level of praise to the work done in the private schools, as evidenced by its endorsement of the school operated by Miss Jeane Ashe, a black Mobilian. In calling attention to the advertisement for her school, the *Nationalist* noted: "Her work is a glorious one and we hope that she will be well sustained."[29] Hence, competition between schools that operated independently of the Freedmen's Bureau and schools that received outside financial support never bothered most black Mobilians as it did Buckley.

Educational access mattered; educational type did not. Both school types, though, fulfilled the community's overarching desire to become a literate people. Hence, both types could co-exist without difficulty.[30]

Moreover, the independent schools illustrated that black Mobilians were not solely dependent upon their white educational partners. While they recognized the importance of such partnerships, black Mobilians' desire for self-determination encouraged the schools' creation and coexistence. They utilized all forums and channels in order to ensure educational access for interested individuals. Their initiative showed that the Freedmen's Schools were not merely the result of outside influences but instead from their self-expression of the meanings of freedom and citizenship after Confederate defeat. They sought compromises over matters that did not threaten their chief objective and fought those that did. Pragmatism guided their struggle.

Intense hostility from white Mobilians overshadowed the debate over independent or federal schools. Indeed, white opposition represented a major obstacle in black Mobilians' struggle for education. White Mobilians often coped with Confederate defeat through violence directed at the first African American schools in the city. Some white residents characterized the African American and white teachers working in the Freedmen's Schools as a "pack of thieves," and "little dirty schoolmasters and schoolmistresses."[31] Dr. Josiah C. Nott, physician and dean of the Medical College, led the opposition movement. Prior to the Civil War, Nott received notoriety for his promotion of polygenism, or the belief of multiple origins, as a justification for slavery and repression of African Americans. He now attempted to thwart the nascent system by encouraging the destruction of the Medical College where he had served as the dean. Nott publicly declared that he "would rather see the building burned down, than used for its present purposes." His bold proclamation reverberated among white residents opposed to the Freedmen's Schools. They viewed eradication and property destruction as the only possible solutions to the postwar expansion of African American education.[32]

Several arsonists acted upon Nott's call to action. By the end of the summer of 1865, the Methodist Church and Presbyterian Church fell victim to "acts of incendiary violence." Throughout the 1865–66 academic year, arson plagued other churches that housed a Freedmen's School. According to Major General Swayne's report to O. O. Howard, commissioner of the Freedmen's Bureau, arson even destroyed the Zion Methodist Church in late 1865 "directly after a military order restoring possession to the congregation previously excluded by white Trustees." Arsonists found great support among white residents. In March 1866, the *Nationalist* reported the remarks made by a white citizen after the destruction of another church as being "glad of it, and he hoped the Medical college would go next." Ultimately, the resident felt that "when all places of resort for the negroes shall be destroyed, and the troops withdrawn, the whites would be able to manage them."[33] As evidenced by remarks of white citizens and Dr. Nott, and the actions of the arsonists, white Mobilians desired a swift end to the African American postwar educational gains, even if it meant the destruction of property that were seen as "places of resort."[34]

Nott's attack on African American education and the resulting arson never yielded the desired effects. After calling for its destruction, Nott argued for the restoration of the confiscated property to school trustees, thereby removing the Medical College as a "Negro school." He formally requested the school's return in a letter to O. O. Howard in late 1865. While extracts of the letter appeared locally, the London *Popular Magazine of Anthropology* published the entire letter in its July 1866 edition.[35] Entitled "The Negro Race," Nott employed scientific and historical evidence to argue that African Americans lacked the intellectual facilities and capabilities necessary for full citizenship and equality as whites. Ultimately, he concluded that the Freedmen's Bureau efforts could not overcome African Americans' natural inferiority, intellectual deficiencies, smaller brain sizes, and lack of a history worthy of study. Thus, Nott advised Howard to "remove your bureau and the United States troops (particularly blacks) as speedily as possible from our soil, and leave the relations between the races to regulate themselves." The publication of private correspondence, "The Negro Race" and its reprints in the Southern press, prompted swift and well-developed intellectual responses from black Mobilians and their educational partners. The nature of their responses directly challenged Nott's characterizations of African Americans' intellectual abilities and their access to education, citizenship, and equality in postwar Mobile.[36]

Instead of remaining silent as under slavery, black Mobilians responded directly to Nott's arguments against their right to education, citizenship, and equality as articulated in "The Negro Race." An anonymous letter to the *Nationalist* elaborately detailed the flaws in Nott's argument. First, the letter's author addressed the racial underpinnings of Nott's argument:

> The Dr.'s entire letter is predicated upon a theory in regard to the negro race. All facts that are not in accordance with this theory are ignore by him, while his deductions from this theory lead him to repudiate all the results of the war in regard to this race, and to condemn all the measures of the government based upon these results. There was a time, in the

history of our world, when the white race were not only not [*sic*] the
dominant race, but had not up to that time, had any history at all.[37]

In ignoring the significance of the Civil War, the author felt that Nott had
failed to acknowledge the gains achieved by African Americans in the war's
immediate aftermath: "According to Dr. Nott's logic, the struggles of our
ancestors for a place in history should have been discarded as the futile
schemes of an inferior race, which should have been consigned to permanent subordination." However, the author concluded that the reality of Reconstruction and the Freedmen's Schools revealed another reality. Postwar
achievements demonstrated that African Americans had not been "consigned to permanent subordination" as suggested by Nott. Instead, they had
accepted their rightful place in postwar Mobile as equals and not as racial
subordinates.[38]

The author then turned his attention to Nott's demand for the removal
of the Freedmen's Bureau from Mobile and the entire state of Alabama. The
author argued: "Dr. Nott demands that the Bureau shall be removed and
that he and his compeers be permitted to settle the matter with the colored people themselves. This settlement would, of course, be made upon
the basis of the Dr's theory of the permanent inferiority and subordination
of the colored people."[39] To this demand, the author forcibly and cogently
responded: "We tell the Dr., and all others, that the hope of any such settlement is perfectly visionary. There will be no settlement of matters here
but upon the basis of perfect reciprocity of rights and privileges between
the two races." The author predicted that there would be "a war of races at
hand, compared to which Hayti was mere boy's play" if anyone suppressed
their efforts to become an educated people in Mobile or elsewhere in the
state. Nott's arguments did not persuade them. Through his prediction of a
race war, the author expressed black Mobilians' absolute refusal to give up
their postwar gains. For the African American intellectual and lay community, Nott's arguments lacked merit. Indeed, they would wage another military engagement on the scale of the Civil War first instead of giving up their
newly acquired rights.[40] Yet the author still hoped for a peaceful resolution.

Through this engaged response, the author defined the terms with which
black Mobilians and their partners would deal with local white elites. They
maintained that the end of the antebellum white elites' infringement on African Americans' educational decisions was a nonnegotiable term. In their
eyes, emancipation ended their subservience. They fully embraced their
rights of citizenship in which educational attainment was at its core. Nott

and other white Mobilians simply had to come to terms with the new urban landscape that included the African American schoolhouse.[41]

Black Mobilians' relationship with the Freedmen's Bureau strengthened as a result of Nott's public denouncements and the resulting arson. Swayne demanded justice from the unreconstructed Confederates. He insisted that Mobile's mayor conduct a thorough investigation of the arson using the city's police department. In compliance, the mayor offered a reward "for the detection and proof to conviction, of the guilty perpetuators."[42] Although no arrests resulted, Swayne's overwhelming support of African American education placed Nott, arsonists, and other hostile white Mobilians on notice. If necessary, Swayne would use the full weight of the federal government in combating the opposition. Moreover, Swayne's swift response showed that the Freedmen's Bureau fully approved of black Mobilians' expressions of freedom and citizenship through education. The African American schoolhouse embodied the bureau's efforts to assist African Americans in their transition from slavery to freedom. Failure in Mobile was not an option. By not tolerating the actions of arsonists, the partnerships between the Freedmen's Bureau and black Mobilians strengthened.[43]

Overall, Nott's proclamation and the resulting arson galvanized black Mobilians' activism. They viewed their fight as a continuation of the Civil War. A March 1866 *Nationalist* article outlined the rationale behind their war:

> Ours is a moral war. The collision of arms, mighty as it was, illustrated the might or moral forces, which had been gathering in this country since the pilgrims came and planted the free state, the free church, and the free school. We say the war illustrated those powers, but it did not measure them. . . . The popular education of the North made it necessary that the war should come, and that it should be triumphant. The war simply put down the insurrection of barbarism against civilization, and opened the way for education which is the real liberation. The sword may make the freedman, but only the truth makes the freeman.[44]

In defining their plight as a war for protection and education, they saw their white partners as essential allies against hostile combatants like Nott and his followers. These enemies needed to be defeated in order to secure the fruits of their emancipation. Once they became an educated people, African Americans would truly achieve liberation from their slave past and be full citizens of the nation. The overwhelming support from their partners assured African Americans that they were not alone in the war. The arson and Nott's proclamations, therefore, increased their resolve.[45]

Thus, school operations continued amid the crisis. Unscathed by the arsonists' wrath, the Medical College absorbed several schools destroyed by fire. St. Louis Street School, Methodist Church School on St. Michaels Street, and the Presbyterian Church on Dauphin Street either temporarily or permanently moved into the building. As a result, the Medical College's enrollment increased accordingly.[46] Moreover, the Medical College's closing exercises in June 1866 received support from the community, in terms of attendance and media coverage. The extensive *Nationalist* coverage proudly named the scholars who received awards for scholastic achievement and those who performing remarkably well in the exercises. By highlighting success despite the tumultuous year, the *Nationalist* concluded that the "seeds of knowledge have germinated in hundreds of minds, and all that is now needed is that the young plants may receive the needed culture for a few years longer, and then our *Tribune* neighbor will cease to write about teaching them mechanically."[47] These public events held at the Medical College validated the community's continued activism against Nott and the arsonists. Neither arson nor other expressions of the local white opposition deterred them. It only spurred them into action.

During the 1866–67 academic year, a minor shift in organizational alliances occurred that would have major ramifications for the Mobile school system. The American Missionary Association took over operations of the schools at the Medical College. The organization pushed E. C. Branch and his host missionary association out of the school system. While Branch's opinions regarding the American Missionary Association's maneuvering is not clear, it is evident that Branch's commitment to the city's African American community never waned. He opened a grocery store that catered to African Americans' educational and noneducational needs and participated in the development of the city's Republican Party alongside former educational partners. Branch's presence and continued activism demonstrated his commitment to black Mobilians' educational quest, even after his departure.[48] The existing sources suggest that the organizational changes had few effects. Under new leadership, the Medical College remained the cornerstone of African American educational pursuits. The continued existence of the Medical College schools cemented the community's trust in the American Missionary Association. As a result, black Mobilians continued their activism against Nott with a new partner. This partnership proved beneficial in maintaining the Medical College within the Freedmen's School system.

Ultimately, Nott's proclamation and resulting arson prevented the return of the confiscated Medical College property to the school's former trustees. Dr. Nott petitioned the Freedmen's Bureau for the restoration of the Medical College to the school's antebellum Board of Trustees. Recalling Nott's involvement in the arson, Swayne refused. After causing some alarm among his superiors in Washington, DC, Swayne remained obstinate in his refusal, even to O. O. Howard, "unless so intimated in orders to resolve this building to applicants at present."[49] Instead, Swayne brokered a sale with the American Missionary Association for the property. A large monetary donation from Ralph Emerson Jr. to the American Missionary Association in early 1867 facilitated the sale and subsequent opening of Emerson College in the former Medical College. Whether acting alone or together, the community's educational partnerships strengthened because of local white opposition. Instead of abandoning the cause of African American education, the network successfully resolved the obstacles posed by arson and other expressions of opposition.[50]

White opposition did not present the only obstacle to black Mobilians' struggle for education. Internal division, specifically the divide between Creoles of Color and African Americans, posed another challenge. Dating from French and Spanish colonial rule, the social structure of Mobile and the surrounding county included Creoles of Color who claimed an African ancestry mixed with French and/or Spanish ancestry. The population was characterized by their light complexion, Catholicism, general acceptance of mixed-race ancestry, and pride in their European heritage. In ceding their land to the United States, colonial officials in Mobile ensured the continued existence of this group with the Louisiana Purchase in 1803 and the Adams-Onis Treaty in 1819. The Adams-Onis Treaty had the greatest impact by stipulating that African Americans and their descendants who could claim French or Spanish descent would be recognized as full citizens by the state of Alabama. As full citizens, the treaty guaranteed Creoles of Color their civil, social, and legal rights by elevating this mixed-race group into a new social status, widely known as the "treaty population." This treaty and the benefits bestowed upon Creoles of Color fostered the hostilities between Creoles and black Mobilians.[51]

Creoles of Color carved a space within Mobile's antebellum racial order. Living predominantly in Mobile, they represented approximately one-third of the city's population of free persons of color. They ensured the continuation of their rights by regularly invoking the Adams-Onis Treaty. According to historian Michael Fitzgerald, Creoles enjoyed rights not afforded to free or enslaved African Americans. These social and economic advantages caused the Creole community to disavow any association with free and enslaved African American communities in Mobile. As historian Virginia Meacham Gould indicated, Creoles also "fiercely protected their identities and status" through exclusive, by-invitation-only social and civic organizations such as the Creole Fire Company no. 1.[52]

Furthermore, Creoles used their access to education as a way to distinguish themselves from black Mobilians. When educational opportunities constricted for African Americans after Nat Turner's rebellion, Creole education legally expanded. Creole children typically received an education in private academies or parochial schools. Mobile's Catholic archdiocese established tuition-funded schools for Creoles under the direction of the Brothers of Sacred Heart and Sisters of Charity. In 1849 Rev. Alexander Mc-Glashen established the Bethel Free School for Creoles. Financed by special offerings and events, seventy students quickly enrolled in the school. The Mobile press deemed the school "greatly needed" for Creoles who "had certain of the rights and privileges of American citizens secured to them by the treaty." Reverend McGlashen later established the Creole Academy. Members of the Creole community oversaw both schools' operations and served as the administrators. By 1860 the Creole schools had 114 pupils, which represented the majority of the free persons of color attending school.[53]

The establishment of a public school system in Mobile further encouraged the division. The school system extended to the Creole population, but only at their insistence that city officials upheld their status mandated by the Adams-Onis Treaty. The city assumed the management of the Creole School in 1852 and maintained the school until the beginning of the Civil War at taxpayers' expense. The Creole Fair continued as a financial source for the school's operations. This "important cultural outgrowth" of the common school movement developments reinforced Creoles' unique antebellum identity as the school system maintained exclusive admission policies and excluded black Mobilians. Some exceptions existed though. Although the mayor required school administrators to provide the names of eligible children, some elite free African American children managed to receive an education from the Creole School. Lack of consistent enforcement of antiliteracy laws, and the occasional intraclass cooperation permitted these few exceptions. Overall, Mobile's antebellum educational developments reinforced Creoles' social status over black Mobilians.[54]

After the Civil War, the Creole School remained a source of division. The school was the only nonwhite school officially recognized by the Mobile school system. It remained outside of the Freedmen's School system, whose existence Mobile school officials did not recognize. Recognition and separation reinforced a feeling of superiority in Creoles over African Americans. Rather than remain silent on the issue, black Mobilians attacked the logic of Creoles' educational superiority because the Freedmen's Schools and access to education invalidated their claims. "A Subscriber" observed in a January 1866 letter to the editor of the *Nationalist* that "many of our best informed Creoles [are] falling into the ranks with their less favored brethren." The high tensions resulted in verbal and written insults and social ostracism between the communities.[55]

Events following the 1866 annual parade of the Creole Fire Company no. 1 forced a change in relations, which permitted the cooperation between John Carraway and Ovide Gregory at the 1867 Alabama constitutional convention. Founded by John A. Collins Sr., Lawrence Broux, Augustus Nicholas, and other Creoles in 1819, the Creole Fire Company no. 1 annually celebrated its anniversary with a parade. Festivities regularly included elaborate displays of the fire equipment for community review and approval, music performed by the fire company's band, and speeches delivered by Creole and white dignitaries.[56] One year after Confederate defeat, the Creole Fire Company no. 1 celebrated its forty-seventh anniversary. According to the *Mobile Daily Advertiser and Register*, the evening parade opened with a Creole brass band performing "Dixie" and other musical selections. The finely dressed firemen displayed their gleaming fire equipment and the Confederate flag in the procession. In the meeting preceding the torchlight parade, Creoles relished in the official recognition received by the antebellum white elites. Mayor Withers, several white Mobile fire companies, and other white dignitaries toasted the company. Each praised the Creole Fire Company no. 1 with speeches, which extolled on Creoles' patriotism as well as allegiance to the antebellum social hierarchy and the former Confederacy. The conservative white press also featured two full-length articles on the celebration.[57]

However, not everyone was impressed by the celebration. In the pages of the *Nationalist*, black Mobilians attacked Creoles' refusal to accept postwar racial realities and their place within the African American community. In response to the festivities, the newspaper rebuked the Creoles: "You may toady to white men till doomsday without becoming any whiter, and will only increase the stain by bringing yourselves individually into contempt. There is only one thing, which you can do, however, which is both sensible and honorable, and that is elevate your own race."[58] Black Mobilians limited their criticisms to the printed page instead of resorting to physical violence. However, a group of young white men showed no such restraint. Enraged by

the spectacle, several young white males went into interracial crowds viewing the procession and attacked any African American or Creole encountered. The men viewed both groups as being the same race and made no
distinction between African Americans and Creoles. In their indiscriminate
attacks, the young white men killed an African American bystander who
resisted. Horrified by the events, the mayor ordered their arrest. Instead of
imprisonment, the convicted youth received a fine for their actions.[59]

After the riot, a shift occurred. Although the schools remained separated, Creoles and black Mobilians reconciled some of their differences.
Shared experiences with white supremacy and burgeoning political activism fostered the initial attempts at reconciliation. The *Nationalist* implored its readers: "But if the sensible portion of both Creoles and freedmen
resolve to rise superior to their prejudice and to cultivate a spirit of amity
to work *together* in all good undertakings, their combined efforts secure to
both classes the more undisturbed exercise of all the rights of manhood."
While sources remain silent upon the details of the behind-the-scenes discussions, it is evident that reconciliation between the communities began
within the year. Subsequent Creole Fire Company no. 1 events received
positive commentary from the *Nationalist*. Ovide Gregory, future constitutional convention delegate, and other Creoles collaborated with African
Americans in a mass convention held in Mobile in May 1867. Together,
Creoles and black Mobilians advocated for the creation of an inclusive common school system throughout Alabama.[60] Shared experiences with racism
made Creoles align themselves with their African American brethren. To be
sure, this cooperation never truly eliminated tensions between the groups.
However, both groups willingly put them aside for the benefit of the entire
nonwhite community. They began seeing their postwar experiences as being a common rather than a separate one.[61]

This cooperation continued during the drafting and ratification of the
Alabama constitution. The *Nationalist* proved instrumental in unifying
and encouraging cooperation between the Creole and African American
communities. The newspaper sought to minimize class divisions among
African Americans and Creoles in order to secure their approval for the
convention and during the ratification process. Albert Griffin, the *Nationalist* editor, appealed to the communities prior to the convention by guar-
anteeing that the new constitution would include provisions for a public
school system. However, his assurances did not always eliminate speculation and anxiety as illustrated in an 1867 letter to the editor. The unknown
author leveled four charges against the newspaper. First, it argued that the
newspaper did not advocate for the creation of public schools. Second, the

newspaper wanted the schools, if created, to maintain class distinctions between Creole elites and nonelites. Third, under the new constitution the newspaper's editor would restore antebellum school commissioners. Fourth, the newspaper was advocating for separate schools and continued racial discrimination in the city. Griffin refuted all of these charges and attempted to diminish the class factionalism. He began by asserting that the newspaper fully supported public schools. He then argued that black and white Republicans, not Democrats, would fill the new school boards. He concluded by arguing that parents, rather than the convention, would decide upon the separate school debate. He felt that parents would vote for the constitution and public schools if the constitution did not make class and racial distinctions. The newspaper would continue to publish a barrage of articles and editorials dismissing these charges during its coverage of the convention and preratification election. The *Nationalist* actively pursued the Creole and African American communities for their support of the new constitution. Griffin and his staff recognized that the wounds of the antebellum divide remained not fully healed. Only unity would secure the education of both Creole and African American children in the new constitution, and ratification would ensure the future of education for nonwhites in Alabama.[62]

After failure of the constitution's ratification, the *Nationalist* devoted its attentions to alleviation of divisions between the communities.[63] Editors felt that their Republican allies in Congress would approve the constitution and allow Alabama's readmission without requiring another convention. Thus, the newspaper devoted little coverage to the subsequent ratification debate in order to fully bridge the divide between the African American and Creole communities. The strength of white conservatives' hegemony provoked the necessity of unity in order for African American education and other postwar gains to remain a reality.[64]

The African American and Creole communities now proved receptive to the *Nationalist*'s vision for inclusivity and state-funded public schools. Fear of conservative white Democrats regaining political saliency and power motivated many. Intimidation, violence, and other extralegal measures had allowed for failure in the ratification election. In an open letter to Mayor Caleb Price, several members of the African American and Creole elite appealed to the white community to lessen the violence against African Americans and Republicans during the congressional ratification debate and the 1868 elections. The violent restoration attempts threatened the new constitution. This threat made unity a pressing need as a strategy against the aggressive political adversaries. Solidarity, as historian Michael Fitzgerald demonstrated, permitted the prior factionalism to cease in the educational and political advancements in the city. The willingness to put aside class and color differences, Fitzgerald concluded, proved to be an effective strategy for the next two decades. Although social divisions still existed, the once-prevalent Creole and African American divide was minimized in the political and educational realm shortly after the ratification debate. Events surrounding the Creole Fire Company no. 1 anniversary parade and the ratification crisis revealed the necessity of a unified black community. Therefore, Creoles and black Mobilians put aside their antebellum differences in order to secure their vision for education, freedom, and citizenship over the postwar landscape.[65]

In April 1865 black Mobilians embarked on their long and arduous quest for education. A vocal white opposition and internal division within the city's black community quickly tempered the initial success of the schools. Despite these obstacles, they successfully established an educational foundation based upon an extensive network of relationships. In the process, black Mobilians and their educational partners never failed to remember the system's vulnerability. The extreme manifestations of local white hostility convinced them that only a strong relationship with federal agencies and suffrage would give the system any possible future. Undeterred, they continued their fight to become an educated people.

Within two years, black Mobilians had established a system of schools in the city but not everyone had access to them due to intimidation by whites and bleak economic realities. They, like their southern urban counterparts, remained dependent upon federal agencies and outside organizations to some degree. Even the private schools of Mobile required the Freedmen's Bureau protection against arsonists. As long as African Americans lacked the ability to fully exercise their freedom, the nascent school system remained vulnerable. It would take federal mandates for readmission to the Union in order to achieve the long-term sustainability desired by black Mobilians. Therefore, article 11, section 6 provided the necessary framework for transforming African American education into a legitimate state right of citizenship. To be sure, it did not end the challenges as African Americans worked with the state in developing the public schools. The new article, though, enshrined postwar educational advances by ensuring access for all Alabamians, not merely black Mobilians, irrespective of race and/or former servitude. It legitimated the African American schoolhouse and permitted its continuation with state funding. Ultimately, black Mobilians' definition of freedom and citizenship prevailed in the new landscape wrought by the Civil War.

━━━━

NOTES

1. Alabama Constitution (1868), art. 11, sec. 6, http://www.legislature.state.al.us/misc/history/constitutions/1868/1868_11.html (accessed on October 17, 2012).

2. Lawrence S. Berry, William V. Turner, and R. D. Wiggins, "Untitled," *Nationalist*, May 16, 1867, 3.

3. "Letter from Montgomery," *Mobile Daily Register*, November 10, 1867, 2.

4. Alabama Constitution (1868), art. 11, sec. 6; Eric Foner, *Reconstruction: America's Unfinished Revolution, 1863–1877* (New York: Harper and Row, 1988), 276; Arthur W. Bergeron Jr., *Confederate Mobile* (Jackson: University Press of Mississippi, 1991), xi.

5. Howard Rabinowitz, *Race Relations in the Urban South, 1865–1890* (rpt., Athens: University of Georgia Press, 1996), 156–57.

6. Foner, *Reconstruction*, 97–102; Rabinowitz, *Race Relations in the Urban South*, 157.

7. Heather Williams, *Self-Taught: African-American Education in Slavery and Freedom* (Chapel Hill: University of North Carolina Press, 2005), 87–89; Jacqueline Jones, *Saving Savannah: The City and the Civil War* (New York: Knopf, 2008), 216–18, 227–28, 257.

8. Foner, *Reconstruction*, 97–102; Hannah E. Stevenson, April 9, 1865 letter, folder 15, box 5, Curtis-Stevenson Family Papers, 1775–1920, Massachusetts Historical Society, Boston, Massachusetts; "New England Report of the Teacher's Committee," *American Freedmen* 1, no. 2 (May 1866): 29.

9. Heather Andrea Williams, "'Clothing Themselves in Intelligence': The Freedpeople, Schooling, and Northern Teachers, 1861–1871," *Journal of African American Education* 87 (Fall 2002): 372–73.

10. Foner, *Reconstruction*, 144–48.

11. Rabinowitz, *Race Relations in the Urban South*, 153–54; Foner, *Reconstruction*, 428.

12. Michael W. Fitzgerald, *Urban Emancipation: Popular Politics in Reconstruction Mobile, 1860–1890* (Baton Rouge: Louisiana State University Press, 2002), 9–25.

13. The historiography of the postwar African American educational efforts is extensive. Henry Swint, *The Northern Teacher in the South, 1862–1870* (1941; rpt., New York: Octagon Books, 1967). Swint's early conclusions of vindictive nature of "Yankee schoolmarms" was overturned by the following revisionist works: Jacqueline Jones, *Soldiers of Light and Love: Northern Teachers and Georgia Blacks, 1865–1873* (Chapel Hill: University of North Carolina Press, 1980); Ronald Butchart, *Northern Schools, Southern Blacks, and Reconstruction: Freedmen's Education, 1862–1875* (Westport, CT: Greenwood Press, 1980); Robert Morris, *Reading, 'Riting, and Reconstruction: the Education of Freedmen in the South, 1861–1870* (Chicago: University of Chicago Press, 1981). Scholars have turned their attention to African American participation, see James Anderson, *The Education of Blacks in the South, 1865–1935* (Chapel Hill: University of North Carolina Press, 1988), and Williams, *Self-Taught*. Building on the revisionist scholarship, Ronald Butchart's *School the Freed People: Teaching, Learning, and the Struggle for Black Freedom, 1861–1876* (Chapel Hill: University of North Carolina Press, 2010) is one of the definitive works available to date.

14. E. C. Branch, "Report of Our Schools," *The Nationalist*, January 18, 1866, 2; John B. Myers, "The Education of the Alabama Freedmen during Presidential Reconstruction, 1865–1867," *Journal of Negro History* 40, no 2 (Spring 1971): 165.

15. Harriett Amos, *Cotton City: Urban Development in Antebellum Mobile* (Birmingham: University of Alabama Press, 1985), 7, 22–24, 26–47, 196.

16. Karl Kaestle, *Pillars of the Republic: Common Schools and American Society 1780–1860* (New York: Hill and Wang, 1983), 64, 68–71, 76, 82, 91–92, 105, 113, 192.

17. Amos, *Cotton City*, 189–90; Christopher Nordmann, "Free Negroes in Mobile County, Alabama" (PhD diss., University of Alabama, 1990), 204–5, 210–12. Eighth Census statistics: US Census Bureau, "Statistics of the United States (Including Mortality, Property, &c.,) in 1860: Compiled from the Original Returns and Being Final Exhibit of the Eighth Census, Under the Direction of the Secretary of the Interior" (Washington, DC: Government Printing Office, 1866), 507.

18. Kenneth B. White, "The Alabama Freedmen's Bureau and Black Education: The Myth of Opportunity," *Alabama Review* 34, no. 2 (April 1981): 109; Kenneth White, "Wager Swayne: Racist or Realist?," *Alabama Review* 31, no. 2 (April 1978): 93–95.

19. "Mr. E. C. Branch," *Nationalist*, April 5, 1866, 3.

20. White, "Alabama Freedmen's Bureau and Black Education," 109; Horace Mann Bond, *Negro Education in Alabama: A Study in Cotton and Steel* (1939; rpt., Tuscaloosa: University of Alabama Press, 1994), 81–83.

21. Rabinowitz, *Race Relations in the Urban South*, 153–58.

22. Branch, "Report of Our Schools," 2; "Monthly Reports of District Superintendents, September 1865–June 1870," microfilm roll 5, Bureau of Refugees, Freedmen, and Abandoned Lands, *Records of the Superintendent of Education for the State of Alabama, Bureau of Refugees, Freedmen, and Abandoned Lands, 1865–1870*, National Archives Microfilm Publication M810, Record Group 105, National Archives and Records Service, General Services Administration, 1972 (hereafter AL-BRFAL-ED). For a history of the *Nationalist*, see Kimberly Bess Cantrell, "A Voice for the Freedmen: The Mobile *Nationalist*, 1865–1869" (master's thesis, Auburn University, 1989).

23. Branch, "Report of Our Schools," 2.

24. Ibid.

25. Ibid.

26. Williams, *Self-Taught*, 152–55; Foner, *Reconstruction*, 96.

27. C. W. Buckley, Draft Report Made to Major General Swayne Relative to Colored Schools, March 30, 1866, microfilm roll 1, AL-BRFAL-ED.

28. "Mr. E. C. Branch," 2.

29. "Private School," advertisement, *Nationalist*, December 27, 1866, 3.

30. "School Exhibition," *Nationalist*, April 19, 1866, 2; "Untitled," *Nationalist*, December 27, 1866, 2; "Private School," 3.

31. Quoted in Wager Swayne, Report to Major General O. O. Howard Concerning the Continued Occupancy of the Medical College in Mobile and the Reasons Therefore, January 24, 1866, microfilm roll 3, AL-BRFAL-ED (hereafter Swayne, report to Howard, January 24, 1866).

32. Reginald Horsman, *Josiah Nott of Mobile: Southerner, Physician, and Racial Theo-*

rist (Baton Rouge: Louisiana State University Press, 1987), 170–221, quoted in Swayne, report to Howard, January 24, 1866.

33. "The Recent Fires," *Nationalist*, March 18, 1866, 2; quoted in Swayne, report to Howard, January 24, 1866.

34. White, "The Alabama Freedmen's Bureau and Black Education," 118, 123–24.

35. Horsman, *Josiah Nott of Mobile*, 296–301.

36. Josiah Nott, "The Negro Race," *Popular Magazine of Anthropology* 1, no. 3 (July 1866): 102–6, 116–18.

37. "Letter of J. C. Nott, M.D.," *Nationalist*, March 1, 1866, 2.

38. Ibid.

39. Ibid.

40. Ibid.

41. Ibid.

42. Swayne, report to Howard, January 24, 1866; "Proclamation," *Nationalist*, March 8, 1866, 2.

43. C. W. Buckley, Draft Report Made to Major General Swayne by the Superintendent of Colored Schools, April 20, 1866, 3, microfilm roll 1, AL-BRFAL-ED.

44. "Education of the Freedmen," *Nationalist*, March 29, 1866, 2.

45. Ibid.

46. Branch, "Report of Our Schools," 2; Swayne, report to Howard, January 24, 1866.

47. "First of January," *Nationalist*, January 11, 1866, 2; "School at the College," *Nationalist*, June 28, 1866, 2.

48. "Glorious News," advertisement, *Nationalist*, April 18, 1867, 2; "Union Meeting," *Nationalist*, March 7, 1867, 2.

49. Swayne, report to Howard, January 24, 1866.

50. George Tracey to C. W. Buckley, January 11, 1867, George Tracey to C. W. Buckley, January 24, 1867, and William A. Talcott to C. W. Buckley, February 5, 1867, all microfilm roll 3, AL-BRFAL-ED; Charles A. Church, *History of Rockford and Winnebago County Illinois: From Settlement in 1834 to the Civil War* (Rockford, IL: New England Society of Rockford, Illinois, 1900), 334.

51. Amos, *Cotton City*, 185, 189–90; Fitzgerald, *Urban Emancipation*, 10–11; Ira Berlin, *Slaves without Masters: The Free Negro in the Antebellum South* (New York: Vintage Books, 1976), 131.

52. Fitzgerald, *Urban Emancipation*, 11–13; Virginia Meacham Gould, "Free Creoles of Color in Mobile and Pensacola," in *Creoles of Color in the Gulf South*, ed. James H. Dorman (Knoxville: University of Tennessee Press, 1996), 43–44.

53. Amos, *Cotton City*, 185, quoted in Nordmann, "Free Negroes in Mobile County," 201–2; Peter Kolchin, *First Freedom: The Responses of Alabama's Blacks to Emancipation and Reconstruction* (Westport, CT: Greenwood Press, 1972), 79–80; *Eighth Census Statistics*, 507. For Alabama codes regarding African American literacy after the rebellion, see Williams, *Self-Taught*, 208.

54. Amos, *Cotton City*, 189–90; Nordmann, "Free Negroes in Mobile County," 204–5, 210–12; Kolchin, *First Freedom*, 79; *Eighth Census Statistics*, 507.

55. Mobile City Directory, 1865–1866, Mobile Municipal Archives, Mobile, Alabama; A Subscriber, "Letter to the Editor," *Nationalist*, January 25, 1866, 2.

56. "Forty-Seventh Anniversary of Creole Fire Company No. 1," *Mobile Daily Register and Advertiser*, April 28, 1866, 3; Fitzgerald, *Urban Emancipation*, 12–13.
57. "Forty-Seventh Anniversary of Creole Fire Company No. 1," 3; "The Symposium of the Creole Fire Company," *Mobile Daily Register and Advertiser*, April 29, 1866, 3.
58. "A Talk with the Creoles," *Nationalist*, May 1, 1866, 2.
59. Fitzgerald, *Urban Emancipation*, 73.
60. "Time Makes No Changes," *Nationalist*, May 10, 1866, 2; "Ball of the Creole Fire Co.," *Nationalist*, January 31, 1867, 2; "Creole Fire Co. No. 1," *Nationalist*, May 2, 1867, 2; "Colored State Convention," *Nationalist*, April 4, 1867, 3; "Colored Mass Convention of the State of Alabama," *Mobile Daily Advertiser and Register*, May 4, 1867, 2.
61. "The Colored Men," letter to the editor, *Nationalist*, July 11, 1867, 2.
62. Albert Griffin, "The School Question," *Nationalist*, October 3, 1867, 2; Cantrell, "A Voice for the Freedmen," 58–60.
63. Cantrell, "A Voice for the Freedmen," 57, 67–68. Although the majority of the votes approved ratification, the election failed to receive the 85,000 votes required by the Second Reconstruction Act. This technicality blocked ratification. After a congressional intervention, a presidential veto, and a congressional override, the constitution eventually received recognition and approval for readmission.
64. Alpha, "What's Next," *Nationalist*, February 27, 1868, 2; Cantrell, "A Voice for the Freedmen," 64–68.
65. L. S. Berry, R. D. Wiggins, John Bryant, John Carraway, and James Bragg, "Protest of the Colored People," *Nationalist* (Mobile), September 5, 1868, 2–3; Fitzgerald, *Urban Emancipation*, 128–31.

PART 5

A New Urban South

CHAPTER TEN

Invasion, Destruction, and the Remaking of Civil War Atlanta

WILLIAM A. LINK

Few cities in the slave South became as much defined by the Civil War as Atlanta. Although not especially populous—ranking ninety-ninth in size among American cities in 1860 and sixty-first a decade later—the city proved crucial to the Confederacy. It was as important to the Rebel cause, according to Georgia governor Joseph E. Brown, "as the heart is to the human body."[1] Historian Liddell Hart called the city the "foundation of the hostile power and will of the Confederacy."[2] Atlanta's surrender on September 2, 1864, dealt a serious blow to southern fortunes. The Union invaders, as one historian concludes, penetrated the "very vitals of the Confederacy."[3] At the time, Union victory bolstered morale and greatly aided Lincoln's standing in public opinion on the eve of the presidential election in November 1864.

For the most part, scholars of the Civil War era have had more to say about the immediate military dimensions of William T. Sherman's Atlanta Campaign, and less about what the war meant for the city. Implicitly, they have focused more on the war than how the war transformed southern society. Subsequently, Atlanta became defined as a community that arose out of the ashes of destruction. From wartime destruction, Henry Grady declared in 1886, Atlantans "raised a brave and beautiful city" and achieved a "fuller independence for the South than that which our fathers sought to win in the forum by their eloquence or compel on the field by their swords."[4]

Using the instance of Atlanta, this chapter considers how the Civil War shaped the urban South, and how southern cities affected the war. The massive Yankee invasion of north Georgia in 1864 fundamentally remade the city, during the war and thereafter. Conditions of war altered the social landscape, drawing in population, creating new wealth, and, in particular, altering the basis of the slave system. The Civil War also changed Atlanta's social and economic structure, remaking what one historian calls an "over-grown town that was not even on the map" into a vital strategic center.[5]

Many years after it ended, the Civil War continued to shape how At-lanta understood itself. The searing experience of war meant destruction; Atlanta was invaded, besieged, destroyed, and depopulated. Subsequently, how Atlantans came to regard wartime destruction helped them to under-stand what the war meant, and how they regarded the future. While Atlanta was relatively unimportant as an urban entity before 1861, its physical and cultural importance depended on its wartime experience.

Atlantans today think of Sherman's invasion as a moment that helped to identify their city's particular position in the failed southern nation. In-vasion and destruction thus left a dual legacy. Like other Georgians, Atlan-tans demonized Sherman, making him into a symbol of callous disregard of helpless civilians and the depredations of the Yankee invaders. But destruc-tion also provided another, more powerful trope about a city reimagining it-self. Atlanta became a New South icon only because of the extent to which it suffered destruction, only because it was a Phoenix rising out of the ashes of destruction.[6]

Atlanta, a northern visitor wrote during the 1850s, was the "most unat-tractive place that I had seen."[7] Even so, it was a city on the move during the late antebellum era. By the 1850s, four railroad lines converged in the town, which renamed itself "Marthasville" in 1843 and "Atlanta" two years later. With nearly 10,000 inhabitants by the Civil War's outbreak, the town was growing into a significant urban center.[8] Driving Atlanta's growth was its insistent capitalist ethos. Early on, the city embraced the market revolution and uninhibitedly advocated itself as a center of commercial and mercan-tile activity. Like another city that during the same era that became a domi-nant transportation and marketing center—Chicago—Atlanta attracted a group of merchant-capitalists with an ambitious vision of their future in what historian Don Doyle calls a "northern enclave on foreign soil." Many of them were not Georgia natives, with a large percentage from the North. With this energized group of boosters leading the way, antebellum Atlanta relentlessly promoted growth, enterprise, and industry.[9]

With nearly fifty stores in the 1850s selling whiskey to thirsty residents, drunkenness and crime were common. Atlanta boosters eagerly abandoned its identity as a disorderly frontier town. In municipal elections in 1850, boosters organized a Moral Party, which competed with a Rowdy Party. After Moral Party candidate Jonathan Norcross, a Maine native who ran a sawmill and dry-goods store, was elected mayor, the Rowdies rebelled, shooting a small cannon loaded with grass and dirt at Norcross's office.[10]

The boosters suppressed the rebellion and arrested its ringleaders, using a posse of 100 men.[11] Yet antebellum Atlanta continued to have an unsavory reputation. Insults to honor frequently resulted in violence. "A rougher village I never saw," remembered one resident. The prevalent disorder and violence made boosters acutely aware of their fragile past—and the need to stabilize the social and political order.[12]

Rather than stalling Atlanta's boosters, secession and Civil War created new opportunities. Municipal leaders adopted the Confederate cause—even advancing an unsuccessful bid to make the town the capital of the new southern nation. In May 1862 Atlanta became a military post, formalizing the city's strategic importance.[13] On August 12, 1862, Confederate authorities declared martial law, enabling them to regulate civilian behavior and marshal economic resources.[14] Two years into the war, the city had become, according to the St. Louis Republican, the "most vital point in rebeldom."[15] On the city's western side, by August 1862 the Confederate arsenal produced 75,000 rounds a day and employed over 5,400 workers.[16] Workers manufactured field pieces, shell casings, casting shots, fuses, tents, swords, as well as whiskey, clothing, shoes, saddlery, leather goods, and belt buckles. Gunsmiths milled and rifled barrels; the Western and Atlantic shops produced the famous Joe Brown Pike, named for Georgia's governor. Mills in Atlanta ground wheat for flour; workshops produced hardtack to feed Confederate armies. Railroad shops manufactured cars and serviced them. Atlanta's furnaces and foundries made iron for Confederate gunboats and ironclads, along with other war supplies essential to the cause. The Atlanta Rolling Mill became second only to the Tredegar Works in Richmond in the production of rolled and rerolled rail that sustained the Confederate transportation system. By early 1862 the city had become what one historian called "one of the most important workshops of the Confederacy."[17]

But the wartime boom sorely tested the ability of the city fathers to govern. As Union armies pushed into the southern interior, refugees streamed in.[18] Railroads became overwhelmed by the demands of passengers and freight. Traffic clogged the railroads, and military needs competed with civilian passengers and freight. Tracks and rolling stock were so overused that maintenance became impossible. Western and Atlantic trains ran so closely together, according to one historian, "that there appeared to be one continuous line of box cars and locomotives from Atlanta to Marietta."[19]

Wartime expansion fanned a culture of speculative capitalism. Shortages of critical resources—raw materials, labor, and housing—became endemic. Civilians were victims of rampant inflation. "Times is very hard here," wrote a local woman.[20] Speculation, declared the Atlanta Daily Intelligencer, had become "now the curse of our country," the result of a "set of vampires, who will neither fight for the South nor contribute a cent to the support of those who are in the field."[21] The *Intelligencer* worried especially about the rising price of salt, an essential ingredient in food preservation. The "heartless extortion" of the salt supply badly affected rural Georgians, who "must perish" if speculator-driven price inflation continued.[22]

Rising crime and disorder—a throwback to Atlanta's frontier days— threatened the city's social order during wartime. According to one estimate, there were as many as 8,000–10,000 draft dodgers in the area, foraging for food and terrorizing residents in the suburbs.[23] With wages unable to keep pace with prices, labor unrest periodically erupted. In October 1862 workers at the Confederate arsenal struck for higher wages, but the strike collapsed when authorities threatened to conscript the workers. Similarly, a printer strike in 1863 failed in the face of threatened conscription.[24] Spurred on by rising prices and food shortages, civil unrest led by women erupted in 1863 in Richmond, Salisbury (North Carolina), Macon, and Augusta, especially so among soldiers' wives. On March 18, 1863, as many as twenty Atlanta women stormed local grocers, seizing bacon, meal, and vegetables. They took food because they needed it; "their suffering condition," they explained to onlookers, justified their actions. Although the Atlanta women attracted some sympathy for their actions, some Atlantans worried about a breakdown of law and order. They took property just as government had seized it, commented Atlanta's *Southern Confederacy*, and their actions imitated governmental tyranny. Was it any wonder that people had become "imbued with a spirit of lawlessness"?[25]

The disorder spawned by the war tested the boosters' ability to maintain a coherent identity. The wartime boom also opened opportunities for social conflict and differentiation inside the city, considerations that historians have often neglected. The war raised basic questions about loyalty and the support for the war among civilians, about the increasingly ambiguous position of African Americans, and about the security and sanctity of the slaveholding regime. In many ways, the centrifugal forces of war fractured social and ideological unity.

As in other parts of the South, conditional Unionists in Atlanta had opposed secession until Fort Sumter and the onset of military conflict. At the same time, there were also members of what historian Thomas Dyer calls a "small, but significant minority" of "Secret Yankees" who remained unconditional Unionists. Dyer estimates that perhaps a hundred Atlantans fell into this category.[26] Some residents were suspected of disloyalty. The *Atlanta Daily Intelligencer* warned of Fifth Columnists in the city, some of whom might become incendiaries. Southerners worried about arson in the presecession era, though the perpetrators they most often feared were resistant slaves. During the war, white fears shifted to traitors who might burn their businesses and homes. "The people, in country and town, should keep a bright look out for these prowling scoundrels," said the *Intelligencer*. These subversives were "to be found almost every where." The newspaper so feared incendiaries that it favored hanging them on the spot if caught in the act.[27]

There was some basis for Confederate paranoia. Unionist James L. Dunning refused to permit his Atlanta Machine Company Works to be used in the war effort. Confederate authorities responded by seizing the facility. Most Unionists kept their views to themselves. There was "no safety in talking in public," recalled one of them. Christian Kantz, a German who immigrated and owned a farm, ran a brewery two miles north of Atlanta. He privately described himself as "a Union man & opposed to the Confederacy." Once Sherman conquered Atlanta, Kantz worked with the invaders to identify loyal people in the city.[28]

Cyrena Bailey Stone, a Vermont native who moved to Atlanta with her husband in 1854, participated in a network of underground Unionists and kept a detailed diary of her activities. Her husband, Amherst Stone, a lawyer and entrepreneur, was arrested in 1863 in New York as a Confederate sympathizer. Although an ardent Unionist, Amherst was imprisoned twice in Fort Lafayette, New York, and then prohibited from returning south.[29] Alone in Atlanta, Cyrena Stone retained a stubborn loyalty to the Union. "Ye who dwell in that old North-land," she wrote in early 1864, "can ever know as it is known here—how little life and earthly possession are worth, without a Gover[n]ment to cling to." This "Strife between Truth & Treason must soon end—triumphantly for Truth."[30]

Stone emphasized dissatisfaction with the Confederacy and the war's hardships for ordinary people. As the war progressed, southern authorities began conscripting men in their forties. She cited the case of one Atlanta resident, older than the legal age limit of forty-five, who was pressed into military service while visiting Savannah. Obtaining a week's furlough, he informed Stone that he would "die before he will ever fight for this cause." At his request, Stone produced a secret "starred treasure"—an American flag—that she kept hidden. "When it was spread before him," she wrote, "he did not speak, for a minute or two," and his eyes brimmed with tears. "O God!" he declared, "when shall we see this dear old flag waving in triumph over this wretched land!"[31]

Stone welcomed a coming Armageddon. "The days go by with a strange quiet at home & the Front," she wrote about a month before Sherman's invasion, and springtime seemed "loth to adorn the land with sweet flowers when they are so soon, perhaps, to be bathed in blood—to be trampled in the dust by fierce warriors rushing on to victory or defeat." The "long expected battle" excited "wild hopes" on her part for Confederate defeat and redemption from the Rebel cause. The rumors of war were so near "that we almost put our ears to the Earth, and with finger on the lips—listen breathlessly" for an army that would "proclaim Liberty indeed."[32]

Stone looked forward to northern invasion, though she acknowledged the chaos accompanying it. These were "days of strange & thrilling interest, solemn too as death." There was a "wild up-heaving" with "encampments & fortifications appearing everywhere" and tent fires "gleaming in the dark forests, near & far—bugles sounding, solders coming and going; every thing & every body in a delirium of fear & excitement." She reported "fears & tremblings" among the residents because the "*Yankees* are coming, & they must go somewhere!"[33]

White Atlantans worried about the disloyalty of residents like Cyrena Stone, but a much more threatening specter of disloyalty lay in the enslaved and free black population. In antebellum Atlanta, black people remained on the margins. Slavery was weakly established compared with plantation regions.[34] The city had a tiny free black population, with only nineteen free negroes in 1850 and thirty-one a decade later. The frontier town largely excluded black people, as white artisans feared the competition of a larger black population. The city council imposed a $200 fine on free blacks entering the city in 1855. Atlanta also worried about hired slaves. A group of white mechanics complained to the city council in March 1858 about "Negro mechanics whose masters reside in other places," and who could "afford to underbid the regular resident citizen mechanics of your city." The white mechanics appealed to the city council to limit the use of unsupervised black labor.[35]

During the wartime boom, however, slave labor became critically important. Slave dealers ran a highly profitable business, with rising prices and skyrocketing demand.[36] Although compared to coastal or central Georgia the African American population in antebellum Atlanta remained small, in sheer numbers African Americans became a much more significant part of the city, increasing from 20 to 46 percent of the population between 1860 and 1870.[37] The war also presented new opportunities for black Atlantans. Cyrena Stone described black aspirations as gravitating naturally toward freedom, "a wild yearning for what every heart craves." Though an ardent Unionist, Stone expressed racial attitudes that assumed black inferiority and submissiveness. Although loyal to the Stars and Stripes, she owned six slaves and leased a seventh.[38] Nonetheless, Stone realized that the war was eroding slaveholder control.[39]

As war reached Atlanta, slaves responded enthusiastically. For several mornings in late May 1864, when few residents heard gun and cannon fire, Stone's slaves asked her about the sounds of battle. "I always answer no, and tell them it is all their imagination," Stone wrote. The next day, the slaves insisted that Cyrena go outside to listen. "There! Just listen way yonder!" they declared. "Didn't you hear that?" After some effort, she heard, far to the north, the "faintest echo of booming guns." When Stone realized what these noises were, they "awakened the wildest joy I have ever known." "O that music!," she wrote, "the first notes of our redemption anthem."[40]

The war remade Atlanta into an urban community in which black people played a more central economic role. As the wartime city expanded, its demography and racial dynamics changed. Doors now cracked open for some black people. Roderick Badger, a free black dentist, became the subject of white protests because of his "professional pretensions," but he succeeded in amassing property during the war. Similarly, six other black barbers also acquired belongings and wealth.[41] Others gradually acquired a more modest amount of property and nudged themselves closer to economic independence. Polly Beedles, a free person of color, married Henry, a slave, in 1861. During the course of the war, the Beedles accumulated property in her name.[42] Jefferson Simons, a slave blacksmith, found his services in high demand once the war began. Hiring his time from his master, "I owed nobody for it," he recalled. Buying his tools in 1860 and a wagon the next year, Simons later paid $325 in Confederate currency for a mule and $200 for a horse. By the end of the war, he owned enough property to make a claim for compensation from the northern government for a lost mule, horse, wagon, and tools.[43]

Other slaves also achieved greater autonomy. Joseph Holland, owned by banker and railroad man E. W. Holland, worked in Atlanta as a drayman. He acquired enough property to purchase himself and his wife from his master. In addition, Joseph saved enough money to buy his own stock—two mules and a horse—which he used in his hauling business. As a result of wartime prosperity, Holland also bought a house and lot. A decade after the war, the Southern Claims Commission certified that Holland's ownership of property was "fully & satisfactorily proved." When Sherman occupied Atlanta, although Yankee soldiers confiscated his mules and horse, Holland followed the northern army, and worked for them as they marched through Georgia and the Carolinas.[44] Prince Ponder, enslaved before the war, bought his freedom from an Atlanta widow out of profits from a successful grocery business, where he sold provisions, tobacco, and whiskey. A local white described him as "unusually energetic, industrious & money making" and owning "as much if not more property" as any black Atlantan. Julius Hayden, a local judge, owned Ponder's wife, and they lived on the Hayden farm about three miles from the city. In August 1864, once Sherman laid siege to Atlanta, Judge Hayden fled the farm, leaving Ponder in charge in exchange for serving as caretaker. Ponder owned a substantial amount of property: two mules, a bay horse, a horse and buggy with harness, and a wagon, along with stores of whiskey, tobacco, wheat, rye, hogs, and bacon.[45]

Among the more interesting instances of African American accomplishment was Austin Wright, an enslaved tinsmith. Born in Virginia about 1820, he moved to the city as a young man. Long before the war, with his master's endorsement he hired himself out, maintaining a tinshop in the city, acquiring property as a "man of energy and sagacity." The war pushed matters along further. Soon Wright operated a business that was outside of the control of his master, a "red hot rebel" who no longer even collected hiring wages from him. In 1863, hearing of Lincoln's Emancipation Proclamation, Wright declared himself as free and working "in his own name." He secured control of a downtown building, renting it from Lucien B. Davis, a white man. Wright then sublet rooms in the building to other black people.

Wright made canteens, tin cups, and other materials for the Confederate army. The wartime boom was a boon, as Wright's tinsmith trade took off, producing, according to one account, a "very considerable business for a colored man." Wright scoured the city for tin, a scarce wartime commodity, securing stocks from second-hand sources. Becoming an important leader in the black community, during the war Wright spread the word about freedom to other slaves. He also lent money to other enslaved and free African Americans in Atlanta.

Early in the war, moreover, Wright helped to organize three "negro balls," ostensibly to raise money for Confederate soldiers and their black servants. In December 1861 the *Atlanta Daily Intelligencer* charged that the negro balls had "become so frequent in our city, that they amount to a nuisance." At the balls, a "big buck negro, with a gold watch in his pocket, and a gold chain around his neck . . . acts as master of ceremonies." The *Intelligencer* complained that the money raised rarely benefited soldiers but became a pretext for local black leaders to accumulate capital.[46] To many whites, the negro balls had careened out of control, and in 1863 the city council prohibited them.

Seven years after the war ended, in 1872, Wright petitioned the Southern Claims Commission for nearly $6,400—an astonishingly large amount—in restitution for property from his tinshop, which he claimed that the Union army had confiscated when they occupied Atlanta in September 1864. Like most other black people, he remained loyal to the Union; a fellow African American described him as "always a Union man" who was "just like every other colored man—loyal." But Wright's petition encountered an incredulous response: How could a black man have acquired so much property? It was "barely possible that this negro may have had a few articles of Tin when the soldiers entered the beleaguered town," said an army officer present in Atlanta in September 1864, but he found highly unlikely that Wright possessed this much wealth. The leading tinsmith in Atlanta, a white man, reported that Wright owned no more than $2,000. The Claims Commission concluded that it was impossible to validate Wright's claim, though it declared itself "fully satisfied" that some property was taken by Union troops. It awarded him $500 in compensation.[47]

The Civil War helped to create a black middle class in Atlanta, laying a lasting foundation for their future in the city. The accumulation of wealth, however modest, provided a basis for expanding economic, cultural, and political leadership. From a city that during the antebellum years had few blacks, either enslaved or free, Atlanta became a city that, as a result of the wartime boom, possessed a visible presence of black people. Not only did the racial demographics change, but also the racial balance of power was altered. By undermining the system of slavery, the pressures of war created fissures that blacks could exploit but that also thoroughly alarmed whites.

Whites recognized that the most important implication of increased black economic freedom was the erosion of the slave system. Particularly troublesome was the increasingly common practice by which masters permitted slaves to hire themselves out. Self-hiring was widely condemned during the antebellum years. During the war, white fears grew about black economic freedom. In September 1862 fifteen male slaves were arrested when they were discovered unsupervised in quarters above a downtown storehouse. "That negroes, slaves, should be permitted to hire rooms to sleep in, away from their owner," said the *Atlanta Daily Intelligencer*, was a "new feature of toleration in our city." The newspaper called for officials to suppress this practice because it was "corrupting to our negro population." As late as April 1864, however, the Fulton County grand jury maintained that self-hiring was "on the increase and constantly abused."[48]

Whites worried about the loyalties of their slaves, who made clear their sympathies. "My only fear is [that] there may be some trouble with our negroes," wrote an Atlanta woman in November 1861. She warned of a "diabolical plot" intending to increase the numbers of free blacks "to try to excite our slaves to rebellion."[49] There were various attempts, mostly unsuccessful, to restrict black autonomy. In 1863 the city council prohibited slaves from renting horses or carriages without slaveholders' approval. The council also banned slaves and free blacks from selling beer, cakes, fruits, or confectioneries, and prevented them from walking with a cane, club, or stick, or from smoking tobacco in public places.[50] The mayor's court, which regulated petty crime, cracked down on self-hiring erratically. In May 1861 ten slaves were charged with "living separate and apart from their owners and hiring their own time," and the court responded by fining their masters. Similarly, in February 1862, the court fined a white man twenty dollars for "allowing your slave to hire her time and enjoy the privilege of labor for her self & c." The court avoided prosecuting self-hiring because of the law's ambiguity and because of the difficulty of enforcement. By early 1862 the court had decided that there was "no penalty prescribed by the ordinance against the hiring of their time, by slaves to be inflicted upon the Slave for such offence."[51]

A basic problem in any crackdown was that many Atlanta whites profited from the underground economy. In February 1862 the mayor's court fined a white man, Thomas Clince, ten dollars for "allowing your slave Nancy to keep an eating house & c."[52] In August 1863 another white, Harris Fuller, was fined ten dollars for permitting his slave, Louisa, to maintain an eating house "on her own account or the account of another person."[53] The generally lax attitude toward self-hiring, combined with greater attention to independent black entrepreneurs, continued during the remainder of the war.[54]

White fears about the disintegrating system of slavery focused on crime. Freedom for slaves, to whites, meant a threat to property. Whites complained about an epidemic of theft that was caused by "negroes [brought] from a distance . . . who are too frequently left in the charge of no responsible party."[55] About the rise in theft, the *Atlanta Daily Intelligencer* commented: "We have no doubt that most if not all this pilfering is done by negroes."[56] In another indicator of the disturbing public presence of unregulated black people, the white city government attempted to prevent the sale of liquor to black people. In July 1861, when Randall, a hired slave, was charged with selling liquor to another slave, Isaac, the mayor's court responded with the harsh sentence of thirty-nine lashes.[57] In February 1864 another slave, Edward, was convicted of a similar crime and received an identical sentence.[58]

Fears of crime melded with a more defiant and resistant black community. Freedpeople simply seemed more assertive. In March 1861 John Parker, a free black man, facing charges of unruliness, received twenty lashes.[59] Disorderly conduct on Atlanta streets became a common charge of African Americans hauled before the mayor's court.[60] Especially disturbing was a rising incidence of defiant disregard of racial etiquette—what whites called "impudence" and "insolence." In October 1861 a slave, Lucy, was charged with "disorderly conduct by using impudent language to a white person & c." She was sentenced to thirty-nine lashes.[61] In February 1863 a hired slave, Bill, who rode a horse on the sidewalk and used insolent language, received fifteen lashes.[62] In February 1864 another slave, Stephen, was charged with yelling at midnight and "mocking the Policeman."[63]

The war raised new questions about master-slave relationships and about the institution of slavery itself. Black people experienced the wartime boom, just as did whites, and they exploited the opportunities before them. But they also faced considerable hardship. Confederates freely impressed slaves to maintain defenses and trenches, and regularly exposed them to military danger. In the late stages of the war, northern invaders made little distinction between white and black, and in spite of prospect of liberation African Americans also confronted danger, deprivation, and loss.

For whites, invasion and destruction meant social disintegration. The experiences of Thomas Maguire, a cotton planter living northeast of the city, are illustrative. Born in Ireland in 1801, Maguire immigrated to Gwinnett County, near Atlanta, and in 1860 owned twenty-six slaves. As the invaders moved into northern Georgia, Maguire angrily denounced the Yankee intrusion. On July 29 Union troops arrived and confiscated his corn, though much of it remained hidden; he observed that his family hated the "mean Yankees." A neighbor noted that the troops appeared to have left the neighborhood—"he hopes to Hell." Maguire hid his bacon; "to keep it in the smoke house," he explained, "is to invite the Yankees to take it if they come this way." While hearing rumors, probably untrue, that the Yankees had suffered a "whipping" in Atlanta, Maguire described his anxiety about the uncertainty of invasion. "I long to hear what our army is doing in Atlanta but we must wait," he wrote in his diary. "To be without news regular is a great hardship." Later, someone from Atlanta passed through and claimed that things were "all right" there. "I hope he tells the truth," Maguire wrote skeptically. His slaves, he recounted, were "all demoralized," with "everything going wrong or nothing going right."[64]

Throughout August, Maguire heard the Union bombardment of Atlanta. "Would like to know the result," he recorded on August 2. Three days later, he reported a lull in the fighting; "no firing last night or this morning in Atlanta," he wrote, though it resumed in the afternoon. Anxious about the result, he said he did "not know what to do." Yet the sounds of cannon fire kept him guessing. "Heavy firing about Atlanta last night," he wrote on August 16, followed by "little firing" the following morning. "Would like to know the reason," he said, but he predicted that "our flag is there still waving bravely to the breeze." As the cannon quieted in late August, Maguire speculated about the news of the battle. He reported the rumor that the Yankees were "badly whipped" at Jonesboro and had left Atlanta, "but where they are gone is unknown." For the last week of August, he ended many of his entries with the disappointed inscription, "No news."[65]

What Maguire and others saw as hopeful signs of Yankee defeat was actually the beginning of the end for Confederate Atlanta. Rather than withdrawing, during the last week of August 1864 Sherman began a flanking maneuver in which he moved six of his seven infantry corps, 60,000 men, between Rough and Ready and Jonesboro, sixteen miles south of the city. In a battle on August 31, northern forces succeeded in capturing the Macon and Western Railroad and in cutting the remaining rail link from Atlanta.[66] Once this connection was closed, Atlanta's fate was sealed, and Confederate forces evacuated the city on September 1, 1864.

Maguire soon learned of Atlanta's fall. He described a "great fire" consuming Atlanta and burning "all the public stores . . . that could not be got away." Distraught about defeat, Maguire was comforted by the clarity of the news. It was reported, he wrote, "that Atlanta is given up and our army falling back." This was a "great misfortune to Georgia but it cannot be helped." White Georgians were now "in a bad fix." But he remained worried about what the victors would do, and rumors abounded among the locals immediately outside Atlanta. "Plenty of rumors about the Yankees," he wrote, with "lots of folks moving back their stock, etc., etc."[67]

Occupying Atlanta with little resistance, the Union army moved into the city on the morning of September 2. Sherman did not enter Atlanta until the morning of September 3, quietly arriving from southwest of the city. Atlantans watched him, according to one account, "eager to catch a glance of the man whose name had now become so famous." A lone black man exclaimed: "I just wanted to see de man what made old massa run."[68] Atlanta, Sherman telegraphed Halleck, "is ours, and fairly won." He could later proudly report to Grant on September 6 that he was "feeding high on the corn-fields of the Confederacy."[69]

Two months later, on November 15, 1864, the northern invaders left Atlanta. As the 33rd Massachusetts's band played "John Brown's Body," Atlanta's northern occupiers, after a two-month occupation, left the city, torching the downtown, singing as they marched out of town. "I have never

heard that noble anthem when it was so grand, so solemn, so inspiring,"
declared a Vermonter. The heavens were "one expanse of lurid fire."[70] Atlanta's burning, commented Sherman's aide Henry Hitchcock, presented
the "grandest and most awful scene." He described "great tongues of flame,
then huge waves of fire" shooting up beyond rooftops, while collapsing
walls sent up cinders. From Union headquarters, Hitchcock watched "immense and raging fires, lighting up the whole heavens." "The whole region
for miles was lighted up with a strange and indescribable glare," an Ohio
soldier remembered. "Atlanta on fire—Ah cruel war," echoed another Buckeye, "and cruel it has become."[71]

After the war, acutely sensitive to his image as a rampaging Vandal,
Sherman offered an evasive interpretation of policies toward civilians. In
his memoirs, he discounted civilian depredations and destruction of property as the result of "bummers" operating on the fringes.[72] Rather than
deliberately destroying Atlanta when he left in November 1864, Sherman
claimed that he intended only to burn public buildings in the city center.
"As far as burning the city in the sense of wanton destruction," Sherman
told an interviewer in 1881, "I never thought of such a thing."[73]

In the circumstances of the Atlanta Campaign, Sherman avidly pursued
military objectives that led to the bombardment of the city and the expul-
sion of its citizens. In terms of the military standards of the time, these
two decisions, combined with his fabled March to the Sea, were perfectly
legitimate, perhaps unjustly earning him the enmity of white southerners for many generations. But whether Sherman was militarily justified in
waging his sort of warfare is of less concern than how he became a symbol
for invasion and destructiveness. The truth lay less in an objective than
in perceived reality. For there is little question that white Atlantans ral-
lied around the notion that Sherman meant invasion, and invasion meant
destruction.

A few weeks after Sherman left Atlanta, Yankee troops again visited
Thomas Maguire. Before they came, he wondered about his future but was
careful to hide tools, horses, and buggies. "What will become of us," he lamented, "God only knows."[74] After the Yankees camped around his house,
Maguire fled to the woods. "At every side," he wrote, "hogs and sheep are
being shot down and skinned to regale Yankee palates." Spending two nights
in the woods, Maguire returned to discover much of his property in ruins.
"Gin house and screw burned, stables and barn all in ashes, fencing burned
and destruction visible all around," he wrote. His carriage and wagon were
burned, with livestock, feed, and equipment taken. Engaged in the "gathering
up the fragments of the spoils," Maguire concluded that it was useless to try

to calculate the extent of destruction. This was, he declared, "the destruction of Jerusalem on a small scale."[75]

In the aftermath of war, northern visitors portrayed Atlanta's ruin as just retribution. The "Babylon of the South" had fallen, wrote a reporter, with its deserted "splendid houses and broad streets." Its future seemed clear: "The streets will soon be overgrown with grass, and sportive children will play through them and furtively peep through the piles of brick and the ruins of factories, foundries, and railroad depots, peopling the deserted halls with ghastly legends." Atlanta was nothing more than "a deserted city of ruins" whose "growing grandeur and loveliness" had disappeared. The city stood as a "lesson to rebels of the fruits of their wicked efforts to rend their country in pieces."[76]

The Yankee conquest of Atlanta and fiery departure all created physical destruction. As the lifeline of Atlanta's economic existence, the railroad infrastructure became a primary target during the campaign. Sherman's commanders ravaged the Western and Atlantic railroad lines as they moved southward from east Tennessee toward Atlanta.[77] Sherman cheered on the devastation of the transportation network, and troops were specifically instructed about how the rail lines should be destroyed. "Let details of men . . . begin at your very front and break up and destroy the railroad absolutely back to and including Decatur," Sherman wrote to Gen. John A. Logan in July 1864.[78] "I want you to do the best job of railroad destruction on record," he told another general. Sherman instructed that cuts in the railroad lines be filled with logs and trees and then covered with dirt so that "we may rest perfectly satisfied as regards the use of this railroad during the remainder of this campaign."[79]

Observers frequently commented about how the Atlanta Campaign wreaked havoc on the landscape. When Sherman's army left Atlanta, wrote memoirist F. Y. Hedley, the area between Atlanta and Chattanooga was laid to waste, where months before that area had been "alive with masses of fiercely contending human beings." After a "demon of destruction" had passed by, the landscape stood "still and desolate." Although most of the graves of the dead remained unmarked, noted Hedley, there were other "monuments testifying to the fearful struggle": trees destroyed by cannon, along with destroyed caissons. There was, he reflected, "no time for sentiment, and death's work had no novelty here."[80]

Union photographer George N. Barnard documented the effects of Sherman's campaign after September 11, 1864, when he arrived in Atlanta. For the next month, he photographed empty battlefields, fortifications, denuded forests, barren fields, pockmarked houses, and the burned ruins of downtown Atlanta. Barnard's images show how the invaders and defenders reshaped the forests, valleys, and farms that stood in the path of war. The city "suffered much from our projectiles," wrote a journalist accompanying Sherman, with many burned-out and destroyed houses. "Almost every house in the centre and the north and west ends of the town bear testimony to the skill and execution of our gunnery."[81] A reporter who visited the route of Sherman's invasion a year after his campaign noted that the 136 miles between Chattanooga and Atlanta were marked by ruined buildings and destroyed property, showing "what a desolation war is."[82]

Strolling through central Atlanta a year after its destruction, a reporter described "many things curious and striking." The city hall had survived. The large square, two-story brick building was occupied by troops and served as a jail, its ground windows barricaded with iron rails. Nearby, though located in the worst areas of the bombardment, five churches fared well; only the Episcopal church burned. The buildings around these churches bore the marks of war. City residents were still in shock, according to this account, "too exhausted or paralyzed . . . to have attempted anything toward rebuilding." One brick building was "covered rudely with boards," and a barber ran his business there. With some exception, there was "nothing in Atlanta that deserves the name of business."[83]

Eyewitnesses agreed about destruction and devastation affecting Atlanta. A newspaper correspondent from Richmond wrote in August 1864 that the Western and Atlantic route between Dalton and Atlanta was devastated for four miles on either side.[84] The property of north Georgia was completely destroyed, wrote a Wisconsin soldier in early June 1864; nothing could "escape the scrutiny of the boys." The country was "desolate" and "fearful."[85] "Our army is destroying all the Crops as we go along," wrote a soldier in the Ohio 94th Regt.[86]

An Atlantan returning during the fall of 1864 described the environmental damage. Approaching the city from Stone Mountain, or from Kennesaw Mountain, the vista was unobstructed by the dense forest which had previously blocked the view. For many miles around the city, "scarcely a tree is standing, and near and within a few miles of the city fire and the axe have destroyed the habitations of the rich and the poor, and laid waste the ground." Animal carcasses lay everywhere, "while the stench . . . filled the air, producing a loathing on the part of all who ventured into the city, unutterably disgusting." On downtown streets lay charred remains of railroad ties that were "so numerous and spread out to such an extent, as to remind of the ocean when the waves are raised by a brisk wind." This was "an ocean of ruins."[87]

Atlanta's rebuilding during the post–Civil War decades became part of its psyche as an urban community able to remake itself into a center of modern capitalism in a New South. But the city's revival was intimately connected to wartime developments, and Atlanta's fate depended on northern involvement. As William Thomas shows, during 1865 the US Military Railroad Corps repaired and rebuilt the devastated Western and Atlantic immediately after the war, installing 140 miles of new track and constructing sixteen bridges. The effort relied on a massive effort of human and financial resources, which the US government provided, resulting, according to Thomas, in an "entirely redeveloped railroad network." Business activity was significant; 338 new firms were licensed in the city during the last half of 1865 alone. Atlanta's retail district possessed 250 brick buildings by late 1866, most of them new or reconstructed structures. Railroads rebuilt depots and shops; new machine shops and foundries supported a railroad boom. The city's political leadership constructed two new market houses, enlarged and refenced the city cemetery, widened and improved streets, and removed the debris and trash left over from the war.[88]

As was true throughout its history, Atlanta welcomed migrants, and, while residents' businesses failed, outsiders opened new enterprises. Atlanta had traditionally been friendly to northern investment and businessmen; this remained true during the postwar years. Although northerners joined the ranks of migrants, many were native-born white southerners. S. R. McCamy moved from Chattanooga to Atlanta sometime in 1866. "A sharp shrewd trader," he was reported as having "considerable means which he has not lost." He began a merchandising business with partners from Athens, Kentucky, and Atlanta. Judged as "high toned honorable gentleman and worthy of credit," McCamy apparently had a "fair run of trade and a large stock."[89]

Wartime devastation laid a basis for postwar economic expansion. Agents of the credit-reporting agency, R. G. Dun, described widespread economic devastation, resulting in the extinction of many of its entrepreneurs. But those surviving the cataclysm often did so because they had profited from the war. Some Atlantans made handsome fortunes because of their close relationship with the Confederate government in supply and distribution. Merchants Cox and Hill emerged from the war "probably with more than before," according to the Dun agent, because of profits from Confederate Quartermaster business. Somehow, they saved these profits, perhaps by storing their wealth in gold abroad. Despite the collapse of Confederate currency, the most successful entrepreneurs were those possessing capital that they could plow back into their businesses after the war.[90]

The connections between pre- and postwar economic successes also appeared in the instance of George Washington Adair, an antebellum capitalist who expanded his business after Confederate defeat. Though a Unionist prior to 1861, Adair enthusiastically adopted the Rebel cause, editing the pro-Confederate *Southern Confederacy*. Late in the war, he demonstrated his credentials by enlisting in a cavalry regiment, serving under the fabled Gen. Nathaniel Bedford Forest. Adair became one of postwar Atlanta's most successful real estate entrepreneurs, but the foundation of his wealth lay earlier. A railroad conductor first moving to Atlanta in 1854, Adair began a successful trading and auctioneering business. But the Dun agent reported a business about which Adair subsequently said little—slave trading. In January 1857 he and his partner were described as "negro brokers" who were "keen & shrewd traders" who were "good for all contracts." The wartime demand for slaves in Atlanta added to Adair's capital resources and provided a basis for postwar expansion and wealth.[91]

How did the Civil War shape the urban South, and how did southern cities affect the war? Atlanta was hardly typical of the antebellum urban South. It was a smallish interior city, even for the South, whose existence depended on railroads. It was dwarfed in the antebellum era by cities such as Baltimore, Savannah, New Orleans, and Richmond. But these qualities made Atlanta a leading example of what postwar urban southern cities would look like, as railroads, industry, and finance defined economic significance. Atlanta became an exemplar of what boosters would call the "New South."

In this sense, the Civil War became key in transforming Atlanta's status as an urban center. The Civil War itself exposed division and conflict, not unity, raising expectations, creating wealth, and opening doors previously closed. In particular, the war expanded the African American presence even while it undermined the stability of the institution of slavery. The destruction of the city by Confederates and Yankees was vivid, but it helped lay a basis for a subsequent remaking and reimagining of the Atlanta's position in the New South.

NOTES

1. Quoted in Grigsby Hart Wooton Jr., "New City of the South: Atlanta, 1843–1873" (PhD diss., Johns Hopkins University, 1973), 91.

2. B. H. Liddell Hart, *Sherman: Soldier, Realist, American* (New York: Dodd, Mead, and Co., 1929), 233.

3. Albert Castel, *Decision in the West: The Atlanta Campaign of 1864* (Manhattan: University Press of Kansas, 1992), 539, 547.

4. http://www.anselm.edu/academic/history/hdubrulle/civwar/text/documents/doc54 .htm (accessed May 2, 2010). On Grady's speech, see Raymond B. Nixon, *Henry W. Grady: Spokesman of the New South* (New York: Alfred A. Knopf, 1943), chap. 11; Harold E. Davis, *Henry Grady's New South: Atlanta, A Brave and Beautiful City* (Tuscaloosa: University of Alabama Press, 1990), chap. 6.

5. Castel, *Decision in the West*, 547.

6. On destruction, see Megan Kate Nelson, *Ruin Nation: Destruction and the American Civil War* (Athens: University of Georgia Press, 2012); Lisa M. Brady, *War upon the Land: Military Strategy and the Transformation of Southern Landscapes during the American Civil War* (Athens: University of Georgia Press, 2012).

7. Carlton Rogers was the visitor. Wooton, "New City of the South," 14.

8. Harvey K. Newman, *Southern Hospitality: Tourism and the Growth of Atlanta* (Tuscaloosa: University of Alabama Press, 1999), 11–20; Georgina Hickey, *Hope and Danger in the New South City: Working-Class Women and Urban Development in Atlanta, 1890–1940* (Athens: University of Georgia Press, 2003), 9ff.; Wooton, "New City of the South," chap. 1.

9. Don Harrison Doyle, *New Men, New Cities, New South: Atlanta, Nashville, Charleston, Mobile, 1860–1910* (Chapel Hill: University of North Carolina Press, 1990), 34. Also see Mary A. Decredico, *Patriotism for Profit: Georgia's Urban Entrepreneurs and the Confederate War Effort* (Chapel Hill: University of North Carolina Press, 1990).

10. Thomas H. Martin, *Atlanta and Its Builders: A Comprehensive History of the Gate City of the South*, 2 vols. (Atlanta: Century Memorial Publishing Company, 1902), 1:77.

11. Wallace Putnam Reed, *History of Atlanta, Georgia* (Syracuse, NY: D. Mason and Co. Pub., 1889), 32–33.

12. "The place," wrote early historian Thomas H. Martin, "was nothing if not bustling." "At a very early period in her history," he declared, "Atlanta laid the foundation of her great commercial supremacy and rapid upbuilding." Also see James Michael Russell, *Atlanta, 1847–1890: City Building in the Old South and the New* (Baton Rouge: Louisiana State University Press, 1988), 72; Reed, *History of Atlanta*, 45–46; Martin, *Atlanta and Its Builders*, 1:100; Wooton, "New City of the South," 48.

13. "Military Regulations in Atlanta," *Atlanta Daily Intelligencer*, May 15, 1862; "Atlanta as a Military Post," *Atlanta Daily Intelligencer*, January 15, 1863.

14. "Martial Law," *Atlanta Daily Intelligencer*, August 14, 1862.

15. Quoted in *Natchez Daily Courier*, November 24, 1863.

16. Ralph Benjamin Singer Jr., "Confederate Atlanta" (PhD diss., University of Georgia, 1973), 240–41.

17. Arthur Reed Taylor, "From the Ashes: Atlanta during Reconstruction, 1865–1876" (PhD diss., Emory University, 1973), 3.

18. "An Influx to Atlanta," *Atlanta Daily Intelligencer*, February 27, 1862.

19. Reed, *History of Atlanta*, 106; Franklin M. Garrett, *Atlanta and Environs: A Chron-*

icle of Its People and Events, 2 vols. (Athens: University of Georgia Press, 1954),
1:509–10; Singer, "Confederate Atlanta," 108, 148–49; Elizabeth Bowlby, "The Role
of Atlanta during the War between the States," *Atlanta Historical Quarterly* 5 (1940):
179–81. There were also complaints about Confederate seizures of supplies in northern Georgia. "More Outrages—A Remedy Applied," *Southern Confederacy*, February 27, 1863.

20. Elizabeth Wiggins to her mother, September 7, 1861, Elizabeth Wiggins Papers, Duke
University Library, Durham, NC.

21. "Speculation," *Atlanta Daily Intelligencer*, November 5, 1861; see also November 27, 1861.

22. "Speculation," *Atlanta Daily Intelligencer*, November 5, 1861.

23. Singer, "Confederate Atlanta," 216–17, 229–31; *Atlanta Daily Intelligencer*, February 5, 1863.

24. Singer, "Confederate Atlanta," 164–65; Garrett, *Atlanta and Environs*, 1:573; "The
Wages of Labor," *Atlanta Daily Intelligencer*, June 26, 1862.

25. "Crinoline Imitations of the Habits of Certain Officials," *Southern Confederacy*,
March 19, 1863; Singer, "Confederate Atlanta," 189–90; Stephanie McCurry, *Confederate Reckoning: Power and Politics in the Civil War South* (Cambridge, MA:
Harvard University Press, 2010), 180–82. McCurry describes the riot as "highly
organized, premeditated, and disciplined" (181).

26. Thomas G. Dyer, *Secret Yankees: The Union Circle in Confederate Atlanta* (Baltimore, MD: Johns Hopkins University Press, 1999), 5.

27. "Incendiaries Abroad," *Atlanta Daily Intelligencer*, December 14, 1862.

28. Claim of Christian Kantz, Southern Claims Commission, Allowed Claims, Fulton
County, GA, RG 217, microfilm no. M1658 (hereafter cited as SCC).

29. Dyer, *Secret Yankees*, 120–33.

30. Cyrena Stone diary, January 1, 1864, University of Georgia Library, Athens.

31. Ibid., February 14, 1864.

32. Ibid., May 6, 1864.

33. Ibid., May 24, 1864.

34. Wooton, "New City of the South," table 5, p. 59. On slavery and race in Georgia, see
Watson W. Jennison, *Cultivating Race: The Expansion of Slavery in Georgia, 1750–
1860* (Lexington: University Press of Kentucky, 2012).

35. W. E. B. Du Bois and Augustus Granville Dill, eds., *The Negro American Artisan*,
Atlanta University Publications no. 17 (Atlanta: Atlanta University Press, 1912), 34.

36. Singer, "Confederate Atlanta," 143–44. A "successful end to this war," Samuel Rich-
ards predicted, would mean even higher demand and prices for his slaves. In a mental
note in his diary in May 1863 he wrote: "I must make out descriptive lists of my
darkies and record in my journal for future reference." Garrett, *Atlanta and Environs*,
1:557.

37. Tera W. Hunter, *To 'Joy My Freedom: Southern Black Women's Lives and Labors
after the Civil War* (Cambridge, MA: Harvard University Press, 1997), 21.

38. Dyer, *Secret Yankees*, 22.

39. Stone Diary, January 20, 1864.

40. Ibid., May 27, 1864.

41. James Michael Russell, *Atlanta, 1847–1890: City Building in the Old South and the New* (Baton Rouge: Louisiana State University Press, 1988), 70; Wooton, "New City of the South," 60; Allison Dorsey, *To Build Our Lives Together: Community Formation in Black Atlanta, 1875–1906* (Athens: University of Georgia Press, 2004), 23–26.
42. Claim of Henry and Polly Beedles, allowed claims, SCC.
43. Jefferson Simons, January 30, 1872, allowed claims, Fulton County, GA, SCC.
44. Joseph Holland, January 6, 1872, allowed claims, Fulton County, GA, SCC. Holland's brothers, Thomas and William Holland, also self-hired themselves from the same master. Thomas Holland, February 11, 1873, allowed claims, Fulton County, GA, SCC; William Holland, February 11, 1873, ibid. For another example of a slave able to carve out freedom during the war, see Dyer, *Secret Yankees*, 22–23.
45. Prince Ponder, January 15, 1873, allowed claims, Fulton County, GA, SCC. Ponder was awarded $3,666.25 out of an original claim of $4,341.25—a substantial allowance by the SCC's stingy standards.
46. "Negro Balls," *Atlanta Daily Intelligencer*, December 13, 1861.
47. Claim of Austin Wright, May 31, 1872, allowed claims, Fulton County, GA, SCC; Russell, *Atlanta, 1847–1890*, 110; "A Concert by Negroes," *Southern Confederacy*, August 21, 1861.
48. Garrett, *Atlanta and Environs*, 1:511–12, 571; "Strange," *Atlanta Daily Intelligencer*, September 25, 1862.
49. S. P. Yancey to Benjamin Yancey, November 11, 1861, Benjamin C. Yancey Papers, Duke University Library, Durham, NC.
50. Garrett, *Atlanta and Environs*, 1:553.
51. [Atlanta] Mayor's Court Record, May 21, 23, 1861, and February 14, 1862, Atlanta History Center.
52. Ibid., February 12, 1862.
53. Ibid., August 25, 1863.
54. Strikingly, on the same day in March 1864, the mayor's court dismissed several cases of self-hiring while, at the time, it fined a white, P. L. Howard, for his slave keeping an eating house "on his own accord." Mayor's Court Record, March 23, 1864.
55. Russell, *Atlanta*, 110.
56. Quoted in Singer, "Confederate Atlanta," 190–91.
57. Mayor's Court Record, July 5, 1861.
58. Ibid., February 8, 1864.
59. Ibid., March 29–30, 1861.
60. Ibid., May 15, 1861.
61. Ibid., October 18, 1861; *Southern Confederacy*, October 20, 1861.
62. Mayor's Court Record, February 21, 1863. Henry, a slave owned by H. L. Lockhart, was charged with "riding a horse in a gallope [sic] and in a faster gait than a walk across the Bridge in Market Street near city market" (March 25, 1864).
63. Ibid., February 23, 1864.
64. Thomas Maguire Diary, July 29 and 30, and August 1 and 7, 1864, Atlanta History Center.
65. Ibid., August 2, 5, 11, 24, 25, and 29, 1864.

66. Russell S. Bonds, *War like a Thunderbolt: The Battle and Burning of Atlanta* (Yardley, PA: Westholme, 2009), 243–51.

67. Maguire Diary, September 2 and 16, 1864.

68. Castel, *Decision in the West*, 548.

69. Sherman to Halleck, September 3, 1864, *O.R.*, ser. 1, vol. 38 (pt. 5), p. 777, and Sherman to Grant, September 6, 1864, p. 808.

70. "Burning of Atlanta," *Vermont Chronicle*, January 7, 1865; George Ward Nichols, *The Story of the Great March from the Diary of a Staff Officer* (New York: Harper and Brothers, 1865), 41; F. Y. Hedley, *Marching through Georgia: Pen-Pictures of Every-Day Life* (Chicago: Donohue, Henneberry, and Co., 1890), 257.

71. M. A. DeWolfe Howe, ed., *Marching with Sherman: Passages from the Letters and Campaign Diaries of Henry Hitchcock* (New Haven, CT: Yale University Press, 1927), 57; Noah Andre Trudeau, *Southern Storm: Sherman's March to the Sea* (New York: HarperCollins, 2008), 85–89. See original of Henry Hitchcock's diary in Library of Congress.

72. Carol Reardon, "William T. Sherman in Postwar Georgia's Collective Memory, 1864–1914," in *Wars within a War: Controversy and Conflict over the American Civil War*, ed. Joan Waugh and Gary Gallagher (Chapel Hill: University of North Carolina Press, 2009), 228.

73. "Direct Questions," *Atlanta Daily Constitution*, January 1, 1881.

74. Maguire Diary, November 1, 2, and 3, 1864.

75. Ibid., November 17, 1864.

76. "The Devastation at Atlanta, November 15, 1864," *Daily National Intelligencer*, November 22, 1864.

77. For a detailed description of the Western and Atlantic line, see G. W. Lee to Joseph E. Brown, March 25, 1864, Brown Family Papers, box 1, folder 3, University of Georgia, Athens.

78. Sherman to Logan, July 23, 24, 1864, *O.R.*, ser 1, 38, pt. 1, 237–38, 242–43.

79. Sherman to Howard, August 28, 1864, ibid., 695.

80. Hedley, *Marching through Georgia*, 256.

81. David P. Conyngham, *Sherman's March Through the South* (New York: Sheldon and Company, 1865), 216–23.

82. "The South as It Is," *New York Times*, August 22, 1865.

83. Ibid.

84. *Richmond Daily Dispatch*, August 30, 1864.

85. William Wallace to Sarah Wallace, June 6 and July 1, 1864, in "William Wallace's Civil War Letters: The Atlanta Campaign," ed. John O. Holzhueter, *Wisconsin Magazine of History* 57 (Winter 1973–74): 99–100.

86. John Herr to his mother, June 12, 1864, Herr Papers, Duke University, Durham, NC.

87. "The Devastation at Atlanta, November 15, 1864."

88. William G. Thomas, *The Iron Way: Railroads, the Civil War, and the Making of Modern America* (New Haven, CT: Yale University Press, 2011), 182–86.

89. Entries for S. R. McCamry and Co., February 3, 1866, R. G. Dun & Co Collection, Historical Collections, Baker Library, Harvard Business School, Harvard University.

90. Entries for Cox, Hill, and Co., August 15 and October 28, 1859, Georgia (Fulton County), vol. 13, R. G. Dun and Co. Collection, Historical Collections, Baker Library, Harvard Business School. The same was true for other merchants closely associated with the war trade. W. B. Lowe and Co. "made considerable money" during the war, and their capital provided a jumpstart over competitors. Entry for W. B. Lowe and Co., March 3, 1866, Dun Collection. I much appreciate the helpful direction of Mary Decredico in using this source.

91. Entry for Adair and Chisholm, January 8, 1857, Dun Collection; Martin, *Atlanta and Its Builders*, 627–28.

CHAPTER ELEVEN

Freeing the Lavish Hand of Nature: Environment and Economy in Nineteenth-Century Hampton Roads

JOHN MAJEWSKI

Strategically located at the intersection of the Chesapeake Bay and the mouth of the James River, Virginia's Hampton Roads constitutes one of the longest stretches of protected anchorages in the world. The deepwater channel (what geographers call a roadstead, or road) seemingly had the potential to capture America's lucrative trade in tobacco, cotton, and other key raw materials. Antebellum Virginians frequently touted the natural advantages of the Hampton Roads area, often declaring that it would soon rival New York City for commercial supremacy. In 1806 Thomas Jefferson predicted that Norfolk (the principal city of Hampton Roads) would soon surpass Boston, New York, and Philadelphia as the major port of the East Coast.[1] In 1853 Norfolk booster William S. Forrest praised the "lavish hand of nature" for creating Hampton Roads. "The relative position of the place is exceedingly favourable. For the various purposes of trade and commerce, both foreign and domestic, the port of Norfolk and Portsmouth stands almost unrivalled."[2] Forrest approvingly cited the work of Mathew F. Maury, an internationally renowned oceanographer who served in the US Navy. Maury believed that Norfolk was not only positioned to attract the growing western trade, but could also serve as a gateway for the commerce of Brazil and Amazon River Valley. As sectional tensions deepened, southern secessionists added a political twist to Maury's argument. Once the South secured its independence—and federal policies stopped subsidizing northern commercial interests—Norfolk would finally become that imposing commercial center that nature had intended. In 1860 secessionist Edmund Ruffin (who hailed from the Hampton Roads area) predicted in his futuristic novel *Anticipations of the Future* that once the South secured its independence, Norfolk would see "its population triple and its commerce increase fivefold" so that it would become "the chief seaport and commercial mart on the Atlantic Coast."[3]

Though Virginians frequently highlighted the commercial potential of
Norfolk and Hampton Roads, the area's slow development was a major em-
barrassment. The area's urban growth lagged well behind major northern
cities. In 1800, Norfolk was the tenth largest city in the United States;
by 1860 it ranked as the sixty-first largest city. Even combining Norfolk's
population with that of nearby Portsmouth produced a population of just
over 24,000 in 1860, which would rank thirty-seventh in the nation just
behind Worcester, Massachusetts.[4] The relative economic and demographic
decline of Norfolk led antislavery writers to argue that lazy and indolent
Virginians had failed to capitalize on Hampton Roads' superior geography.
In 1842 the English travel writer James Silk Buckingham asserted that slavery deterred industrious and hard-working immigrants from moving to the
South, which in turn hurt Norfolk's trade. If Virginians abolished slavery,
Buckingham wrote, "We should then see the Chesapeake crowded with
ships and vessels."[5] Frederick Law Olmsted, who wrote extensive travel
accounts focusing on the southern economy, observed in the 1850s that
Norfolk had more natural advantages than New York, "yet if the citizens
had always been subject to a deadly enervating pestilence, it could not be a
more miserable, sorry little seaport than it is." In contrast to the lassitude of
Norfolk's slave economy, Olmsted hailed the "skill, enterprise, and energy
of New York merchants" that had built one of the world's great commercial
cities.[6] Virginians resented such criticisms, but even the city's most enthu-
siastic boosters admitted that Norfolk's faltering development reflected a
lack of entrepreneurial drive. "Virginia saw those advantages and *slept upon
them*," wrote Maury. "Nature had placed them there, and she did not dream
that man could take them away. But the enterprise of New York has taken
them away."[7]

After the Civil War, however, Hampton Roads began to reach its full
commercial potential. By the early 1880s three trunk-line railroads connected Hampton Roads to Appalachian coal mines and Deep South cotton
fields. Reflecting rapid technological change in railroads and shipping, these
large-scale networks made cities such as Norfolk and Newport News leading coal and cotton ports. Networks of railroads and steamships also transformed other local industries, such as truck farming and oyster production,
which grew impressively in the late nineteenth century. Northern visitors
in the late nineteenth century, in sharp contrast to antebellum visitors,
marveled at the spirit of enterprise and industry that pervaded Norfolk. In
1882 journalist Charles Burr Todd delighted "in the air of bustle and activity that prevails [in Norfolk], so different from the dullness and languor of
many southern towns. The city is literally overflowing with life and vigor."[8]

This chapter seeks to understand this remarkable transformation. How did Hampton Roads become a New South success story after its notable failures in the antebellum period?

The answer lies in the complex interaction of institutions and environment. In the antebellum period, the environment of Hampton Roads conspired with slavery to limit the region's development. The "lavish hand of nature," it turned out, was far less generous than many observers had supposed. Two key environmental factors offset Norfolk's superior geographical position: poor soils and a warm, humid climate. The acidic soils of the Hampton Roads region discouraged the growth of densely populated hinterlands that could support industry and commerce. Most farmers and planters in the region used shifting cultivation, in which old-growth forest was burnt to produce ash that could neutralize acidic soils. Shifting cultivation required much of the land to be in long-term fallow. Most land in the region remained uncultivated, resulting in a sparsely settled countryside that deterred urban growth. Slavery added to these woes—its stark inequality contributed to the lack of local markets, which further inhibited industrialization. The warm, humid climate presented another set of problems—Hampton Roads was well suited for mosquitoes that carried yellow fever. Norfolk and Portsmouth experienced one of the worst epidemics in the antebellum period when more than 3,000 residents died of yellow fever in the summer and autumn of 1855. The yellow fever epidemic cemented the long-standing reputation of Hampton Roads as fundamentally unhealthy, thus undermining business confidence and deterring emigration. Nature, it seems, was more of a curse than a blessing for Norfolk and its environs.

In indirect but significant ways, the Civil War helped free "the lavish hand of nature" and unleash the economic potential of Hampton Roads. In narrow economic terms, the war itself had little direct impact. Occupied by northern military forces early in the conflict, the region's commerce generally stagnated during the war years. Indirectly, though, the war resulted in a flood of northern capital that underwrote the commercial infrastructure of Hampton Roads. Before the war, northern investment in Hampton Roads was minimal—most of the capital from the area's struggling railroads in the antebellum period came from local merchants, nearby planters, and local and state governments. After the war, northern capitalists poured tens of millions of dollars into new railroads, new steamships, new dock facilities, and even new cities. Northern capitalists such as Collis P. Huntington treated Hampton Roads as something akin to a blank slate, which they happily filled with a commercial infrastructure that would finally harness the region's geographic potential. The creation of truly national capital markets and networks meant that outsiders controlled Hampton Roads economy, but these outsides provided for more growth and opportunity (for both whites and blacks) than the old antebellum order. Northern capital, in other words, allowed the cities of Hampton Roads to escape the confines of their sparsely settled hinterland to realize the commercial ambitions of their early boosters.

SHIFTING CULTIVATION AND HINTERLAND DEVELOPMENT

Hampton Roads itself is situated near the entrance of Chesapeake Bay. What is known as the "Virginia Peninsula" is located immediately to the north of the Roads. Consisting of the counties of York, Charles City, James City, and New Kent, the Virginia Peninsula was the initial site of colonial settlement; Jamestown is only a short distance away from Hampton Roads. Unlike most US seaports, Hampton Roads is not a single unified urban entity, but rather an urban region composed of several cities with no dominant central node. This distinctive pattern of urbanization grew stronger overtime. By 2010 Hampton Roads ranked as the sixth largest metropolitan area in the South with a population of nearly 1.7 million, but that urban population is divided among a number of different cities, including Virginia Beach (2010 population of 437,994), Norfolk (242,803), Chesapeake (222,209), Portsmouth (95,535), Newport News (180,719), and Hampton (137,436).[9] The concentration of smaller cities—rather than the dominant presence of a Boston, New York, Philadelphia, or Charleston—stems from the geographic nature of a roadstead as opposed to a harbor. A harbor contains a single point of protected anchorage, while a roadstead is a lengthier channel in which a number of different points may become ports. Comparisons of Hampton Roads to New York or Philadelphia, while popular in the antebellum era, were bound to be somewhat misleading. Hampton Roads would have its own distinctive pattern of urban development that successfully took advantage of its long stretch of deepwater anchorage.

It would take time—and a great deal of northern capital—to develop the many cities that now compose the Hampton Roads region. In the antebellum period, economic development in the Hampton Roads region focused on the cities of Norfolk and Portsmouth, in part because they were the most convenient place to tap the trade of southern Virginia. The cities not only shared a superb harbor, but they could also conceivably capture the trade of southern Virginia and adjoining counties of North Carolina. Norfolk even-

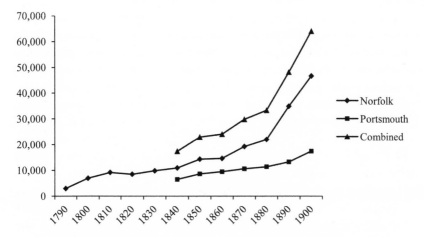

Fig. 11.1. The population of Norfolk and Portsmouth in the nineteenth century.

tually became Virginia's largest city in the colonial period, with an estimated population of 6,000 on the eve of the Revolution. While historians
have described Norfolk as "thriving" relative to other Virginia cities (the
next largest competitor was the colonial capital at Williamsburg, with 2,000
residents), it was already well behind northern cities such as Philadelphia
(30,000 residents) and New York (25,000 residents).[10]

Norfolk fortunes took a decided turn for the worse in 1775, when Royal
Governor Lord Dunmore burned the town to the ground in retaliation for
the rebel uprising. With Norfolk destroyed, Baltimore dominated the trade
of the Chesapeake region, leaving Norfolk the difficult task of catching
up. It would take Norfolk until 1800 to regain the same size it had in the
colonial period (see fig. 11.1). For most of the antebellum period, Norfolk
would continue to grow, but at a rate far behind many other cities. Direct
comparisons with the great northern port cities cast Norfolk's ambitions
in an almost comical light—in 1860 New York (population 1.1 million),
Philadelphia (population 565,529), and Baltimore (population 212,418) all
dwarfed the combined population of Norfolk and Portsmouth (just over
24,000 residents). The small size of the cities of Hampton Roads was tied to
their rather limited trade. In 1860 Norfolk's merchants shipped goods worth
$3.89 million. Almost all of the city's trade (85 percent) was part of the large
coastal trading network that connected US ports. Foreign trade amounted
to just under $600,000, a tiny fraction of nation's $334 million export trade.
The few foreign ships that visited the port (only forty-three called on the

port in 1860) generally hailed from the Caribbean, as Norfolk was too small
to warrant regular visits by European traders. Corn, which accounted for
31 percent of Norfolk's exports, was the single largest item of trade. Norfolk
exported some cotton (worth $874,000), but the total amount was small fry
compared to the booming cotton markets of the antebellum period.[11]

The key problem for Norfolk was that relatively few people lived in the
adjoining countryside, which meant that Norfolk had little in the way of a
hinterland that could provide markets for merchants and manufacturers.
The sparsely settled countryside caught the attention of the editor of *The
Hive*, a literary magazine published in Waltham, Massachusetts, who took
an excursion to Norfolk and Richmond in 1832. One of the things the editor noticed was the surprisingly sparse settlement. Even near Norfolk itself,
"The shore of each side of the Elizabeth River to the city is lined with pine
woods, with now and then a negro hut." When making his way to Richmond via the James River, he saw "wood all along in great abundance." As
the trip progressed, the journalist became increasingly scornful. The character of the countryside—dotted with plantations and "miserable log huts
peopled with hosts of dirty, ragged negroes"—was a far cry from the "pleasant villages" and "well cultivated fields" of New England.[12]

A visit to the ruins of Jamestown reinforced the sense of decline and
degeneracy. "Jamestown is the site of the earliest English settlements in the
United States; and while places of recent origin have grown into a state of
magnitude, equaling the great cities of Europe, Jamestown has gone to decay."[13]

Such accounts highlight a recurring problem for the Hampton Roads
region: most of the countryside was uncultivated and underdeveloped. According to census statistics, the eleven counties that made up the Hampton
Roads region and its immediate hinterland, 5,514 farms and plantations, collectively cultivated 656,605 acres in 1860, which constituted 40 percent of
the acreage within farms or plantations.[14] Keep in mind that large swaths of
the Hampton Roads region were so unproductive that that they remained un-
claimed, including the Great Dismal Swamp, which stretched for nearly one
million acres to the south of Norfolk. Observers frequently noted the large
percentage of uncultivated land. A correspondent to the *Farmer's Register*
reported in 1843 that "the proportion of cleared to uncleared land must be
small. The Great Dismal, and other large swamps, are spread over a large
proportion of the county, and besides there is an immense quantity of land
covered with trees of a second growth."[15] Even Norfolk newspaper editor
William Forrest, a prominent Norfolk booster, noted that "there is much
uncultivated and unimproved land," though he characteristically turned

the lack of settlement into an opportunity to buy "picturesque and handsome sites for farms with a few miles from the city."[16]

The uncultivated landscape created problems for the industrial development of Hampton Roads. In the North dense rural populations created markets that sustained early industrialization. In 1860 the six counties in the immediate vicinity of Philadelphia, for example, contained 29,498 farms and 1.8 million improved acres. Farmers near Philadelphia cultivated 83 percent of their acreage, which was considerably more than the 40 percent of the farmers and planters in the Hampton Roads region. Not surprisingly, the population densities were far higher in Philadelphia's hinterland. Nearly a half million people lived in Philadelphia's hinterland in 1860, a figure that does not include Philadelphia or its immediate suburbs. In contrast, 125,000 residents lived in the entire Hampton Roads region (Norfolk included).[17] Philadelphia was emblematic of a northern model of development, in which strong demand from the hinterland supported urban trade and manufacturing, which in turn intensified agricultural production and further increased rural demand. The lack of intensive agriculture prevented Norfolk from doing the same.[18]

One simple fact explains why so much acreage in the Hampton Roads area was unimproved: the land itself was not very fertile. The soils in the Hampton Roads region, like soils throughout much of the South, tended to be highly acidic. Planters and farmers employed what historian Jack Temple Kirby has called "fire culture," in which forest growth was burned before planting.[19] The resulting ash, which was high in calcium content, helped neutralize the natural acidity. The ash, however, leached out of the soil after four or five years, forcing cultivators to burn a new plot. In the meantime, the old land remained in long-term fallow for up to thirty years. That is why "fire culture" is more commonly known today as "shifting cultivation"—after the fertility of one plot has been depleted farmers shift their efforts to the next field. The "old fields" limited economic utility: Farmers and planters could allow cattle and swine to roam the forests unattended, and sometimes used forest growth for firewood, fences, and buildings. Such economic production—especially when it constituted the output of about two-thirds of the land—could hardly fuel urban growth. Cattle and swine left to fend in marshlands and pine forests were often small and scrawny; they became emblematic of agricultural self-sufficiency rather than new export markets.[20] The shipment of unprocessed wood—which producers elsewhere would turn into furniture, fences, barns, and homes—was also insufficient to sustain economic development.[21]

Slavery further blunted the development of markets in Hampton Roads. In 1860 nearly 39 percent of the population of Hampton Roads was enslaved, which further decreased the ability of Hampton Roads to generate consumer demand for its cities. Slaves, especially skilled workers hired out in Norfolk, might have purchased some consumer goods, and it is also possible that slaves working their own small plots of land grew enough produce to finance small purchases of cloth, tobacco, and coffee. It is difficult to imagine, though, that the collective purchasing power of Hampton Roads' slave population kept pace with the consumption of northern families who increasingly participated in the consumer culture of the market revolution. In an age when transportation costs were a critical economic variable, the combination of large swaths of empty land and a large enslaved population would make it particularly difficult for the Hampton Roads to develop local manufacturing. In 1860 Norfolk County ranked eighty-third within the South in per capita manufacturing (as measured in terms of value added).[22] The lack of manufacturing in Norfolk was most telling in the decade between 1810 and 1820, when the city's population declined by nearly 8 percent because of trade disruptions stemming from the Napoleonic Wars. The same trade disruptions hurt other port cities as well, but merchants in New England and the Middle Atlantic region diversified into manufacturing. Norfolk's sparsely populated hinterland prevented similar diversification.

Norfolk's trade also suffered because of its small hinterland. As noted above, European merchants and manufactures avoided Norfolk because its small size generated little of the consumer demand that would have made such trade worthwhile. Rather than trade directly with Europe, Norfolk sent its products to New York and other northern cities, where they could be either consumed locally or re-exported. For many southerners, the lack of direct trade with Europe and dependence on northern merchants smacked of economic colonialism—northerners, it seemed, unfairly profited from southern trade. Norfolk's merchants sponsored commercial conventions and other meetings that promoted ambitious plans to jump-start direct European trade, including subsidies to steamship lines that served European ports.[23] In 1851 Norfolk booster William M. Burwell advocated that the various cities of Virginia form a joint-stock company to finance a line of steamers to Norfolk, which would essentially allow Norfolk to replace New York.[24] Such plans went nowhere, partly because (as we will see in more detail below) of intense commercial rivalries among Virginia cities. Even if such an enterprise somehow became operational, could a single steamship line radically reconfigure the trade relations of the Atlantic World? Northerners laughed at such notions. New York merchants, Olmsted wrote, "can *command* commerce, and need not petition their Legislature, or appeal to mean sectional prejudices to obtain it."[25]

Shifting cultivation, it is important to stress, was not the fault of indolent or tradition-bound Virginia farmers. Cultivators in the Hampton Roads region frequently adopted new crops and innovative techniques. In the eighteenth century, farmers and planters began to cycle out of tobacco and focus more on grains and corn. By 1860 agricultural production had become increasingly diversified into a mix of tobacco and grains. Hampton Roads planters also took steps to overcome the high acidity of their soils. Edmund Ruffin, a leading proponent of the scientific study of the soil chemistry, pioneered the use of marl (a clay mixed with fossilized shell) to help reduce the acidity of southern soils. The calcium in marl, Ruffin hypothesized, helped neutralize the acidity of southern soils. A number of planters in the Hampton Roads region utilized marl, but it barely made a dent in the large acreage of unimproved land, mainly because transporting marl was expensive and time-consuming.[26] No matter how innovative, Hampton Roads cultivators could not overcome the natural infertility of their soil. In 1890—well after the advent of artificial fertilizers—Hampton Roads farmers still cultivated only 44 percent of their land.[27]

RAILROADS AND ANTEBELLUM NORFOLK

Norfolk might have overcome its underpopulated hinterland and the impact of slavery had railroads and canals penetrated more deeply to the interior. Norfolk's relatively small size, though, lowered the potential for profits and made financing more challenging. With significant assistance from the federal government, the Dismal Swamp Canal was completed in 1805. Running along the eastern edge of the swamp, the waterway connected Norfolk to North Carolina's Albemarle Sound. While wood products and farm produce shipped via the canal became a major source of trade for Norfolk's merchants, the canal could not fuel the dramatic expansion that Norfolk's boosters so ardently desired.[28] Another appealing option was to build a railroad that would connect with Roanoke River, which flowed from the Shenandoah Valley southeast to North Carolina. A connection to the Roanoke River—less than a hundred miles from Norfolk—would allow the city to vastly expand its hinterland. Hampton Roads residents organized the Portsmouth and Roanoke Railroad Company in 1834, with the cities of Portsmouth and Norfolk contributing a combined $150,000 to the project. Although the company received generous state aid, it was chronically undercapitalized. The initial tracks were laid with iron-plated wooden rails

instead of solid metal; the foundation of the track was built with timber instead of stone. The company had to borrow heavily to rebuild the track and
build an important bridge over the Roanoke. Revenues proved consistently
disappointing, especially during the difficult economic conditions of the
late 1830s and early 1840s. The company eventually fell into bankruptcy. In
1846 northern investors eventually purchased the railroad and reorganized
it as the Seaboard and Roanoke.[29]

The failure of the Portsmouth and Norfolk Railroad did not stop Hampton Roads residents from pushing even more ambitious projects. They
dreamed of a railroad built along the James that would connect Norfolk to
the Ohio River. Given Norfolk's small size, building such a project would
require a massive infusion of state funds. Politicians from the Hampton
Roads region argued that a vigorous program of state internal improvements
would turn Norfolk into a great commercial city. With a railroad built to the
west, Northampton politician Joseph Segar argued in 1838, Virginians could
finally avoid the "enormous tax" of trading through northern cities. Segar
recognized that Virginia's cities need an extensive "back country trade" if
they were to become "importing cities." Such a trade could only come from
an extensive system of state-financed internal improvements that could
turn Virginia's cities into powerful commercial centers that would break
up the commercial thralldom that now renders us abject tributaries to the
North." Although the state legislature periodically funded the Virginia Central Railroad and the Ohio and Covington Railroad to link the Ohio River
to Richmond (where Norfolk boosters hoped that it would be extended to
their city), the funding was never enough to finish the improvement.[30] In
1853 Segar asked what would have happened to Richmond and Norfolk if
twenty years ago Virginia had built a central improvement to the Ohio: "Sir,
they would be at this moment far ahead of Baltimore, large market towns
for our people, and the seats of flourishing commerce and manufacturers,
of the mechanic arts, of busy industry in all its forms, while our political
influence in the national confederacy would have been preserved."[31]

Given the importance of the state aid, Norfolk's problems were political
as well as economic. Norfolk faced stiff competition over internal improvements from the fall-line towns of Richmond (located on the James) and Petersburg (located on the Appomattox, which was a tributary of the James).
Each city had its own dreams of commercial greatness, and both had important geographic advantages over the Hampton Roads area. Richmond and
Petersburg were closer to the far more productive lands of the Virginia Piedmont and the Shenandoah Valley, which gave them a big leg up in securing

grains and tobacco. Richmond, in particular, became a major milling center (exporting tobacco to Australia and South America), as well as the nation's largest tobacco producer. With excellent access to coal and iron, Richmond was also home to the famous Tredegar Iron Works, the South's largest producer of rails, cannon, and other iron commodities. Richmond, not surprisingly, ranked first within the South in manufacturing output per capita. Petersburg, while significantly behind Richmond, nevertheless was still far ahead of Norfolk. The two fall-line towns—centrally located and better connected (both economically and politically) to the Piedmont and Shenandoah Valley—would consistently have a leg up on Norfolk in the political battles over state investment. To make matters worse, the primary geographic advantage of Hampton Roads—its superior deepwater anchorage—was of limited value during most of the antebellum period. The relatively small sailing and steam vessels of the area could bypass Norfolk and Portsmouth and proceed up the James directly to Richmond and Petersburg. There appeared to be little value of extending railroad connections to the east when most trade could be conducted without the ports and merchants of Hampton Roads.

The fate of the Portsmouth and Roanoke Railroad demonstrated how the fall-line cities consistently undermined Norfolk's attempt to build better western connections. Building its own railroad to capture the trade of the Roanoke River Valley, Petersburg interests worked hard to prevent the Portsmouth and Roanoke Railroad from receiving additional state investment. Facing a chronic shortage of capital, the Hampton Roads company borrowed large sums of money to build a strategic bridge. A Petersburg businessman secretly purchased the debt and then forced the company into insolvency. At one point residents from Petersburg and Portsmouth/Norfolk almost engaged in a pitched battle. Such episodes demonstrated the tensions over state investment decisions. When the Virginia legislature refused to fund a western railroad, Norfolk boosters threatened to secede from Virginia and become part of North Carolina.[32] While it was always convenient to blame the state legislature for the city's disappointing growth, the political difficulties of the Hampton Roads cities were more often a symptom than a cause of economic stagnation. Without a populous hinterland to jump-start growth initially, Norfolk and Portsmouth lacked the political and economic power to shape Virginia's commercial policy. Whereas New York, Philadelphia, and Baltimore could shape internal improvement policy in their states, Norfolk was just another one of the smallish Virginia cities competing for state funds.[33]

YELLOW FEVER AND HAMPTON ROADS

The ships that Norfolk residents so eagerly sought to attract to its waters sometimes brought a deadly passenger: the yellow fever virus. Yellow fever is carried by certain species of mosquitoes that thrive in Africa and South America. In the nineteenth century, though, most medical observers believed that yellow fever, malaria, and other tropical diseases resulted from a "miasma" that spread the disease through the air. In North America, yellow fever epidemics often occurred in commercial centers in the summer and fall, when ships in the Caribbean carried infected sailors and mosquitoes to port (the disease was nicknamed "yellow jack," denoting its close association with sailors and ships). Although yellow fever epidemics sometimes struck northern cities—Philadelphia experienced a particularly severe epidemic in 1793—the disease was far more common in southern port cities where the warm, humid climate and later autumn frosts provided a friendlier environment to mosquitoes. Many persons experienced yellow fever as nothing worse than a bout with the flu. For others, it was a death sentence. Death via yellow fever was gruesome—three to six days after being infected, patients suffered violent headaches, high fever, and aching joints. Severely infected persons turned jaundiced, a tell-tale sign that the disease was attacking the liver. In many severe cases, the disease continued to attack the liver and other vital organs until the patient vomited black bile, which almost always meant impending death. Yellow fever devastated entire cities and destroyed entire armies, especially if a large part of the exposed population had not been previously exposed to the disease. The hemispheric repercussions were staggering. When rebellious slaves claimed Haitian independence, Napoleon attempted to recapture the colony in 1802. After initial military success, the French forces and subsequent reinforcements faced a brutal yellow fever epidemic that killed an estimated 50,000 troops. Napoleon was forced to grant Haiti independence, which in turn led him to sell his Louisiana territories to the United States.[34]

Norfolk, like other southern ports, frequently suffered from yellow fever outbreaks. Northern newspapers published reports about the appearance of yellow fever in the Norfolk area in the 1790s and early 1800s—precisely the moment Norfolk was trying to recover from the economic upheaval of the American Revolution. The influx of new residents, in fact, may have contributed to the outbreaks. In the nineteenth-century South, yellow fever was known as a "Stranger's Disease" because newcomers were far more vulnerable. Newcomers that clustered together—unseasoned troops in a barracks, prisoners of war in a camp, recent immigrants in a tenement building—were especially vulnerable, as they lived near other potential carriers.[35] Dr. Robert Archer, a Norfolk health officer who wrote a lengthy report on an 1821 epidemic that killed 160 residents, noted that "Europeans, and particularly the Irish, were most obnoxious to the disease: next to these, the natives of northern and eastern states. The emigrants from the West Indies suffered comparatively nothing, and very few of the old inhabitants were affected."[36] Long-term residents, even if they had not been exposed to the disease, stood a far better chance of avoiding infection via what epidemiologists call "herd" immunity. The immune system of a survivor would kill the virus, which meant that subsequent mosquito bites would not spread the disease. Nineteenth-century southerners thus mistakenly believed that simply having lived in an area with yellow fever would confer immunity.

Norfolk residents learned of their mistake in the worse way possible when the steamer *Benjamin Franklin* arrived in Norfolk from the Virgin Islands in June 1855. The ship was immediately quarantined, which was common practice for vessels hailing from the Caribbean during the yellow fever seasons of summer and fall. Yet after twelve days in quarantine, the ship was allowed to dock. The captain (always unnamed in the various accounts of the episode) claimed that no passengers or crew members were infected. Port officials (including the city's health inspector) allowed the *Benjamin Franklin* to dock in Portsmouth as long as its hold remained closed. The captain apparently disregarded the order regarding the hold and emptied the ship's bilge water to facilitate repairs. The ship's crew, according to accounts collected afterwards, tried to hide the evidence of the disease: crew members furtively buried bodies in the middle of the night, and several sailors swam ashore, preferring to risk drowning than to face yellow fever.[37]

The decision of the port officials—and the duplicity of the captain—proved disastrous. Portsmouth workers, especially those living in crowded neighborhoods near the shipyards, first contracted the disease. Some of the panicked workers fled to working-class tenements in Norfolk, thus further spreading the fever. While alarmed, residents in Norfolk and Portsmouth did not panic; that yellow fever struck initially tenements housing poor Irish immigrants gave hope that the epidemic would be contained to the slums surrounding docks. It was not. By the end of July, thousands had fallen ill and hundreds had died. Officials in Portsmouth and Norfolk took a number of drastic actions—the tenements were evacuated and then razed to the ground; the streets of Portsmouth were covered with lime; tar fires were set in the streets to clear the noxious air that was thought to spread the disease. Nothing helped, and in early August residents fled in panic and terror. By mid-August almost all business came to a halt and food became increasingly difficult to find. Coffins were also in short supply—sometimes two or three bodies had to be stacked in a single coffin so burials could proceed at a rapid pace. Simply collecting the dead became a major logistical problem; Norfolk officials declared martial law so they could confiscate wagons and carriages to transport the dead. Only fall frosts, which arrived in October, halted the epidemic. By the time the epidemic had run its course, approximately 3,000 residents of Portsmouth and Norfolk had died.[38]

The tremendous loss of life aside, the epidemic was a disaster for the Hampton Roads economy. The population of Norfolk and Portsmouth grew less than 5 percent from 1850 to 1860, which was well behind the growth of most other Virginia cities. The short-term slowing of population growth hurt the economy of Hampton Roads, but the loss of life did not necessarily have devastating long-term consequences. Many US cities that experienced tragic yellow fever epidemics—including Philadelphia in the 1790s and Memphis in the 1870s—quickly recovered. Perhaps more important, the epidemic solidified images that Portsmouth and Norfolk were fundamentally unhealthy places. News of the epidemic spread far and wide; northern periodicals made it a major national story. The front- page headline of the *New York Daily News* on September 11, 1855, for example, was "YELLOW FEVER. Fearful Progress of the Disease at Norfolk. Statements of Medical Eye-Witness. Latest Telegraphic Accounts."[39] Northern relief organizations raised hundreds of thousands of dollars and sent scores of doctors and nurses, many of whom died in their effort to help Hampton Roads residents. Instead of eliciting sympathy, the yellow fever epidemic led writers such as Olmsted to connect slavery to disease. Slothful and ignorant southerners— the product of the region's slave economy—had neglected basic sanitation. The city's "undrained and filthy condition," Olmsted wrote, insured that "this dreadful visitor certainly did not come uninvited."[40] The yellow fever epidemic seemingly confirmed that the South was backward, underdeveloped, and foreign.

Norfolk boosters knew that a reputation as an unhealthy city would severely damage their city's commercial ambitions. Ships would be less likely to dock, emigrants would be less likely to come, and investors would be less likely to invest. City officials failed to report on the epidemic for nearly six weeks for fear of damaging the city's commercial prospects.[41] Norfolk's sense of denial reflected a long-standing tradition. In 1853 William S. Forrest, one of the paper's editors, claimed in his promotional book *Descriptive Sketches of Norfolk and Vicinity* that the city was fundamentally healthy. The "myth" that Norfolk was sickly, Forrest hinted, was part of a campaign of rival cities to undermine the city's commercial interests. Forrest admitted that the town suffered yellow fever outbreaks in 1821, 1826, and 1852, but Forrest asserted that these episodes had been confined to a small portion of the population. The "bright eyes of the thousands of citizens that thronged the streets" gave lie to the rumors that Norfolk was a dangerous place. Yellow fever had spread so slowly that the editor concluded that "the climate of Norfolk is utterly unsuited for the dissemination of the disease."[42] Three years later Forrest wrote another book, this one entitled *The Great Pestilence*. Forrest was obviously coming to grips with the city's tremendous sense of loss after the 1855 epidemic, yet he took great pains to defend Norfolk against those who believed that the disease originated from the city: "It is a slander upon the place to assert, that this disease, in all its malignity, if in any form, originated in Norfolk."[43] The *Franklin* could have landed anywhere, and the yellow fever epidemic could have just as easily taken place in Charleston, New York, or Philadelphia. Even Forrest, though, admitted that Norfolk's climate might have contributed to the cause of the disease. Forrest invoked a curious metaphor: "As a magazine of gunpowder is harmless and powerless without the application of fire, so the air we breathed here would, in all probability, [have] remained harmless" without the *Franklin*'s arrival.[44] Who would want to live or invest near the epidemiological equivalent of an ammunition depot?

UNLEASHING THE LAVISH HAND OF NATURE

Immediately after the Civil War, a series of technological and institutional changes gradually emerged that finally unleashed the "lavish hand of nature." The war itself immediately transformed the social order of Hampton Roads—almost from the very beginning of hostilities, escaping slaves fled to Fortress Monroe (which was located north of Norfolk, on the other side of the roadstead), where Union commander Benjamin Butler famously labeled them "contraband of war" and prevented local masters from reclaiming their supposed property. In May 1862 Union forces occupied Norfolk during McClellan's peninsula campaign and held the city under martial law for the duration of the conflict. Freed African Americans, working with northern reformers, established new schools in the contraband camps of Hampton Roads. Soon after the war, the Hampton Normal and Agricultural Institute would train thousands of African American teachers, including Booker T. Washington.[45] Despite these tremendous social and political changes, the war's immediate economic impact was hardly transformative. Norfolk and Portsmouth avoided the destruction that engulfed cities such as Atlanta and Richmond, but on the other hand never served as major supply depots in the same way that helped the growth of Louisville, St. Louis, and Nashville. With northern occupation, the coastal trade resumed; cotton trickled into Norfolk, where it was traded (sometimes legally, sometimes not) to northern cities. Overseas trade dwindled. The total value of Norfolk's foreign exports in 1866 amounted to only $411,450.[46]

The long-term changes associated with the war, however, had an immense impact on the economy of Hampton Roads. The population figures in figure 11.1 clearly show that growth accelerated in Norfolk and Portsmouth in the 1860s and continued to accelerate through the late nineteenth century. Why was the decade of the 1860s such an important inflection point? One possibility is that emancipation spurred greater consumption among the area's African American population, which in turn led to more local manufacturing. African Americans workers undoubtedly played a key part in the growing economy of Hampton Roads—observers noted that they loaded ships, worked on truck farms, labored in the growing oyster and shellfish industry, and sold goods as petty retailers and itinerant merchants. Wages, however, remained abysmally low—day laborers in the thriving truck farms surrounding Norfolk received 75 cents per day, far lower than day laborers in the North received. Such low wages and enduring racial discrimination would limit the buying power of African Americans, even if they did participate more directly in the market economy. The rural hinterlands still remained far less developed than those in the North—the percentage of improved land remained at low levels after the Civil War and observers still noted the sparsely settled countryside. In 1885 journalist Ernest Ingersoll, who enthusiastically praised Norfolk's economy, nevertheless noted that "the country about Norfolk is low and flat, and the soil sandy, and in many places sterile. Between the city and the ocean is a great stretch of pine-woods and scrub-oaks, elevated only a little way above tidewater and intersected by many swamps."[47] Given these environmental conditions, hinterland growth remained limited—total consumption may well have increased, but not enough to lead to widespread industrialization.

The key change for Hampton Roads was not so much in the growth of the local hinterland, but the flood of northern capital that transformed the area's railroad network. Before the war, northern capitalists had avoided investing in Virginia railroads. Instead of selling stocks and bonds in Boston, New York, and Philadelphia, most companies cobbled together financing from local investors, municipal governments, and the state government. Northern investors might well have been worried over the low returns of Virginia railroads, as southern railroads (with significantly less traffic than northern enterprises) tended to be significantly less profitable.[48] Northern investors often invested in western enterprises where short-run profits were low but long-term growth prospects were bright. Virginia's economy, however, seemed to be in long-term decline, as least relative to the North and Midwest. The constant critiques of free labor writers and the simmering sectional controversies—what Gavin Wright has called the "economic cold war" between slavery and free labor—may well have convinced northern investors to put their money elsewhere.[49] After the war, however, northern investors eagerly poured money into southern railroads. Postbellum investors had little reason to fear that political upheaval would endanger their investments; southern state governments (not to mention the federal government) became far more pliable to the wishes of corporations after the war. While railroad profits in the South generally remained lower than elsewhere in the country, investors could reasonably believe that the South's economic recovery and plentiful natural resources would eventually make their investments remunerative. Hampton Roads was a major beneficiary of northern capital. Between 1865 and 1885 northern capital largely financed three large rail systems emanating from Hampton Roads. These systems, stretching from Kentucky to Atlanta, would collectively control nearly 3,000 miles of track.

The first great system was the Seaboard Air Line, which was put together by Moncure Robinson and his son, John Moncure Robinson. Moncure Robinson was one of America's great railroad engineers in the nineteenth century. Born in Richmond and educated at William and Mary, Moncure worked as an engineer on several Virginia rail projects, including the Portsmouth and Roanoke Company. His most noted and influential engineering accomplishments, though, were on Pennsylvania lines, including the Philadelphia and Reading Railroad. In 1848 he retired from engineering work and concentrated instead on railroad investing, using his home in Philadelphia as a headquarters.[50] With excellent connections in both the North and the South, he was well positioned to rebuild and expand the southern railroad network after the Civil War. With controlling interest in the old Portsmouth and Roanoke Company (renamed the Seaboard and Roanoke Railroad), Robinson and his son improved the harbor facilities of Portsmouth and Norfolk, even designing railroad cars and harbor tugboats that would make the unloading of freight as efficient as possible. To further rationalize the company's operations, the Robinsons started a steamship company with direct connections to Baltimore and New York. With the Seaboard and the Roanoke serving as a foundation, the Robinsons used stock purchases, family alliances, and contractual relationships to form the Seaboard Air

Line system that eventually connected Hampton Roads to Atlanta, Georgia. While this system was nominally composed of different lines, the Robinsons insured that shippers could seamlessly transport cotton and other goods with a single bill of lading. The Seaboard Air Line proved too efficient for some Portsmouth residents. Fearing that the direct connection from railcar to steamboat bypassed traditional middlemen, in 1867 Portsmouth merchants and allied interests asked the city council to ban the railroad's cars from directly entering the city and port facilities. The city council denied the request. The enormous cotton trade was too valuable to jeopardize.[51]

Another railroad financier, Collis P. Huntington, built a rail system to connect Hampton Roads to the Ohio River. Although a New Englander, Huntington had spent time in the South as a young itinerant merchant. Many decades later, the famous Huntington—best known for managing the Union Pacific—sought to build a direct connection from Richmond to the coal lands of West Virginia and on to the Ohio River. In 1869 Huntington obtained control of several Virginia railroads and turned them into the Chesapeake and Ohio. Huntington, though, faced the daunting challenge of traversing mountainous West Virginia, which in some ways was more difficult than building his transcontinental railroad. The undertaking proved far costlier than Huntington and his New York backers estimated, but the company finally completed a direct connection between Richmond and the Ohio River in 1873. In 1882 Huntington extended the line seventy-five miles to the east to connect with Newport News on the Virginia Peninsula side of Hampton Roads. Newport News was entirely the creation of Huntington—his companies built the railroad facilities, the docks, and the town's large ship-building company.[52] While the high cost of building the Ohio and Chesapeake made the railroad's profitability tenuous, the enterprise gave Hampton Roads direct access to West Virginia's bountiful supplies of coal. Coal became a major export and enhanced Hampton Roads' strategic importance. The combination of deepwater anchorage and plentiful supplies of coal—both crucially important for the large steam-powered warships of the late nineteenth century—helped make Hampton Roads one of the navy's largest bases in the early twentieth century.

William Mahone, a native of Hampton Roads, created the region's third large-scale railroad system. Before the Civil War, Mahone was chief engineer of the Norfolk and Petersburg Railroad. Completed in 1858 the railroad created considerable controversy in Norfolk, as some area residents feared that it would benefit Petersburg more than Norfolk. Such fears proved unfounded. Mahone, who became the railroad's president in 1860, would transform the company into a large-scale system that would serve Norfolk far more than Petersburg. While the Civil War put a temporary halt to Mahone's ambitious plans, in the long run the war helped his cause. Mahone eagerly supported secession, and he rose to the rank of general in the Confederate army. His status as a war hero—he saved the Confederate lines at the Battle of the Crater in 1864—greatly aided his commercial and political ambitions. In 1870 Mahone persuaded the legislature to sell two state-owned lines to the Norfolk and Petersburg line so that he could form the Atlantic, Mississippi, and Ohio (AM&O) in 1870, which stretched 408 miles across Virginia from Norfolk to Bristol, Tennessee. The AM&O had the potential to make even more far-flung connections, but the company ran into financial trouble during the Depression of 1873. In 1880 impatient British bondholders, who had provided the bulk of the financing for AM&O's expansion, finally forced Mahone's enterprise into receivership. Northern capitalists with ties to the Pennsylvania Railroad took control and renamed the company the Norfolk and Western Railroad. They continued Mahone's policy of expansion, and made Roanoke (located in southwest Virginia) the company's headquarters. The Norfolk and Western gave Hampton Roads another connection to large supplies of high-quality coal.[53]

The emergence of these three large rail systems coincided with changing technology in steamship design and construction that put a premium on the core geographic strength of Hampton Roads: protected deepwater anchorage. The growing size and power of ocean-going vessels, with larger hulls and more efficient screw propellers, made them too large to ascend the James River for Richmond and Petersburg. In the 1880s new steamships were drawing as much as 19 feet in water, yet the James was only 12.5 to 16 feet deep. New ships were also longer—the average length of a new ship rose from just under 200 feet in 1865 to 400 feet in 1920—which made it far more difficult to handle the curves on the James.[54] Freight coming from or going to the fall-line cities had to be transferred at Norfolk or some other point to lighter, more maneuverable ships. Shipping directly to Norfolk and other Hampton Roads' locales eliminated an expensive transshipment point. This is why all three major rail systems invested in updated port facilities in Hampton Roads: they wanted to make the exchange of good to the large ships as efficient as possible. The changes in steamship design also gave Hampton Roads an advantage on south Atlantic ports such as Charleston, whose shallow harbor made it difficult to safely accommodate the larger vessels.

The railroad lines and improved port facilities helped make Hampton Roads a major export center of cotton and coal. As noted earlier, antebellum Norfolk and Portsmouth had almost no direct trade with Europe before the

Civil War; almost all trade was with other US cities or the Caribbean. After the Civil War, the Caribbean trade receded in significance, which limited the risk of yellow fever. Investing and migrating to Hampton Roads no longer carried the same risk of disease and death. Instead of trading with the Caribbean, the ports of Hampton Roads now shipped directly to Europe. In 1876 Norfolk shipped more than 100,000 bales to Europe. By 1880 the total cotton trade of Norfolk (both coastal and foreign) reached 472,000 bales, which ranked third in the nation. The city's boosters proudly noted that freight cars "run out to our wharves, alongside of which the largest of merchant vessels may lay and receive the bales into their holds." Before the cotton was loaded, "powerful hydraulic presses compress the bales so that ships can carry more than their registered tonnage."[55] The story with coal was similar. In 1886 more than a half million tons of coal was exported at a single pier at Lambert's Point (near Norfolk); the pier was specially designed so that coal cars could directly fill the holds of waiting ships.[56] Railroads, in essence, had dramatically expanded Norfolk's hinterland (at least in terms of exports) to include the cotton fields of the Deep South and the coal fields of Appalachia.

Other industries in Hampton Roads—which arose directly from the region's natural advantages—flourished as more efficient railroads and steamships tied the region more firmly within national and international markets. Truck farming (the cultivation of fruits and vegetables on a large scale) began in the antebellum period. Thanks to the area's earlier growing season, cultivators could ship fruits and vegetables to northern cities via steamship so that they reached market a full month before northern produce.[57] Farmers used lime (often from large deposits of oyster shells that dotted the area) to neutralize acidic soils. Thanks to the improved transportation network, truck farming grew tremendously. In 1889 some 6,000 laborers worked on truck gardens in the Norfolk district year around, while an additional 16,000 worked during the height of the picking and shipping season. In 1879 the value of the area's fruit and vegetable crops was $1.75 million; in 1890 it was $5.77 million.[58] The transformation of truck farming paralleled the changes in the cotton and coal trade. Specialized steamships, built with an extra deck to accommodate large shipments of vegetables and fruits, helped speed the boxes and barrels of fruits and vegetables to Boston, New York, and Philadelphia.

The same general formula helped transform the area's oyster industry, which became another significant source of growth. Oysters thrived in the Hampton Roads region, and they had become a big business in the antebellum period. After the Civil War, the trade grew considerably—oysters were planted in thousands of acres of specialized beds and then harvested by a small flotilla of skiffs and canoes. Thousands of workers (mostly African Americans) laboriously shucked the oysters (separating the shells), so that the shellfish could either be packed raw or steamed before canning. Steamboat lines then took the oysters to northern cities. In 1880 Virginia's oyster industry employed 10,400 workers, mostly concentrated in the Hampton Roads region. Observers noted that northern entrepreneurs provided much of the capital and expertise for the postbellum expansion. According to one report in 1880, much of Norfolk's oyster trade was "in the hands of northern men.... The enterprise and capital of these gentlemen has largely developed this business, which now forms one of the most important branches of Norfolk's trade."[59] This migration of capital and capitalists, which would have been difficult to imagine in the antebellum period, had become a defining feature of this important industry.

CONCLUSION: CIVIL WAR AND COLONIAL DEPENDENCY

As the nineteenth century came to a close, Hampton Roads seemed much closer to fulfilling the great commercial promise that antebellum Virginians foresaw. In complex and unexpected ways, a series of postwar institutional changes (better integration into capital and commodity markets) and technological changes (bigger steamships, improved railroads) allowed Hampton Roads residents to finally take advantage of their region's geographical advantages. In the antebellum period, a combination of slavery (which limited hinterland demand) and poor soils (which stifled population growth in the countryside) slowed the region's development. The Civil War abolished slavery, but wages remained low for most of the African American population while many farmers still used shifting cultivation. After the Civil War, though, the hinterland mattered less—northern capital, via the construction of a modern and efficient railroad network, transformed the economy of Hampton Roads. For decades, Hampton Roads boosters had supported railroads and commercial growth to escape colonial dependency on northern capital. In the end, it was colonial dependence (defined as reliance on northern capital) that allowed Hampton Roads to finally live up to its commercial promise.

Both northern journalists and Virginia's New South boosters celebrated the area's growth, even if each group drew a different lesson. For northerners, Hampton Roads became an example of how the adoption of Yankee values could transform the South. For Virginia's New South boosters, Hampton Roads demonstrated the economic potential of the South. In 1916

Virginia's chapter of the United Daughters of the Confederacy (UDC) published a pamphlet called *Virginia Leads*, which highlighted all of the accomplishments of the Old Dominion. The UDC prominently featured Hampton Roads, including "Greatest coal exporting port in America, Norfolk, Va.," "Heaviest freight trains in the world run into Norfolk," and "Largest dry docks, Newport News."[60] The implication of the UDC is that southern enterprise created these remarkable accomplishments. The boosters of Hampton Roads could be credited with facilitating northern investment, but it was ultimately northern investment that created the infrastructure necessary to fully utilize the area's geographic advantages. No matter how aggressive or enterprising, antebellum Virginians could not overcome the area's significant environmental problems. It took the long-term institutional changes associated with the Civil War—as well as changes in rail and ship technology—to finally free the lavish hand of nature and fully utilize the geographic and environmental advantages of Hampton Roads.

NOTES

1. Thomas C. Parramore with Peter C. Stewart and Tommy L. Bogger, *Norfolk: The First Four Centuries* (Charlottesville: University of Virginia Press, 1994), 149.
2. William S. Forrest, *Historical and Descriptive Sketches of Norfolk and Vicinity* (Philadelphia: Lindsay and Balkiston, 1853), 34.
3. Edmund Ruffin, *Anticipations of the Future, To Serve as Lessons for the Present Times* (Richmond, VA: J. W. Randolph, 1860), 332.
4. Calculated from US Census Bureau, "Population of the 100 Largest Cities and Other Urban Places in the United States: 1790–1990," http://www.census.gov/population/www/documentation/twps0027/twps0027.html (accessed March 8, 2012).
5. James Silk Buckingham, *The Slave States of America*, vol. 2 (London: Fisher, Son, and Co., 1842), 458.
6. Frederick Law Olmsted, *A Journey in the Seaboard Slave States with Remarks on Their Economy* (New York: Mason Brothers, 1859), 137–38.
7. Mathew Maury, quoted in Forrest, *Historical and Descriptive Sketches*, 316.
8. Charles Burr Todd, "Norfolk, Old and New," *Lippencott's Magazine of Popular Literature and Science* 4 (October 1882): 322.
9. "Hampton Roads—Heart of the Mid-Atlantic," http://www.hreda.com/area-profile/hampton-roads-metro-area (accessed August 14, 2012).
10. John J. McCusker and Russel R. Menard, *The Economy of British America, 1607–1789, With Supplementary Bibliography* (Chapel Hill: University of North Carolina Press, 1991), 131.

11. "Commerce of Southern Cities—Norfolk, Va," *Merchants' Magazine and Commercial Review* 42 (April 1, 1860): 480.

12. "Journal of an Excursion by Water to Norfolk, City Point, and Richmond, Virginia," *The Hive* (February 28, 1835): 71, 72, 74.

13. Ibid., 72.

14. These statistics calculated from the 1860 Agricultural Census.

15. J. S. Wise, "Report of the Board of Agriculture: On Norfolk County," *Farmer's Register* (January 1843): 26.

16. Forrest, *Historical and Descriptive Sketches*, 330.

17. These statistics taken from Historical Census Browser (2004). Retrieved from the University of Virginia, Geospatial and Statistical Data Center, http://mapserver.lib .virginia.edu/collections/ (accessed March 18, 2012).

18. David R. Meyer, *The Roots of American Industrialization* (Baltimore, MD: Johns Hopkins University Press, 2003), 162–88; Diane Lindstrom, *Economic Development in the Philadelphia Region, 1810–1850* (New York: Columbia University Press, 1978); John Majewski, *A House Dividing: Economic Development in Pennsylvania and Virginia before the Civil War* (New York: Cambridge University Press, 2000), 141–67.

19. Jack Temple Kirby, *Poquosin: A Study in Rural Landscape and Society* (Chapel Hill: University of North Carolina Press, 1995).

20. For more on the economic consequences of shifting cultivation, see John Majewski, *Modernizing a Slave Economy: The Economic Vision of the Confederate Nation* (Chapel Hill: University of North Carolina Press, 2009), chap. 1.

21. Areas like the Great Dismal Swamp also provided a large source of lumber, which was either exported or used by local shipyards. The shipment of unprocessed wood— which other areas would turn into furniture, fences, barns, and homes—symbolized the uneven development of the region's economy.

22. These statistics calculated from the 1860 Manufacturing Census. I thank Viken Tchakerian for sharing them with me. For more on the market for southern manufacturing, see his "Productivity, Extent of Markets, and Manufacturing in the Late Antebellum South and Midwest," *Journal of Economic History* 54 (1994): 500.

23. Joseph J. Persky, *The Burden of Dependency: Colonial Themes in Southern Economic Thought* (Baltimore, MD: Johns Hopkins University Press, 1992), 61–96.

24. William M. Burwell, *An Address on the Commercial Future of Virginia* (Richmond, VA: Ritchie and Dunnavant, 1851), 15–16.

25. Olmsted, *Journey in the Seaboard Slave States*, 139.

26. Majewski, *Modernizing a Slave Economy*, 151–61.

27. That modest improvement came about because more marginal acreage was no longer cultivated. Total improved acreage in the Hampton Roads region declined from 656,605 in 1860 to 597,560 aces in 1890. Historical Census Browser (2004), Retrieved from the University of Virginia, Geospatial and Statistical Data Center, http:// mapserver.lib.virginia.edu/collections/ (accessed March 18, 2012).

28. Parramore, Stewart, and Bogger, *Norfolk*, 158–60.

29. Peter C. Stewart, "Railroads and Urban Rivalries in Antebellum Eastern Virginia," *Virginia Magazine of History and Biography* 81 (January 1973): 3–22.

30. William Segar, *Speech of Mr. Segar, of Northampton, on the Subject of a General System of Internal Improvements* (Richmond, VA: Bailie and Gallaher, 1838), 9, 21.

31. *Speech of Mr. Segar, of Elizabeth City, On the Bill Authorizing a Loan of State Bonds to the South-Side Rail Road Company* (Richmond: H. K. Ellyson, 1853), 19.

32. David Goldfield, *Urban Growth in the Age of Sectionalism: Virginia 1847–1861* (Baton Rouge: Louisiana State University Press, 1977), 205.

33. For a critique of state legislative aid and urban rivalries in Virginia, see Majewski, *A House Dividing*, 128–39.

34. J. R. McNeill, *Mosquito Empires: Ecology and War in the Greater Caribbean, 1620–1914* (New York: Cambridge University Press, 2010).

35. Peter McCandless, *Slavery, Disease, and Suffering in the Southern Lowcountry* (New York: Cambridge University Press, 2011), 106–24.

36. Dr. Robert Archer, "History of Yellow Fever, as It Appeared in Norfolk during the Summer and Autumn of 1821," *American Medical Recorder* (January 1822): 61.

37. William S. Forrest, *The Great Pestilence in Virginia; Being an Historical Account of the Origin, General Character, and Ravages of the Yellow Fever in Norfolk and Portsmouth in 1855* (New York: Derby and Jackson, 1856), 12–21.

38. For a useful narrative of the epidemic's progression, see Parramore, Stewart, and Bogger, *Norfolk*, 176–92.

39. "Yellow Fever," *New York Daily Times*, September 11, 1855, 1.

40. Frederick Law Olmsted, *A Journey to the Seaboard Slave States in the Years 1853–1854: With Remarks on Their Economy* (New York: G P. Putnam's Sons, 1904), 153.

41. Goldfield, *Urban Growth in the Age of Sectionalism*, 155.

42. Forrest, *Historical and Descriptive Sketches*, 332, 335–36.

43. Forrest, *The Great Pestilence*, 8.

44. Ibid., 8, 12.

45. L. P. Jackson, "The Origin of Hampton Institute," *Journal of Negro History* 10, no. 2 (1925): 131–49.

46. H. W. Burton, *The History of Norfolk, Virginia* (Norfolk, VA: Norfolk Virginian, 1877), 203.

47. Ernest Ingersoll, "Within the Capes of Virginia," *Frank Leslie's Popular Monthly* 20 (1885): 151.

48. Scott Reynolds Nelson, *Iron Confederacies: Southern Railways, Klan Violence, and Reconstruction* (Chapel Hill: University of North Carolina Press, 1999), 11–26.

49. Gavin Wright, *Slavery and American Economic Development* (Baton Rouge: Louisiana State University Press, 2006). It is not clear that Virginia railroads, despite constant complaints about the difficulty in raising capital, were even interested in northern investment. Virginians, for example, constantly feared that Baltimore was trying to steal Virginia's trade from Richmond, Petersburg, and Norfolk.

50. Richard B. Osborne, "Professional Biography of Moncure Robinson," *William and Mary Quarterly* 1 (October 1921): 237–60.

51. Nelson, *Iron Confederacies*, 56, 67–68.

52. Allen W. Moger, "Railroad Practices and Policies in Virginia after the Civil War," *Virginia Magazine of History and Biography* 59 (1951): 427–29.

53. John F. Stover, *The Railroads of the South, 1865–1900* (Chapel Hill: University of North Carolina Press, 1955), 66–68, 204.

54. Steven J. Hoffman, "The Decline of the Port of Richmond: The Congress, the Corps, and the Chamber of Commerce," *Virginia Magazine of History and Biography* 108 (2000): 255–78. See also Nelson, *Iron Confederacies*, 83.

55. Burton, *History of Norfolk*, 200.

56. Robert W. Lamb, *Our Twin Cities of the Nineteenth Century (Norfolk and Portsmouth): Their Past, Present, and Future* (Norfolk, VA: Barcroft Publisher, 1887–88).

57. Parramore, Stewart, and Bogger, *Norfolk*, 171–73.

58. US Census Office, *Reports on the Statistics of Agriculture in the United States, Agriculture by Irrigation in the Western Part of the United States, and Statistics of Fisheries in the United States at the Eleventh Census: 1890* (Washington, DC: Government Printing Office, 1896), 594, 596.

59. Ernest Ingersoll, US Bureau of Fisheries, *The Oyster Industry* (Washington, DC: Government Printing Office, 1881), 186.

60. W. C. N. Merchant, *Virginia Leads* (Richmond: The Virginia Division of the United Daughters of the Confederacy, 1916), 16.

Cities and the History of the Civil War South

ANDREW L. SLAP AND FRANK TOWERS

The phrase "Confederate Cities" has long had different connotations, depending on which word is emphasized. Civil War historians have generally focused on the "Confederate," and discussed cities in the South as places where events like bread riots or sieges occurred. Urban scholars have mostly focused on the "Cities," and used southern cities during the period to explore larger issues of urbanization. One of the goals of this volume is to try giving more equal analytical weight to both words in "Confederate Cities," to consider how southern cities as cities affected the Civil War and in turn how the conflict affected the urban South.

To investigate the neglected connections between urban and Civil War–era history in the South, the contributors focused on a particular aspect of a city or urban network. The essays are purposefully diverse, ranging from the experiences of a Union soldier on one weekend in wartime New Orleans to the economic development of coastal Virginia over the course of decades. The geographic and thematic diversity provides a rich multitude of perspectives about how individual cities or networks of cities affected, or were affected by, the Civil War in specific ways. As a whole, though, the essays suggest some broader interpretations about the relationship between the urban South and the Civil War.

First, many of the essays find major differences between the urban and rural antebellum South. In looking at the language of secession Frank Towers and Lloyd Benson explore the negotiation of urban versus regional and national agendas on the eve of the Civil War. They find that cities served both as symbols for the would-be Confederate nation and, to the extent that cities exerted a claim on their residents' collective identity, that they acted as blocks to national unity. Michael Pierson shows how cities like New Orleans offered Union soldiers surroundings they could recognize and feel a kinship to after a stint in hostile rural Louisiana. As Pierson writes, "No one could ever argue that New Orleans perfectly resembled any northern city (or any other southern city), but its large immigrant populations, the predominance of wage labor, and the mixture of wealth and poverty must have struck many northern soldiers as familiar." In this respect, New Orleans participated in urbanism as such, a cultural formation that cut across regional and national boundaries and made anyone familiar with the life of one city feel at least a little kinship for the life of another. Andrew Slap likewise discusses how a high percentage of foreign-born immigrants helped make Memphis demographically distinct from rural Tennessee. With nearly 31 percent of its population foreign born by 1860, Memphis had established ethnic neighborhoods, while less than 2 percent of all Tennessee residents were foreign born. William Link contends that a different kind of immigrant, ones from the North, helped to make Atlanta different from the Georgia countryside. He explains that "like another city that during the same era which became a dominant transportation and marketing center—Chicago—Atlanta attracted a group of merchant-capitalists with an ambitious vision of their future in what historian Don Doyle calls a 'northern enclave on foreign soil.'" Thus, while Keith Bohannon writes, "the urban South in the late antebellum era did not stand apart from the countryside" and most of the authors acknowledge connections between the two, the consensus is that in important ways the urban and rural South were distinct from each other.

In several ways the differences and tensions between the urban and rural South hurt the Confederate endeavor, the second theme that emerges from the essays. Towers contends that conflict between town and country during the secession movement persisted throughout the Civil War and directly hurt the Confederacy's ability to unite as a nation. Although Benson thinks the Confederacy was able to resolve these differences, they still consumed some of white southerners' limited time and energy at the beginning of the conflict. On a material level, Link shows how a city like Atlanta could help supply the Confederate war machine, but Gallman argues that the South's relatively underdeveloped cities were poorly prepared to carry the weight of the war's demands. Gallman, Link, and Bohannon also find that the urban characteristics of southern cities made them particularly well suited as centers of war resistance the Confederacy could ill afford. On the other hand, David Moltke-Hansen finds that cities and towns played a critical role in Confederate communications, and, in this respect, led "intentional efforts at the intellectual transformation of an American region into a separate nation." This is all not to revive the debate over whether the Confederacy lost because of an internal collapse, but suggest new aspects to the southern homefront and their effect on the course of the Civil War.

The third theme that emerges from the essays is that Confederate defeat lessened the differences between the urban and rural South, making the postbellum South more homogenous than its antebellum predecessor. This should probably not come as a surprise, since historians have long paraphrased Robert Penn Warren that the South was born at Appomattox, arguing that the crucible of war brought white southerners together while the un-American experience of defeat made them distinct. Moltke-Hansen contends that the vibrant print culture of the antebellum and wartime southern cities moved to New York after the Civil War, with the ironic consequence of promoting an "orientalized" narrative of the South as tradition-bound outlier to the rapidly changing society of the United States. In reality, after the Civil War many southern cities rapidly expanded their industry and transportation systems, enmeshing large swathes of the countryside in regional networks. John Majewski describes how the growing transportation network around Norfolk encouraged the growth of truck farming and other economic activities that increasingly linked the urban center to the rural hinterland. Norfolk also benefited from investments in transportation that were occurring elsewhere in the South, particularly the upcountry interior and Texas where booms in oil, coal, and manufacturing spurred the growth of new cities. Despite Norfolk's success, as Moltke-Hansen notes, the major cities of the Confederacy, most of them eastern and Gulf Coast ports, declined in relation to these new postwar boomtowns like Birmingham, Alabama, and Dallas, Texas. Atlanta, of course, was the ultimate boomtown and Link shows how it became the economic hub just not for Georgia but for much of the entire Southeast. The increasing linkages between cities and the country helped to make the postbellum South more homogeneous.[1]

The greatest change in the South after the Civil War, however, was emancipation and its profound effect on the region's cities is the last theme of the volume. The ability of freed African Americans to move to southern cities that had previously been overwhelmingly white made the urban and rural South much more similar. For instance, by 1870 African Americans comprised 36 percent of Memphis's population, comparable to the 38 percent of African Americans throughout the South then. Significantly, Hilary Green, Justin Behrend, and Slap all discuss how African Americans' migration to cities helped create new connections between the urban and rural South, reinforcing the economic ties discussed by Majewski and Link. African Americans social networks in the greater Memphis urban region are central to Slap's essay. Behrend starts his essay with a postwar Fourth of July celebration in which thousands of African Americans from the surrounding countryside gathered in Natchez and then, with urban African Americans, paraded out to a planation to demonstrate their political mobilization. Green shows how educational reforms that started in Mobile quickly spread throughout Alabama as African Americans asserted their own definitions of citizenship and freedom. Link echoes many of these ideas in asserting that the Civil War "presented new opportunities for black Atlantans." The optimistic tone of these essays in regard to African Americans in the postbellum urban South departs from previous pessimistic assessments of race in southern cities after the Civil War. During Reconstruction, according to Eric Foner, blacks "believed 'freedom was freer,'" in cities but "often encountered severe disappointment," while Howard Rabinowitz contended that postwar cities served as the incubators of segregation and the larger structure of Jim Crow. Behrend, Green, Link, and Slap come down on the side of Richard Wade's thesis that cities offered more political, educational, and community building opportunities for African Americans in the decades after the Civil War.[2]

Recalling the new urban history brings to mind a final contribution of this volume to the history of Confederate cities. As the notes to our essays show, the current generation of southern urban historians has drawn deeply on the findings of scholarship produced between the 1960s and 1980s. Nevertheless, these essays also show how the study of the Civil War urban South has changed since then. Interest in gender and the environment, themes explored herein by Pierson and Majewski, have come to the forefront, whereas other questions about urbanization, such as occupational mobility, have faded from view. In addition to new themes, this volume is perhaps more concerned with the Civil War itself than were earlier histories that looked at the broader sweep of nineteenth-century history. Although interested in the big picture, this volume's closer attention to the 1860s shows how cities impacted aspects of the war, such as the debate over national identity and the process of emancipation, that earlier generations of Civil War historians had studied without reference to the urban context. Going forward, students of the South's Civil War can do more to bring cities into the history of the Confederacy just as specialists on the history of cities have the opportunity to look back to the Civil War era for new insights into what it meant to be urban.

NOTES

1. James C. Cobb, *Away Down South: A History of Southern Identity* (New York: Oxford University Press, 2005), 60; David Goldfield, *Southern Histories: Public, Personal, and Sacred* (Athens: University of Georgia Press, 2003), 6–7.

2. Eric Foner, *Reconstruction: America's Unfinished Revolution, 1863–1877* (New York: Harper and Row, 1988), 81–82; Howard N. Rabinowitz, *Race Relations in the Urban South, 1865–1890* (New York: Oxford University Press, 1978); Richard C. Wade, *Slavery in the Cities: The South, 1820–1860* (New York: Oxford University Press, 1964).

JUSTIN BEHREND is an associate professor of history at the State University of New York at Geneseo. He is the author of *Reconstructing Democracy: Grassroots Black Politics in the Deep South after the Civil War* (University of Georgia Press, 2015) and numerous articles, including "Rebellious Talk and Conspiratorial Plots: The Making of a Slave Insurrection in Civil War Natchez," *Journal of Southern History* (February 2011), and "Rumors of Revolt," *New York Times*, September 15, 2011.

T. LLOYD BENSON is the Walter Kenneth Mattison Professor of History at Furman University. In addition to many articles and essays, he is the author of *The Caning of Senator Sumner* (2003). His current manuscript is "Planters and Hoosiers: The Development of Sectional Society in Antebellum Indiana and Mississippi."

KEITH S. BOHANNON is an associate professor of history at the University of West Georgia. He is the coeditor of *A Georgian with "Old Stonewall" in Virginia: The Letters of Ujanirtus Allen, Company F, 21st Regiment, Georgia Volunteer Infantry* (Louisiana State University Press, 1998), and the author of nine essays published by the University of Georgia Press, the University of North Carolina Press, Indiana University Press, and the University of Alabama Press.

J. MATTHEW GALLMAN is a professor of history at the University of Florida. He is the author of four books, including *Mastering Wartime: A Social History of Philadelphia during the Civil War* (Cambridge University Press, 1990), *The North Fights the Civil War: The Home Front* (Ivan Dee, 1994), *Receiving Erin's Children: Philadelphia, Liverpool, and the Irish*

Famine Migration, 1845–1855 (University of North Carolina Press, 2000), and *America's Joan of Arc: The Life of Anna Elizabeth Dickinson* (Oxford University Press, 2006). He is currently working on a study of political rhetoric and satire in the North during the Civil War.

DAVID GOLDFIELD is the Robert Lee Bailey Professor of History at the University of North Carolina, Charlotte. He has published sixteen books on various aspects of southern and American history, including the award-winning *Cotton Fields and Skyscrapers: Southern City and Region* (Johns Hopkins University Press, 1989) and *Still Fighting the Civil War: The American South and Southern History* (Louisiana State University Press, 2002). His latest book is *America Aflame: How the Civil War Created a Nation* (Bloomsbury Press, 2011).

HILARY N. GREEN is an assistant professor of history in the Department of Gender and Race Studies at the University of Alabama, Tuscaloosa. She is the author of *Educational Reconstruction: African American Education in the Urban South, 1865–1890* (Fordham University Press, 2015). Her current research focuses on African American memory of the Civil War.

WILLIAM A. LINK is the Richard J. Milbauer Professor of History at the University of Florida, a position which he has held since 2004. His publications include, most recently, *Roots of Secession: Slavery and Politics in Antebellum Virginia* (2003), *Righteous Warrior: Jesse Helms and the Rise of Modern Conservatism* (2008), and *Links: My Family in American History* (2012). His latest book is *Atlanta, Cradle of the New South: Race and Remembering in the Civil War's Aftermath* (2013).

JOHN MAJEWSKI is a professor of history and associate dean of the division of Humanities and Fine Arts at the University of California Santa Barbara. He is the author of *A House Dividing: Economic Development in Pennsylvania and Virginia before the Civil War* (Cambridge University Press, 2000) and *Modernizing a Slave Economy: The Economic Vision of the Confederate Nation* (University of North Carolina Press, 2009).

DAVID MOLTKE-HANSEN is the general editor, with Mark Smith, of Cambridge Studies on the American South, and general editor of the five volumes of the selected writings of Elizabeth Fox-Genovese for the University of South Carolina Press. His recent articles have been published in *Historically Speaking, Studies in the Literary Imagination*, the *Journal of the Historical Society,* and *Mississippi Quarterly.* He is currently writing a brief generational history of the Civil War South for the Johns Hopkins University Press and the selected writings of William Henry Trescot for the Southern Texts Society at the University of Georgia Press.

MICHAEL PIERSON is a professor of history at the University of Massachusetts at Lowell. He is author of *Free Hearts and Free Homes: Gender and American Antislavery Politics* (2003) and *Mutiny at Fort Jackson: The Untold Story of the Fall of New Orleans* (2008).

ANDREW L. SLAP is a professor of history at East Tennessee State University. He is the author of *The Doom of Reconstruction: The Liberal Republicans in the Civil War Era* (Fordham University Press, 2006). He is also the editor of *Reconstructing Appalachia: The Civil War's Aftermath* (University Press of Kentucky, 2010) and coeditor of *This Distracted and Anarchical People: New Answers for Old Questions about the Civil War Era North* (Fordham University Press, 2012). His current book project is "African American Communities during Slavery, War, and Peace: Memphis in the Nineteenth Century."

FRANK TOWERS is an associate professor of history at the University of Calgary and specialist in the history of slavery, politics, and cities in the nineteenth-century United States. He is the author of *The Urban South and the Coming of the Civil War* (University of Virginia Press, 2004), coeditor of *The Old South's Modern Worlds: Slavery, Region, and Nation in the Age of Progress* (Oxford University Press, 2011), and more than twenty essays for peer-reviewed journals and scholarly anthologies. His current research project is titled "The Slave Power's Grassroots: Federal Proslavery Politics and Local Electorates in the United States, 1840–1861."

HISTORICAL STUDIES OF URBAN AMERICA

Edited by Lilia Fernández, Timothy J. Gilfoyle, Becky M. Nicolaides, and Amanda Seligman
James R. Grossman, editor emeritus

Series titles, continued from frontmatter